Foundations of Component-Based Systems

This collection of articles by well-known experts is intended for researchers in computer science, practitioners of formal methods, and computer programmers working in safety-critical applications or in the technology of component-based systems. The work brings together, for the first time, several elements of this area that are fast becoming the focus of much current research and practice in computing.

The introduction by Clemens Szyperski gives a snapshot of the current state of the field. About half the articles deal with theoretical frameworks, models, and systems of notation; the rest of the book concentrates on case studies by researchers who have built prototype systems and present findings on architecture verification. The emphasis is on advances in the ideas behind component-based systems; how to design and specify reusable components; and how to reason about, verify, and validate systems from components.

Gary T. Leavens is Associate Professor in the Department of Computer Science at Iowa State University. He received his Ph.D. from MIT in 1989 and has taught at Iowa State University ever since. Dr. Leavens has written for such journals as *ACM TOSEN*, *ACM TOPLAS*, *Theoretical Computer Science*, *Acta Informatica*, and *Theory and Practice of Object Systems*. He serves on the program committees of well-known conferences such as OOPSLA and ICSE. His research has been funded by the U.S. National Science Foundation.

Murali Sitaraman is Associate Professor in the Department of Computer Science and Electrical Engineering at West Virginia University. He received his Ph.D. at Ohio State University and has taught at West Virginia University since 1990. Dr. Sitaraman has written for such journals as *IEEE Transactions on Software Engineering*, *Software Practice and Experience*, *Formal Aspects of Computing*, and *IEEE Software*. He was program chair of the IEEE Computer Society International Conference on Software Reuse in 1996 and has served on program committees for several major conferences.

Foundations of Component-Based Systems

Edited by

GARY T. LEAVENS
Iowa State University

MURALI SITARAMAN
West Virginia University

CAMBRIDGE
UNIVERSITY PRESS

CAMBRIDGE UNIVERSITY PRESS
Cambridge, New York, Melbourne, Madrid, Cape Town, Singapore,
São Paulo, Delhi, Dubai, Tokyo, Mexico City

Cambridge University Press
The Edinburgh Building, Cambridge CB2 8RU, UK

Published in the United States of America by Cambridge University Press, New York

www.cambridge.org
Information on this title: www.cambridge.org/9780521155694

© Cambridge University Press 2000

First published 2000
First paperback edition 2010

A catalogue record for this publication is available from the British Library

Library of Congress Cataloguing in Publication Data

Foundations of component-based systems 1 edited by Gary T. Leavens, Murali Sitaraman.
    p.cm.
  ISBN 0-521-77164-1
  1. Component software. 2. System design. I. Leavens, Gary T. II. Sitaraman, Murali.

QA76.76.C66 F68 2000
005.1-dc21   99-049686

ISBN 978-0-521-77164-1 Hardback
ISBN 978-0-521-15569-4 Paperback

Contents

Preface

Component-based software construction has become a central focus of software engineering research and computing practice. There is a near-universal recognition in the field that development of high-quality systems on time is possible only through assembly of well-conceived and prefabricated software components.

This volume brings together, for the first time, programming and specification issues as well as framework, architecture, and distributed computing issues that should be considered in designing component-based systems. It simultaneously tries to lay a foundation to bridge a spectrum of approaches that span current component-based technology and formal foundational research. The technological chapters focus on component structure and integration issues, providing a basis for the latter chapters that focus on component semantics in sequential and concurrent setting. Taken together, these chapters should benefit software engineering practitioners in enhancing component-based construction practice and researchers in establishing a connection to practical technology. They should also provide new research directions to computer science and engineering graduate students for advancing the field.

The volume begins with a chapter by Szyperski, which summarizes current technologies, including COM, CORBA, and JavaBeans. This chapter highlights the importance and role of component-based construction for modern computing. It also outlines essential problems to be solved for component-based software to become both reliable and effective.

Following this initial chapter, Part One of the volume focuses on elements of frameworks and architectures for component-based composition. Though the chapters in this section use particular languages and notations to illustrate the ideas, the central themes of the chapters are generally applicable to all component-based software construction.

In Part One, the chapter by Luckham, Vera, and Meldal explains that an architecture is a specification of the components and communication among them, and elaborates on the concepts needed to support this view. Garlan, Monroe, and Wile introduce ACME as a common representation for software architectures and as an enabler to integrate systems built using alternative architecture definition languages.

The chapter by Lumpe, Achermann, and Nierstrasz defines the requirements of a flexible software composition language and provides formal semantic foundations to facilitate precise specification and formal reasoning. Chen and Cheng describe criteria for matching specifications and explain what constitutes a reuse-ensuring match.

Part Two deals with aspects of formal specification and verification, with emphasis on object-based software construction. The chapters discuss behavioral subtyping, specification and verification, and preservation of behavior when objects of one type are converted to another. Leavens and Dhara give a background and survey of behavioral subtyping, which is a relationship between types that allows modular specification and verification of object-oriented software. Müller and Poetzsch-Heffter explain a modular technique for specifying and verifying object-oriented components. Wing and Ockerbloom's chapter focuses on guaranteeing consistent observable behavior when converting objects of one type to another.

Part Three concentrates on formal models and formal semantics of components and compositions. The chapters in this part describe complementary approaches for understanding components and compositions.

In Part Three, the chapter by Bergner, Rausch, Sihling, Vilbig, and Broy gives a formal model that encompasses both components and object-oriented features of programming languages. They use this model to describe the meaning of commonly used graphical description techniques (such as some diagram forms in the UML). Gibson, Weide, Pike, and Edwards provide a formal model of parameterized component-based (software) systems that facilitates modular reasoning about collections of interacting components. Goguen and Tracz describe an algebraic approach to software engineering. Their chapter introduces module expressions to compose components and provides an implementation-oriented semantics for composition.

Part Four of the volume contains chapters on reactive and distributed computing, two critical aspects of component-based systems, and modern software practice. The chapter by Lano, Bicarregui, Maibaum, and Fiadeiro describes a modular, declarative approach for specification of reactive systems. The approach is suitable for model-based design notations such as VDM and B. Garland and Lynch's chapter presents a new language for structured modeling of distributed computing systems, using a mathematical I/O automaton model as the basis. The chapter also provides an overview of design and analysis tools that can be developed using the model.

Though we have organized this volume beginning with issues on languages and frameworks, and proceeding to techniques for specification, verification, formal models, and distribution, the individual parts and chapters in this volume are self-contained. A reader or teacher should be able to choose the order in which to read or discuss the chapters.

The chapters in this volume have not been previously published. They were particularly solicited for this volume from experts in the field. To ensure high quality, all chapters were peer reviewed. Every chapter, except for one, had at least two reviewers. In every case, the reviewers provided detailed and timely feedback to the authors for revision. Our sincere thanks are due to the reviewers, including: Franz Achermann, Uwe Assmann, Gerald Baumgartner, Manfred Broy, Jack Callahan, Betty Cheng, Paolo Ciancarini, James Donahue, Stephen Edwards, Bernd Fischer, Rustan Leino, Ali Mili, Anna Mikhajlova, Oscar Nierstrasz, John Penix, Johannes Sametinger, Oleg Sheyner, Judith Stafford, and Raymie Stata.

Our sincere thanks to Lauren Cowles at Cambridge University Press for her support and advice during this project, and to Ernie Haim for his careful eye and help in the production of this book. We thank Addison-Wesley for giving permission to Szyperski to derive his chapter from his book *Component Software: Beyond Object-Oriented Programming* (Addison-Wesley, 1998). We also thank the U.S. National Science Foundation, the U.S. Defense Advanced Research Projects Agency, and our institutions for supporting this editorial work. Thanks to Janet from Gary and to Susan and Nathan from Murali for their love and support.

Gary T. Leavens, Ames, Iowa
Murali Sitaraman, Morgantown, West Virginia
January 14, 2000

1
Component Software and the Way Ahead

Clemens Szyperski

Microsoft Research
One Microsoft Way, Redmond, WA 98053 USA
cszypers@microsoft.com

Abstract

Components capture the deployment nature of software; objects capture its runtime nature. Components and objects together enable the construction of next-generation software. However, as discussed in this chapter, many problems still need to be solved before component software can become ubiquitous. One important step to be taken is to move from component introversion to component extroversion and to adopt component-based software architecture on a much broader basis. To avoid the many traps on that way, it is useful to emphasize: Components are units of deployment and versioning but the atoms of configuration. To control the complexity explosion of peer-to-peer component architectures, component frameworks need to be pursued beyond their current weak foundation.

1.1 Introduction

From the early days of discovering that software construction ought to be an engineering discipline it has been recognized that the one key concept to learn from other engineering disciplines is the notion of prefabrication of more generic parts and their assembly to form more specific parts. Such "parts" can figure at different levels and stages of a production process—but only if they form isolatable parts of deployed solutions should they be called software components. Parts used to generate the parts that are eventually deployed, should not be called software components to avoid diffusing the component concept to a useless level of generality. In the remainder of this chapter, where unambiguous, software components are simply called components.

The restrictive notion of software components just sketched is, of course, a pragmatic take. From an ontological point of view, everything that can be composed into a composite is a component. Since plenty of compositional concepts are used on the road towards deployable software, all these could be subsumed under the component umbrella. Examples of such compositional concepts are expressions, functions, statements, procedures, classes, and modules. Of these, only modules— and only if carefully institutionalized—form the basis of software components, but merely primordial ones.

Notably, there is a second space of compositional concepts that deserves separate attention: the space of run-time instances. Composition in this space covers concepts such as co-allocation of variables, address indirection (references and pointers), objects, and object composition via forwarding, aggregation, or delegation. Especially in the space of objects, it is a common simplification to not thoroughly distinguish objects from classes—that is, instances from their generating description. However, this distinction is fundamental to the understanding of what software components should be.

Components are on the upswing, while objects have been around for a while. It is therefore understandable but not helpful to see object-oriented programming sold in new clothes by simply calling objects "components." The emerging component-based approaches and tools combine objects and components in ways that show they are separate concepts. In this chapter, some key differences between objects and components are examined to clarify these blurred areas.

The remainder of this chapter is organized as follows: First, some motivating arguments are given for the use of components and the need to have standards. Then, some key terms are unfolded, explained, and justified. Based on this, a refined component definition is reviewed. Following, some light is shed on the fine line between component-based programming and component assembly. In particular, it is shown that approaches based on assembly really assemble objects, not components, but that they create new components when saving the finished assembly. Taking steps beyond objects, concepts of component frameworks and component system architecture are then introduced.

1.1.1 Why Components?

Reference to more mature engineering disciplines cannot and should not be the key argument for pushing software component technology. So, what is the rationale behind component software? Or rather, what is it that components should be? This section introduces a set of key arguments that motivate the use of components, intentionally preceding later sections that cover software components in detail.

Traditionally, closed solutions with proprietary interfaces addressed most customers' needs. Heavyweights such as operating systems and database engines are among the few examples of components that have reached high levels of maturity. Large software-systems manufacturers often configure delivered solutions by combining modules in a client-specific way. However, the interfaces between such modules tend to be proprietary—at most, open to highly specialized independent software vendors (ISVs) that specifically produce further modules for such systems. In many cases, these modules are fused together during a linking step and are no longer distinguishable in deployed solutions.

There are three sets of arguments in favor of component software:

(i) *Baseline argument:* Component-based solutions can combine acquired and purpose-created components. By combining "make" and "buy", components offer to reduce cost by focussing on core competencies and by avoiding excessive reinvention of the wheel. Hence, strategic components are made while non-strategic ones are bought, perhaps even off-the-shelf (COTS). This way, organizations can maintain their competitive edge—an issue of increasing importance as software dominates more and more aspects of modern organizations.

(ii) *Enterprise argument:* Components can be assembled in a variety of different ways. If the component factoring is performed skillfully, then several products of a *product line* can be covered by configuring a core set of components, plus perhaps some more product-specific ones. Product creation is then largely an issue of configuration. Furthermore, by versioning individual components and reconfiguring systems the evolution of products can be controlled.

(iii) *Dynamic computing argument:* Modern software systems are increasingly challenged by an open and growing set of content types to be processed. A web browser is a good example. If well architected, such systems can be dynamically extended to meet new requirements on demand.

The baseline argument is not as strong as it seems: source-level reuse may often be sufficient for this purpose. Likewise, the enterprise argument still allows for final product integration. In both cases it is thus possible to get away without investing into component technology that supports deployment-time components. However, the dynamic computing argument strictly requires components that are units of deployment. It is interesting to observe that the first two scenarios do benefit from deployable components. In the baseline case the argument is increased robustness: source code is a fragile basis for reuse. In the enterprise case the argument is increased flexibility: deployed systems can be upgraded and adapted to changing needs without requiring clients to install a whole new system.

1.1.2 Component Standards

Deployable components need to be shipped in a "binary" form, that is, a form that is machine processable and does not require any further human intervention. Traditionally, this form was a loadable image holding machine code. Alternatively, and long known, such a form can be lifted to match some virtual machine. Java bytecode is the presently most popular binary form for a virtual machine. In addition to binary form, a component standard needs to be established that—at this binary level—defines interoperation between components from independent providers. Traditionally, this task was performed by operating systems that defined a *calling convention*. With components that should go beyond simple procedural interfaces, new standard infrastructure is needed to effectively standardize more general calling conventions.

Attempts to create low-level connection standards or wiring standards are either product- or standard-driven. The Microsoft standards, resting on its Component Object Model (COM) [Mic97, Box98, Cha96], have always been product-driven and are thus incremental, evolutionary, and to a degree legacy-laden by nature. Standard-driven approaches usually originate in industry consortia. The prime example here is the Object Management Group (OMG)'s effort. However, OMG's Common Object Request Broker Architecture (CORBA) [Obj98] hasn't contributed much in the component world and is now falling back on JavaSoft's Enterprise Java-Beans (EJB) [Jav98] standards for components, although attempting a CORBA Beans generalization in the CORBA 3 revision. The JavaBeans standard still has a way to go and it is not implementation language-neutral. Re-introducing such neutrality in CORBA Beans—while remaining sufficiently compatible with the evolving EJB specification—is a major challenge. To summarize, the situation is somewhat paradoxical in that it seems there is a choice between platform independence (EJB) and language independence (COM). The CORBA promise of offering both yet remains unfulfilled in the components arena.

At first, it might be surprising that standards for component software are largely pushed by desktop- and Internet-based solutions. On second thought, this should not be surprising at all. Component software is a complex technology to master—and viable, component-based solutions will only evolve if the benefits are clear. Traditional enterprise computing has many benefits, but they all depend on enterprises that are willing to evolve substantially.

In the desktop and Internet worlds, the situation is different. Centralized control over what information is processed when and where is not an option in these worlds. Instead, contents (such as web pages or documents) arrive at a user's machine and need to be processed there and then. With a rapidly exploding variety of content types—and open encoding standards such as XML, monolithic applications have long reached their limits. Beyond the flexibility of component software is its capability to dynamically grow to address changing needs: Components are key to the extensibility and evolvability of software systems. This is the dynamic computing argument introduced above.

1.2 Terms and Concepts

1.2.1 What a Component Is and Is Not

The terms "component" and "object" are often used interchangeably. In addition, constructions such as "component object" are used. Objects are said to be instances of classes or clones of prototype objects. Objects and components both make their services available through interfaces. Language designers add more confusion by discussing namespaces, modules, packages, and so on. It is, therefore, useful to unfold and explain these terms. To remain goal-oriented, here is a first definition of components:

Component A component's characteristic properties are that it is a unit of independent deployment; a unit of third-party composition; and it has no persistent state.

These properties have several implications. For a component to be independently deployable, it needs to be separated from its environment and from other components. A component, therefore, encapsulates its constituent features. In addition, since a component is a unit of deployment, it is never deployed partially.

If a third party needs to compose a component with other components, the component must be self-contained. (A third party is one that cannot be expected to access the construction details of all the components involved.) In addition, the component needs to come with clear specifications of what it provides and what it requires. In other words, a component needs to encapsulate its implementation and interact with its environment through well-defined interfaces and platform assumptions only. It is also generally useful to minimize hard-wired dependencies in favor of externally configurable providers. If all hard-wiring is avoided, then a component is fully connectable (or "pluggable"): it can be used in any context where the required and provided interfaces can be properly connected. See Section 1.4 for a detailed discussion of connections and assembly.

Finally, observe that a component without any persistent state cannot be distinguished from copies of its own—an important and useful property. (Exceptions to this rule are attributes not contributing to the component's functionality, such as serial numbers used for accounting.) Without state, a component can be loaded into and activated in a particular system—but in any given process, there will be at most one copy of a particular component. So, while it is useful to ask whether a particular component is available or not, it is meaningless to ask about the number of copies of that component. (Note that a component may simultaneously exist in different versions. However, these are not copies of a component, but rather related components.) Not copying components does not mean that components cannot support multiple instances. For example, a button component would exist only once in a deployment context, but it could support any number of button instances (see Section 1.2.2 below).

In many current approaches, components are heavyweights. For example, a database server could be a component. If there is only one database maintained by this class of server, then it is easy to confuse the instance with the concept. In the example, the database server, together with the database, can be seen as a component with persistent state. According to the definition described previously, this instance of the database concept is not a component. Instead, the static database server program is and it supports a single instance: the database object. This separation of the immutable plan from the mutable instances is key to avoid massive maintenance problems. If components could be mutable, that is, have state, then no two installations of the same component would have the same properties. The differentiation of components and objects is thus fundamentally about differentiating between static properties that hold for a particular configuration and dynamic properties of any particular computational scenario. Drawing this line carefully is essential to curbing manageability, configurability, and version control problems.

1.2.2 Objects

The notions of instantiation, identity, and encapsulation lead to the notion of objects. In contrast to the properties characterizing components, an object's characteristic properties are that it is a unit of instantiation (it has a unique identity), it has state that can be persistent, and it encapsulates its state and behavior.

Again, several object properties follow directly. Since an object is a unit of instantiation, it cannot be partially instantiated. Since an object has individual state, it also needs a unique identity so it can be identified, despite state changes, for the object's lifetime. Consider the apocryphal story about George Washington's axe, which had five new handles and four new axe-heads—but was still George Washington's axe. This is typical of objects: nothing but their abstract identity remains stable over time.

Since objects get instantiated, a construction plan is needed that describes the new object's state space, initial state, and behavior before the object can exist. Such a plan may be explicitly available and is then called a class. Alternatively, it may be implicitly available in the form of an object that already exists, that is close to the object to be created, and can be cloned. Such a preexisting object is called a prototype object [Lie86, US87, Bla94].

Whether using classes or prototype objects, the newly instantiated object needs to be set to an initial state. The initial state needs to be a valid state of the constructed object, but it may also depend on parameters specified by the client asking for the new object. The code that is required to control object creation and initialization could be a static procedure, usually called a constructor. Alternatively, it can be an object of its own, usually called an object factory, or factory for short.

1.2.3 Object References and Persistent Objects

The object's identity is usually captured by an object reference. Most programming languages do not explicitly support object references; language-level references hold unique references of objects (usually their addresses in memory), but there is no direct high-level support to manipulate the reference as such. (Languages like C provide low-level address manipulation facilities.) Distinguishing between an object—an identity, state, and implementing class—and an object reference (just the identity) is important when considering persistence. As described later, almost all so-called persistence schemes just preserve an object's state and class, but not its absolute identity. An exception is CORBA, which defines Interoperable Object References (IORs) as stable entities (which are really objects). Storing an IOR makes the pure object identity persist.

1.2.4 Components and Objects

Typically, a component comes to life through objects and therefore would normally contain one or more classes or immutable prototype objects. In addition, it might contain a set of immutable objects that capture default initial state and other component resources. However, there is no need for a component to contain only classes or any classes at all. A component could contain traditional procedures and even have global (static) variables; or it may be realized in its entirety using a functional programming approach, an assembly language, or any other approach. Objects created in a component, or references to such objects, can become visible to the component's clients, usually other components. If only objects become visible to clients, there is no way to tell whether a component is pure object-oriented inside, or not.

A component may contain multiple classes, but a class is necessarily confined to a single component; partial deployment of a class wouldn't normally make sense. Just as classes can depend on other classes (inheritance), components can depend on other components (import). The superclasses of a class do not necessarily need to reside in the same component as the class. Where a class has a superclass in another component, the inheritance relation crosses component boundaries and objects created by instantiating such a class are effectively instances carried by multiple components. Whether or not inheritance across components is a good thing is the focus of heated debate. The theoretical reasoning behind this clash is interesting and close to the essence of component orientation [Szy98], but it is beyond the scope of this chapter.

1.2.5 Modules

Components are rather close to modules, as introduced by modular languages in the early 1980s. The most popular modular languages are Modula-2 and Ada. In Ada, modules are called packages, but the concepts are almost identical. An important hallmark of modular approaches is the support of separate compilation, including the ability to properly type-check across module boundaries.

With the introduction of the Eiffel language, the claim was that a class is a better module [Mey88]. This seemed justified based on the early ideas that modules would each implement one abstract data type (ADT). After all, a class can be seen as implementing an ADT, with the additional properties of inheritance and polymorphism. However, modules can be used, and always have been used, to package multiple entities, such as ADTs or classes, into one unit. Also, modules do not have a concept of instantiation, while classes do. (In module-less languages, this leads to the construction of static classes that essentially serve as simple modules.)

Recent language designs, such as Oberon, Modula-3, and Component Pascal, keep the modules and classes separate. (In Java, a package is somewhat weaker than a module and mostly serves namespace control purposes.) Also, a module can contain multiple classes. Where classes inherit from each other, they can do so across module boundaries. Modules can be seen as minimal components. Even modules that do not contain any classes can function as components. It is important though that the modules that should function as components are individually and separably present at deployment time.

Nevertheless, module concepts don't normally support one aspect of full-fledged components. A module does not come with persistent immutable resources, beyond what has been hardwired as constants in the code. Resources seem to parameterize a component—replacing these resources allows one to make a new version of a component without needing to recompile it, for example, for purposes of localization. Modification of resources may look like a form of a mutable component state. Since components are not supposed to modify their own resources (or their code), the component definition remains useful: resources fall into the same category as the compiled code that forms part of a component.

Component technology unavoidably leads to modular solutions. The software engineering benefits can thus justify initial investment into component technology, even if component markets are not foreseen.

1.3 Components Beyond Modules

It is possible to go beyond the technical level of reducing components to better modules. To do so, it is helpful to define components differently.

A Definition: Component "A software component is a unit of composition with contractually specified interfaces and explicit context dependencies only. A software component can be deployed independently and is subject to composition by third parties." (Workshop on Component-Oriented Programming at ECOOP 1996 [SP97].)

This definition covers the characteristic properties of components as discussed. It covers technical aspects such as independence, contractual interfaces, and composition, and also market-related aspects such as third parties and deployment. It is the unique property of components, not only of software components, to combine technical and market aspects. One possible—and purely technical—interpretation of this view maps this component concept back to that of modules, as illustrated in the following.

• A *component* is a set of simultaneously deployed atomic components. An atomic component is a module plus a set of resources.

This distinction of components and atomic components caters to the fact that most atomic components are not deployed individually, although they could be. Instead, atomic components normally belong to a set of components, and a typical deployment will cover the entire set. Atomic components are the elementary units of deployment, versioning and replacement; although it is not usually done, individual deployment is possible. A module is thus an atomic component with no separate resources.

ActiveX, JavaBeans, and CORBA components come packaged in a form that satisfies this component definition. While none of these approaches uses the term "module", constructs of the same meaning are easily identified. For example, in Java packages are not modules. But the atomic units of deployment aren't modules either; they are class files and resources. A single package is compiled into many class files—one per class. However, a set of class files and a set of resources are combined into a JAR (Java archive) file to be shipped as a Java component.

• A *module* is a set of classes and possibly constructs that are not object-oriented, such as procedures or functions.

Modules may statically require the presence of other modules in order to work. Hence, a module can be deployed if all the modules it depends on are available. The dependency graph must be acyclic or else a group of modules in a cyclic-dependency relation would always require simultaneous deployment, violating the defining property of modules. Also, modules that underly components should not have a persistent state, as argued in Section 1.2.1.

• A *resource* is a frozen collection of typed items.

The resource concept could include code resources to subsume modules. The point is that there are resources besides the ones generated by a compiler compiling a module or package. In a pure-objects approach, resources are serialized immutable objects. They're immutable because components have no persistent identity. Duplicates cannot be distinguished.

1.3.1 Interfaces

A component's interfaces define its access points. These points let a component's clients, usually components themselves, access the component's services. Normally, a component has multiple interfaces corresponding to different access points. Each access point may provide a different service, catering to different client needs. It is important to emphasize the interface specifications' contractual nature. Since the component and its clients are developed in mutual ignorance, the standardized contract must form a common ground for successful interaction. What nontechnical aspects do contractual interfaces need to obey to be successful?

First, undue market fragmentation must be avoided, as it threatens the viability of components. The redundant introduction of similar interfaces should also be minimized. In a market economy, such a minimization is usually either the result of early standardization efforts in a market segment, or the result of fierce eliminating competition. In the former case, the danger is suboptimality due to committee design; in the latter case, it is suboptimality due to the nontechnical nature of market forces.

Second, to maximize the reach of an interface specification, and of components implementing this interface, common media are needed to publicize and advertise interfaces and components. If nothing else, this requires a small number of widely accepted unique naming schemes.

1.3.2 Explicit Context Dependencies

Besides specifying provided interfaces, the previous definition of components also requires components to specify their needs. That is, the definition requires specification of what the deployment environment will need to provide, such that the components can function. These needs are called context dependencies, referring to the context of composition and deployment. If there were only one software-component world, it would suffice to enumerate required interfaces of other components to specify all context dependencies [OB97]. For example, a mail-merge component would specify that it needs a file system interface. Note that with today's components even this list of required interfaces is not normally available. The emphasis is usually just on provided interfaces.

In reality, several component worlds coexist, compete, and conflict with each other. Currently there are at least three major worlds emerging, based on OMG's CORBA, Sun's Java, and Microsoft's COM. In addition, component worlds are fragmented by the various computing and networking platforms. This is not likely to change soon. Just as the markets have so far tolerated a surprising multitude of operating systems, there will be room for multiple component worlds. Where multiple such worlds share markets, a component's context dependencies specification must include its required interfaces and the component world (or worlds) it has been prepared for.

There will also be secondary markets for cross-component-world integration. In analogy, consider the thriving market for power-plug adapters for electrical devices. Thus, bridging solutions, such as OMG's COM and CORBA Interworking standard, mitigate chasms.

1.3.3 Component Weight

Obviously, a component is most useful if it offers the right set of interfaces and has no restricting context dependencies; that is, if it can perform in all component worlds and requires no further interface. However, few components, if any, could perform under such weak environmental guarantees. Technically, a component could come with all required software bundled in, but that would defeat the purpose of using components in the first place.

Note that a part of the environmental requirements is the machine the component can execute on. In the case of a virtual machine, such as the Java Virtual Machine, this is a straightforward specification. On native code platforms, a mechanism such as Apple's fat binaries, which packs multiple binaries into one file, would still let a component run everywhere.

Instead of constructing a self-sufficient component with everything built in, a component designer may have opted for maximal reuse. Although maximizing reuse has many oft-cited advantages, it has one substantial disadvantage: the explosion of context dependencies. If component designs were frozen after release, and if all deployment environments were the same, this would not pose a problem. However, as components evolve and different environments provide different configurations and version mixes, it becomes a showstopper to have a large number of context dependencies. *Maximizing reuse minimizes use.* In practice, component designers have to strive for a balance.

1.4 Component-based Programming Versus Component Assembly

Component technology is sometimes used as a synonym for visual assembly of prefabricated components. Indeed, for relatively simple applications, "wiring" components is surprisingly productive—for example, JavaSoft's BeanBox lets a user connect beans visually and displays such connections as pieces of pipe work: plumbing instead of programming.

It is useful to look behind the scenes. When wiring ("plumbing") components, the visual assembly tool registers event listeners with event sources. For example, if the assembly of a button and a text field should clear the text field whenever the button is pressed, then the button is the event source of the event "button pressed" and the text field is listening for this event. While details are of no importance here, it is clear that this assembly process is not primarily about components. (Although, when adding the first object of a kind, an assembly tool will need to locate and possibly load an appropriate component.) The button and the text field are instances, that is, objects not components.

However, there is a problem with this analysis. If the assembled objects are saved and distributed as a new component, how can this be explained? The key here is to realize that not the graph of objects is actually saved. Instead, the saved information suffices to generate a new graph of objects that happens to have the same topology (and, to a degree, the same state) as the originally assembled graph of objects. However, the newly generated graph and the original graph will not share common objects: the object identities are all different.

1.4.1 Assembling Objects, Not Components

The stored graph should then be viewed as persistent state but not as persistent objects. Therefore, what seems to be assembly at the instance rather than the class level—and thus fundamentally different—becomes a matter of convenience.

In fact, there is no difference in outcome between this approach of assembling a component out of subcomponents and a traditional programmatic implementation that "hard codes" the assembly. Indeed, visual assembly tools are free to not save object graphs, but to generate code that when executed creates the required objects and establishes their interconnections.

It would seem that a key difference is that the saved object graph could easily be modified at run time, after deploying the component, while the generated code would be harder to modify. Easy or not, such a modification of the graph is quite equivalent to self-modifying code, something that is usually not seen as desirable since the resulting management problems immediately outweigh the gained flexibility.

1.4.2 Component Objects

Components carry instances that act at run-time as prescribed by their generating component. In the simplest case, a component is simply a class and the carried instances are objects of that class. However, most components (whether COM or JavaBeans) will consist of many classes.

A Java Bean is externally represented by a single class and thus a single kind of object representing all possible instantiations or uses of that component. A COM component is more flexible. It can present itself to clients as an arbitrary object collection, whose clients only see sets of interfaces that are unrelated.

In JavaBeans or CORBA, multiple interfaces are ultimately merged into one implementing class. This prevents proper handling of important cases such as components that support multiple versions of an interface, where the exact implementation of a particular method shared by all these versions needs to depend on the version of the interface the client is using. The CORBA Components proposal promises to fix this problem.

1.5 Component Introversion Versus Component Extroversion

When probing the repertoire of software engineering, the support for component-based systems is almost void. Practically all methods and tools have been devised with an expectation that there is the final deliverable. The need to split such a deliverable across machines and, in general, the need to resolve deployment requirements is almost always seen as a late step in the process. Software engineers approaching the construction of solutions under such premises are "component introverted": they excel at producing individual components. Where such a component is an application—the application—that solves the given problem, this is fine. The established operating systems then take care of the component model (they define what it is that makes a piece of software an application—and requiring it to be unit of deployment is always one of the requirements).

To move ahead and create solutions based on components (more than one), the software engineer needs to become a "component extrovert." Methods and tools are required that support the architecting of systems based on components as well as the long-term maintenance (versioning!) of component-based solutions. The extroverted approach is naturally open: there is a need to consider the factoring into components at early stages of the design process to enable incorporation of existing components. Componentization forms a major feature of a solution—if done well, clients benefit from extensibility and evolvability in unprecedented magnitude. However, to be truly useful, the dimensions of evolvability and the coverage of available components need to match the clients' needs. Therefore, components and component-based architectures need to even enter early requirements and analysis phases. Once this step is accepted—and the justification for (certain) components communicated to clients—the old idea of turning waterfalls into cyclical models might finally bear full fruit.

Even when researchers clearly isolate problems as being related to the composite and possibly extensible nature of systems, the emphasis is often on the introvert's problem of constructing individual components. Often, these approaches fall into the category of generative approaches. A generative approach takes some higher-level description of what is required and then uses a generator to synthesize highly specific software solutions based on generic "components" and the requirements. However, these "components" do not survive the generative process and, following the line of this chapter, it is appropriate to consider the generated artifact a single component. An example in this category are the weavers of aspect-oriented programming [Kic97] as well as many other generators—including the most conventional ones: compilers. While generative approaches clearly have their place—it is not easy to produce good components—they do not help to build component-based systems in large.

A word of caution at this point: there are a large number of software systems in productive use that is based on a systems integration approach. The programming of such systems is often called scripting and the components integrated across are heavyweights such as complete applications and servers. The integrated pieces can rightfully be called components and it would thus seem appropriate that those software engineers focusing on such integration activities are component extroverts already. Unfortunately, the situation is rather sobering in current practice. Critical questions for overall architecture typically remain unanswered. Technical approaches addressing the key issue of versioning and evolution over time are usually covered by hand waving. Indeed, among the three current candidates for component models, only COM offers a sound answer to the versioning problem. However, even in the case of COM the practice tends to be to not use COM properly and therefore to not solve the versioning problem. The discipline and best practice still have to evolve to embrace the component extroverts' point of view!

1.6 Conceptualization—Beyond Objects?

At a conceptual level, it is obviously useful to introduce layers, to single out components, and to separate concerns. How much of this needs to "survive" in a concrete realization of an architecture? More provocative: are granularities beyond objects (or classes) really needed? Interestingly, it is sometimes claimed that a prime strength of objects is the isomorphism of objects and object relations as they show up in requirements, analysis, design, and implementation (for example [GR95]). This is true if either nothing but objects count in all these phases, or if everything that is more than one object can be isolated and represented by just one object. Doing so is largely the main thrust of "pure" object-oriented approaches.

It is obviously not true that everything is just an object. However, it is true that anything that requires a group of objects to interact can be abstracted by designating a representative object that stands for the interacting group. In this context, it becomes essential to distinguish between has-a (or contains-a) relations and uses-a relations. The representative object has a group of objects while the objects in the group, possibly mediated by the representative, use each other. Relations between objects can be modeled as graphs, where objects are nodes and a relation introduces directed edges between such nodes. Distinguishing has-a from uses-a allows distinguishing between intergraph and intragraph edges. Consider an externalization service that supports transfer of objects between contexts in time and space. Storing a compound document is an example. Intragraph edges need to be followed in typical externalization activities. Intergraph edges are not followed but abstractly maintained as "links," where links symbolically represent the target node of a directed edge. As a special case, links can also occur within a graph.

Unless special care is taken, all objects are potentially in arbitrary uses-a or has-a relations. Arbitrary uses-a relations can introduce cyclic dependencies and threaten organizational structure. Arbitrary has-a relations can even be unsound: the has-a relation must be acyclic. Hierarchical design is the key to mastering complexity. Unless objects are conceptually allowed to contain other objects in their entirety, there is little hope to master complexity in a pure object-oriented approach. As soon as hierarchical designs are introduced, the question arises how parts of such hierarchical designs could be units of deployment. It is, therefore, and quite paradoxically, nontrivial to introduce the notion of components into object systems.

1.7 Structures beyond objects

This section introduces definitions of structures at levels beyond objects (classes). The terms defined help to construct an architectural terminology.

- A *component-system architecture* consists of a set of platform decisions, a set of component frameworks, and an interoperation design for the component frameworks.

A *platform* is the substrate that allows for installation of components and component frameworks, such that these can be instantiated and activated. A platform can be concrete or virtual. Concrete platforms provide direct physical support, that is, implement their services in hardware. Virtual platforms—also called platform abstractions or platform shields—emulate a platform on top of another, introducing a cost-flexibility tradeoff. In practice, all platforms are virtual to some degree and a sharp distinction is academic. The conceptual distance, or gap, between a virtual platform and its underlying platform generally has a tremendous impact on expected performance. Understanding this distance is thus important.

- A *component framework* is a dedicated and focused architecture, usually around a few key mechanisms, and a fixed set of policies for mechanisms at the component level.

Component frameworks often implement protocols to connect participating components and enforce some of the policies set by the framework. The policies governing the use of the mechanisms that are used by the framework itself are not necessarily fixed. Instead, they can be left to higher-level architectures.

A good example of component frameworks are the application servers that are presently emerging to support transactional multitier applications, such as Microsoft Transaction Server and Enterprise JavaBeans compliant servers. Still, practical examples component frameworks remain rare; some are briefly mentioned in Section 1.9, a more detailed discussion can be found in [Szy98].

- An *interoperation design* for component frameworks comprises the rules of interoperation among all the frameworks joined by the system architecture.

Such a design can be seen as a second-order component framework, with the (first-order) component frameworks as its plug-in (second-order) components. It is quite clearly established by now that this second order is required—a single component framework for everything is illusory. An architectural approach to this situation is described in the next section.

Good examples for general interoperation designs are hard to come by. The OMG Object Management Architecture (OMA) aims in this direction, but much of the OMA remains sketchy and many aspects of interoperation across services and facilities have yet to be resolved. The current state of the art is to concentrate on interoperation aspects at the 'plumbing' level; for example, by concentrating on interoperation between ORBs (IIOP) or between COM and CORBA (CORBA InterWorking bridging standard).

1.8 A Tiered-Component Architecture

A fundamental notion of traditional software architecture is that of layers. Layers and hierarchical decomposition remain useful in component systems. Each part of a component system, including the components themselves, can be layered; components may be located within particular layers of a larger architecture. To master the complexity of larger component systems, architecture itself needs to be layered. It is important to clearly distinguish between the layers formed by an architecture and those formed by a meta-architecture. The layers formed by a meta-architecture are thus called tiers. Multitier client/server applications are an example of tiered architectures, where the subsystems residing at each tier can be and often are themselves layered.

This section proposes a notion of tiers that is different from the one found in client/server architectures. A component-system architecture, as introduced in the previous section, arranges an open set of component frameworks. This is a second-tier architecture, where each of the component frameworks introduces a first-tier architecture. In this sense, all parts of a client/server architecture reside in the same tier and an overarching management structure, if one exists, could be seen as residing at the next higher tier.

It is important to notice the radical difference between tiers and traditional layers. Traditional layers, as seen from the bottom up, are of increasingly abstract and increasingly application-specific nature. Each layer abstracts from details present at the layer below. In a well-balanced layered system, all layers have their performance and resource implications. To the contrary, tiers need to be of decreasing performance and resource relevance, but of increasing structural relevance, to avoid scaling problems. Different tiers focus on different degrees of integration, but all are of comparable application relevance.

Instances carried by components can communicate directly with each other, for example, using COM Connectable Objects, Microsoft Message Queue, CORBA events, or Java Beans events. However, they can also interact indirectly through a component framework that mediates and regulates component interaction. The same choice reoccurs when component framework instances interact; the mediator in this case is a tier-three instance. It is important that not every single interaction at a lower tier needs to be observed and mediated by a higher tier. Hence, lower tiers need to abstract interaction to curb load on higher tiers and thus allow the architecture to scale.

Beside tiering, component frameworks can also be used in a layered (or nested) fashion. In this case a component framework with all inserted components is used to construct a single component that is then received by another component framework. The inner component framework perfectly abstracts its framework nature and the outer framework is in no way special: both frameworks really exist in the same tier. Such a layered (or nested) approach can easily be recursively applied without introducing new complexity. Only where a component framework reveals its framework nature—and thus its inserted components—will mediation by another component framework force this mediating framework into a higher tier.

In a world still largely dominated by monolithic software, not even first-tier architectures are commonplace. Note that objects and class frameworks do not form the lowest tier; the tier structure starts with deployable entities: components! Traditional class frameworks merely structure individual components, independent of the placement in a tiered architecture. Historically, class frameworks are also called application frameworks, with an assumption that applications are monolithic.

Objects and class frameworks can be found within components where, depending on the components' complexity, they can well form their own layering and hierarchies, for example, MFC in OLE. However, all of a class framework's structure is flattened out when compiling a component. Unlike component frameworks, the line between a class framework and its instantiation is blurred, since the framework is immaterial at runtime, while the instances do not exist at compile-time. This duality may explain the common confusion of the terms class and object.

As in the preceding section, it can be seen as clearly established that a single first-tier architecture satisfying all demands of all components and all component applications will never emerge. Obviously, if it did, the tier model would be superfluous. What is more important, it is not even desirable to focus on a single unified first-tier architecture. Lightweight architectures that intentionally focus on one problem—rather than trying to be everything for all—enable the construction of lightweight components. Such components can be constructed with restrictive assumptions in mind. Lightweight components are most economical if their guiding architecture opens an important degree of extensibility while fixing other decisions.

The possibility to have lightweight components is important; it creates richness in a market in which heavier weights can also blossom. For example, the many ActiveX "heavyweights" get truly useful when combined with the many more lightweight components, including controls in the original sense. Lightweight components can be made possible in two ways: by using multiple, specialized component frameworks, or by allowing components to leave those features unimplemented that they do not require. In the first case, the question of interoperation among component frameworks arises, and thus the concept of tiered architectures. In the second case, it becomes difficult to compose components, as it is never clear which aspects are implemented. Indeed, most systems following the second approach simply do not even have a guiding first-tier architecture: there is no component framework at all.

1.9 Component Frameworks and Component-System Architecture

Component frameworks are the most important step to lift component software off the ground. Most current emphasis has been on construction of individual components and on the basic "wiring" support of components. It is thus highly unlikely that components developed independently under such conditions are able to cooperate usefully. The primary goal of component technology—independent deployment and assembly of components—is not reached.

A component framework is a software entity that supports components conforming to certain standards and allows instances of these components to be "plugged" into the component framework. The component framework establishes environmental conditions for component instances and regulates the interaction between component instances. Component frameworks can come alone and create an island for certain components, or they can themselves cooperate with other components or component frameworks. It is thus natural to model component frameworks themselves as components. As detailed in the previous section, it is also possible to postulate higher-tier component frameworks that regulate the interaction between component frameworks.

Today, there are only a few component frameworks on the market. Higher-tier component frameworks seem necessary and unavoidable in the longer run, but certainly do not exist on the markets today. Examples of component frameworks for visual components are the late OpenDoc and BlackBox [Obe97]. A nonvisual component framework for hard real-time control applications is JBed [Esm98]. Important emerging kinds of component frameworks are application servers such as MTS (Microsoft Transaction Server) and EJB-compliant servers. With the clear need to simplify the realization of component-based transactional applications, the aim of application server designs is to factor transaction binding and isolation.

1.10 Closing Remarks

While components capture software fragment's static nature, objects capture its dynamic nature. Simply treating everything as dynamic can eliminate this distinction. However, it is a time-proven principle of software engineering to try to strengthen the static description of systems as much as possible. One can always superimpose dynamics where needed. Modern facilities such as metaprogramming and just-in-time compilation simplify this soft treatment of the boundary between static and dynamic. Nevertheless, it is advisable to explicitly capture as many static properties of a design or an architecture as possible. This is the role of components and architectures that assign components their place. The role of objects is to capture the dynamic nature of the arising systems built out of components. Component objects are objects carried by identified components—frequently it is useful to identify a set of objects in conjunction as a component object. Components and objects together enable the construction of next-generation software. However, as sketched in this chapter, the road ahead is still long and winding—many problems still need to be solved before component software can become ubiquitous. One important step to be taken is to move from component introversion to component extroversion and adopt component-based software architecture on a much broader basis. To avoid the many traps on that way, it is useful to emphasize: components are units of deployment; as such, they do not nest (although the instances they support typically do). Components are also the units of versioning but the atoms of configuration. Since naive peer-to-peer component architectures lead to a complexity explosion and thus do not scale, it is important to pursue component frameworks and component system architectures much further.

Acknowledgments

This work is partially based on the author's book Component Software [Szy98]. Opinions expressed in this chapter are the author's and are not necessarily shared by or represent Microsoft Corporation.

Bibliography

a94]   Blaschek, G. *Object-Oriented Programming with Prototypes.* Springer-Verlag, Berlin, 1994.

)x98]   Box, D. *Essential COM.* Addison-Wesley, Reading, Mass., 1998.

na96]   Chappel, D. *Understanding ActiveX and OLE.* Microsoft Press, Redmond, Wash., 1996.

;m98]   Esmertec, Inc. *JBed real-time operating system and IDE.* www.esmertec.com, 1998.

R95]   Goldberg, A. and Rubin, K. S. *Succeeding with Objects—Design Frameworks for Project Management.* Addison-Wesley, 1995.

v98]   JavaSoft. *Enterprise JavaBeans Specification.* java.sun.com/products/ejb/, 1998.

ic97]   Kiczales, G. *AOP: Going beyond objects for better separation of concerns in design and implementation.* Xerox PARC, Slides of invited talk, www.parc.xerox.com/aop/invited-talk/, 1997.

e86]   Lieberman, H. Using prototypical objects to implement shared behavior in oo systems. In *OOPSLA86, SIGPLAN Notices*, volume 21:11, pages 214–223. ACM Press, November 1986.

ey88]   Meyer, B. *Object-Oriented Software Construction.* Prentice-Hall, Englewood Cliffs, NJ, 2nd, 1997 edition, 1988.

ic97]   Microsoft Corporation. *The Component Object Model Specification.* www.microsoft.com/com/, 1997.

B97]   Olafsson, A. and Bryan, D. On the need for required interfaces of components. In Mühlhäuser, M., editor, *Special Issues in Object-Oriented Programming—ECOOP96 Workshop Reader*, pages 159–171, Heidelberg, 1997. dpunkt Verlag.

[Obe97]   Oberon Microsystems, Inc. *BlackBox Component Builder*. www.oberon.ch, 1997.

[Obj98]   Object Management Group. *CORBA 2.2 Specification*. www.omg.org, 1998.

[SP97]   Szyperski, C. and Pfister, C. Workshop on component-oriented programming (wcop96), summary. In Mühlhäuser, M., editor, *Special Issues in Object-Oriented Programming—ECOOP96 Workshop Reader*, pages 127–130, Heidelberg, 1997. dpunkt Verlag.

[Szy98]   Szyperski, C. *Component Software: Beyond Object-Oriented Programming*. Addison-Wesley, Harlow, UK, 1998.

[US87]   Ungar, D. and Smith, R. B. Self: the power of simplicity. In *OOPSLA87, SIGPLAN Notices*, volume 22:10, pages 227–241. ACM Press, October 1987.

Part One

Frameworks and Architectures

2

Key Concepts in Architecture Definition Languages

David C. Luckham

Stanford University

James Vera

Stanford University

Sigurd Meldal

Cal Poly

Abstract

An *architecture* is a specification of the *components* of a system and the *communication* between them. An architecture guarantees certain behavioral properties of a conforming system and can be a powerful tool to aid the processes of predicting behavior of systems with that architecture, managing the construction of a system, and maintaining it.

This paper presents three alternative concepts of architecture: *object connection architecture*, *interface connection architecture*, and *plug and socket architecture*. While the first kind can be represented in standard programming languages, the two latter kinds require new language features. We describe the features of an ADL called *Rapide* that are designed to represent the different concepts of *interface* and *connection* in each of the three kinds of architecture. Simple examples are given to illustrate the relative merits of each kind of architecture in guaranteeing properties of conforming systems, and in supporting efficient techniques for correctly modifying a conforming system.

The power of architectures depends upon the concept of *conformance* of a system to an architecture. We define conformance in terms of two principles: *interface conformance* (individual components behave correctly), and *communication integrity* (components communicate correctly). We indicate how plug and socket architectures reduce the complexity of architecture definitions and in many cases guarantee that if the components of a system obey interface conformance, then the system obeys communication integrity.

The presentation is independent of any particular formalism, since the concepts can be represented in widely differing architecture definition formalisms, varying from graphical languages to event-based simulation languages.

23

2.1 Introduction

In recent years, object-oriented techniques have caused a paradigm shift in systems development. As a result, we have become much more efficient at building objects—the components of systems.

However, object-oriented techniques do not solve the conspicuous problem of planning the complete system *before* constructing its components. Large-scale software systems continue to be plagued with a variety of development problems which have been amply discussed in the literature (see, for example, [Gib94]). First on the list of lessons learned [Mar96] is the need for a "Meta-Model" that "deals with basic notions such as how objects communicate with other objects." The use of commercial middleware such as CORBA ORBs [Gro91] to facilitate building distributed object systems increases the need for Meta models of the systems.

There are several attempts within the software engineering community to find new technologies that augment object-oriented methods to provide planning and prototyping of systems at a global level, *before* component objects are built—for example "patterns" [GHJV95] and "architecture" [GS93]. Unfortunately, although the word "architecture" appears as frequently as "system" or "object," the term "architecture" often has little meaning other than a graphical diagram consisting of boxes and arrows that serves as a pictorial table of contents for detailed design and code documents. Moreover, its ambiguity is often compounded by different uses of "architecture" – for example, to describe different views of a system, a hierarchical abstraction view [Int87], a modular decomposition view [SNH95, Mel90], and so forth. Also, "style" (for example, client-server, pipe-and-filter, and so forth, see [GS93]) and "architecture" tend to be confused. Style refers to the roles played by components; concepts of "architecture" are common to all styles of architecture.

The most common answer given to the question *"what is architecture?"* is *"interfaces* and *connections."* This is not a bad answer, but the devil is in the details of what the properties of "interfaces" and "connections" are, how they are related to the system, and what use can be made of them in various processes of system development. The primary issue is to define precisely different concepts of *architecture* and their relation to *system.* A second important issue is to show how the various concepts of architecture can be expressed in formalisms (graphical or textual) with precisely defined semantics.

In this paper we present three concepts of architecture: *(i) object connection architecture, (ii) interface connection architecture,* and *(iii) plug and socket* architecture. These are different kinds of architectures that specify the components of systems and the communications between those components.

Object connection architectures are the most familiar kind since they can be defined in standard programming languages such as C++. But this kind of architecture has limited usefulness. It cannot be used as a metamodel to guide building a system, for example. *Interface connection* architectures, on the other hand, are intended to be used as meta models to guide system development, and to guarantee certain properties of systems that conform to them. *Plug and socket* architectures are a specialization of interface connection architectures to deal with practical issues that arise in the use of architectures to build systems. These issues include *(i)* scalability (that is, defining large architectures), *(ii)* refinement (that is, *processes* of refining or modifying an architecture), and *(iii)* guaranteeing properties of conforming systems (that is, an ability to infer from the architecture that a conforming system will have certain properties). The concept of plug and socket architectures is derived from the hardware domain—it uses the simple notion of a *plug* as a grouping of related interface features, and a complementary notion of the *dual* of a plug, called a *socket*. Simple examples are given to illustrate the relative merits of each kind of architecture.

The power of architectures depends upon the concept of *conformance* of a system to an architecture. The stricter the concept of conformance between a system and its architecture, the more one can infer about the system from analysis of its architecture. We define conformance in terms of the following criteria:

(i) **hierarchical decomposition**: For each interface in the architecture there should be a unique module corresponding to it in the system (that is, the component implementing that interface).†

(ii) **interface conformance**: Each component in the system must conform to its interface. This conformance requirement is, in general, stronger than the purely syntactic interface conformance usually required by programming languages since behavioral constraints can be part of interfaces.

(iii) **communication integrity**: The system's components interact only as specified by the connections in the architecture.

Whether or not a system obeys either *interface conformance* or *communication integrity* is an undecidable problem in the general case. However, we describe how plug and socket architectures not only reduce the complexity of architecture definitions, but can in many cases guarantee that if the components of a system obey interface conformance, then the system obeys communication integrity.

Rapide [LKA+95, LV95, LVB+93] is a widely applicable architecture definition language suitable for defining constraint-based architectures whose purpose is to constrain a system to obey certain design criteria, or defining executable architectures for event-based simulation of system behavior. The features discussed in this article are all supported by *Rapide*.

---

† *Rapide* enables the use of more sophisticated notions of decomposition (such as allowing subarchitectures or groups of modules to implement a particular interface in the architecture, or even to be satisfied by the existence of an abstraction mapping from the system to the architecture), but these are beyond the scope of this presentation.

2.2 Some Terminology

To discuss concepts of architectures in general and *Rapide* in particular we need a small amount of terminology. The following concepts are explained in general terms so as not to imply any particular language or semantics; different languages, (for example, C++ [ES90], VHDL[VHD87], Ada [Ada83], UML [RJB98], ACME [GMW97], and *Rapide* [LVB+93, LKA+95]) define some of these concepts using their own semantics. Key relationships, "is a component of" and "conforms to" are illustrated in Figure 2.1.

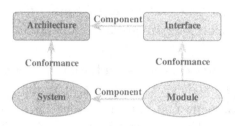

Fig. 2.1. Two Key Relationships.

component: Components of architectures are *interfaces*; components of systems are *modules*.

feature: A computational element of a component, for example, a function or port or action.

specification: A set of structural or behavioral constraints expressed in a formal language.

uses: A relationship between components and features. A component uses a feature by, for example, calling a function, or sending a message to a port.

interface definition: A definition of a set of features of a component, together with a specification of their behavior. Interface features of a component can be used by other components to communicate with the component. Examples can be the public part of a C++ or Java class, an Ada package specification, a Java interface, or a *Rapide* interface type.

interface: An architectural component about which the only known fact is that its realization conforms to a given interface definition.

module: An executable computational entity containing a set of features, possibly with an internal computational- and data structure, for example an Ada package body, a *Rapide* module, or a C++ or Java class. Modules may compute independently of, or concurrently with, one another. A module implementing an interface is called a *system component,* and must give a realization of the features of its corresponding *architecture component*—the interface.

connection: A relation between components, implying potential interaction. For example, one component uses a feature of another component.

conformance: A relationship between a specification and a realization. A system may conform to an architecture in a manner analogous to that of modules conforming to an interface definition.

interface conformance: A relationship between a module and an interface definition. A module *conforms* to an interface definition if (1) it contains the features specified by the interface definition, and (2) their behavior satisfies the behavior specification given in the interface definition.

architecture: A specification of a system, identifying its components and the interactions between them, by means of interfaces, connections, and constraints.

2.3 Object Connection Architectures

An *object-oriented interface* specifies the features that must be *provided* by modules conforming to the interface. Typically, a feature is a function, an interface specifies the name and signature of the function, and a module contains an implementation of a function with that name and signature. Examples are SmallTalk, Java and C++ classes, Java interfaces, Ada package specifications, UML class diagrams, and VHDL entity interfaces.†

An *object-oriented system* consists of *(i)* object-oriented interfaces, *(ii)* a set of modules, each conforming to an interface by providing an implementation of the features specified in that interface, and *(iii)* connections between the modules. The connections define how each module uses the features specified in the interfaces of other modules. An *object connection architecture* consists of the interfaces and connections of a system. Figure 2.2 shows a simple system and its object connection architecture. In this figure, interfaces are shaded "lids" of the boxes, and the boxes represent modules that conform to the "lids"; connections are shown as directed arcs from a module to a feature in an interface of another module. The direction of a connection indicates which interface specifies a feature being used; the vertical lines indicate the association between an interface feature and its implementation in a module (often simply association by name). The system here, which is a very simple compiler, could be a C++ program, for example, in which features are functions, interfaces are classes (public parts), and connections are function calls. It could also be a Java system hosted on a CORBA ORB, in which the connections are rpc's facilitated by the ORB.

The architecture in Figure 2.2 is called an *object connection architecture* because the connections are from object to object. It has the major disadvantage that the

---

† These examples of interfaces differ in some respects, for example, packages and entities are not types in Ada or VHDL; but each allows the interface features of a module to be visible outside the module, and permits the module to encapsulate or hide other features from outside use.

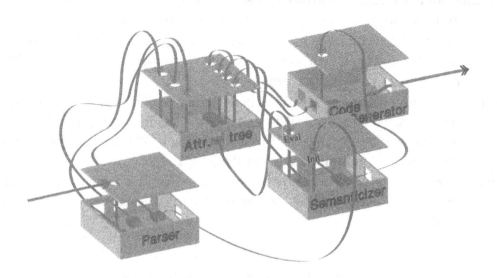

Fig. 2.2. An Object Connection Architecture (with Two Interface Elements Identified).

modules must be built before the architecture is defined, so it cannot be used to lay out the plan for the system. It is, however, a very common (mis)conception of "architecture."

Conformance to an object connection architecture is usually enforced to a limited extent by the language in which the system is implemented. For example, decomposition is satisfied in most programming languages by naming rules for associating an interface with a unique module. Interface conformance is usually checked by compiletime syntactic rules for types and parameter lists, but conformance to semantic constraints is not guaranteed at all. Communication integrity for object connection architectures is trivial since the connections are defined, after the system is built, to consist of all the interactions between the modules.

Examples

To illustrate the ease or difficulty of determining properties of a system from the kind of architecture it has, we take the well-known paradigm example of a compiler. Our simple compiler has four components; a Parser, a Semanticizer, a Code Generator, and an Attributed Tree.

Consider two common programming problems that frequently occur during the development or maintenance of any system.

Problem 1: Determine Which Modules Are Affected by a Change to an Interface.

We might wish to remove or change a function in the Semanticizer interface. First, the Semanticizer module that implements that interface will have to be modified to conform to the new interface. But to determine the effects of this change we must also identify the modules that use that function, and decide if these require modifications as well. We need to trace the connections from other modules to *Eval* that function. But these architecture connections are not defined separately from the system itself. So, we must examine all modules in the system.

Problem 2: Determine Whether We Can Replace a Module by Another One that Conforms to the Same Interface.

Suppose we want to upgrade our compiler by substituting a new parser for the existing one. Assume the new parser conforms to the Parser interface just as the the old parser did. Object-oriented subtyping such as in C++ allows this kind of change, while maintaining some level of error checking. But does the changed system have the same functional behavior? Suppose, for example, the original Parser module made a call to the initializing function, *Init*, of the Semanticizer. There is nothing in the interface definition of the Parser that requires it to make this call—so the new Parser might not, with misbehavior of the Semanticizer and the consequent failure of the entire compiler system as the likely consequence. So even interchanging modules that conform to the same interface in an object-oriented system may have disastrous effects.

These two examples illustrate some of the problems with object connection architectures. First, discovering the connections of the architecture requires inspecting the whole system—and is not an easy task in the presence of pointers, and so forth. Secondly, object-oriented interfaces do not specify system components sufficiently to guarantee that connections will not change when one module that conforms to an interface is substituted for another module that conforms to the same interface.

2.4 Interfaces for Defining Architecture

The motivation for defining an architecture is to provide a precise plan (or Meta Model [Mar96]) suitable for predicting system behavior before a system is built, and for guiding the development of a system. An architecture must specify components in *sufficient detail* that their interactions can also be specified in the architecture. While "sufficient detail" may be vague, we know from the examples in Section 2.3 that object-oriented interfaces do not provide sufficient detail. What is missing?

Definition of Connections. First is the ability to define module interactions when one knows only their interfaces. Part of the failing of object-oriented interfaces is that they specify only the features *provided* by modules. The concept of interface in ADLs should define also those features that modules *require* from their environment.

Substitutivity of Conforming Components. Second, we would like to be able to interchange any two modules that conform to (or "implement") the same interface without changing the system in some "essential" way. So, an interface must contain specifications of the semantics of its features, not just signature information. Those specifications must logically imply any "essential" behavior.

Consequently, ADL interfaces should contain five varieties of specifications:

 (i) A list of the features *provided* by the module;

 (ii) A list of the features *required* by the module;

(iii) A specification of the *behavior of the provided features*;

(iv) A specification of the *behavior of the required features*;

 (v) A specification of any *interaction between two or more features*.

By specifying all of the required features used by a module, an ADL interface explicitly expresses the dependencies a conforming module has on its environment. We say the interface is *contextualized*. Specification of interactions among features adds additional constraints on how a module depends upon context; for example, the *Semanticizer* interface in our example compiler could specify that an initialization function *Init* must be called before calls to *Eval* will return values.

Object-oriented interfaces such as in Java and C++ have traditionally only contained specifications of provided features, with the other four kinds of specification, (ii), (iii), (iv), and (v) left to informal comments or buried in the implementation of the module associated with the interface. As a result, the object-oriented notion of subtyping (substitutivity) is based only on the provided features. This is probably due in part to the influence of the original Simula Class design [OJD66], but also due to an emphasis on the design of the interfaces to support *information hiding* [Par75]. We would argue that in leaving out the features a module requires, object-oriented interfaces have hidden too much to be useful for architecture definition (cfr. [Lak96].

2.5 Interface Connection Architectures

An *interface connection architecture* defines *all* connections between the components of a system using only the interfaces. Interfaces need to specify both *provided* and *required* features. Such an architecture, and a system conforming to it, is shown in Figures 2.3 and 2.4.

A connection associates a provided feature with a required feature. A connection from a using module to an interface feature of a providing module in Figure 2.2 is represented in Figure 2.3 as an arc from a required feature specified in the interface of a user to a provided feature specified in the interface of a provider. Thus all of

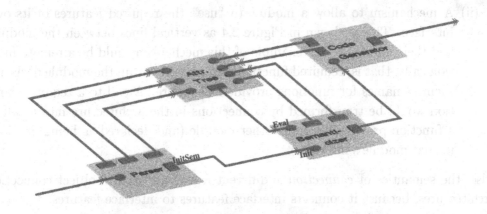

Fig. 2.3. An Interface Connection Architecture.

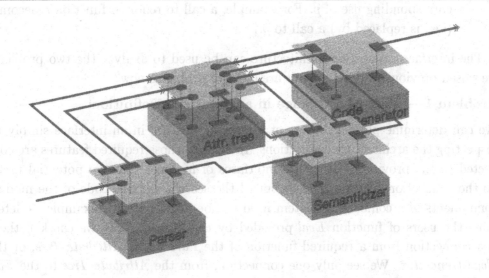

Fig. 2.4. An Interface Connection Architecture with a Conforming System.

the connections between modules in the object connection system are defined as *connections between interface features* in the interface connection architecture.

Two new ADL mechanisms are needed to define connections in interface connection architectures that are not available in present-day programming languages such as Java, C++, or Ada:†

(i) A mechanism to define connections between required features of one interface and provided features another interface. Connections could be as trivial as identifying pairs of names in interfaces (having a semantics similar to pin connections in hardware modeling languages), or as powerful as the pattern-triggered reactive rules of *Rapide*[LVB+93].

† Hardware simulation languages such as Verilog and VHDL contain rudimentary forms of such features.

(ii) A mechanism to allow a module to "use" the required features of its own interface. This is shown in Figure 2.4 as vertical lines between the modules and their interfaces. An example of this mechanism could be a remote function call—that is, required functions are treated within the module declaring them as names for functions provided elsewhere. A call to a required function would be transformed by connections in the architecture into a call to a function provided by some other module (and declared as being provided in that module's interface).

Also, the semantics of *connection* is different from that used in object connection architectures, because it connects interface features to interface features:

interface connection: An association between a required interface feature, r, and a provided interface feature, p, such that any use of r is associated with a corresponding use of p. For example, a call to required function r becomes (i.e., is replaced by) a call to p.†

The interface connection architecture can be used to analyze the two problems we raised previously. How difficult are our two problems now?

Problem 1—Effect of a Change in an Interface Definition:

We can determine potential users of a provided feature in an interface simply by inspecting the architecture connections. Interfaces whose required features are connected to the provided feature are interfaces of modules that are potential users. So the connections can be used to bound the search, and the code of the module components of a conforming system need not be inspected. For example to determine the users of function *Eval* provided by the *Semanticizer*, we check if there is a connection from a required function of the *Parser*, the *Attribute Tree*, or the *Code Generator*. We see only one connection, from the *Attribute Tree* to the *Eval* function of the *Semanticizer*.

To determine whether a potential user actually makes use of an interface feature we would only need to analyze specifications in the interface of the potential user—our assumption that components conform to their interfaces ensures that we have identified all components that are users of *Eval*.

Problem 2—The Effect of Replacing One Module with Another:

Suppose, for example, in some compiler that conforms to our architecture, we want to replace the *Parser* module with another parser. We are concerned about the effect of this change on initializing the *Semanticizer*. We can answer this problem by analyzing the architecture without looking at the code of components.

The connection, from *Parser.InitSem* to *Semanticizer.Init* means that the Parser

---

† CCS [Mil80] makes use of a degenerate version of this in its synchronization primitives, requiring an event with name "e" to be synchronized with an event with name "$\overline{e}$" when composing processes. In an ADL, connection by name correspondences is not powerful enough—a more dynamic mechanism is needed.

can initialize the Semanticizer. Essentially, the architecture specifies a "plan" by specifying the two interface functions and the connection between them: the plan is for the parser in any conforming compiler system to initialize the semanticizer. But, must all parsers do it?

Since interfaces for interface connection architectures must specify required features, as well as provided features, formal specifications in interfaces can specify relationships between the provided and required features as well as properties of each feature individually. This allows more powerful specifications than in object-oriented interfaces. *Rapide* interfaces include a "constraints" part. The *Parser* interface contains a simple constraint that its interaction with its environment must start with a call to its *InitSem* function. So, all parsers *must* initialize the semanticizer before doing anything else. Therefore, in this example, assuming that the compiler's modules conform to their interface specifications, any two parsers can be interchanged and the semanticizer will always be properly initialized.

But what if a connection between two interface functions is not in the architecture? Then neither the old nor new *Parser* can initialize the *Semanticizer* (by communication integrity). So the system must function correctly without the *Parser* initializing the *Semanticizer*.

Finally, if there is no constraint in the parser interface requiring it to call *InitSem* then we must assume that the system will function correctly in either case—both when the parser does initialize the semanticizer, and when it does not.

These examples illustrate a general approach to our two common problems: they can be resolved in systems with interface connection architectures by analysis of the interfaces and connections without inspecting the implementation. Therefore, these problems are easier to solve in systems with interface connection architectures than object connection architectures. But this approach works only if we assume that *(i)* modules conform to interfaces, and *(ii)* modules obey communication integrity.

2.6 ADL Features for Scale and Connectability

Interface connection architectures allow us to define models of the communication of a system *before* building the system. They can be used early in the development process to simulate the behavior of different possible architectures. Interface connection architectures can also be used to manage system development, for example, the detailed definitions of the interfaces and connections can be used to predict how a proposed modification to one interface will propagate to other interfaces and which groups of implementors will be affected (see tactic 2, [Gil96]). They can also be used to define conformance tests for the final product system. Interface connection architectures do, however, raise new issues of *scale* and *connectability*.

For ADLs, the new *scale* issues are how to express succinctly:

(i) Large numbers of features in interfaces.

(ii) Large numbers of connections between interfaces.

Architectures at more detailed levels can often have on the order of 100 features in an interface, with each kind of feature being connected to several others in different interfaces (for example, the Sparc V9 instruction set architecture in *Rapide* [SP95]). This situation has been accentuated in *Rapide* by introducing *requires* features into interfaces, and also by making the connections between interfaces explicit—whereas they were implicitly defined inside the modules of module connection systems. Proliferation of interface ports and port-to-port connections is already a problem in representing hardware models in present simulation languages such as Verilog [TM91] and VHDL [VHD87]†.

To put it simply, an object connection system tends to hide a complex spaghetti of connections inside the modules, whereas an interface connection architecture will raise the level of visibility of connections so that they become an immediately apparent property of the architecture. Indeed, complexity of connections is exactly the kind of issue one wants to reveal as early as possible in system planning. But now, ADLs must find ways of coping with this complexity.

A second issue, related to scale, is *connectability* of interface features:

(i) Connectability of interface features.
(ii) Correctness of connections.

An ADL should not allow interface features to be connected if there is no possibility that the resulting communication will make any sense —for example, if the data communicated would violate type requirements at either end of the connection or if two ends of a connection obey incompatible protocols. An ADL should be sufficiently expressive that one can state the conditions under which a two interface features are *connectable*, and conditions under which a connection between them is *correct*:

Connectability: Two interface features are *connectable* if the implied transfer of data is compatible with all type constraints of the features.

Correct: A connection is *correct* if the implied transfer of data is consistent with all constraints of the features being connected.

Connectability is intended to be a compile time check, involving, for example, compatibility of the types of functions, or the signatures of ports. For example, in strongly typed ADLs (such as *Rapide*), one can check that the data type requirements of both ends of a connection are compatible. *Correctness of connections* is a logically stronger requirement, involving semantic constraints of the features, such as checking whether the stated protocols of two features are compatible. Correctness of connections may be undecidable in some cases.

† For example, VHDL has an iterative loop-like *generate* construct to define connections over enumerable sets of entities.

Examples

(i) Suppose interface features are functions in *Rapide*. Each function has a type determined by the type of its arguments and the type of its return value. Suppose a connection between f and g is defined as identification of f with g, so that any call to f is handled by a call to g with the same arguments. Connectability could be defined as the type of a *provided* function g must be a subtype of the type of a *required* function, f, i.e., $Type(g) <: Type(f)$. On the other hand, *correctness* of a connection could be a much stronger requirement, say, for example, that both functions f and g return prime numbers.

(ii) Suppose interface features are ports as in VHDL. A port has a mode, *in* or *out*, and a type that defines the data carried on the port. Connectability could depend only on the modes, simply requiring an *out* port to be connected only with an *in* port. *Correctness* in VHDL is stronger, requiring the data types of the ports to be the same type and in the same representation.

(iii) In a graphical formalism for defining architectures such as one finds in Java beanboxes and similar component-based IDEs, features could be represented by colored shapes such as circles and triangles in boxes representing interfaces. Connections could be represented as directed lines joining features in different boxes. Two features might be *connectable* only if they are the same shape and color.

(iv) In [AG94] a feature is a port represented as a CSP [Hoa85] process, which may be viewed as a formal specification of the events at the port. A connector is a set of *role* processes together with a process that coordinates (or schedules) the roles, called the *glue*. The concept of connectability is associated with a port and a role: the port process must be a refinement of the role process and have certain properties, such as freedom from deadlock. A correct connection between a set of ports by means of a connector is a binding of ports to roles of the connector to which they are connectable so that the instance of the connector has certain properties, freedom from deadlock being one of them.

In the first and last examples above we see that, in general, correctness of a connection in an architecture depends upon the semantics of the features it connects, and not simply upon some syntactic property such as the signature of a function. Just as determining whether or not a module in a system conforms to its interface in general is an undecidable problem, so is determining the correctness of a connection in an architecture, given a reasonably rich language for expressing feature semantics. With the rich type- and subtype-relations expressible in modern languages such as *Rapide*, even the simple notion of (sub-)type checking becomes a rather powerful tool for identifying incorrect connections. In cases where such automatic checking at the time of the architecture's definition is infeasible, a precise statement of semantic constraints allows semiautomatic tools to be applied in analyzing and checking properties of an architecture as part of the conformance checking or during the system's actual execution. *Rapide*'s event-oriented constraint language is a case in point: one can monitor a system's execution, recognizing violations of the constraints if they occur.

2.7 Plug and Socket Architectures

The approach to complex connection topologies taken in *Rapide* is to provide new language constructs analogous to plugs and sockets in hardware. These constructs allow subsets of interface features to be grouped together, and connections between individual features in related groups to be defined by one connection between the groups. These constructs are a software version of the hardware paradigm in which many signal wires connecting two components are grouped into a single cable, with the appropriate plugs and sockets at each end.

The *Rapide* service construct allows features in an interface to be structured into "subinterfaces." A service in an interface identifies a subset of the features of that interface and names them together. A service has a *type*, and can be connected to a service of another component if the other service is of a *dual* type. Such a single connection is shorthand for a set of connections between the dual features of a service. Duality captures the notion of plugs and sockets: dual services (services whose types are duals of each other) can be connected in a manner reminiscent of how plugs and sockets may be connected in hardware. Consequently, in *Rapide*, a service is often called a *plug* and a dual service a *socket*.

Constraints given in a service definition are identical to those of the dual of the service, since they constrain equally the provided as well as the required features and their use (this requirement can be relaxed under certain conditions, but a discussion of that is beyond the scope of this presentation).

A large interface with a large number of features being provided or required can be partitioned into services with associated constraints. Each service should contain a subset of features that are related in some way, for example, the features whose purpose is communication between this interface and one particular type of interface.

As a simple illustration, return to the interfaces for our compiler, and consider the connections between the various components (see Figures 2.3 and 2.4). Even in this simplified architecture we have to keep track of a significant number of connections, and we have to rely on the naming scheme of the various interfaces to ensure that the correct connections are made. For instance, the connections show that the *Parser* requires three communication paths to the *Attribute Tree*. So we might expect to group those into a service that specifies communication between parsers and trees, and similarly grouping the features communicating with other components.

Structuring the interfaces with these services *contextualizes* the interfaces so that if an architecture contains a semanticizer component, one expects to see a tree component with a dual service to which the semanticizer can be connected.

As with physical cables, services can be nested so that interfaces can be hierarchically structured.

The connection between the dual services in the Parser object and the Attribute tree object is called a *service connection*.† It connects the dual features with the same name in each service and replaces the three connections between the two objects in Figure 2.3. Note that a service connection defines a potentially bi-directional communication subsystem. We discuss its correctness in the next section.

Plug and socket architectures are interface connection architectures in which interfaces are structured by services, and dual services are connected by service connections:

Service connection: A single connection between a pair of dual services, representing the set of interface connections between each pair of dual features in the services.

A service connection is notationally as simple as a connection between a pair of interface features. One service connection therefore reduces the notation required for a set of interface connections to the same complexity as the notation for a single member of that set—rather like a set of separate wires being bundled together into a single cable.

Correctness of Service Connections

In complex architectures connections between components involve sets of sets of interface features. Often, there is a protocol relating the order and the use of features in the sets. A *correct* connection must satisfy both the formal constraints on individual interface features and also the protocols relating dataflow among different features in the set.

Correct service connection: If the constraints of two components connected by a service connection together are sufficient to ensure that the constraints given in the service definition are satisfied then the connection is *correct*.

Correctness of a connection between interface features requires both connectability and conformance to semantic constraints. Connectability of dual interface features is implied by the definition of duality. So, a service connection is correct if the semantic constraints in its plug and socket are always satisfied—under the assumption that the modules it connects conform to their interfaces. For example, an RS-232 connection is correct if the two units being connected both adhere to the protocol of when wires go high or low, as well as satisfying the more "syntactic" property of having the correct number of wires.

---

† Also, a *plug and socket* connection.

If the constraints given in the service definition are sufficiently strong then simple interface conformance ensures that connections are correct. Such constraints are often on the "assume–guarantee" form [Jon83], where each side of the connection guarantees certain behavior under the assumption of the other end satisfying its end of the constraint. By inductive reasoning one can usually show that when both sides of the connection each conforms to "their" part of the constraints then the connection itself is correct.

For many common examples of plug and socket pairs, it is easy to show that a plug and socket connection between them is correct. This is true for common kinds of protocols which constrain the order in which interface features are used, for example. In such cases, if the two modules having the plug and the socket respectively conform to their service type definition, then they will communicate correctly on a connection between them.†

The concepts of **dual types** and **connectable interface features** can be generalized to allow for object-oriented subtyping, but we omit that discussion here.

A Plug and Socket Architecture for Our Compiler

One of the advantages of structuring interfaces into services is that the service types and duality give some hints about how the interfaces are intended to be connected (contextualizing). Many connection errors are avoided.

For example, by looking at the interfaces in Figure 2.3 one cannot tell which functions are intended to be connected. One cannot easily decide which other module is intended to use the Semanticizer's *Init* function, or whether the *Init* and *Eval* functions (in the *Semanticizer*) were expected to be used by the same module. If there is an error in the connections (very common in hardware modelling languages), there is no easy cross check. Indeed, one is typically reduced to relying on style guides and naming conventions as the means to identify the end points of connections. In general it is difficult to tell which feature in one interface was intended to be connected to what other features in a different interface, or which features in a particular interface were meant to be associated together for the purpose of connection —that is, are part of a communication protocol.

Using service connections we can reorganize the interface connection architecture in Figure 2.3 as depicted graphically in Figure 2.5. Each interface contains only two or three plugs or sockets, with each of these encapsulating the communication between a specific pair of interfaces; each pair of interfaces contains duals, indicating correct connections between them.

Advantages of plugs and sockets are illustrated in this and the previous example. First, an interface is structured into groups of features (the plugs and sockets) that indicate which other types of interfaces it should be connected to in architectures—

---

† A general characterization of the semantic constraints for which plug and socket connections are known to be correct is beyond the scope of this paper.

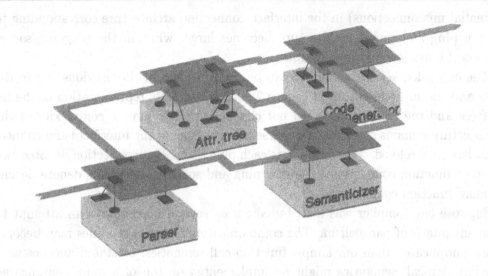

Fig. 2.5. A Plug and Socket Architecture and Conforming System.

that is, those with duals. So plugs and sockets indicate context with more precision than before. Second, plug connections are less prone to trivial syntactic errors because they connect duals—not simply individual features. Third, as indicated by the previous example, plug connections can often result in correct sets of connections where the correctness is easy to determine.

Refining Communication in the Compiler Architecture

Plugs and sockets are also useful in the process of *refining* the detail in the communication between components of an architecture without increasing the complexity of its connection topology. As the detail in specifying the communication between the components increases, the number of features in each of the plugs and sockets increases as well. But while the plugs become more complex, the plug and socket architecture as shown in Figure 2.5 remains unchanged.

For example, one could refine the plugs and socket pair defining the communication between the Semanticizer and the Tree. The Tree could supply a more fine-grained interface to the Semanticizer, allowing the Semanticizer to ask for specific symbol table information. And vice versa, the Semanticizer could offer different semanticization schemes. The service definition might become so rich that we subdivide its features even further into Symbol Table features and Semanticize features. Similar expansions in detail could be made in the other plugs and sockets in our compiler architecture. The Parser interface could add features which select among different grammars (C, C++, etc). The Code Generator could provide features which control its heuristics (fast generation of inefficient code, slow generation of efficient code) or its target instruction set (i486, Sparc, etc). The number of connections (and potential misconnections) in the interface connection architecture corresponding to such a plug and socket architecture becomes large, while in the plug-and-socket version it stays low and manageable.

The expanded service definition can be used in place of the previous one in the plug and socket architecture in Figure 2.5. The syntactic representation of the interfaces and the connections need not change, so the syntactic complexity of the architecture remains constant. Of course, the meaning of the interfaces and connections has been refined. Whereas before each plug and socket connection denoted two or three function connections, the new plug and socket connections denote dozens or more function connections.

Suppose our compiler was distributed across several machines in an attempt to take advantage of parallelism. The communication between modules may become more complicated than our simple function-call semantics, or stated another way, our function-call semantics might be implemented on top of a more complicated mechanism which hides the details of distributed communication. Instead of complicating each interface with the details of this new means of communication, we could encapsulate the mechanism inside of a plugs and sockets and use that service in our interfaces.

Furthermore, this way of refining plug definitions maintains a high degree of confidence in the correctness of the resulting connections. If one end of a connection has not been correctly changed to accommodate the new plug definition then the check for connectability of the two ends of the connection will identify the problem.

Services have been used successfully as a tool to avoid undue complexity in architectural definitions, and as a handy unit for abstraction and refinement as architectures evolve [ML98].

Plug and socket connections are not restricted to being one-to-one or static. We may have architectures in which one plug is connected to several sockets, and plug-to-socket connections may depend upon execution time variables (see [VPL99] for a discussion of dynamic architectures).

2.8 Conformance to Interface Connection Architectures

Our approach to problem 2—analyzing the effect of replacing one module with another—relies on the conformance of the system to the connections in the interface connection architecture, *communication integrity*. Communication integrity is important in ensuring that the development of the system follows the plan laid out in the architecture.

Communication integrity implies that all interaction between architecture components as implemented in the system is specified by the connections of the interface connection architecture.

This is a powerful constraint on the implementation of a system, but not quite as onerous for the system builder as it may seem at first glance.

Note, first of all, that only communication between *components* is constrained. The implementation of an architecture component may rely on system modules not explicitly occurring in the architecture, provided such modules are not used to communicate with another component. For example, the implementation of some architecture component could make calls to an arithmetic module (which usually would not represent an architecture component, that is, would not correspond to an interface of the architecture).

Note, secondly, that architecture connections may themselves be realized as system connectors or whole communication subsystems. When there is a connection between two architecture components then the implementation may make use of *connector* modules in the system to realize the connection. For example, direct communication between architecture components may be implemented as indirect or even asynchronous information flow via buffers, networks or other means not explicitly mentioned in the architecture. The only constraint is that whatever behavioral properties required of the connections and their use (for example, what the protocols for use are) be satisfied by the system modules implementing the connectivity.

Given this, in addressing how one can maintain communication integrity when constructing a system from an architecture we look at two concerns: on the one hand avoiding cluttering the architecture with extraneous components, whose presence may be dictated only by the fact that other components interact with them (and thus they would represent connections if they were not explicitly introduced). On the other hand, that system modules interacting with modules realizing distinct architecture components should not open communication paths that are not sanctioned by the architecture.

Both aspects deal with the problem of determining (and limiting) when a system module can serve as a communication conduit between architecture components, in which case it must be represented in thh architecture either as a component in its own right, or as (part of) a connection between the two components.

There are a number of different approaches to addressing these concerns. These can involve language restrictions, or various "sufficient" programming style rules. The strictest conformance-ensuring discipline would be:

Strict Component Partitioning: *A module realizing an architecture component is allowed to interact with other such modules only by using the defined interface features.*

This is a style of programming that syntactically prohibits module connections being programmed between components where there is no connection between those components in the architecture.

This style has as a consequence that distinct system components initially do not share *any* modules at all—no data structures, no functional modules, and so on are shared. In this case the architecture serves as a partitioning of the system into disjoint module sets—one for each architecture component—and the interaction among components is only direct (by whatever means the implementation technology offers), and along the lines defined by the connections of the architecture.

This is a disciplined, but easily enforced programming style, analogous to plugging hardware chips into a board. It requires interfaces to be carefully constructed to declare required features of components. It avoids explicit connections that are not specified in the architecture. But it does not, by itself, ensure against surreptitious or accidental communication. Furthermore, it is much too harsh a discipline for most practical purposes—it would disallow shared libraries, communication subsystems, and others.

If the features of a module are used by two or more components of a system, or the module (or access to it) is passed as a parameter of communication between components, then we say that the module is *shared* between the components. Moving from syntactic to more semantic criteria for conformance to the communication integrity requirement, one implementation style or rule which relaxes the discipline of strict component partitioning is to require that a shared module should offer only a *safe feature set*:

Safe Feature Set: *A feature set is safe if its constraints require that the use of a feature does not influence the behavior of future uses of that or other features of the set.*

The requirement that all features of a shared module be without memory of previous invocations of itself or other features of the module is often still too strict for many purposes. The idea of using modules that have safe feature sets, either as shared modules or as system components, can be modified and relaxed further in various ways. For example,

Safely Partitioned Modules: *A module is safely partitioned if its constraints require that the use of a feature by one module does not influence the behavior of future uses of that or other features of the interface by other modules.*

When a module is *not* safe then it is called a *communication module*:

Communication Module: *A module is a communication module if it allows the use of a feature by one component to influence the behavior of future uses by other components of that or other features of the interface.*

Communication integrity forces an interface connection architecture to define the communication of a system "completely." If system components are to share a file system, for example, the possible communication between them must be represented. This raises issues of scale and complexity of interface communication architectures. This is good, because now we are forced to face some of the complexity issues of systems at the architecture design stage. Without this strong conformance requirement, "architecture" can misrepresent systems communication issues which at later stages in the development cycle may become sources of error.

2.9 Conclusion

This paper presented key concepts in three approaches to defining decomposition architectures: *(i)* the *module connection architecture*; *(ii)* the *interface connection architecture*, and *(iii)* the *plug and socket architecture*; and the requirements that must be satisfied by an ADL in order to be useful in defining such architectures.

The first two approaches differ in the way they are related to systems. A module connection architecture, typical of many object-oriented systems, is fully entangled with the implementation of the system it is supposed to describe.

The interface connection architecture overcomes this problem by requiring that all communication into and out of a component go through that component's interface. This allows the communication architecture to be defined purely in terms of the interfaces, before components are constructed to implement those interfaces. We have indicated how interface connection architectures can be templates for system development and modification. Interface connection architectures have the effect of raising the communication topology of the system to the level of the architecture, thus introducing concerns about scale early in the development process.

The refinement of the architecture notion, moving from interface connection architectures to plug and socket architectures, preserves the advantages that the interface connection architecture has over the module connection architecture while introducing some ways of dealing with the scale and conformance problems of the interface connection architecture. Through the use of *plugs and sockets* and the notion of *duality*, an interface's specification may be kept manageably compact. We have indicated how plugs and sockets may be used to lessen the burden of proof for system/architecture conformance.

Further works lies in determining more powerful and useful concepts of architecture, and in incorporating connection topology into the notion of architectural class (or type).

Acknowledgments

This project was funded by DARPA under ONR contract N00014-92-J-1928 and AFOSR under Grant AFOSR91-0354, and by NFR under contract 100426/410

Bibliography

[Ada83]   US Department of Defense, US Government Printing Office. *The Ada Programming Language Reference Manual*, February 1983. ANSI/MIL-STD-1815A-1983.

[AG94]   Allen, R. and Garlan, D. Formalizing architectural connection. In *Proceedings of Sixteenth International Conference on Software Engineering*, pages xx–yy. IEEE Computer Society Press, May 1994.

[ES90]   Ellis, M. A. and Stroustrup, B. *The Annotated C++ Reference Manual.* Addison-Wesley, 1990.

[GHJV95]   Gamma, E., Helm, R., Johnson, R., and Vlissides, J. *Design Patterns.* Addison-Wesley, 1995.

[Gib94]   Gibbs, W. W. Software's chronic crisis. *Scientific American*, 271(3):86, September 1994.

[Gil96]   Gillette, W. Managing mega projects: A focused approach. *IEEE Software*, 13(4):2, July 1996.

[GMW97]   Garlan, D., Monroe, R. T., and Wile, D. Acme: An architecture description interchange language. In *Proceedings of CASCON'97*, pages 169–183, Toronto, Ontario, November 1997.

[Gro91]   Group, T. O. M. *The Common Object Request Broker: Architecture and Specification.* The Object Management Group, revision 1.1 edition, December 1991.

[GS93]   Garlan, D. and Shaw, M. *An Introduction to Software Architecture*, volume I. World Scientific Publishing Company, 1993.

[Hoa85]   Hoare, C. *Communicating Sequential Processes.* Prentice-Hall, 1985.

[Int87]   International Organization for Standardization. *Information processing systems – Open Systems Interconnection – Specification of Basic Encoding Rules for Abstract Notation One (ASN.1)*, December 1987. International Standard 8825.

[Jon83]   Jones, C. B. Specification and design of (parallel) programs. In *Proceedings IFIP 1983*, pages 321–332. North Holland, 1983.

[Lak96]   Lakos, J. *Large-Scale C++ Software Design.* Addison Wesley, 1996.

[LKA+95]   Luckham, D. C., Kenney, J. J., Augustin, L. M., Vera, J., Bryan, D., and Mann, W. Specification and analysis of system architecture using Rapide. *IEEE Transactions on Software Engineering*, 21(4):336–355, April 1995.

[LV95]   Luckham, D. C. and Vera, J. An event-based architecture definition language. *IEEE Transactions on Software Engineering*, 21(9):717–734, September 1995.

[LVB+93]   Luckham, D. C., Vera, J., Bryan, D., Augustin, L., and Belz, F. Partial orderings of event sets and their application to prototyping concurrent, timed systems. *Journal of Systems and Software*, 21(3):253–265, June 1993.

[Mar96]   Maring, B. Object-oriented development of large applications. *IEEE Software*, 13(3):33–40, May 1996.

[Mel90]   Meldal, S. Supporting architecture mappings in concurrent systems design. In *Proceedings of Australian Software Engineering Conference*. IREE Australia, May 1990.

[Mil80]   Milner, R. *A Calculus of Communicating Systems.* Lecture Notes in Computer Science 92. Springer–Verlag, 1980.

[ML98]   Meldal, S. and Luckham, D. C. Missi reference architecture – from prose to precise specification. In Broy, M. and Rumpe, B., editors, *Requirements Targeting Software and Systems Engineering*, volume 1526 of *LNCS*, pages 293–329. Springer-Verlag, 1998.

[OJD66]   O-J. Dahl, K. N. Simula – an algol-based simulation language. *Comm. A.C.M.*, 9(9):671–678, 1966.

[Par75]   Parnas, D. L. The influence of software structure on reliability. In *Proceedings of the International Conference on Reliable Software*, pages 358–362, April 1975.

[RJB98]   Rumbaugh, J., Jacobson, I., and Booch, G. *The Unified Modeling Language Reference Manual.* Addison-Wesley, 1998.

[SNH95]   Soni, D., Nord, R. L., and Hofmeister, C. Software architecture in industrial applications. In *Proceedings of the 17th International Conference on Software Engineering*, pages 196–207. ACM, April 1995.

[SP95]   Santoro, A. and Park, W. SPARC-V9 architecture specification with Rapide. to appear, Stanford CSL Technical Report, 1995.

[TM91]   Thomas, D. E. and Moorby, P. R. *The Verilog hardware description language*. Kluwer Academic Publishers, 1991.

[VHD87]   IEEE, Inc., 345 East 47th Street, New York, NY, 10017. *IEEE Standard VHDL Language Reference Manual*, March 1987. IEEE Standard 1076–1987.

[VPL99]   Vera, J., Perrochon, L., and Luckham, D. C. Event-based execution architectures for dynamic software systems. In Donohue, P., editor, *TC2 First Working IFIP Conference on Software Architecture (WICSA1)*, pages 303–317. Kluwer Academic, February 1999.

3

Acme: Architectural Description of Component-Based Systems

David Garlan

Computer Science Department, Carnegie Mellon University
Pittsburgh, PA 15213-3890 USA

Robert T. Monroe

Computer Science Department, Carnegie Mellon University
Pittsburgh, PA 15213-3890 USA

David Wile

USC/Information Sciences Institute
4676 Admiralty Way
Marina del Rey, CA 90292 USA

Abstract

Over the past decade there has been considerable experimentation with the design of architecture description languages that can provide a formal basis for description and analysis of the architectures of component-based systems. As the field has matured there has emerged among the software architecture research community general consensus about many aspects of the foundations for architectural representation and analysis. One result has been the development of a generic architecture description language, called *Acme*, that can serve as a common representation for software architectures and that permits the integration of diverse collections of independently developed architectural analysis tools. In this paper we describe the Acme language and tools, and our experience in using it to integrate architecture analysis tools and to describe component-based systems.

3.1 Introduction

An important problem for component-based systems engineering is finding appropriate notations to describe those systems. Good notations make it possible to document component-based designs clearly, reason about their properties, and automate their analysis and system generation.

One approach to describing component-based systems is to use object modeling notations (for example, as in [Szy98]). Each component can be represented by a class, component interfaces can be represented by class interfaces, and interactions between components can be defined in terms of associations.

Object modeling of component-based systems has a number of nice features. Ob-

47

ject notations are familiar to an increasingly large number of software engineers. They provide a direct mapping to implementations. They are supported by commercial tools. They have well-defined methods for developing systems from a set of requirements.

But object modeling notations have a number of drawbacks with respect to the description of component-based systems. First, they provide only a single form of primitive interconnection – method invocation. This makes it difficult to represent richer types of component interaction as first class design elements. Second, they have weak support for hierarchical description, making it difficult to describe systems at increasing levels of detail. Third, they do not support the definition of families of systems. While they can be used to describe patterns and to define a vocabulary of object types, they don't have explicit syntactic support for characterizing a class of system in terms of the design constraints that each member of the family must observe. Fourth, they do not provide direct support for characterizing and analyzing non-functional properties. This makes it difficult to reason about critical system design properties, such as system performance and reliability.

An alternative approach, and one that overcomes these problems, is to use an architecture description language (ADL). Over the past decade a number of languages have been developed to handle the high-level description of complex software systems, exposing their gross structure as a collection of interacting components, and allowing engineers to reason about system properties at a high level of abstraction. Typical properties of concern include protocols of interaction, bandwidths and latencies, locations of central data stores, conformance to architectural standards, and anticipated dimensions of evolution [GP95, GS93, MT97, PW92].

While different ADLs focus on different aspects of architecture, as the field has matured there has emerged among the software architecture research community general consensus about many aspects of the foundations for architectural representation and analysis. One result has been the development of a generic, second-generation architecture description language, called *Acme*, that can serve as a common representation for software architectures, and that permits the integration of diverse collections of independently developed architectural analysis tools. In the remainder of this paper we describe the Acme language and tools, and our experience using it. We begin by surveying the conceptual basis for architecture description. Then we describe Acme as a concrete example of a language for architecture description. Finally, we summarize current experience with Acme and outline directions for future research.

3.2 Architectural Description

The software architecture of a system defines its high-level structure, exposing its gross organization as a collection of interacting components. A well-defined architecture allows an engineer to reason about system properties at a high level of abstraction [GP95, GS93, PW92]. Typical properties of concern include compatibility between components [AG97], conformance to standards [AGI98], performance [SG98], schedulability [BV93], and reliability.

Architectural design has always played a strong role in determining the success of complex software-based systems: the choice of an appropriate architecture can lead to a product that satisfies its requirements and is easily modified as new requirements present themselves, while an inappropriate architecture can be disastrous.

Despite its importance to software systems engineers, the practice of architectural design has been largely ad hoc, informal, and idiosyncratic. As a result, architectural designs are often poorly understood by developers; architectural choices are based more on default than solid engineering principles; architectural designs cannot be analyzed for consistency or completeness; architectural constraints assumed in the initial design are not enforced as a system evolves; and there are few tools to help architectural designers with their tasks.

In response to these problems a number of researchers in industry and academia have proposed formal notations for representing and analyzing architectural designs. Generically referred to as "Architecture Description Languages" (ADLs), these notations usually provide both a conceptual framework and a concrete syntax for characterizing software architectures. They also typically provide tools for parsing, unparsing, displaying, compiling, analyzing, or simulating architectural descriptions written in their associated language.†

Examples of ADLs include Aesop [GAO94], Adage [CS93], C2 [MORT96], Darwin [MDEK95], Rapide [LAK+95], SADL [MQR95], UniCon [SDK+95], Meta-H [BV93], and Wright [AG97]. While all of these languages are concerned with architectural design, each provides certain distinctive capabilities: Adage supports the description of architectural frameworks for avionics navigation and guidance; Aesop supports the use of architectural styles; C2 supports the description of user interface systems using an event-based style; Darwin supports the analysis of distributed message-passing systems; Meta-H provides guidance for designers of real-time avionics control software; Rapide allows architectural designs to be simulated, and has tools for analyzing the results of those simulations; SADL provides a formal basis for architectural refinement; UniCon has a high-level compiler for architectural designs that support a mixture of heterogeneous component and connector types; Wright supports the formal specification and analysis of interactions between architectural components.

Although there is considerable diversity in the capabilities of different ADLs, all share a similar conceptual basis, or ontology [Gar95, MT97], that determines a common foundation of concepts and concerns for architectural description. The main elements of this ontology are:

- *Components* represent the primary computational elements and data stores of a

---

† In this paper we use the term "ADL" to refer to both the language and its supporting toolset.

system. Intuitively, they correspond to the boxes in box-and-line descriptions of software architectures. Typical examples of components include such things as clients, servers, filters, objects, blackboards, and databases. In most ADLs components may have multiple interfaces, each interface defining a point of interaction between a component and its environment.

- *Connectors* represent interactions among components. Computationally speaking, connectors mediate the communication and coordination activities among components. That is, they provide the "glue" for architectural designs, and intuitively, they correspond to the lines in box-and-line descriptions. Examples include simple forms of interaction, such as pipes, procedure call, and event broadcast. But connectors may also represent more complex interactions, such as a client-server protocol or a SQL link between a database and an application. Connectors also have interfaces that define the roles played by the various participants in the interaction represented by the connector.

- *Systems* represent configurations (graphs) of components and connectors. In modern ADLs a key property of system descriptions is that the overall topology of a system is defined independently from the components and connectors that make up the system. (This is in contrast to most programming language module systems where dependencies are wired into components via import clauses.) Systems may also be hierarchical: components and connectors may represent subsystems that have "internal" architectures.

- *Properties* represent semantic information about a system and its components that goes beyond structure. As noted earlier, different ADLs focus on different properties, but virtually all provide *some* way to define one or more extra-functional properties together with tools for analyzing those properties. For example, some ADLs allow one to calculate overall system throughput and latency based on performance estimates of each component and connector [SG98].

- *Constraints* represent claims about an architectural design that should remain true even as it evolves over time. Typical constraints include restrictions on allowable values of properties, topology, and design vocabulary. For example, an architecture might constrain its design so that the number of clients of a particular server is less than some maximum value.

- *Styles* represent families of related systems. An architectural *style* typically defines a vocabulary of design element types and rules for composing them [SG96]. Examples include dataflow architectures based on graphs of pipes and filters, blackboard architectures based on shared data space and a set of knowledge sources, and layered systems. Some architectural styles additionally prescribe a framework† as a set of structural forms that specific applications can specialize.

---

† Terminology distinguishing different kinds of families of architectures is far from standard. Among the terms used are "product-line frameworks," "component integration standards," "kits," "architectural patterns," "styles," "idioms," and others. For the purposes of this paper, the distinctions between these kinds of architectural families is less important than the fact that they all represent a set of architectural instances.

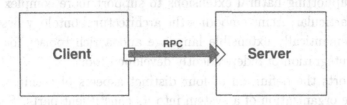

Fig. 3.1. Simple Client-Server Diagram.

Examples include the traditional multistage compiler framework, 3-tiered client-server systems, the OSI protocol stack, and user interface management systems.

As a very simple illustrative example, Figure 3.1 depicts a system containing a client and server component connected by a RPC connector. The server itself might be represented by a subarchitecture (not shown). Properties of the connector might include the protocol of interaction that it requires. Properties of the server might include the average response time for requests. Constraints on the system might stipulate that no more than five clients can ever be connected to this server and that servers may not initiate communication with a client. The style of the system might be a "client-server" style in which the vocabulary of design includes clients, servers, and RPC connectors.

This ontological basis of ADLs has a natural map to the descriptive needs of component-based systems. First, ADLs allow one to describe compositions of components precisely, making explicit the ways in which those components communicate. Second, they support the use of multiple component interfaces, a key feature of many component-based systems approaches. Third, they support hierarchical descriptions and encapsulation of subsystems as components in a larger system. Fourth, they support the specification and analysis of non-functional properties. Fifth, many ADLs provide an explicit home for describing the detailed semantics of communication infrastructure (through specification of connector types). Sixth, ADLs allow one to define constraints on system composition that make clear what kinds of compositions are allowed. Finally, architectural styles allow one to make precise the differences between kinds of component integration standards.

3.3 Acme

To elaborate on how architectural description allows one to characterize component based systems, we now describe a particular ADL, called Acme.† As a second-generation ADL, Acme has the distinctive property that it builds on the experience of other ADLs, providing in a simple language the essential elements of architectural

---

† In this paper we provide a high-level view of the language, emphasizing aspects that are particularly relevant to the description of component-based systems. For a more detailed treatment see [Mon98].

design, and supporting natural extensions to support more complex architectural features. In particular, Acme embodies the architectural ontology described above, providing a semantically extensible language and a rich toolset for architectural analysis and integration of independently developed tools.

Acme supports the definition of four distinct aspects of architecture. First is structure—the organization of a system into its constituent parts. Second is properties of interest—information about a system or its parts that allow one to reason abstractly about overall behavior (both functional and nonfunctional). Third is constraints—guidelines for how the architecture can change over time. Fourth is types and styles—defining classes and families of architecture. We now consider each in turn.

3.3.1 Structure

Architectural structure is defined in Acme using seven core types of entities: *components, connectors, systems, ports, roles, representations, and rep-maps*.† The first five are illustrated in Figure 3.2.

Consistent with the ontology outlined earlier, Acme *components* represent computational elements and data stores of a system. A component may have multiple interfaces, each of which is termed a *port*. A port identifies a point of interaction between the component and its environment, and can represent an interface as simple as a single procedure signature. Alternatively, a port can define a more complex interface, such as a collection of procedure calls that must be invoked in certain specified orders, or an event multicast interface.

Acme *connectors* represent interactions among components. Connectors also have interfaces that are defined by a set of *roles*. Each role of a connector defines a participant of the interaction represented by the connector. Binary connectors have two roles such as the *caller* and *callee* roles of an RPC connector, the *reading* and *writing* roles of a pipe, or the *sender* and *receiver* roles of a message passing connector. Other kinds of connectors may have more than two roles. For example an event broadcast connector might have a single *event-announcer* role and an arbitrary number of *event-receiver* roles.

Acme *systems* are defined as graphs in which the nodes represent components and the arcs represent connectors. This is done by identifying which component ports are *attached* to which connector roles.

Figure 3.3 contains an Acme description of the simple architecture of Figure 3.1. The *client* component is declared to have a single *send-request* port, and the server has a single *receive-request* port. The connector has two roles designated *caller* and *callee*. The topology of this system is defined by listing a set of *attachments* that bind component ports to connector roles. In this case, the client's requesting port

---

† In earlier presentations, this part of the language was referred to as "Kernel Acme."

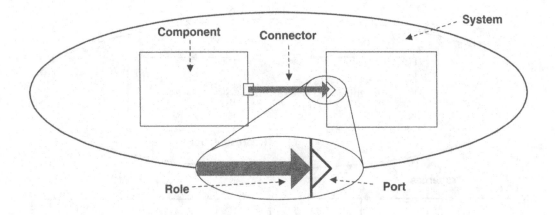

Fig. 3.2. Elements of an Acme Description.

```
System simple_cs = {
  Component client = { Port sendRequest }
  Component server = { Port receiveRequest }
  Connector rpc  = { Roles {caller, callee} }
  Attachments : {
      client.sendRequest to rpc.caller ;
      server.receiveRequest to rpc.callee }
}
```

Fig. 3.3. Simple Client-Server System in Acme.

is bound to the rpc's caller role, and the servers's request-handling port is bound to the rpc's callee role.

To support hierarchical descriptions of architectures, Acme permits any component or connector to be represented by one or more detailed, lower-level descriptions. Each such description is termed a *representation*. Representations of a component are illustrated abstractly in Figure 3.4.

The ability to associate multiple representations with a design element† allows

---

† We use the term "design element" to refer to any of the Acme building blocks: components, connectors, and so on.

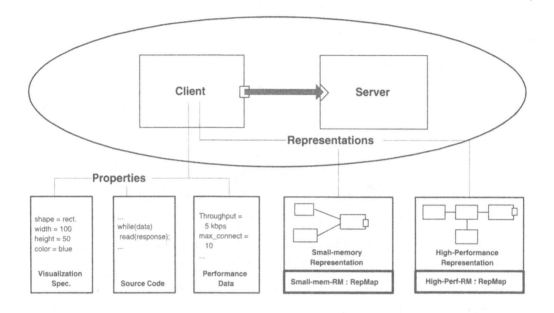

Fig. 3.4. Representations and Properties of a Component.

Acme to encode multiple views of architectural entities (although there is nothing currently built into Acme that supports resolution of inter-view correspondences).

When a component or connector has an architectural representation there must be some way to indicate the correspondence between the internal system representation and the external interface of the component or connector that is being represented. A *rep-map* (short for "representation map") defines this correspondence. In the simplest case a rep-map provides an association between internal ports and external ports (or, for connectors, internal roles, and external roles).† In other cases the map may be considerably more complex.

Figures 3.5 and 3.6 illustrate the use of representations in elaborating the simple client-server example. In this case, the *server* component is elaborated by a more detailed architectural representation.

---

† Note that rep-maps are not connectors: connectors define paths of interaction, while rep-maps identify an abstraction relationship between sets of interface points.

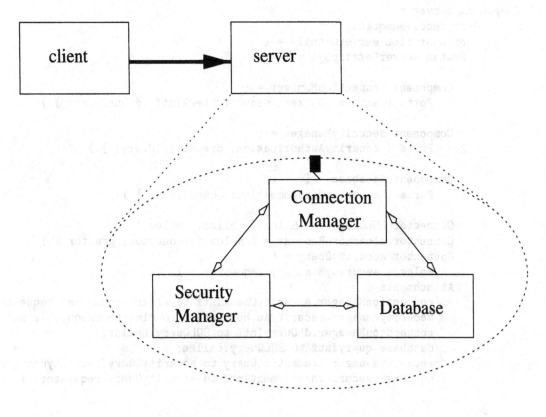

Fig. 3.5. Hierarchical Client-Server System.

3.3.2 Properties

The seven classes of design element outlined above are sufficient for defining the *structure* of an architecture as a graph of components and connectors. Explicit description of structure is useful for documenting systems as compositions of components.

However, there is much more to architectural description than structure. But what exactly? Looking at the range of first-generation ADLs, each typically has its own forms of auxiliary information that determines such things as the run-time semantics of the system, protocols of interaction, scheduling constraints, and resource consumption.

Clearly, the needs for documenting extra-structural properties of a system's architecture depend on the nature of the system, the kinds of analyses required, the tools at hand, and the level of detail included in the description.

To accommodate the open-ended requirements for specification of auxiliary information, Acme supports annotation of architectural structure with arbitrary lists

```
System simpleCS = {
  Component client = { ... }
  Component server = {
        Port receiveRequest;
        Representation serverDetails = {
          System serverDetailsSys = {

            Component connectionManager = {
               Ports { externalSocket; securityCheckIntf; dbQueryIntf } }

            Component securityManager = {
               Ports { securityAuthorization; credentialQuery; } }

            Component database = {
               Ports { securityManagementIntf; queryIntf; } }

            Connector SQLQuery = { Roles { caller; callee } }
            Connector clearanceRequest = { Roles { requestor; grantor } }
            Connector securityQuery = {
               Roles { securityManager; requestor } }
            Attachments {
               connectionManager.securityCheckIntf to clearanceRequest.requestor;
               securityManager.securityAuthorization to clearanceRequest.grantor;
               connectionManager.dbQueryIntf to SQLQuery.caller;
               database.queryIntf to SQLQuery.callee;
               securityManager.credentialQuery to securityQuery.securityManager;
               database.securityManagementIntf to securityQuery.requestor; }

        }
        Bindings { connectionManager.externalSocket to server.receiveRequest }
    }
  }
  Connector rpc  = { ... }
  Attachments { client.send-request to rpc.caller ;
                server.receive-request to rpc.callee }
```

Fig. 3.6. Client-Server System with Representation.

of properties. Each property has a name, an optional type, and a value. Any of the seven classes of Acme architectural design entities can be annotated with a property list.

Figure 3.4 pictures several properties that might be associated with the example architecture, and Figure 3.7 shows the simple client-server system elaborated with several properties in Acme. In the latter figure, properties document such things as the client's expected request rate and the location of its source code. For the *rpc*

```
System simple_cs = {
  Component client = {
      Port sendRequest;
      Properties { requestRate : float = 17.0;
                   sourceCode : externalFile = "CODE-LIB/client.c" }}

  Component server = {
      Port receiveRequest;
      Properties { idempotent : boolean = true;
                   maxConcurrentClients : integer = 1;
                   multithreaded : boolean = false;
                   sourceCode : externalFile = "CODE-LIB/server.c" }}

  Connector rpc  = {
      Role caller;
      Role callee;
      Properties { synchronous : boolean = true;
                   maxRoles : integer = 2;
                   protocol : WrightSpec = "..." }}

  Attachments {
     client.send-request to rpc.caller ;
     server.receive-request to rpc.callee }
}
```

Fig. 3.7. Client-Server System with Properties.

connector, properties document the protocol of interaction described as a Wright specification [AG97] (elided in the figure).

Properties serve to document details of an architecture relevant to its design and analysis. However, from Acme's point of view properties are uninterpreted values—that is, they have no intrinsic semantics. Properties become useful, however, when tools use them for analysis, translation, display, and manipulation.

The types of properties are defined using a set of built-in primitive property types (including integer, string, and boolean), and type constructors for records, sets, and lists.

3.3.3 Design Constraints

One of the key ingredients of an architecture description is a set of design constraints that determine how an architectural design is permitted to evolve over time. Such constraints can be considered a special kind of property, but since they play such a central role in architectural design, Acme provides special syntax for describing them. (Of course, this also permits the creation of tools for checking constraint satisfaction of an architectural description.)

Connected(comp1, comp2)	True if component comp1 is connected to component comp2 by at least one connector
Reachable(comp1, comp2)	True if component comp2 is in the transitive closure of Connected(comp1, *)
HasProperty(elt, propName)	True if element elt has a property called propName
HasType(elt, typeName)	True if element elt has type typeName
SystemName.Connectors	The set of connectors in system SystemName
ConnectorName.Roles	The set of the roles in connector ConnectorName

Fig. 3.8. Sample Functions for Constraint Expressions.

Acme uses a constraint language based on first order predicate logic (FOPL).[†] That is, design constraints are expressed as predicates over architectural specifications. The constraint language includes the standard set of FOPL constructs (conjunction, disjunction, implication, quantification, and others). It also includes a number of special functions that refer to architecture-specific aspects of a system. For example, there are predicates to determine if two components are connected (both directly and indirectly), and if a component has a particular property. Other functions return the set of components in a given system, the set of ports of a given component, the set of representations of a connector, and so forth. Figure 3.8 lists a representative set of example functions. (For a detailed description see [Mon99].)

Constraints can be associated with any design element of an Acme description. The scope of the constraint is determined by that association. For example, if a constraint is attached to a system then it can refer to any of the design elements contained within it (components, connectors, and their parts). On the other hand, a constraint attached to a component can only refer to that component (using the special keyword *self*, and its parts (that is, its ports, properties, and representations).

To explore a few examples, consider the following constraints that might be associated with a system:

> *connected(client, server)*

will be true if the components named *client* and *server* are connected directly by a connector.

> *Forall conn : connector in systemInstance.Connectors @ size(conn.roles) = 2*

will be true of a system in which all of the connectors are binary connectors.

---

† Acme constraints were initially developed in the Armani system [Mon99, Mon98], and recently incorporated into the language.

```
System messagePathSystem = {
  ...
  Connector MessagePath = {
      Roles {source; sink;}
      Property expectedThroughput : float =  512;
      Invariant (queueBufferSize >= 512) and (queueBufferSize <= 4096);
      Heuristic expectedThroughput <= (queueBufferSize / 2);
  }
}
```

Fig. 3.9. *MessagePath* Connector with Invariants and Heuristics.

> *Forall conn : connector in systemInstance.Connectors @*
> > *Forall r : role in conn.Roles @*
> > > *Exists comp : component in systemInstance.Components @*
> > > > *Exists p : port in comp.Ports @ attached(p,r) and (p.protocol = r.protocol)*

will be true when all connectors in the system are attached to a port, and the attached (port, role) pair share the same protocol. Here the port and role protocol values are represented as properties of the port and role design elements.

Constraints can also define the range of legal property values, as in

> *self.throughputRate >= 3095*

and indicate relationships between properties, as in

> *comp.totalLatency =*
> > *(comp.readLatency + comp.processingLatency + comp.writeLatency)*

Constraints may be attached to design elements in one of two ways: as an *invariant* or a *heuristic*. In the first case, the constraint is taken to be a rule that cannot be violated. In the second case, the constraint is taken to be a rule that should be observed, but may be selectively violated. Tools that check for consistency of an Acme specification will naturally treat these differently. A violation of an invariant makes the architectural specification invalid, while a violation of a heuristic is treated as a warning.

Figure 3.9 illustrates how constraints might be used for a hypothetical *MessagePath* connector. In this example an invariant prescribes the range of legal buffer sizes, while a heuristic prescribes a maximum value for the expected throughput.

3.3.4 Types and Styles

An important general capability for the description of architectures is the ability to define styles—or families—of systems. Styles allow one to define a domain-specific or application-specific design vocabulary, together with constraints on how that

```
Component Type Client = {
    Port Request = {Property protocol: CSPprotocolT};
    Property request-rate: Float;
    Invariant Forall p in self.Ports @ p.protocol = rpc-client;
    Invariant size(self.Ports) <= 5;
    Invariant request-rate >= 0;
    Heuristic request-rate < 100;
}
```

Fig. 3.10. Component Type "Client."

vocabulary can be used. This in turn supports packaging of domain-specific design expertise, use of special-purpose analysis and code-generation tools, simplification of the design process, and the ability to check for conformance to architectural standards.

The basic building block for defining styles in Acme is a type system that can be used to encapsulate recurring structures and relationships. In Acme an architect can define three kinds of types: property types, structural types, and styles. Property types were discussed earlier.

Structural types make it possible to define types of components, connectors, ports, and roles. Each such type provides a type name and a list of required substructure, properties, and constraints. Figure 3.10 illustrates the definition of a *Client* component type. The type definition specifies that any component that is an instance of type *Client* must have at least one port called *Request* and a property called *request-rate* of type float. Further, the invariants associated with the type require that all ports of a *Client* component have a *protocol* property whose value is *rpc-client*, that no client more than 5 ports, that a component's request rate is larger greater than 0. Finally, there is a heuristic indicating that the request-rate should be less than 100.

The third kind of type is a style, which (for historical reasons) is called a *family* in Acme. Just as structural types represent sets of structural elements, a family represents a set of *systems*.

An Acme family is defined by specifying three things: a set of property and structural types, a set of constraints, and default structure. The property and structural types provide the design vocabulary for the family. The constraints determine how instances of those types can be used. The default structure prescribes the minimal set of instances that must appear in any system in the family.

Figure 3.11 illustrates the definition of a "Pipe and Filter" family, together with a sample system declaration using the family. The family defines two component types, one connector type, and one property type. The single invariant of this family prescribes that all connectors must be pipes. No default structure is declared in

```
Family PipeFilterFam = {

  Component Type FilterT = {
        Ports { stdin; stdout; };
        Property throughput : int;
  };
  Component Type UnixFilterT extends FilterT with {
        Port stderr;
        Property implementationFile : String;
  };
  Connector Type PipeT = {
        Roles { source; sink; };
        Property bufferSize : int;
  };
  Property Type StringMsgFormatT = Record [ size:int; msg:String; ];
  Invariant Forall c in self.Connectors @ HasType(c, PipeT);

}

System simplePF : PipeFilterFam = {

    Component smooth : FilterT = new FilterT
    Component detectErrors : FilterT;
    Component showTracks : UnixFilterT = new UnixFilterT extended with {
        Property implementationFile : String = "IMPL_HOME/showTracks.c";
    };

    // Declare the system's connectors
    Connector firstPipe : PipeT;
    Connector secondPipe : PipeT;

    // Define the system's topology
    Attachments { smooth.stdout to firstPipe.source;
                  detectErrors.stdin to firstPipe.sink;
                  detectErrors.stdout to secondPipe.source;
                  showTracks.stdin to secondPipe.sink; }
}
```

Fig. 3.11. Definition of a Pipe-Filter Family.

the family. The system *simplePF* is then defined as an instance of the family. This declaration allows the system to make use of any of the types in the family, and it must satisfy all of the family's invariants.

Figure 3.11 also illustrates several other points about the use of types and families. First, types can be used to create default instances with the *new* keyword (as in *new FilterT*). This causes the value of the instance to have the minimal structure defined by type. But an instance can also add to this default structure, as illustrated in the definition of the *showTracks* component. That component adds a new property (*implementationFile*).

This raises an important question: what does it mean for an instance to satisfy a type? In Acme, types are interpreted as predicates, and asserting that an instance satisfies a type is the same as asserting that it satisfies the predicate denoted by the type. The predicate associated with a type is constructed by viewing declared structure as asserting the *existence* of that structure in each instance. In other words, a type defines the *minimal* structure of its instances.† (Hence, in the example of Figure 3.11 it is essential to include the invariant asserting that all connectors have type *pipe*.)

The use of a predicate-based type system has several important consequences. First, design elements (and systems) can have an arbitrary number of types. For example, the fact that a structural element is declared to be of a particular type, does not preclude it from satisfying other type specifications. This is an important property since it permits, for example, a system to be considered a valid instance of a style, even though it was not explicitly declared as such.

Second, the use of invariants fits smoothly within the type system. Adding a invariant to a structural type or family simply conjoins that predicate with the others in the type. This means that the type system becomes quite expressive – essentially harnessing first order predicate logic (FOPL) to create useful type distinctions.

Third, the process of type checking becomes one of checking satisfaction of a set of predicates over declared structures. Hence, types play two useful roles: (a) they encapsulate common, reusable structures and properties, and (b) they support a powerful form of checkable redundancy.

The use of predicates does, however, raise the issue that, in general, checking for satisfaction of FOPL predicates is not decidable. Therefore, systems that rely on predicate-based type systems usually do so with the aid of a theorem prover (for example, PVS [ORS92]). In Acme, however, we constrain the expressiveness of types so that type checking remains decidable. This is done by ensuring that quantification is only over finite sets of elements. Finiteness comes from the fact that Acme structures can only declare a finite number of subparts (components, ports, representations, and others).

3.4 Using Acme

The success of any system description language is ultimately defined by its impact on the practice of developing complex software systems. While Acme is still relatively

---

† The semantics of the Acme type system is similar to – but considerably simpler than – that of other predicate-based type systems, such as the one used by PVS [ORS92]. For a formal treatment of the semantics, see [Mon98].

young, as such languages go it has already begun to play several key roles in the software architecture community.

The first role is as an architecture description language. As a second-generation ADL, Acme has attempted capture the essential elements of architectural modeling. Hence the language presents a relatively simple core set of concepts for defining system structure, coupled with the ability to extend those concepts using properties, constraints, types, and styles that are appropriate to the context of use. A number of case studies have been carried out using Acme, including a substantial missile guidance system, and a global tracking system for the U.S. Department of Defense (carried out by Lockheed-Martin Corporation).

The second role is as a basis for new architecture design and analysis tools. Currently over a dozen tools and three design environments have been built to operate on Acme descriptions. The tools perform a variety of tasks, including type checking Acme (including satisfaction of invariants and constraints) [Mon99], generation of Web-based documentation, automated graph layout, animation of runtime behavior in architectural terms [GB99, LAK+95], dependence analysis for predicting the impacts of changes [SRW98], and performance and reliability analyses (for certain styles) [SG98].

The environments provide graphical front ends for creating Acme descriptions and support various analysis capabilities. The primary environment, called AcmeStudio, provides a Windows-based front end, together with capabilities for customizing the environment to support style-specific visualizations and tool invocation. A second prototype environment, called Armani, uses a commercial graphical front end (Visio) and a Java back end. It developed the initial implementation of the constraint checker for Acme descriptions. A third, more experimental environment designed at ISI emphasizes the creation of domain-specific architectural styles and analyzers. It uses the Microsoft's PowerPoint editor for graph manipulation coupled with analyzers reacting to changes to a DCOM representation of the architectural elements and their attached properties [GB99].

The third role of Acme is as a basis for integrating existing tools. As noted earlier, a large number of ADLs have been developed, each with their own stand-alone toolset. Acme can be used to integrate many of these tools by providing a common representation for interchanging architectural descriptions. (Indeed, historically, this was the initial motivation for creating Acme.) The basis for tool integration using Acme is the ability of other tools to read and write Acme descriptions. This is accomplished by encoding ADL-specific information as properties, attached to a generic structural skeleton. To the extent that tools share properties, they can exchange semantically relevant information for analysis.

To take one example, described in detail in [GW99], both Rapide and Wright are ADLs that model abstract behavior of architectural designs in terms of event traces. Rapide tools are primarily used to simulate event-based behavior, while Wright tools use a model checker to perform static behavioral analysis. The complementary capabilities of the two systems were combined by using Acme as an interchange language.

Naturally, the ability to perform such integration depends both on the ability of existing ADLs to read and write Acme, and on the ability to relate semantic information from one ADL to another. With respect to the first issue, a number of ADLs can handle Acme, including UniCon, Wright, Aesop, C2, and SADL. With respect to the second, work is underway to define common property sublanguages that will be accessible to several tools. Examples include property languages for visualization, for representation of events and event patterns, and for timing information.

The fourth role of Acme is as a starting point for the development of new domain-specific ADLs. Many companies are recognizing the importance of product-line frameworks, often based on external component integration standards. Ideally developers of such systems would use tools and environments tailored to those frameworks and standards. Unfortunately, there is little available commercially. Practitioners must therefore rely on either general purpose modeling notations (such as UML) or domain-specific tools that may not match their domain. Acme provides an alternative by supporting a path along which one can produce more specialized ADLs by tailoring the general descriptive framework provided by Acme to the needs of the specific domain (for example, using the ISI Acme environment or AcmeStudio).

3.5 Conclusion and Future Work

We have argued that architecture description languages provide an appropriate foundational basis for describing component-based systems designs. We then illustrated the nature of such description by presenting Acme. Finally, we described the roles that languages such as Acme are starting to play. While we would not claim that architectural descriptions should supplant all other means for specifying component-based systems, experience to date demonstrates that they are a useful adjunct to existing mechanisms, especially for specifying and reasoning about nonfunctional properties of a system.

However, much remains to be done both in practice and in research. On the practical side of things, it will clearly be important to experiment further with architectural descriptions in real settings. It will also be important to develop new tools that are useful to practicing software architects, and to continue to integrate existing tools.

On the research side a number of avenues are worth exploring. First is extensions of the type system to support parameterized and higher-order types.† An initial proposal for this has already been sketched out.

---

† An earlier version of Acme had a rudimentary form of this, called "templates" that appeared in earlier documentation, but was never fully implemented or integrated with the current tools.

Second is extensions to support the definition of structural patterns. These extensions would permit class diagram-like patterns to be added to family definitions.

Third is better integration with external tools and notations. In particular, it is important to be able to relate architectural descriptions, such as Acme's, to notations such as UML. Several proposals have been published on how to do this (for example, [MR99, HNS99]), but it is not yet clear what aspects of object modeling are best exploited in this mapping.

Fourth is the development of an "ADL Toolkit" that would provide meta-tools for producing new architecture description languages. While this can be done now, for example, using Acme's extension mechanisms, the capabilities would be more accessible to practicing system designers if there were better tool support for the process.

3.6 Acknowledgments

The development of Acme has been a community effort, with contributions from many researchers and practitioners. We thank the many people who have informed the language design and worked to incorporate Acme into their tools and development environments.

The research reported here was sponsored by the Wright Laboratory, Aeronautical Systems Center, Air Force Materiel Command, USAF, and the U.S. DoD Advanced Research Projects Agency (DARPA) under grants F30602-97-2-0031, and F33615-93-1-1330; and by National Science Foundation under Grant CCR-9357792. Views and conclusions contained in this document are those of the authors and should not be interpreted as representing the official policies, either expressed or implied, of Wright Laboratory, the U.S. Department of Defense, the United States Government, or the National Science Foundation. The U.S. Government is authorized to reproduce and distribute reprints for Government purposes, notwithstanding any copyright notation thereon.

Bibliography

[AG97]   Allen, R. and Garlan, D. A formal basis for architectural connection. *ACM Transactions on Software Engineering and Methodology*, July 1997.

[AGI98] Allen, R., Garlan, D., and Ivers, J. Formal modeling and analysis of the HLA component integration standard. In *Proceedings of the Sixth International Symposium on the Foundations of Software Engineering (FSE-6)*, Lake Buena Vista, Florida, November 1998. ACM.

[BV93]   Binns, P. and Vestal, S. Formal real-time architecture specification and analysis. In *Tenth IEEE Workshop on Real-Time Operating Systems and Software*, New York, NY, May 1993.

[CS93]   Coglianese, L. and Szymanski, R. DSSA-ADAGE: An Environment for Architecture-based Avionics Development. In *Proceedings of AGARD'93*, May 1993.

[GAO94]   Garlan, D., Allen, R., and Ockerbloom, J. Exploiting style in architectural design environments. In *Proceedings of SIGSOFT'94: The Second ACM SIGSOFT Symposium on the Foundations of Software Engineering*, pages 179–185. ACM Press, December 1994.

[Gar95]   Garlan, D., editor. *Proceedings of the First International Workshop on Architectures for Software Systems*, Seattle, WA, April 1995. Published as CMU Technical Report CMU-CS-95-151, April 1995.

[GB99]   Goldman, N. M. and Balzer, R. M. The isi visual design editor. In *Proceedings of the 1999 IEEE International Conference on Visual Languages*, September 1999. To appear.

[GP95]   Garlan, D. and Perry, D. Introduction to the special issue on software architecture. *IEEE Transactions on Software Engineering*, 21(4), April 1995.

[GS93]   Garlan, D. and Shaw, M. An introduction to software architecture. In Ambriola, V. and Tortora, G., editors, *Advances in Software Engineering and Knowledge Engineering*, pages 1–39, Singapore, 1993. World Scientific Publishing Company.

[GW99]   Garlan, D. and Wang, Z. A case study in software architecture interchange. In *Proceedings of Coordination '99*. Springer Verlag, April 1999.

[HNS99]   Hofmeister, C., Nord, R. L., and Soni, D. Describing software architecture with UML. In *Proceedings of the First Working IFIP Conference on Software Architecture (WICSA1)*, San Antonio, TX, February 1999.

[LAK+95] Luckham, D. C., Augustin, L. M., Kenney, J. J., Veera, J., Bryan, D., and Mann, W. Specification and analysis of system architecture using Rapide. *IEEE Transactions on Software Engineering, Special Issue on Software Architecture*, 21(4):336–355, April 1995.

[MDEK95] Magee, J., Dulay, N., Eisenbach, S., and Kramer, J. Specifying distributed software architectures. In *Proceedings of the Fifth European Software Engineering Conference, ESEC'95*, September 1995.

[Mon98]   Monroe, R. T. Capturing software architecture design expertise with armani. Technical Report CMU-CS-163, Carnegie Mellon University, October 1998.

[Mon99]   Monroe, R. T. *Rapid Development of Custom Software Design Environments*. PhD thesis, Carnegie Mellon University, July 1999.

[MORT96] Medvidovic, N., Oreizy, P., Robbins, J. E., and Taylor, R. N. Using object-oriented typing to support architectural design in the C2 style. In *SIGSOFT'96: Proceedings of the Fourth ACM Symposium on the Foundations of Software Engineering*. ACM Press, October 1996.

[MQR95]   Moriconi, M., Qian, X., and Riemenschneider, R. Correct architecture refinement. *IEEE Transactions on Software Engineering, Special Issue on Software Architecture*, 21(4):356–372, April 1995.

[MR99]   Medvidovic, N. and Rosenblum, D. S. Assessing the suitability of a standard design method for modeling software architectures. In *Proceedings of the First Working IFIP Conference on Software Architecture (WICSA1)*, San Antonio, TX, February 1999.

[MT97]   Medvidovic, N. and Taylor, R. N. Architecture description languages. In *Software Engineering – ESEC/FSE'97*, volume 1301 of *Lecture Notes in Computer Science*, Zurich, Switzerland, September 1997. Springer.

[ORS92]   Owre, S., Rushby, J. M., and Shankar, N. PVS: A prototype verification system. In Kapur, D., editor, *11th International Conference on Automated Deduction (CADE)*, volume 607 of *Lecture Notes in Artificial Intelligence*, pages 748–752. Springer-Verlag, June 1992.

[PW92]   Perry, D. E. and Wolf, A. L. Foundations for the study of software architecture. *ACM SIGSOFT Software Engineering Notes*, 17(4):40–52, October 1992.

[SDK+95]   Shaw, M., DeLine, R., Klein, D. V., Ross, T. L., Young, D. M., and Zelesnik, G. Abstractions for software architecture and tools to support them. *IEEE Transactions on Software Engineering, Special Issue on Software Architecture*, 21(4):314–335, April 1995.

[SG96]   Shaw, M. and Garlan, D. *Software Architecture: Perspectives on an Emerging Discipline*. Prentice Hall, 1996.

[SG98]   Spitznagel, B. and Garlan, D. Architecture-based performance analysis. In *Tenth International Conference on Software Engineering and Knowledge Engineering (SEKE'98)*, San Francisco, CA, June 1998.

[SRW98]   Stafford, J., Richardson, D., and Wolf, A. Aladdin: A Tool for Architecture-Level Dependence Analysis of Software. Technical Report CU-CS-858-98, Department of Computer Science, University of Colorado, Boulder, CO, April 1998.

[Szy98]   Szyperski, C. *Component Software: Beyond Object-Oriented Programming*. Addison-Wesley, 19998.

4

A Formal Language for Composition

Markus Lumpe, Franz Achermann, and Oscar Nierstrasz

Software Composition Group,
University of Berne,
Institute for Computer Science and Applied Mathematics
IAM, Neubrückstrasse 10, CH-3012 Bern, Switzerland
{lumpe, acherman, oscar}@iam.unibe.ch

Abstract

A composition language based on a formal semantic foundation will facilitate precise specification of glue abstractions and compositions, and will support reasoning about their behavior. The semantic foundation, however, must address a set of requirements like *encapsulation, objects as processes, components as abstractions, plug compatibility, a formal object model,* and *scalability.* In this work, we propose the $\pi\mathcal{L}$-calculus, an extension of the π-calculus, as a formal foundation for software composition, define a language in terms of it, and illustrate how this language can be used to plug components together.

4.1 Introduction

One of the key challenges for programming language designers today is to provide the tools that will allow software engineers to develop robust, flexible, distributed applications from plug-compatible software components [NM95]. Current object-oriented programming languages typically provide an ad hoc collection of mechanisms for constructing and composing objects, and they are based on ad hoc semantic foundations (if any at all) [Nie93]. A language for composing open systems, however, should be based on a rigorous formal foundation in which concurrency, communication, abstraction, and composition are primitives. In fact, the development of both the formal foundation and the language will be driven by a set of key requirements for a composition language [NM95]: *encapsulation, objects as processes, components as abstractions, plug compatibility, a formal object model,* and *scalability.*

Now, by defining the translation of higher-level language elements by means of a mapping to a mathematical calculus, we get non-ambiguous semantic interpretations of these constructs. Moreover, the language is open, since further language extensions can be handled the same way. Using this approach, we argue that it is possible to add newly defined higher-level abstractions and composition mechanisms. Finally, we are also able to reason about composition and check valid compositions.

We have previously used the π-calculus to model object composition and generic synchronization policies as an example for wrapping [LSN96, SL97, Var96]. The inherent problem, however, is the limited reusability and extensibility due to position-dependent parameters. We propose $\pi\mathcal{L}$ as a variant of the π-calculus that is inherently extensible. In the polyadic π-calculus [Mil91], sender and receiver processes need to agree on the number of communicated names and the interpretation of each of these. This schema of contracts between two components is too rigid, since it often requires the propagation of extensions of one part to the other. This propagation, however, can be reduced in many cases if we replace the polyadic communication of tuples by monadic communication of forms.

Dami has tackled a similar problem in the context of the λ-calculus, and has proposed λN [Dam94, Dam98], a calculus in which parameters are identified by names rather than positions. The resulting flexibility and extensibility can also be seen in HTML forms, whose fields are encoded as named (rather than positional) parameters in URLs, and in Python [vR96], where functions can be defined to take arguments by keywords.

In the next section, we informally present the $\pi\mathcal{L}$-calculus. In Section 4.3 we define PICCOLA by extending a core language step-by-step with higher-level language constructs that simplify programming with component agents. In the Sections 4.4 and 4.5 we show how to implement a composition mechanism and some glue paradigms. We conclude with some remarks about future work and directions.

4.2 The $\pi\mathcal{L}$-Calculus

In this section we introduce the $\pi\mathcal{L}$-calculus [Lum99], an offspring of an asynchronous fragment of the (polyadic) π-calculus [Mil91, MPW92]. The asynchronous sublanguage was proposed first by Boudol [Bou92] and Honda and Tokoro [HT92]. Sangiorgi [San95] extended the proposal by allowing polyadic communication.

4.2.1 Syntax

In the $\pi\mathcal{L}$-calculus we replace the communication of names or tuples of names by communication of so-called *forms*, a special notion of extensible records. More precisely, the $\pi\mathcal{L}$-calculus is an offspring of the asynchronous π-calculus, where polyadic communication is replaced by monadic communication of forms.

We use a, b, c to range over the set $\mathcal{N}$ of names. As in the π-calculus literature, we use the words "name," "port," and "channel" interchangeably. Unlike the π-

calculus where names are both subject and object of a communication in a sender or receiver, in the $\pi\mathcal{L}$-calculus names are only used as subject of a communication. The role of the object of a communication is taken by forms. Forms are finite mappings from an infinite set $\mathcal{L}$ of labels to an infinite set $\mathcal{N}^+ = \mathcal{N} \cup \{\mathcal{E}\}$, the set of names extended by $\mathcal{E}$ that denotes the empty binding. We use x, y, z to range over $\mathcal{N}^+$, the extended set of names, F, G, H to range over forms, X, Y, Z to range over form variables, and l, m, n to range over $\mathcal{L}$. The syntax for forms is defined as follows:

$$
\begin{array}{lll}
F & ::= \ \mathcal{E} & \textit{empty binding} \\
& | \ \ X & \textit{form variable} \\
& | \ \ F\langle l{=}V\rangle & \textit{binding extension} \\
& | \ \ FX & \textit{polymorphic extension}
\end{array}
$$

$\textit{where}$

$$
\begin{array}{lll}
V & ::= \ x & \textit{simple name} \\
& | \ \ X_l & \textit{name projection}
\end{array}
$$

The most notable elements of forms are *form variables* and *name projections*. *Form variables* are used for both as formal agent parameter in an input agent and as *polymorphic placeholders* in the *polymorphic extension*.

Projections denote locations of names in the $\pi\mathcal{L}$-calculus. A projection X_l has to be read as selection of the parameter named by l.

To formulate how projection works, we need the notion of *variables of a form* and *closed forms*.

Definition 4.2.1 (Variables of a Form) *The set of variables of a form F, written* $\mathcal{V}(F)$, *is defined as:*

$$
\begin{array}{rcl}
\mathcal{V}(\mathcal{E}) & = & \emptyset \\
\mathcal{V}(X) & = & \{X\} \\
\mathcal{V}(F\langle l{=}x\rangle) & = & \mathcal{V}(F) \\
\mathcal{V}(F\langle l{=}X_k\rangle) = \mathcal{V}(FX) & = & \{X\} \cup \mathcal{V}(F)
\end{array}
$$

Definition 4.2.2 (Closed Form) *We say that a form F is closed if it does not contain any form variable, so that $\mathcal{V}(F) = \emptyset$.*

Now we can define the notion of *name projection* as follows.

Definition 4.2.3 (Name Projection) *If a form F is closed, then the application of a label $l \in \mathcal{L}$ to form F (mapping from $\mathcal{L}$ to $\mathcal{N}^+$), written F_l, is called name projection and is defined as:*

$$\mathcal{E}_l = \mathcal{E}$$
$$(F\langle l{=}x\rangle)_l = x$$
$$(F\langle m{=}x\rangle)_l = F_l \quad if\ m \neq l$$

If a binding is defined for label l then F_l yields x, otherwise it yields the empty binding ($\mathcal{E}$). The reader should note that projection F_l can yield the empty binding $\mathcal{E}$ either if $l \notin \mathcal{L}(F)$ or $x = \mathcal{E}$ since $x \in \mathcal{N}^+$. A form may have multiple bindings for label l. In this case F_l extracts the rightmost binding.

The class A of $\pi\mathcal{L}$-calculus agents is built using the operators of inaction, input prefix, output, parallel composition, restriction, and replication. We use A, B, C to range over the class of agents. The syntax for agents is defined as follows:

$$
\begin{array}{llll}
A & ::= & \mathbf{0} & \textit{inactive agent} \\
  & | & A \mid A & \textit{parallel composition} \\
  & | & !V(X).A & \textit{replicated input} \\
  & | & (\nu\, a)A & \textit{restriction} \\
  & | & V(X).A & \textit{input (receive form in X)} \\
  & | & \overline{V}(F) & \textit{output (send form F)}
\end{array}
$$

$\mathbf{0}$ is the inactive agent. An input-prefixed agent $V(X).A$ waits for a form F to be sent along the channel denoted by value V and then behaves like $A\{F/X\}$, where $\{F/X\}$ is the substitution of all form variables X with form F. An output $\overline{V}(F)$ emits a form F along the channel denoted by value V. Unlike in the π-calculus, the value V in both the input prefix and the output particle can be either a simple name or a projection. Parallel composition runs two agents in parallel. The restriction $(\nu\, a)A$ makes name a local to A, that is, it creates a *fresh* name a with scope A. A replication $!V(X).A$ stands for a countably infinite number of copies of $V(X).A$ in parallel.

4.2.2 Terminologies and Notions

Both the input prefix and the restriction operator are binders for names in the π-calculus. In the $\pi\mathcal{L}$-calculus, however, only the operator $(\nu\, a)A$ acts as binder for names occurring free in an agent. In $\pi\mathcal{L}$ the input prefix $V(X)$ is the binding operator for form variables. We use fn(A) and bn(A) to denote the set of *free* and *bound names* of an agent and fv(A) and bv(A) to denote the set of *free* and *bound form variables* of an agent, respectively. Similarly, n(A) and v(A) stand for all names and variables in A, respectively.

The sets fv(A) and bv(A) give rise the the following definition.

Definition 4.2.4 (Closed Agent) *We say that an agent A is closed if it does not contain any free form variables, so that* fv(A) $= \emptyset$.

In contrast to the π-calculus, we strictly distinguish between constants and variables. In the $\pi\mathcal{L}$-calculus names are always constant, that is, names are constant locations and are not subject of substitution (α-conversion is still possible). On the other side, *projections* denote variables in the $\pi\mathcal{L}$-calculus.

We write $A\{F/X\}$ for the substitution of all free occurrences of form variable X with form F in A. Substitutions have precedence over the operators of the language.

Finally, we adopt the usual convention of writing $x(X)$ when we mean $x(X).\mathbf{0}$. Additionally, an agent $\overline{x}(\mathcal{E})$ sending an empty form can just be written $\overline{x}$, a form $\langle \mathcal{E}\langle l{=}x \rangle \rangle$ is just written $\langle l{=}x \rangle$, and we abbreviate $(\nu\ x)(\nu\ y)A$ with $(\nu\ x,y)A$ and $(\nu\ x_1)\ldots(\nu\ x_n)A$ with $(\nu\ \tilde{x})A$, respectively.

4.2.3 Operational Semantics

The operational semantics is given using the reduction system technique proposed by Milner [Mil90, Mil91]. In the reduction system technique, axioms for a structural congruence relation are introduced prior the definition of the reduction relation. Basically, this allows us to separate the laws which govern the neighbourhood relation among agents for the rules that specify their interaction. Furthermore, this simplifies the presentation of the reduction relation by reducing the number of cases that we have to consider.

Definition 4.2.5 *The structural congruence relation,* $\equiv$, *is the smallest congruence relation over agents that satisfies the following axioms:*

$$\begin{aligned}
&(1) && A \mid B \equiv B \mid A,\ (A \mid B) \mid C \equiv A \mid (B \mid C),\ A \mid \mathbf{0} \equiv A; \\
&(2) && (\nu\ a)\mathbf{0} \equiv \mathbf{0},\ (\nu\ a)(\nu\ b)A \equiv (\nu\ b)(\nu\ a)A; \\
&(3) && (\nu\ a)A \mid B \equiv (\nu\ a)(A \mid B),\ \textit{if a not free in } B; \\
&(4) && !V(X).A \equiv V(X).A \mid !V(X).A; \\
&(5) && \mathcal{E}(X).A \equiv \mathbf{0},\ \overline{\mathcal{E}}(F) \equiv \mathbf{0}.
\end{aligned}$$

The axioms (1)–(4) are standard and are the same as for the π-calculus. The only "new" axiom is (5), which defines the behavior if an *empty binding* appears in subject position of the leftmost prefix of an agent. For example, if we have the agent $a(X).X_l(Y)$ and this agent receives along channel a the form $\langle m{=}V_1 \rangle\langle n{=}V_2 \rangle$, then $(X_l(Y))\{\langle m{=}V_1 \rangle\langle n{=}V_2 \rangle/X\}$ yields $\mathcal{E}(Y)$ since label l is not defined in the received form. In this case the agent is identical with the *inactive agent*. This means that a system containing such an agent may reach a deadlock. In general, if the name $\mathcal{E}$ occurs as subject in the leftmost prefix of an agent, this may be interpreted as a runtime error.

The reduction system describes the reduction of $\pi\mathcal{L}$-terms. In fact, the *reduction rules* define the interaction of $\pi\mathcal{L}$-agents. Note, however, that the reduction relation is only defined for closed agents (that is, $\mathrm{fv}(A) = \emptyset$).

Definition 4.2.6 *Let A, B two $\pi\mathcal{L}$-agents and $\mathrm{fv}(A|B) = \emptyset$. Then the one-step reduction $A \longrightarrow B$ is the least relation closed under the following rules:*

$$\text{PAR: } \frac{A \longrightarrow A'}{A \mid B \longrightarrow A' \mid B} \qquad\qquad \text{RES: } \frac{A \longrightarrow A'}{(\nu\, a)A \longrightarrow (\nu\, a)A'}$$

$$\text{COM: } a(X).A \mid \bar{a}.(F) \longrightarrow A\{F/X\}$$

$$\text{STRUCT: } \frac{A \equiv A' \quad A' \longrightarrow B' \quad B' \equiv B}{A \longrightarrow B}$$

The first two rules state that we can reduce under both parallel composition and restriction. (The symmetric rule for parallel composition is redundant, because of the use of structural congruence.)

The communication rule takes two agents which are willing to communicate on the channel a, and substitutes all form variables X with form F in A. The communication rule is the only rule which directly reduces a $\pi\mathcal{L}$-term. A reduction is not allowed underneath an input prefix. Furthermore, closed agents evolve to closed agents [Lum99].

The communication assumes that agents are in a particular format. The structural congruence rule allows us to rewrite agents so that they have the correct format for the communication rules.

4.3 Towards a Composition Language

In this section we develop a first version of the composition language PICCOLA. In order to define PICCOLA, we use the scheme that has been successfully used for the definition of PICT [Pie95], that is, we define a language core and extend it step by step with higher-level syntactic forms that are translated into the core language.

4.3.1 The Core Language

The core is presented in Table 4.1. For describing the syntax, we rely on a meta notation similar to the Backus-Naur Form that is commonly employed for language definitions. Keywords and symbolic constants appear inside quotes. Optional expressions are enclosed in square brackets. Furthermore, we reuse the PICT convention to denote the different types of agents using special symbols. We use ! to stand for output prefixes, ? to stand for input agents, and ?* to stand for replicated input agents.

The reader should note that a parallel composition of agents extends to the right as far as possible, that is, the parallel agent is right associative. Therefore, if an input-prefixed agent is built using parallel composition of subagents, these subagents

Declarations	::=	*Declaration* [*Declarations*]
Declaration	::=	'new' *NameList*
		'run' *Agent*
Agent	::=	*PrimaryAgent* ['|' *Agent*]
PrimaryAgent	::=	'null'
		Location '!' *Form*
		Location '?' '(' [*Variable*] ')' 'do' *Agent*
		Location '?*' '(' [*Variable*] ')' 'do' *Agent*
		'let' *Declarations* 'in' *Agent* 'end'
		'if' *BoolExpression* 'then' *Agent* ['else' *Agent*] 'end'
		'(' *Agent* ')'
NameList	::=	*Name* [, *NameList*]
BoolExpression	::=	*Value Built-in-BoolOperator Value*
Location	::=	*Name*
		Variable '.' *Label*
Form	::=	'<' [*FormElementList*] '>'
		Variable
FormElementList	::=	*FormElement* [',' *FormElementList*]
FormElement	::=	*Variable*
		Label '=' *Value*
Value	::=	*Location*
		String
		Number

Table 4.1. *The core of* PICCOLA.

have to be written in parentheses (for example, the agent (a?(X) do b! <Y>) | c! <Z> is different from the agent a?(X) do b! <Y> | c! <Z>).

In PICCOLA the syntax for forms has been simplified. A form X extended with a sequence of bindings $< l_1 = V_1 >< l_2 = V_2 >$ is now written as a list of form elements: $< X, l_1 = V_1, l_2 = V_2 >$.

In the following, we iteratively extend the syntax by defining higher-level abstractions. These higher-level abstractions come with a set of small examples that will motivate the newly introduced concepts or aspects of the higher-level language. Throughout this section, we use $[\![\cdot]\!]$ as interpretation of a higher-level construct denoted by · in terms of the core language. The complete syntax definition of PICCOLA is given in the Appendix.

4.3.2 Procedures

Assume we have implemented a simple person database service that is located at a global channel `lookup`. In order to query information about a person, we have to send a form containing the labels **name** and **result**. The label **name** binds a string denoting the name of the person while the label **result** maps a channel along which the query result is returned. In the following example, we query information about a person "Smith" and display the received information on the screen using a built-in display agent located at channel **print**.

```
new result                                    // create reply channel
run    lookup!<name="Smith",result=result>    // invoke query
    | result?(Info) do                        // wait for information
                    print!Info                // print information
```

This definition, however, can immediately be simplified, because form variables can host arbitrary forms. In fact, instead of using a newly created reply channel **result**, we can directly bind the channel **print** to label **result**, such that the query result is directly passed to the display agent. The simplified definition is shown in the following:

```
run lookup!<name="Smith",result=print>
```

Now, we would like to provide this behavior as a single service that is parameterized with the person string to be queried. Therefore, we define a replicated input agent that listens at channel **printPerson** waiting for a form containing at least a label **name** and displays the corresponding information on the screen.

```
new printPerson                                        // service channel
run printPerson?*(ArgForm) do lookup!<ArgForm,result=print>  // perform lookup
```

In order to invoke this service, we can send a form to channel **printPerson** that must contain at least the label **name**:

```
printPerson!<name="Smith">
```

In fact, the above service definition is a parameterized agent abstraction. The structure of the definition is so common that we provide a new element for the syntactic domain *Declaration*; we extend the language with a *procedure declaration*:

$$[\![\text{ `\textbf{procedure}' } Name \text{ `(' } [\text{ } Variable \text{ }] \text{ `)' } \text{ `\textbf{do}' } Agent]\!]$$
$$= \text{ `\textbf{new}' } Name$$
$$\text{ `\textbf{run}' } Name?*( [ \text{ } Variable \text{ } ] ) \text{ `\textbf{do}' } Agent$$

Having the procedure declaration available, we also want to have a convenient way to invoke procedures. Therefore, we add an *application*† as additional syntactic form to primary agents:

$$[\![\text{ } Location \text{ `(' } Form \text{ `)' }]\!] \quad = \quad Location!Form$$

---

† The reader should note that we allow arbitrary locations to denote procedure names. For example, an agent can get access to a procedure by receiving a form that contains a binding which maps to the procedure's name.

Now, assuming that the service `lookup` was also defined as procedure, the above `printPerson` service can be rewritten using the new syntax:

```
procedure printPerson(ArgForm) do lookup(<result=print,ArgForm>)
```

The reader should note that in the above declaration we have changed the order of the elements in the form used as argument for the procedure *lookup*. In fact, using this scheme we can define so-called *default arguments*. In case of the procedure *lookup* we have one default argument represented by the binding *result = print* which guarantees that the result of *lookup* is passed to an agent located at channel *print*. To override this default behavior we can simply add a new binding for label *result* to the argument form of the procedure *printPerson*. For example, if we have a user-defined print agent located at channel *printnew*, we can redirect the output produced by procedure *lookup* with the following invocation of *printPerson*:

```
printPerson(<ArgForm,result=printnew>)
```

This example uses polymorphic extension which is technically spoken *asymmetric record concatenation* [CM94] and which is a feature that is extremely useful to model compositional abstractions [Sch99].

4.3.3 Value Declaration

So far, new form variables can only be introduced by input-prefixed agents or procedures. However, it is often convenient to make some variables globally accessible, such that they appear "free" somewhere in the program text and provide a value throughout the rest of that program. To define such variables and to assign them values, we introduce a *value declaration* which is defined as follows:

$$\text{' let' } [\!\![\text{ 'value' } Variable \text{ '=' } Form]\!\!] \text{ 'in' } Agent \text{ 'end'}$$
$$= \text{ 'let' 'new' } r \text{ 'in' } r!Form \mid r?(\ Variable \ ) \text{ 'do' } Agent \text{ 'end'}$$

4.3.4 Complex Forms

All form expressions that we have encountered so far have been built up in a simple way, using just variables and bindings from labels to core values. If we, however, want to define updatable data structures, we need a packing technique that allows us to define data and operations over them in one syntactic construct. Therefore, we extend the syntax of forms and allow local declarations and call these construct *complex forms*:

$$Location! \ [\!\![\text{ 'let' } Declaration \text{ 'in' } Form \text{ 'end' }]\!\!]$$
$$= \text{ 'let' } Declaration \text{ 'in' } Location!Form \text{ 'end'}$$

For example, this syntactic construct together with the value declaration allows us to define a storage cell as follows:

```
value AStorageCell =
  let
    new cell
    run cell!<>
    procedure Read(Args) do cell?(Val) do (Args.result!Val | cell!Val)
    procedure Update(Val) do cell?(OldVal) do cell!Val
  in <Read=Read,Update=Update> end
```

In fact, this declaration defines a simple object **AStorageCell** that maintains a private instance variable denoted by channel *cell* and provides two member functions **Read** and **Update** to get and set the contents of the object **AStorageCell**, respectively. The reader should note that this object encoding uses asynchronous method invocation. In the next section, we define function abstractions. Using functions to implement **Read** and **Update** will allow us to execute these methods synchronously.

4.3.5 Functions

Each time we have applied a form in an output agent or a call expression, we have used "static" forms. To get a greater flexibility and even a more compact specification, we add abstractions for "dynamic" forms. The term "dynamic" means that forms are either generated by agents that act as functions or that have themselves dynamic elements. For functions, we extend *Declarations* as follows:

$$\begin{aligned} &[\![\text{'function'}\ Name\ '('\ [\ Variable\ ]\ ')'\ '='\ Form\ ]\!] \\ =\ &\text{'new'}\ Name \\ &\text{'run'}\ Name?^*(\ \text{X}\ )\ \text{'do'}\ \text{X.result!}Form \end{aligned}$$

with variable **X** being either *Variable* or a fresh wildcard if *Variable* has been omitted in the function declaration. The reader should note that by convention the label **result** maps the name (channel) along which the function result is sent.

In order to call a function, we also add the syntactic domain *Application* to forms (see Section 4.3.2). However, in contrast to procedures, the translation of functions uses **result** as default label to return the function result. Therefore, a function call

```
AFun( AForm )
```

is transformed into

```
AFun( <AForm,result=AResultChannel> )
```

where **AResultChannel** denotes the actual result channel to be used.

The result of a function may be available before the complete function body has been processed. To stress this fact, we extend the syntax domain *Form* with a *return expression*:

$$[\![\text{'return'}\ Form\ ]\!] = \text{X.result!}Form$$

where X denotes the actual formal function parameter.

This expression, however, is only allowed to be used within a function declaration, because the return expression is translated to an output process that sends the form expression along a channel mapped by label **result**. If a return expression is specified within a procedure it will evaluate to the **null** agent, because the necessary label **result** is not defined.

4.3.6 Nested Forms

Up to now, forms are flat values, that is, there is no support to add an additional structure to forms. However, it is often necessary to keep things separated. For example, if a service expects both a channel and a value, we have to send both in one form which is typically written like

```
<channel=cname,AFormValue>
```

Unfortunately, this definition merges the channel and the form value, such that the original structure information is lost. Therefore, we introduce so-called *nested forms*, that is, we extend *Value* to denote also forms:

$$
\begin{aligned}
& \text{`<' } \textit{Label} \text{ `=' } [\![\ \textit{Value} ::= \textit{Form}\ ]\!] \text{ `>'} \\
= \ & \text{`let' } [\![\ \text{`function' } f\ (\ X\ ) = \textit{Form}\ ]\!] \text{ `in' `<' } \textit{Label} \text{ `=' } f \text{ `>' `end'}
\end{aligned}
$$

with f being a fresh function name.

The above form can now be rewritten as follows:

```
<channel=cname,form=AFormValue>
```

Nested forms add, however, one level of indirection. Therefore, to access the form bound by label *form* we need to use function application. For example, if form variable X denotes the above form then the application $X.form()$ yields the form mapped by label *form*.

4.3.7 Active Forms

Active forms are forms that contain active elements, that is, they have function or procedure specifications or function calls in place of bindings. This concept allows us to define form expressions that can act as objects. Therefore, we add *procedures*, *functions*, and *function call* to the syntax category of *FormElement*:

'<' ⟦ '**procedure**' *Name* '(' [*Variable*] ')' '**do**' *Agent* ⟧ '>'
= '**let**' ⟦ '**procedure**' *Name* '(' [*Variable*] ')' '**do**' *Agent* ⟧
        '**in**' '<' *Name* '=' *Name* '>' '**end**'

'<' ⟦ '**function**' *Name* '(' [*Variable*] ')' '=' *Form* ⟧ '>'
= '**let**' ⟦ '**function**' *Name* '(' [*Variable*] ')' '=' *Form* ⟧
        '**in**' '<' *Name* '=' *Name* '>' '**end**'

'<' ⟦ *Location* '(' *Form* ')' ⟧ '>'
= '**let**' ⟦ '**value**' X '=' *Location* '(' *Form* ')' '**in**' '<' X '>' '**end**'

The functions and procedures are translated using the scheme for nested forms. Function calls are transform into a complex form using X as fresh variable.

However, we allow not only form elements to be active, but also forms. Therefore, we extend forms with *conditionals*.

'<' ⟦ '**if**' *BoolExpression* '**then**' *Form*$_1$ ['**else**' *Form*$_2$] '**end**' ⟧ '>'
= '<' ⟦ PrIf '(' bool '=' ⟦ *BoolExpression* ⟧ ','
        t '=' *Form*$_1$ ',' f '=' *Form*$_2$ ')' ⟧ '>'

Roughly spoken, conditional forms are transformed into a function call. The function PrIf is a built-in function (that is, it is part of the runtime system of PICCOLA) that expects a form that contains the labels bool, t, and f. If the else part has been omitted, then the translation replaces *Form*$_2$ with the empty form. Further information on the complete treatment of conditional forms can be found in [Lum99].

4.3.8 Sequencing

In fact, the form <> can be considered as a *continuation signal*, that is, it carries no information but tells the calling agent that its request has been satisfied. Using this signal, we can synchronize parallel running agents. Therefore, we provide a convenient syntax to specify "invoke operation, wait for a signal as a result, and continue":

⟦ *Form* ';' *PrimaryAgent* ⟧
= '**let**' '**value**' X '=' *Form* '**in**' *PrimaryAgent* '**end**'
⟦ *Form*$_1$ ';' *Form*$_2$ ⟧
= '**let**' '**value**' X '=' *Form*$_1$ '**in**' *Form*$_2$ '**end**'

The first abstraction denotes an agent while the latter denotes a form. In both, however, the lefthand-side form (the variable X is fresh) is evaluated before the righthand-side agent or form becomes active. This means that the value of the lefthand-side form is lost; we are only interested in the fact that this form has been evaluated, so that it is now safe to proceed.

4.3.9 External Services

In order to incorporate components that have not been developed in PICCOLA, we provide an *external declaration*:

$$Declaration \quad ::= \quad \text{`\textbf{extern}'} \; String \; Name$$

In this declaration *String* denotes a Java class that provides the interface implementation to the external service while *Name* can be an arbitrarily chosen name that maps the Java class to a channel name. For example, a print service located at `print` is declared as follows:

```
extern "Piccola.builtin.print" print
```

The PICCOLA runtime system provides several Java classes to map external components. However, a detailed description of them is beyond the scope of this work.

4.3.10 Composition Scripts

Finally, we add the facility to define separate modules or composition scripts. A script is itself a component, that is, it can be composed with other composition scripts.

Composition scripts can be separately compiled. The result is stored in a composition library. Composition scripts can load other scripts that have been previously compiled. This implies, however, that composition scripts cannot have circular dependencies which is, in our opinion, the most natural way to support *black-box* reuse of components.

A composition script is defined as follows:

$$Script \quad ::= \quad \text{`\textbf{module}'} \; ModuleName \; [\; Imports \;] \; Declarations \; [\; Main \;]$$

$$Imports \quad ::= \quad \text{`\textbf{load}'} \; NameList \; \text{`;'}$$

$$Main \quad ::= \quad \text{`\textbf{main}'} \; Agent$$

Inspired by Python [Lut96], the main declaration specifies the agent that has to be started in the PICCOLA environment when the script is executed at the top level. Main declarations of imported scripts are ignored.

4.4 An Object Model

In this section we show how objects can be implemented in PICCOLA. Our development is based on the basic object model of Pierce and Turner [PT95]. Adapting this model, we specify an object as a composition of parallel running agents which are bundled with some restricted locations that serve as the state of the object.

Using the higher-level syntax, a storage cell can be implemented as follows:

```
load Blackboard;

function newStorageCell( X ) =
    let
        value cell = newBlackboard()
    in
        cell.Write( <val = X.init> );
        <
            function Update( Args ) = cell.Remove(); cell.Write( <val = Args> ),
            function Read() = cell.Read()
        >
    end
```

In fact, the function **newStorageCell** implements an object generator. The instance variable **cell**, in contrast to the example in Section 4.3.4, is implemented using a Linda-like blackboard abstraction [CG89] (imported by the load statement). Since each new storage cell has its own restricted blackboard we guarantee the invariant that a storage cell can store only a single value.

Now we are ready to define a class abstraction. This abstraction implements a simple metaobject protocol that allows us to create objects. Basically, the definition of a class abstraction follows the scheme similar to those found in [AC96] and [SL97]. Furthermore, the class abstraction can be solely implemented in PICCOLA. There is no need to extend the language†.

The object model defined by the abstraction **Class** that supports single inheritance and private and protected features. This abstraction provides three functions: **newInstance**, **selfbinder**, and **allocate**. The function **newInstance** is responsible for creating new object instances while the others are metaobject operations that establish inheritance and the correct binding of **self**.

```
function Class( Body ) =
    let
        value super = Body.super()

        function allocate ( Init ) =
            Body.allMethods( <super.allocate( Init ), init = Init> )

        function selfbinder( Self ) =
            Body.public( <super = super.selfbinder( Self ), self = Self> )

    in
        <
            function newInstance( Init ) = selfbinder( <allocate(Init)> ),
            selfbinder = selfbinder,
            allocate = allocate
        >
    end
```

The (function) abstraction **Class** expects a form that has three labels: **super**, **allMethods**, and **public**. In fact, all labels denote functions. The function **super** returns the actual super object.

The function **allMethods** returns a "pre-object," that is, **allMethods** extends its

---

† The reader should note that future extensions of PICCOLA will contain builtin language features for classes and objects.

argument form (i.e, the super object) with all newly defined class features (methods and instance variables).

The function `public` is built in the same way as `allMethods`. The function `public` expects a form that maps `super` and `self`. In fact, the values bound to `super` and `self` are also forms. Basically, the function `public` returns the public interface of an object and establishes the correct binding of `self`.

Finally, we have to define the root of the inheritance tree. The root of a class hierarchy is the class `Object`. The class metaobject for `Object` is defined as follows:

```
value Object =
  <
     function newInstance() = <>,
     function selfbinder() = <>,
     function allocate() = <>
  >
```

Using the function `Class`, a metaobject for a storage cell can be implemented as follows. A storage cell class inherits from class `Object`. The function `allMethods` returns a "pre-object" that extends `super` with the pre-methods `preSet` and `preGet` and a binding for the protected feature `blackboard`. Finally, the function `public` returns a fresh storage cell object.

```
value StorageCellClass = Class(
   <
     super = Object,

     function allMethods( Super ) =
       let
          value Init = Super.init()
          value Blackboard = newBlackboard()
       in
          Blackboard.Write( <val = Init> );
          <
            Super,
            function preSet( Args ) =
              let
                 value B = Args.self().blackboard()
              in
                 B.Remove(); B.Write( Args )
              end,
            function preGet( Args ) = Args.self().blackboard().Read(),
            blackboard = Blackboard
          >
       end,

     function public( Pre ) =
       <
          Pre.super(),
          function set( A ) = Pre.self().preSet( <Pre, val = A> ),
          function get() = Pre.self().preGet( Pre )
       >
   > )
```

The abstraction `Class` illustrates how a complex composition mechanism can be defined in PICCOLA. Compared with the object encodings in the polyadic π-calculus [LSN96, SL97], the new formulation of inheritance is much more compact.

Furthermore, in [LSN96, SL97] we had to explicitly name all methods in the process of binding self, even those methods that were not modified in the subclass.

4.5 Generic Wrapper

In the previous section we illustrated how to define a composition mechanism in PICCOLA. In this section we present the definition of a wrapping mechanism. More precisely, we show how a Readers-Writers synchronization policy can be defined using a generic wrapper.

The Readers-Writers policy is a family of concurrency control designs that apply when any number or readers can be executing simultaneously as long as there are no writers, but writers require exclusive access.

It is relatively straightforward to implement a Readers-Writers policy for a given set of reader and writer methods. However, it is problematic to implement it generically, but not impossible. For example, Doug Lea [Lea96] has given a generic implementation of a Readers-Writers policy using an abstract Java class. This implementation defines pre- and post-methods for both reader and writer methods. Using a template method `read_()`, the method `read()` executes `beforeRead()`, possibly blocking until the reader is allowed to enter its critical region. The critical region is implemented in `read_()` and must be provided by a subclass. Then a method `afterRead()` does some cleanup. By subclassing, a programmer provides its own implementation of `read_()`. Unfortunately, it is not possible to subclass the read method so that it can take arguments. However, it is possible to add new methods, but then it is the programmer's responsibility to correctly call `beforeRead()` and `afterRead()` for each reading method and analogously for writer methods.

Using forms, we can define a generic wrapper which wraps any service with arbitrary arguments with pre- and post-methods. A wrapped service is created using the following steps:

- The pre-function `pre` is invoked with the arguments for the service. The returned form is stored in `PreService`.
- The service is invoked with the arguments and its result is returned.
- Finally, the post-function `post` is invoked using `PreService` (the result of the pre-function) as argument.

We define this wrapping operation by the function `wrap` as follows:

```
function wrap( Service ) =
   < function val( X ) =
      let
          value PreService = Service.pre( X )
      in
          return Service.val( X ); Service.post( PreService )
      end >
```

Now we want to build a Readers-Writers policy wrapper. This wrapper enables the wrapping of arbitrary agents by either declaring them as **reader** or **writer**. An agent wrapped with **reader** (**writer**) becomes then a reader (writer) agent. They apply to the following constraints:

- When no writer agent is active, an arbitrary number of reader agents can be concurrently active,
- There is at most one writer active. When a writer is active, no active reader is allowed.

A Readers-Writers policy can now be built up using four agents. These agents work on two private resources, one with a semaphore for the writers, and the other containing the number of currently active reader agents. Initially, the semaphore allows agents to enter, and the value 0 is written onto the blackboard **count** since no reader is active.

The function **preRead** removes the count. If the count is zero, then the writer semaphore is grabbed. Finally, an incremented count is written back to the channel keeping track that one reader-agent is active.

The function **postRead** removes the count from the blackboard. If the count equals one, then the last reader has finished and the writer semaphore is released. Finally, the decremented count is written back to the blackboard.

The function **preWrite** grabs the writer semaphore and the function **postWrite** releases the semaphore.

Creating a reader writer wrapper then means to define two wrappers **reader** and **writer** which wrap an arbitrary agent using the corresponding pre- and post-agents:

```
load Blackboard, Semaphore;

function newReaderWriter() =
  let
    value Writer = newSemaphore()
    value count = newBlackBoard()
    run count.Write( <val = <val = 0>> );

    function preRead() =
      let
        value n = count.Remove()
      in
        if n.val = 0 then Writer.p() end; count.Write( <val = <inc( n )>> )
      end

    function postRead() =
      let
        value n = count.Remove()
      in
        if n.val = 1 then Writer.v() end; count.Write( <val = dec( n )> )
      end

    function preWrite() = Writer.p()
    function postWrite() = Writer.v()
  in
    < function reader( X ) = wrap( <X, pre = preR, post = postR> ),
      function writer( X ) = wrap( <X, pre = preW, post = postW> ) >
  end
```

In this implementation the `count` blackboard acts as lock for the functions `preRead` and `postRead`. However, it is important to note that we keep access to the pre- and post-functions restricted to the policy. A malicious agent cannot call a post function in isolation.

As an example of using the policy we assume a concurrent queue with methods `put`, `get`, and `getcount`. This queue is fully concurrent meaning that `put` and `get` can be executed concurrently. In order to add a `clone` method we can wrap the whole queue with a Readers-Writers policy, and declare the original methods as readers and the `clone` method as a writer. This way we can guarantee that the clone function has a locked queue, can safely use the count, and use put and get methods to create a clone of the queue. In the following we only show the wrapping part of the definition of a "clonable queue":

```
function newCloneQueue() =
  let
    value queue = newQueue()
    value policy = newReaderWriter()

    function clone() = ...                    // clone functionality
  in
    < put = policy.reader( <val = queue.put> ).val,
      get = policy.reader( <val = queue.get> ).val,
      getCount = policy.reader( <val = queue.getCount> ).val,
      clone = policy.writer( <val = clone> ).val >
  end
```

4.6 Conclusion and Future Work

We have presented the $\pi\mathcal{L}$-calculus and a first design of the composition language PICCOLA based on the $\pi\mathcal{L}$-calculus. Furthermore, PICCOLA provides support such that (i) an application may run on a variety of hardware and software platforms (the runtime system is built in Java), and (ii) open applications may be inherently concurrent and distributed (PICCOLA's formal semantics is based on a process calculus).

We have presented some PICCOLA component scripts that facilitate the specification and modeling of generic glue abstractions for adaptation and composition of software components. Although our examples are neither exhaustive nor canonical, we think they represent the essence of glue code, which is typically concerned with (i) adapting interfaces and behavior of software components, and (ii) composing or connecting components to achieve a combined behavior.

Ultimately we are targeting the development of open, hence distributed systems [NSL96]. Given the ad hoc way in which the development of open systems is supported in existing languages, we have identified the need for composing software from predefined, plug-compatible software components. The overall goal of our work, and hence the development of PICCOLA, is the development of a formal model for software composition, integrating a black-box framework for modelling objects and components, and an executable composition language for specifying components and applications as compositions of software components.

We are planning a further development of the πL-calculus to address various other practical problems. For example: Should labels be first-class values? Generic glue code may need to learn about new labels representing extended interfaces of components. Do first-class forms suffice to model a general reflective behavior? Glue code is often reflective in nature. Is it enough to reflect over messages or do we need more?

For the moment PICCOLA is untyped. However, most component approaches (for example, COM [Rog97], CORBA [OMG96], or Darwin [MDEK95]) equip partly or fully the interface specifications with type annotations. One argument for this decision is that only fully and explicitly typed interfaces can benefit from type checking. Furthermore, an independent development of both the client and the provider side may be more or less impossible without appropriate type information (for example, the current version of PICCOLA already records which names have been used to denote forms). Therefore, a next extension of PICCOLA will support type annotations. Furthermore, missing type annotations will be inferred by a type inference algorithm.

In the field of concurrent and distributed systems, various process calculi have recently been proposed [CG98, FG96, VC98] that incorporate other aspects of distributed computation, such as communication failure, distributed scopes, and security. For the moment, we focus on composed systems within one administrative domain and do not take into account other distribution aspects. But a proper solution that addresses these aspects will play a crucial role when we want to model composition between distributed components.

Acknowledgments

We thank all members of the Software Composition Group especially Jean-Guy Schneider. We also express our gratitude to the anonymous reviewers for their comments on the draft of this work.

Bibliography

[AC96]   Abadi, M. and Cardelli, L. *A Theory of Objects*. Springer, 1996.

[Bou92] Boudol, G. Asynchony and the π-calculus. Technical Report 1702, INRIA Sophia-Antipolis, May 1992.

[CG89]   Carriero, N. and Gelernter, D. How to Write Parallel Programs: A Guide to the Perplexed. *ACM Computing Surveys*, 21(3):323–357, September 1989.

[CG98]   Cardelli, L. and Gordon, A. D. Mobile Ambients. In Nivat, M., editor, *Foundations of Software Science and Computational Structures*, LNCS 1378, pages 140–155. Springer, 1998.

[CM94]   Cardelli, L. and Mitchell, J. C. Operations on Records. In Gunter, C. and Mitchell, J. C., editors, *Theoretical Aspects of Object-Oriented Programming*.

MIT Press, 1994. Also appeared as SRC Research Report 48, and in *Mathematical Structures in Computer Science*, 1(1):3–48, March 1991.

[Dam94] Dami, L. *Software Composition: Towards an Integration of Functional and Object-Oriented Approaches*. PhD thesis, Centre Universitaire d'Informatique, University of Geneva, CH, 1994.

[Dam98] Dami, L. A Lambda-Calculus for Dynamic Binding. *Theoretical Computer Science*, 192:201–231, February 1998.

[FG96] Fournet, C. and Gonthier, G. The Reflexive Chemical Abstract Machine and the Join-Calculus. In *Proceedings of the 23rd ACM Symposium on Principles of Programming Languages*, pages 372–385. ACM, January 1996.

[HT92] Honda, K. and Tokoro, M. On asynchronous Communication Semantics. In *ECOOP'91*, LNCS 612. Springer, June 1992.

[Lea96] Lea, D. *Concurrent Programming in Java: Design Principles and Patterns*. The Java Series. Addison-Wesley, October 1996.

[LSN96] Lumpe, M., Schneider, J.-G., and Nierstrasz, O. Using Metaobjects to Model Concurrent Objects with PICT. In *Proceedings of Langages et Modèles à Objets '96*, pages 1–12, Leysin, October 1996.

[Lum99] Lumpe, M. *A π-Calculus Based Approach to Software Composition*. PhD thesis, University of Bern, Institute of Computer Science and Applied Mathematics, January 1999.

[Lut96] Lutz, M. *Programming Python: Object-Oriented Scripting*. O'Reilly & Associates, October 1996.

[MDEK95] Magee, J., Dulay, N., Eisenbach, S., and Kramer, J. Specifying Distributed Software Architectures. In Schäfer, W. and Botella, P., editors, *Proceedings ESEC '95*, LNCS 989, pages 137–153. Springer, September 1995.

[Mil90] Milner, R. Functions as Processes. In *Proceedings ICALP '90*, LNCS 443, pages 167–180. Springer, July 1990.

[Mil91] Milner, R. The Polyadic Pi-Calculus: a Tutorial. Technical Report ECS-LFCS-91-180, Computer Science Department, University of Edinburgh, UK, October 1991.

[MPW92] Milner, R., Parrow, J., and Walker, D. A Calculus of Mobile Processes, Part I/II. *Information and Computation*, 100:1–77, 1992.

[Nie93] Nierstrasz, O. Composing active objects. In Agha, G., Wegner, P., and Yonezawa, A., editors, *Research Directions in Concurrent Object-Oriented Programming*, pages 151–171. MIT Press, 1993.

[NM95] Nierstrasz, O. and Meijler, T. D. Requirements for a Composition Language. In Ciancarini, P., Nierstrasz, O., and Yonezawa, A., editors, *Object-Based Models and Languages for Concurrent Systems*, LNCS 924, pages 147–161. Springer, 1995.

[NSL96] Nierstrasz, O., Schneider, J.-G., and Lumpe, M. Formalizing Composable Software Systems – A Research Agenda. In *Proceedings 1st IFIP Workshop on Formal Methods for Open Object-based Distributed Systems*, pages 271–282. Chapmann & Hall, 1996.

[OMG96] Object Management Group. *The Common Object Request Broker: Architecture and Specification*, July 1996.

[Pie95] Pierce, B. C. Programming in the Pi-Calculus: An experiment in concurrent language design. Technical report, Computer Laboratory, University of Cambridge, UK, May 1995. Tutorial Notes for Pict Version 3.6k.

[PT95] Pierce, B. C. and Turner, D. N. Concurrent Objects in a Process Calculus. In Ito, T. and Yonezawa, A., editors, *Theory and Practice of Parallel Programming (TPPP)*, LNCS 907, pages 187–215. Springer, April 1995.

[Rog97] Rogerson, D. *Inside COM: Microsoft's Component Object Model*. Microsoft Press, 1997.

[San95] Sangiorgi, D. Lazy functions and mobile processes. Technical Report RR-2515, INRIA Sophia-Antipolis, April 1995.

[Sch99] Schneider, J.-G. *Components, Scripts, and Glue: A conceptual framework for software composition.* PhD thesis, University of Bern, Institute of Computer Science and Applied Mathematics, 1999. to appear.

[SL97] Schneider, J.-G. and Lumpe, M. Synchronizing Concurrent Objects in the Pi-Calculus. In Ducournau, R. and Garlatti, S., editors, *Proceedings of Langages et Modèles à Objets '97*, pages 61–76, Roscoff, October 1997. Hermes.

[Var96] Varone, P. Implementation of "Generic Synchronization Policies" in PICT. Technical Report IAM-96-005, University of Bern, Institute of Computer Science and Applied Mathematics, April 1996.

[VC98] Vitek, J. and Castagna, G. Towards a Calculus of Secure Mobile Computations. In Tsichritzis, D., editor, *Electronic Commerce Objects*, pages 31–46. Centre Universitaire d'Informatique, University of Geneva, CH, July 1998.

[vR96] van Rossum, G. Python Reference Manual. Technical report, Corporation for National Research Initiatives (CNRI), October 1996.

Appendix – PICCOLA **Language Definition**

Script   ::=   '**module**' *Name* [*Imports*] *Declarations* [*Main*]

Imports   ::=   '**load**' *NameList* ';'

NameList   ::=   *Name* [',' *NameList*]

Declarations   ::=   *Declaration* [*Declarations*]

Declaration   ::=   '**extern**' *String Name*
　　　　　　　　　'**new**' *NameList*
　　　　　　　　　'**run**' *Agent*
　　　　　　　　　'**procedure**' *Name* '(' [*Variable*] ')' '**do**' *Agent*
　　　　　　　　　'**value**' *Name* '=' *Form*
　　　　　　　　　'**function**' *Name* '(' [*Variable*] ')' '=' *Form*

Main   ::=   '**main**' *Agent*

Agent   ::=   *PrimaryAgent* ['|' *Agent*]

PrimaryAgent   ::=   '**null**'
　　　　　　　　　Location '!' *Form*
　　　　　　　　　Location '?' '(' [*Variable*] ')' '**do**' *Agent*
　　　　　　　　　Location '?*' '(' [*Variable*] ')' '**do**' *Agent*
　　　　　　　　　'**let**' *Declarations* '**in**' *Agent* '**end**'
　　　　　　　　　'**if**' *BoolExpression* '**then**' *Agent* ['**else**' *Agent*] '**end**'
　　　　　　　　　Application
　　　　　　　　　'(' *Agent* ')'
　　　　　　　　　PrimaryForm ';' [*Agent*]

BoolExpression   ::=   *Value Built-in-BoolOperator Value*

Location   ::=   *Name*
                          Variable '.' *Label*
                          PrimaryForm '.' *Label*

Application   ::=   *Location* '(' [*Form*] ')'

Form   ::=   *SeqForm*

SeqForm   ::=   *PrimaryForm* [';' *SeqForm*]

PrimaryForm   ::=   '<' [*FormElementList*] '>'
                            '**let**' *Declarations* '**in**' *Form* '**end**'
                            Application
                            '**return**' *PrimaryForm*
                            '**if**' *BoolExpression* '**then**' *Form* ['**else**' *Form*] '**end**'
                            '(' *Form* ')'
                            Variable

FormElementList   ::=   *FormElement* [',' *FormElementList*]

FormElement   ::=   *Variable*
                            Application
                            Label '=' *Value*
                            '**procedure**' *Name* '(' [*Variable*] ')' '**do**' *Agent*
                            '**function**' *Name* '(' [*Variable*] ')' '=' *Form*

Value   ::=   *Location*
                      Number
                      String
                      Form

5

A Semantic Foundation for Specification Matching

Yonghao Chen and Betty H. C. Cheng

Department of Computer Science and Engineering
Michigan State University
3115 Engineering Building
East Lansing, MI 48824-1226
E-mail: {chenyong,chengb}@cse.msu.edu

Abstract

Determining the behavioral relationship between software components is a central task for many software engineering activities, such as reuse, maintenance, and object-oriented subtyping. With the increasing interest in formal methods and automated software development techniques, specification matching has been proposed as a means to evaluate component relations at an abstract level. A number of specification matches have been proposed to capture the notion of *behavioral refinement*, or *reusability* in the context of software reuse. Without a rigorous means to establish the relationship between a given specification match and its suitability for reuse, the usefulness of a specification match is questionable. In this paper, based on total correctness of a program with respect to its specification, we establish a semantic foundation for reasoning about the connections between a specification match and its usefulness for determining reusability, and provide a framework to evaluate various specification matches. In particular, we discuss a special type of specification matching, *reuse-ensuring* matches. We prove that the set of all equivalence classes of reuse-ensuring matches together with the logical implication ($\Rightarrow$) operator constitute a complete lattice, thus enabling us to identify the *most general* (or the *best*) reuse-ensuring matches.

5.1 Introduction

Determining the behavioral relationship between software components is a central task for many software engineering activities, such as reuse, maintenance, and object-oriented subtyping. With the increasing interest in formal methods and automated software development, specification matching [RW91, JC92, JC93, JC95, ZW95] has been proposed as a means to evaluate component relations at an abstract level. Specification matching identifies behavioral relationships between software components by checking the logical relations between specifications. Among the possible behavioral relations, one of particular interest is *behavioral refinement*, that is, one component provides all the behavior that another component does. In software reuse, this means that one existing component can be (re)used where a new component is needed. In software maintenance, it means that one component can be substituted for another one without changing the behavior of the whole system. In object-oriented subtyping, the refinement relationship between methods of two classes is an essential requirement for one class to be a behavioral subtype of another [LW90]. In this paper, in order to focus our discussion, we study *behavioral refinement* in the context of software reuse. We have concentrated on the software reuse application since it has been the focus of most of the specification matching work [JC92, JC93, JC95, ZW95, JC94, PA97, SF97, MMM97, CC97b]. In software reuse, a key issue is to determine if an existing component is reusable for implementing a given query specification.

A number of specification matching criteria have been proposed to capture the notion of *behavioral refinement*, or *reusability* in the context of software reuse. One widely used formal specification method is based on Hoare's axiomatic approach [Hoa69]. An axiomatic specification of a component (procedure) C is a 2-tuple of predicates, $\langle C_{pre}, C_{post} \rangle$, where C_{pre} specifies the precondition, and C_{post} specifies the postcondition of the procedure. In the following discussion, consistent with terms of software reuse, Q represents a query specification, $\langle Q_{pre}, Q_{post} \rangle$, and A is a library component specification, $\langle A_{pre}, A_{post} \rangle$. Zaremski and Wing [ZW95] defined *exact pre/post* match, $M_{exact-pre/post} : (Q_{pre} \leftrightarrow A_{pre}) \wedge (A_{post} \wedge Q_{post})$, and *plug-in* match, $M_{plug-in} : (Q_{pre} \rightarrow A_{pre}) \wedge (A_{post} \rightarrow Q_{post})$. Penix and Alexander [PA97], and Schumann and Fischer [SF97] use a more *relaxed plug-in* match in their component retrieval work, $M_{relaxed-plug-in} : (Q_{pre} \rightarrow A_{pre}) \wedge (Q_{pre} \wedge A_{post} \rightarrow Q_{post})$. By defining the characteristic predicate of a component (or specification) as $A_{pre} \rightarrow A_{post}$, Jeng and Cheng [JC92, JC93, JC95, JC94], Zaremski and Wing [ZW95] discussed *exact* and *generalized predicate* matches, $M_{exact-pred} : (A_{pre} \rightarrow A_{post}) \leftrightarrow (Q_{pre} \rightarrow Q_{post})$ and $M_{gen-pred} : (A_{pre} \rightarrow A_{post}) \rightarrow (Q_{pre} \rightarrow Q_{post})$. Zaremski and Wing [ZW95] also suggest an alternative definition of characteristic predicate, $A_{pre} \wedge A_{post}$, and therefore obtain a different form of predicate matches. In defining behavioral subtyping, America [Ame91] and Liskov and Wing [LW94] use *plug-in* match as their method rule that governs the behavioral relationships between methods of two classes (or objects). Dhara and Leavens [DL96] later refine their method rule as *guarded generalized predicate* match, $M_{guarded-gen-pred} : (Q_{pre} \rightarrow A_{pre}) \wedge ((A_{pre} \rightarrow A_{post}) \rightarrow (Q_{pre} \rightarrow Q_{post}))$. Table 5.1 lists some of those specification matches defined in the recent literature [JC95, ZW95, PA97, SF97, Ame91, LW94, DL96].

Behavioral refinement has been an important concept in formal programming methodology [Dij76, Jon80, Gri81, Coh90], particularly in refinement calculus [Bac88,

Match	Definition
$M_{exact-pre/post}$	$(Q_{pre} \leftrightarrow A_{pre}) \wedge (A_{post} \leftrightarrow Q_{post})$
$M_{plug-in}$	$(Q_{pre} \rightarrow A_{pre}) \wedge (A_{post} \rightarrow Q_{post})$
$M_{plug-in-post}$	$(A_{post} \rightarrow Q_{post}$
$M_{weak-post}$	$A_{pre} \rightarrow (A_{post} \rightarrow Q_{post})$
$M_{relaxed-plug-in}$	$(Q_{pre} \rightarrow A_{pre}) \wedge ((Q_{pre} \wedge A_{post}) \rightarrow Q_{post})$
$M_{exact-pred}$	$(A_{pre} \rightarrow A_{post}) \leftrightarrow (Q_{pre} \rightarrow Q_{post})$
$M_{gen-pred}$	$(A_{pre} \rightarrow A_{post}) \rightarrow (Q_{pre} \rightarrow Q_{post})$
$M_{exact-pred-2}$	$(A_{pre} \wedge A_{post}) \leftrightarrow (Q_{pre} \wedge Q_{post})$
$M_{gen-pred-2}$	$(A_{pre} \wedge A_{post}) \rightarrow (Q_{pre} \wedge Q_{post})$
$M_{guarded-gen-pred}$	$(Q_{pre} \rightarrow A_{pre}) \wedge ((A_{pre} \rightarrow A_{post}) \rightarrow (Q_{pre} \rightarrow Q_{post}))$

Table 5.1. *Various specification matches*

Mor87, Mor90, BvW98]. In refinement calculus, programming is a step-by-step development of specifications into (executable) code through the application of refinement laws. A refinement law defines a correctness-preserving refinement relationship between two programs. (In refinement calculus, the term "program" is used polymorphically to represent (abstract) specifications, (executable) code, and intermediate forms between the two.) Although most of refinement laws involve the refinement of a specification to a code segment, several refinement laws only involve specifications, such as the *weaken precondition* and *strength postcondition* laws, which together are actually the *plug-in* match shown in Table 5.1.

The usefulness of a specification match M for determining reuse lies in the following assumption:†

Given a query specification Q and a library component A, if $M(A, Q)$ holds, then A can be reused for implementing Q.

The validity of the above assumption depends on how the logical relationships between A and Q, captured by the match M, are related to the reusability of A for Q. Although the usefulness of those specification matches depicted in Table 5.1 have individually been argued in one way or another, there does not exist a general approach to reason about the connections between a specification match and its usefulness for determining reusability. Due to the lack of such a general approach, some problems regarding specification matching cannot be solved in an efficient way.

---

† This assessment and this paper focuses on the correctness of a reusable candidate for a given query specification. It does not address numerous issues related to component adaptation.

For example, given a specification match that happens to be suitable for determining reuse, it is still an open question as to whether there exist *better* specification matches. Intuitively, one specification match is *better* than another if it can identify reusable components for a given query that the other match fails to identify.‡ For example, is there a specification match better than the *relaxed plug-in* match? Or can we further refine the specification match used by Dhara and Leavens [DL96] in defining object-oriented behavioral subtyping? Another drawback to the lack of a general approach for reasoning about specification matching is that different people may have different perspectives and thus define different matches for capturing certain aspects of reusability, as exhibited in the large variety of proposed specification matches. In this paper, we establish a semantic foundation for reasoning about the connections between a specification match and its usefulness for determining reusability, and provide a framework to evaluate various specification matches. We also study the set of all specification matches suitable for determining reuse, and prove the existence of the *best* equivalence classes among those specification matches.

In order to rigorously reason about the usefulness of a specification match, we need a formal definition of *reusability*. The essential requirement of such a definition is correctness: in order for a component to be reusable with respect to a specification, it must "correctly" implement the specification. In this paper, we only consider components (programs) that terminate, thus by correctness we mean *total* correctness.

The remainder of this paper is organized as follows. Section 5.2 gives a definition for *reusability* in terms of the correctness formula of Hoare logic. Based on this definition, a special type of specification matching, *reuse-ensuring match*, is defined. A reuse-ensuring match will guarantee the reusability of a component for correctly implementing a query specification. Section 5.3 gives an overview of relational semantics that will be used as the basis for reasoning about specifications. Then in Section 5.4 we discuss how to prove a specification match is reuse-ensuring. Our proof technique is based on the relational interpretation of programs and specifications [Hoa69, Cou90, HL74]. This interpretation model addresses universal quantification, thus simplifying the form of the matches at the specification level. In Section 5.5, we discuss the lattice properties of reuse-ensuring matches. We prove that the set of all equivalence classes of reuse-ensuring matches together with the logic implication ($\Rightarrow$) operator constitute a complete lattice. Moreover, we give the lattice's greatest and least element, which are also the most general and most specific equivalence classes of reuse-ensuring matches, respectively. In Finally, we describe related work in Section 5.6 and conclude this paper in Section 5.7.

---

‡ "Better" only refers to the ability to retrieve reusable components; it does not necessarily mean that the retrieved components are a better fit.

5.2 Formalizing and Reasoning About Reusability

In this section, we formalize reusability in terms of program correctness with respect to specifications. We then discuss in general terms how specification matching is related to reuse. We define *reuse-ensuring* matches to capture the notion of using specification matching to determine reusability.

5.2.1 Program Specification and Correctness

The most important property of a program is its functionality, that is, what the program can accomplish. Therefore, a correct functional specification is crucial for the effective (re)use of a program. Many formal specification languages have been proposed [Win90], such as VDM [Jon90], Z [Wor92], and the Larch family [GH93]. In this paper, we do not want to be constrained by the syntactical details of specific specification languages. Instead, we use a general form of specifications that is based on Hoare's axiomatic approach [Hoa69]. An *axiomatic specification* of a program is given by a pair of first order assertions about the values of the relevant variables before and after the execution of the program: the *precondition* specifies the initial values, and the *postcondition* specifies the final values and/or their relations with the initial values. In order to differentiate the values of a variable before and after the execution of a program, we use the primed form of a variable to denote the final value of the variable, whereas the nonprimed form of a variable denotes its initial value.† The precondition of a specification thus is a boolean function of nonprimed variables, and the postcondition is a boolean function of primed and/or nonprimed variables.

Example 1 *The specification for computing the quotient and remainder of integer division looks like the following, where x, y, q, and r are all integers.*

$$\begin{aligned} \textbf{precond:} \quad & x \geq 0 \wedge y > 0 \\ \textbf{postcond:} \quad & q' \times y + r' = x \wedge r' \geq 0 \wedge y > r' \end{aligned}$$

It should be noted that in our specification, we assume that by default, the value of each variable may change unless it is explicitly stated that the final value of a variable is the same as its initial value. Therefore, we do not have to introduce a *frame* (or *modifies* clause in Larch) in a specification to list the variables whose values may change.

In order to facilitate our discussion in the rest of the paper, we introduce the following notations.

---

† The notion of primed variable for representing final value is borrowed from the Larch interface specification language for C [GH93].

V	the set of variables that a program operates on.
V′	the set of primed forms of variables in **V**, that is, $\mathbf{V}' = \{v' \mid v \in \mathbf{V}\}$.
PreAssert	the set of first order assertions over **V**.
PostAssert	the set of first order assertions over $\mathbf{V} \cup \mathbf{V}'$.
Spec	the set of specifications. **Spec = PreAssert × PostAssert**.

A specification is usually written as a 2-tuple $\langle p, q \rangle$, where $p \in$ **PreAssert** and $q \in$ **PostAssert** are the precondition and postcondition, respectively. In this paper, a specification S by default refers to $\langle S_{pre}, S_{post} \rangle$.

The correctness of a program with respect to implementing a specification is captured by a boolean expression, the *correctness formula (CF)* [Hoa69, Cou90, Coh90]. We use **CF** to denote the set of correctness formulas.

$$\mathbf{CF} = \mathbf{PreAssert} \times \mathbf{P} \times \mathbf{PostAssert}$$

where **P** is the set of programs.

Given a program A and a specification $\langle p, q \rangle$, the correctness formula, written as $\{p\}A\{q\}$, is informally interpreted as follows:

$\{p\}A\{q\} \equiv$ truth of *program A begun with p satisfied will terminate with q satisfied.*

It should be noted that this definition captures the total correctness of a program: as long as A starts with p satisfied, (1) A is guaranteed to terminate; and (2) q is satisfied when A terminates.

5.2.2 Reusability

The reusability of a component (program) for a query specification depends on whether the component satisfies the query specification. The correctness formula provides a semantic measure for "satisfaction."

Definition 1 (Reusability) *Given a query specification Q: $\langle Q_{pre}, Q_{post} \rangle$, a component A is reusable for implementing Q, if $\{Q_{pre}\}A\{Q_{post}\}$ holds.*

Definition 1 emphasizes the semantic correctness of a reusable component implementing a query specification. According to Definition 1, a reusable component is guaranteed to correctly implement the target specification. Although it is possible to apply program correctness proof techniques [Cou90] to check the validity of a correctness formula, this usually requires a great deal of knowledge about the program itself, such as its internal structures and implementation details. Unfortunately, this type of knowledge is seldom available. Furthermore, program correctness proof techniques are typically too computationally expensive to be practical for general use.

In this paper, we assume that components intended for reuse are delivered with specifications that the components satisfy [GCC98]. (In related investigations, we have applied reverse engineering techniques to obtain predicate-based specifications from existing code [GCC98].) We use $\langle A_{pre}, A_{post} \rangle$ to denote the specification of component A, that is, $\{A_{pre}\}A\{A_{post}\}$. In the rest of this paper, depending on the context, a component A refers to either its specification $\langle A_{pre}, A_{post} \rangle$ or the component itself. Specification matching is a method for evaluating and finding reusable components for a query specification by matching component specifications to the query specification. Formally, a specification match is a boolean function defined as below.

$$M\colon \mathbf{Spec} \times \mathbf{Spec} \to \{T, F\}$$

Given a match M and two specifications S_1 and S_2, if $M(S_1, S_2) = T$, then we say S_1 matches S_2 according to M.

5.2.3 Reuse-Ensuring Match

For a specification match to be useful, it should guarantee the correctness of a component for fulfilling the given query specification. Therefore, we are only interested in those specification matches that when a component matches a query specification, we can be assured that the component is reusable for implementing the query specification. We call these matches *reuse-ensuring*.

Definition 2 (Reuse-ensuring Match) *A specification match M is reuse-ensuring, that is, it can ensure that a component A satisfies a query specification Q, if and only if for any A and Q, $M(A, Q) \wedge \{A_{pre}\}A\{A_{post}\} \Rightarrow \{Q_{pre}\}A\{Q_{post}\}$.*

Once a specification match is proven to be reuse-ensuring, we can use it to evaluate and select components reusable for a query specification by simply checking its validity when applied to candidate components and the query specification.

As an axiomatic proof system for program correctness, Hoare logic [Hoa69, Cou90] has a set of axiom schemata and inference rules, most of which refer to specific program constructs (statements). However, there is one rule, *consequence rule*, that does not involve the specific constructs of a program, as shown below.

$$\frac{p \to p', \{p'\}C\{q'\}, q' \to q}{\{p\}C\{q\}}$$

The *consequence rule* states that if the execution of a program C under precondition p' ensures the truth of assertion q', then the execution of C under any precondition that logically implies p' also ensures the truth of any assertion logically implied by q'. We can apply the *consequence rule* to prove that certain matches are reuse-ensuring. For example, consider the *plug-in* match, $M(A, Q) = (Q_{pre} \to A_{pre}) \wedge (A_{post} \to Q_{post})$. Apply the *consequence rule* with Q_{pre} for p, A_{pre} for p', A_{post} for q', Q_{post} for q, and A for C, we have $\{Q_{pre}\}A\{Q_{post}\}$. Due to the soundness of Hoare logic, we have $M(A, Q) \wedge \{A_{pre}\}A\{A_{post}\} \Rightarrow \{Q_{pre}\}A\{Q_{post}\}$. Therefore, the *plug-in* match is reuse-ensuring.

Unfortunately, Hoare logic is not generally applicable to prove reuse-ensuring matches without involving the internal structures of a component. Thus we turn to the underlying semantics of program specifications and correctness in search of a basis for reasoning about specification matches. One frequently used approach to expressing semantics is based on Dijkstra's weakest precondition functions, *wp* and *wlp* [Dij76]. Given a command *c*, its semantics is defined by *wp.c.p*, the weakest precondition for command *c* to terminate and establish postcondition *p*, and by *wlp.c.p*, the weakest precondition for command *c* to establish *p* if *c* terminates. Since *wp* and *wlp* act as predicate transformers, this kind of semantics is also called predicate-transformation semantics. Hesselink [Hes92] explored the use of predicate-transformation semantics as a foundation for a formal programming methodology. Although it is possible to use predicate-transformation semantics as a foundation to reason about specification matching, the inclusion of programming language constructs makes it unnecessarily complicated for the purposes of reasoning about specification matching. Therefore in the following discussion, we use a more intuitive method of semantics formalization, called relational semantics, as our basis for reasoning about specification matching. Relational semantics has also been used to interpret Hoare logic [Cou90, HL74].

5.3 Relational Semantics

An execution step of a program can be considered as a transformation from one state to another. The effects of a program execution can be described by the sequence of states. A terminated execution has a finite sequence of states. In general, the observation of the intermediate states in the execution sequence is unnecessary. The semantics of a program can be directly defined as a relation between the initial and final states of terminated executions. In this section, we first give a brief overview of relation calculus [FS90]. Then the relational interpretations of programs and specifications are described. Relevant theorems that will facilitate reasoning about specification matches are also discussed.

5.3.1 Relation Calculus

Definition 3 (Relation) *Given a set X, the Cartesian product $X \times X$ is the set of all pairs $\langle x, x' \rangle$, where $x, x' \in X$. A (binary) relation over X is any subset of $X \times X$. The Cartesian product $X \times X$ itself is a special relation, the universal relation.*

In addition to the common set operations: *subset* ($\subseteq$ or $\subset$), *intersection* ($\cap$), *union* ($\cup$) and so forth, we define the following operations that are specific to relations.

Definition 4 (Domain of a Relation) *Given a relation R, $R \subseteq X \times X$, the domain of R, denoted as Dom.R, is the set of first elements of all pairs in R, that* *is,*

$$Dom.R = \{x \mid x \in X \land \exists x'(x' \in X \land \langle x, x' \rangle \in R)\}$$

Definition 5 (Domain Restriction) *Given a relation $R \subseteq X \times X$, and a set $Y \subseteq X$, the domain restricted relation of R by Y, denoted by $Y \rceil R$, is the set of pairs in R whose first element is in Y, that is,*

$$Y \rceil R = \{\langle x, x' \rangle \mid x \in Y \land \langle x, x' \rangle \in R\}$$

Theorem 1 (Properties of Domain Restriction) *Given a set X, let $R_1, R_2 \subseteq X \times X$, and $X_1, X_2 \subseteq X$, it is not difficult to show the following properties regarding domain restriction.*

1. **Monotonicity of Relations.** *If R_1 is a subset of R_2, then $X_1 \rceil R_1$ is also a subset of $X_1 \rceil R_2$. That is, $R_1 \subseteq R_2 \Rightarrow X_1 \rceil R_1 \subseteq X_1 \rceil R_2$*

2. **Monotonicity of Sets.** *If X_1 is a subset of X_2, then $X_1 \rceil R_1$ is also a subset of $X_2 \rceil R_1$. That is, $X_1 \subseteq X_2 \Rightarrow X_1 \rceil R_1 \subseteq X_2 \rceil R_1$*

3. **Idempotent.** *Domain restricting an already domain-restricted relation by the same set has no effect. That is, $X_1 \rceil (X_1 \rceil R_1) = X_1 \rceil R_1$*

5.3.2 Interpretation of Programs and Specifications

The effects of a program execution are recorded in variables operated on by the program. An axiomatic specification is given by stating the initial and final values of these variables, that is, their values in the initial and final states. In general, each variable v belongs to a type $\mathbf{T}_v$ that defines a set of objects (data). For the set of variables $\mathbf{V}$ that a program operates on, we denote the set of (data) objects that all variables in $\mathbf{V}$ can range over as $\mathbf{D}$, that is, $\mathbf{D} = \bigcup_{v \in \mathbf{V}} \mathbf{T}_v$.

Definition 6 (State) *A state (or valuation) s is a function with the set $\mathbf{V}$ of variables as the domain and the set $\mathbf{D}$ of (data) objects as the range, such that $\forall v \in \mathbf{V}, s(v) \in \mathbf{T}_v$, where $s(v)$ is called the value of variable v in state s. The set of all the possible states of a program constitute the state space of the program, denoted as $\mathbf{S}$.*

The relational semantics of programs and specifications are given in terms of the following definitions.

Definition 7 (Interpretation of Programs) *The relational semantics or interpretation of a program P, denoted as I_P, is a binary relation over the state space $\mathbf{S}$ such that $\langle s, s' \rangle \in I_P$, if and only if there exists an execution of program P that starts in initial state s and terminates in final state s'.*

Example 2 *The relational semantics of a simple program "x:=3" (where assuming x is declared as an* Int*) is* $I_{x:=3} = \{\langle s, s' \rangle \mid s \in \mathbf{S} \wedge s' \in \mathbf{S} \wedge s'(x) = 3\}$*, where* $\mathbf{S} = \{s \mid s : \mathbf{V} \to \text{Int}\}$*,* $\mathbf{V} = \{x\}$*.*

Definition 8 (Interpretation of Preconditions) *A precondition* $p \in \mathbf{PreAssert}$ *is interpreted as a subset of state space* $\mathbf{S}$*.* $S_p = \{s \mid s \in \mathbf{S} \wedge p[\forall v \in \mathbf{V}, v \leftarrow s(v)]\}$*, where* $p[\forall v \in \mathbf{V}, v \leftarrow s(v)]$ *is the predicate obtained by substituting all occurrences of every variable* $v \in \mathbf{V}$ *in* p *with* $s(v)$*.*

Definition 9 (Interpretation of Postconditions) *The interpretation of a postcondition* $q \in \mathbf{PostAssert}$ *is a relation over state space* $\mathbf{S}$*.* $R_q = \{\langle s, s' \rangle \mid s \in S \wedge s' \in S \wedge q[\forall v \in \mathbf{V}, \forall v' \in \mathbf{V}', v \leftarrow s(v), v' \leftarrow s'(v)]\}$*, where* $q[\forall v \in \mathbf{V}, \forall v' \in \mathbf{V}', v \leftarrow s(v), v' \leftarrow s'(v)]$ *is the predicate obtained by substituting all occurrences of every variable* $v \in \mathbf{V}$ *in* q *with* $s(v)$ *and all occurrences of every variable* $v' \in \mathbf{V}'$ *in* q *with* $s'(v)$*.*

Example 3 *The boolean constant* T *(true) is interpreted as either* $\mathbf{S}$ *or* $\mathbf{S} \times \mathbf{S}$*, depending on whether it is a precondition or postcondition, respectively. The interpretation of* F *(false) is* ϕ *(empty set). The assertion* p*:* $x \geq 0$*, if used as a precondition, is interpreted as a set of states,* $S_p = \{s \mid s \in \mathbf{S} \wedge s(x) \geq 0\}$*. The assertion* q*:* $z' \times z' \leq x \wedge (z' + 1) \times (z' + 1) > x$ *is interpreted as a relation over* $\mathbf{S}$*,* $R_q = \{\langle s, s' \rangle \mid s \in \mathbf{S} \wedge s' \in \mathbf{S} \wedge s'(z) \times s'(z) \leq s(x) \wedge (s'(z) + 1) \times (s'(z) + 1) > s(x)\}$*.*

Based on the interpretations of assertions given before, we include the following theorem regarding assertions.

Theorem 2 (Properties of Assertions) *For two assertions,* p_1 *and* p_2*. If both* p_1 *and* p_2 *are in* $\mathbf{PreAssert}$*, then* $p_1 \to p_2 \Leftrightarrow S_{p_1} \subseteq S_{p_2}$*. Or if both* p_1 *and* p_2 *are in* $\mathbf{PostAssert}$*, then* $p_1 \to p_2 \Leftrightarrow R_{p_1} \subseteq R_{p_2}$*.*

Definition 10 (Interpretation of Correctness Formulas) *In terms of relational semantics, a correctness formula has the following interpretation:* $I[\{p\}A\{q\}] = S_p \subseteq Dom.I_A \wedge S_p]I_A \subseteq R_q$*.*

Definition 10 captures the notion of total correctness as described in Section 2.1. The first conjunct states that given p satisfied, A will terminate. The second conjunct ensures that q will be satisfied when A terminates.

An axiomatic specification consists of an assertion of **PreAssert** as the precondition and an assertion of **PostAssert** as the postcondition. However, not any pair of assertions from **PreAssert** × **PostAssert** can form an *implementable* specification. For example, specification $\langle T, F \rangle$ cannot be implemented by any program, since there is not a final state (terminating state) that satisfies F.

Definition 11 (Implementable Specification) *Given a state assertion p and a relation assertion q, the 2-tuple $\langle p, q \rangle$ is an implementable specification if and only if $S_p \subseteq Dom.R_q$.*

As an example, consider specification $\langle T, x \geq z' \times z' \wedge x < (z' + 1) \times (z' + 1) \rangle$. This is not an implementable specification, since there does not exist a program that, given any input (for instance, $x = -2$), will establish the truth of $x \geq z' \times z' \wedge x < (z' + 1) \times (z' + 1)$. In the rest of the paper, we assume all referenced specifications to be implementable.

Theorem 3 *Given two implementable specifications, $\langle p, q \rangle$ and $\langle w, u \rangle$. If $p \wedge q \rightarrow w \wedge u$, then $p \rightarrow w$.*

Proof. Suppose $p \wedge q \rightarrow w \wedge u$ is true. Since both $p \wedge q$ and $w \wedge u$ can be considered assertions in **PostAssert**, according to Theorem 2, we have $R_{p \wedge q} \subseteq R_{w \wedge u}$, which implies $Dom.R_{p \wedge q} \subseteq Dom.R_{w \wedge u}$. Since $S_p \subseteq Dom.R_q$ (by Definition 11), we have $Dom.R_{p \wedge q} = S_p$. Similarly, we have $Dom.R_{w \wedge u} = S_w$. Therefore, we have $S_p \subseteq S_w$, which, according to Theorem 2, means $p \rightarrow w$. $\square$

From Theorem 3, we can immediately derive the following corollary.

Corollary 1 *Given two implementable specifications, $\langle p, q \rangle$ and $\langle w, u \rangle$. If $p \wedge q \leftrightarrow w \wedge u$, then $p \leftrightarrow w$.*

Definition 12 (Interpretation of Specifications) *The interpretation of an implementable specification $\langle p, q \rangle$ is the result of domain restricting R_q by S_p, that is, $R_{\langle p, q \rangle} = S_p \rceil R_q$.*

Theorem 4 *Given an implementable specification $\langle p, q \rangle$, $R_{\langle p, q \rangle} = R_{p \wedge q}$.*
Proof.

   (i) For any $\langle s, s' \rangle \in R_{\langle p, q \rangle}$, it follows that $s \in S_p$ and $\langle s, s' \rangle \in R_{\langle p, q \rangle}$ (by Definition 12),

   (ii) which means both $p[\forall v \in \mathbf{V}, v \leftarrow s(v)]$ and $q[\forall v \in \mathbf{V}, \forall v' \in \mathbf{V}', v \leftarrow s(v), v' \leftarrow s'(v)]$ hold.

   (iii) Since p is a precondition, it does not contain primed variables (that is, variables in $\mathbf{V}'$), therefore $p[\forall v \in \mathbf{V}, v \leftarrow s(v)] = p[\forall v \in \mathbf{V}, \forall v' \in \mathbf{V}', v \leftarrow s(v), v' \leftarrow s'(v)]$.

   (iv) It immediately follows that $(p \wedge q)[\forall v \in \mathbf{V}, \forall v' \in \mathbf{V}', v \leftarrow s(v), v' \leftarrow s'(v)]$ holds, which means $\langle s, s' \rangle \in R_{p \wedge q}$.

   (v) On the other hand, for any $\langle s, s' \rangle \in R_{p \wedge q}$, $(p \wedge q)[\forall v \in \mathbf{V}, \forall v' \in \mathbf{V}', v \leftarrow s(v), v' \leftarrow s'(v)]$ is true.

   (vi) Since $(p \wedge q)[\forall v \in \mathbf{V}, \forall v' \in \mathbf{V}', v \leftarrow s(v), v' \leftarrow s'(v)] = p[\forall v \in \mathbf{V}, \forall v' \in \mathbf{V}', v \leftarrow s'(v)] \wedge q[\forall v \in \mathbf{V}, \forall v' \in \mathbf{V}', v \leftarrow s(v), v' \leftarrow s'(v)] = p[\forall v \in \mathbf{V}, v \leftarrow s(v)] \wedge q[\forall v \in \mathbf{V}, \forall v' \in \mathbf{V}', v \leftarrow s(v), v' \leftarrow s'(v)]$, we have $s \in S_p \wedge \langle s, s' \rangle \in R_q$.

   (vii) It follows that $\langle s, s' \rangle \in S_p \rceil R_q$, that is, $\langle s, s' \rangle \in R_{\langle p, q \rangle}$. $\square$

5.4 Proving Reuse-Ensuring Matches

Relational semantics provides a basis for reasoning about specification matches. In this section, we show how we can prove a specification match is reuse-ensuring based on relational semantics. In order to show that a match M is reuse-ensuring, we need to prove that for any specification Q and component A, as long as A

matches Q according to M, then A will correctly implement Q, that is, $M(A,Q) \wedge$ $\{A_{pre}\}A\{A_{post}\} \Rightarrow \{Q_{pre}\}A\{Q_{post}\}$.

Example 4 *As a first example, we show* $M_{exact-pred-2} : (A_{pre} \wedge A_{post}) \leftrightarrow (Q_{pre} \wedge Q_{post})$ *is reuse-ensuring.*

Proof. Suppose $(A_{pre} \wedge A_{post}) \leftrightarrow (Q_{pre} \wedge Q_{post})$ hold. According to Corollary 1, $A_{pre} \leftrightarrow Q_{pre}$ holds, which implies (1): $S_{A_{pre}} = S_{Q_{pre}}$. In the meantime, according to Theorems 2 and 4, we immediately have (2): $S_{Q_{pre}}]R_{Q_{post}} = S_{A_{pre}}]R_{A_{post}}$ from our assumption. Since $\{A_{pre}\}A\{A_{post}\}$, we have (3): $S_{A_{pre}} \subseteq Dom.I_A \wedge S_{A_{pre}}]I_A \subseteq R_{A_{post}}$. From the second conjunct of (3), we have $S_{A_{pre}}]I_A \subseteq S_{A_{pre}}]R_{A_{post}}$ (according to Theorem 1). Together with (1) and (2), we have (4): $S_{Q_{pre}}]I_A \subseteq S_{Q_{pre}}]R_{Q_{post}}$. Also following the first conjunct of (3) and (1) is (5): $S_{Q_{pre}} \subseteq Dom.I_A$. From (4) and (5) immediately follows $\{Q_{pre}\}A\{Q_{post}\}$. □

Example 5 *Our second example shows that* $M_{relaxed-plug-in} : (Q_{pre} \rightarrow A_{pre}) \wedge$ $(Q_{pre} \wedge A_{post} \rightarrow Q_{post})$ *is reuse-ensuring.*

Proof. Suppose $(Q_{pre} \rightarrow A_{pre}) \wedge (Q_{pre} \wedge A_{post} \rightarrow Q_{post})$ holds. From the first conjunct comes (1): $S_{Q_{pre}} \subseteq S_{A_{pre}}$ (Theorem 2), which immediately leads to (2): $S_{Q_{pre}}]I_A \subseteq S_{A_{pre}}]I_A$ (Theorem 1). Since $\{A_{pre}\}A\{A_{post}\}$, we have (3): $S_{A_{pre}} \subseteq Dom.I_A \wedge S_{A_{pre}}]I_A \subseteq R_{A_{post}}$. From the first conjunct of (3) and (1) immediately follows (4): $S_{Q_{pre}} \subseteq Dom.I_A$. On the other hand, from the second conjunct of (3) and (2), we have $S_{Q_{pre}}]I_A \subseteq R_{A_{post}}$, which implies $S_{Q_{pre}}]I_A \subseteq S_{Q_{pre}}]R_{A_{post}}$ (Theorem 1). From the second conjunct of our assumption, $Q_{pre} \wedge A_{post} \rightarrow Q_{post}$, we have $S_{Q_{pre}}]R_{A_{post}} \subseteq R_{Q_{post}}$ (Theorem 4 and Theorem 2). Therefore, we have (5): $S_{Q_{pre}}]I_A \subseteq R_{Q_{post}}$. Combining (4) and (5) follows $\{Q_{pre}\}A\{Q_{post}\}$. □

As illustrated in the above examples, proving a match is reuse-ensuring directly based on relational semantics may be a cumbersome task. The following theorem may greatly simplify the task.

Theorem 5 *Let* M' *be a reuse-ensuring match. A match* M *is reuse-ensuring if for any* A *and* Q, $M(A,Q) \Rightarrow M'(A,Q)$.

Proof. The truth of the above claim immediately follows the definition of reuse-ensuring match and the transitivity of logical implication ($\Rightarrow$). □

As long as a reuse-ensuring match is known, Theorem 5 simplifies the proof of reuse-ensuring matches by relying on the logical relations between specification matches, rather than involving the semantics-based interpretations of programs and specifications. However, it should be noted that the fact a match does not logically imply a given reuse-ensuring match does not necessarily mean that the match is not reuse-ensuring, unless the given reuse-ensuring match is the most general. We further discuss this issue in the next section.

Example 6 *Consider match* $M_{exact-pre/post}$: $(Q_{pre} \leftrightarrow A_{pre}) \wedge (A_{post} \leftrightarrow Q_{post})$. *It is easy to show that* $M_{exact-pre/post}$ *implies* $M_{exact-pred-2}$: $(A_{pre} \wedge A_{post}) \leftrightarrow (Q_{pre} \wedge Q_{post})$, *which is reuse-ensuring as shown in Example 4. Thus* $M_{exact-pre/post}$ *is reuse-ensuring.*

Example 7 *Consider match* $M_{plug-in}$: $(Q_{pre} \rightarrow A_{pre}) \wedge (A_{post} \rightarrow Q_{post})$. *It can be shown that* $M_{plug-in}$ *does not imply* $M_{exact-pred-2}$: $(A_{pre} \wedge A_{post}) \leftrightarrow (Q_{pre} \wedge Q_{post})$. *However, this does not exclude* $M_{plug-in}$ *from being reuse-ensuring. In fact,* $M_{plug-in}$ *is reuse-ensuring, since it implies reuse-ensuring match* $M_{relaxed-plug-in}$: $(Q_{pre} \rightarrow A_{pre}) \wedge (Q_{pre} \wedge A_{post} \rightarrow Q_{post})$ *(see Example 5).*

Example 8 *Finally, we show that* $M_{guarded-gen-pred}$ *is reuse-ensuring by proving* $M_{guarded-gen-pred} \Rightarrow M_{relaxed-plug-in}$. *In fact,* $M_{guarded-gen-pred}$ *and* $M_{relaxed-plug-in}$ *are logically equivalent.*
Proof. For the sake of readability, we assume the normal precedence of logical connectives, that is, $\neg$, $\wedge$, $\vee$, and $\rightarrow$ in the order of decreasing precedence.

$$
\begin{aligned}
M_{guarded-gen-pred}&(A, Q) \\
=\ & (Q_{pre} \rightarrow A_{pre}) \wedge ((A_{pre} \rightarrow A_{post}) \rightarrow (Q_{pre} \rightarrow Q_{post})) \\
\Leftrightarrow\ & (\neg Q_{pre} \vee A_{pre}) \wedge (\neg(\neg A_{pre} \vee A_{post}) \vee (\neg Q_{pre} \vee Q_{post})) \\
\Leftrightarrow\ & (\neg Q_{pre} \vee A_{pre}) \wedge ((A_{pre} \wedge \neg A_{post}) \vee \neg Q_{pre} \vee Q_{post}) \\
\Leftrightarrow\ & (\neg Q_{pre} \vee A_{pre}) \wedge (A_{pre} \wedge \neg A_{post}) \vee \\
& \neg Q_{pre} \vee (\neg Q_{pre} \vee A_{pre}) \wedge Q_{post} \\
\Leftrightarrow\ & A_{pre} \wedge \neg A_{post} \vee \neg Q_{pre} \vee A_{pre} \wedge Q_{post} \\
\Leftrightarrow\ & A_{pre} \wedge (\neg A_{post} \vee Q_{post}) \vee \neg Q_{pre} \\
\Leftrightarrow\ & Q_{pre} \rightarrow (A_{pre} \wedge (A_{post} \rightarrow Q_{post})) \\
\Leftrightarrow\ & (Q_{pre} \rightarrow A_{pre}) \wedge (Q_{pre} \rightarrow (A_{post} \rightarrow Q_{post})) \\
\Leftrightarrow\ & (Q_{pre} \rightarrow A_{pre}) \wedge (Q_{pre} \wedge A_{post} \rightarrow Q_{post}) \\
=\ & M_{relaxed-plug-in}(A, Q)
\end{aligned}
$$

Therefore, $M_{guarded-gen-pred} \Leftrightarrow M_{relaxed-plug-in}$. $\square$

Figure 5.1 shows the reuse-ensuring matches discussed in this section and their relations. In Figure 5.1, an arrow represents a logical implication between two matches.

5.5 Lattice Properties of Reuse-Ensuring Matches

The set of all reuse-ensuring matches are partitioned into equivalence classes by the logical equivalence operator ($\Leftrightarrow$). Let REM be the set of all equivalence classes of reuse-ensuring matches. We introduce the following operations regarding equivalence class. Let c and m be an equivalence class and a reuse-ensuring match, respectively, then c^m denotes an arbitrary element of c, and m^c denotes the equivalence class to which m belongs. Obviously, we have $(c^m)^c = c$. Furthermore, we extend the logical implication operator ($\Rightarrow$) to equivalence classes of reuse-ensuring matches. For two given equivalence classes, $c_1, c_2 \in REM$, we define $c_1 \Rightarrow c_2$ as $c_1^m \Rightarrow c_2^m$. It is

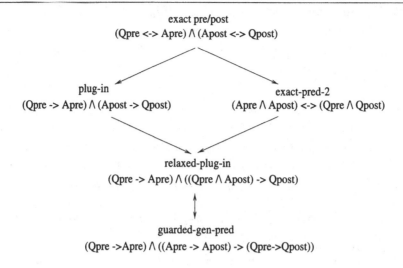

exact pre/post
(Qpre <-> Apre) ∧ (Apost <-> Qpost)

plug-in
(Qpre -> Apre) ∧ (Apost -> Qpost)

exact-pred-2
(Apre ∧ Apost) <-> (Qpre ∧ Qpost)

relaxed-plug-in
(Qpre -> Apre) ∧ ((Qpre ∧ Apost) -> Qpost)

guarded-gen-pred
(Qpre ->Apre) ∧ ((Apre -> Apost) -> (Qpre->Qpost))

Fig. 5.1. Reuse-ensuring Matches and Their Relations.

easy to show that logical implication ($\Rightarrow$) over REM is *reflexive* ($\forall c \in REM, c \Rightarrow c$), *antisymmetric* ($\forall c_1, c_2 \in REM, (c_1 \Rightarrow c_2) \land (c_2 \Rightarrow c_1) \Rightarrow (c_1 = c_2)$), and *transitive* ($\forall c_1, c_2, c_3 \in REM, (c_1 \Rightarrow c_2) \land (c_2 \Rightarrow c_3) \Rightarrow (c_1 \Rightarrow c_3)$), thus $\langle REM, \Rightarrow \rangle$ is a partially ordered set (POSET). Further, we show that $\langle REM, \Rightarrow \rangle$ is a complete lattice [Gra78]. This means that among all the equivalence classes of reuse-ensuring matches, there are two special ones: the most general and the most specific. The former is the greatest element of REM, and the latter is the least element of REM. Specification matches in the most general equivalence class are accordingly called most general reuse-ensuring matches. Therefore, in order to prove if a match is reuse-ensuring, we only need to check if it implies a most general reuse-ensuring match.

Lemma 1 *REM is a finite set.*
Proof. Each match can be regarded as a logical function of four parameters: Q_{pre}, Q_{post}, A_{pre}, and A_{post}, each of which is a predicate with value either *true* or *false*. Thus, the number of all possible input combinations to a match (logical function) is $2^4 = 16$. Given an input, a match can be evaluated to be either *true* or *false*, thus the maximum number of matches that are not logically equivalent is 2^{16}. (Among those matches, only a portion are reuse-ensuring.) Therefore, REM is a finite set. □

Theorem 6 $\langle REM, \Rightarrow \rangle$ *is a complete lattice.*
Proof. For any subset Ψ of REM, we show that the equivalence classes that the conjunction and disjunction of representatives from each member of Ψ belongs to

are the greatest lower bound (glb) and least upper bound (lub) of Ψ, respectively. It should be noted that since REM is finite, and so is Ψ, the above conjunction and disjunction are well-defined.

1. $lub\Psi = (\bigvee_{\psi \in \Psi} \psi^m)^c$: the equivalence class that the disjunction of representatives from each member of Ψ belongs to is the least upper bound (lub) of Ψ.

We claim that $(\bigvee_{\psi \in \Psi} \psi^m)^c \in REM$ is true, because $\forall \psi \in \Psi$, $\psi^m(A, Q) \Rightarrow \{Q_{pre}\}A\{Q_{post}\}$. This yields $\bigvee_{\psi \in \Psi} \psi^m(A, Q) \Rightarrow \{Q_{pre}\}A\{Q_{post}\}$, that is, $\bigvee_{\psi \in \Psi} \psi^m$ is reuse-ensuring. Since $\forall \varphi \in \Psi$, $\varphi^m \Rightarrow \bigvee_{\psi \in \Psi} \psi^m$, that is, $(\varphi^m)^c = \varphi \Rightarrow (\bigvee_{\psi \in \Psi} \psi^m)^c$, therefore $(\bigvee_{\psi \in \Psi} \psi^m)^c$ is an upper bound of Ψ. Next we show that $(\bigvee_{\psi \in \Psi} \psi^m)^c$ implies any upper bound of Ψ. Let φ be an arbitrary upper bound of Ψ. For $\forall \psi \in \Psi$, we have $\psi \Rightarrow \varphi$, and thus $\bigvee_{\psi \in \Psi} \psi^m \Rightarrow \varphi^m$, which means $(\bigvee_{\psi \in \Psi} \psi^m)^c \Rightarrow (\varphi^m)^c = \varphi$. Thus $(\bigvee_{\psi \in \Psi} \psi^m)^c$ is the lub of Ψ.

2. $glb\Psi = (\bigwedge_{\psi \in \Psi} \psi^m)^c$: the equivalence class that the conjunction of representatives from each member of Ψ belongs to is the greatest lower bound (glb) of Ψ.

Obviously, $\bigwedge_{\psi \in \Psi} \psi^m$ is a reuse-ensuring match, that is, $(\bigwedge_{\psi \in \Psi} \psi^m)^c \in REM$. Since $\forall \varphi \in \Psi$, $\bigwedge_{\psi \in \Psi} \psi^m \Rightarrow \varphi^m$, that is, $(\bigwedge_{\psi \in \Psi} \psi^m)^c \Rightarrow (\varphi^m)^c = \varphi$, therefore $(\bigwedge_{\psi \in \Psi} \psi^m)^c$ is a lower bound of Ψ. Next we prove that $(\bigwedge_{\psi \in \Psi} \psi^m)^c$ is implied by any lower bound of Ψ. Let φ be an arbitrary lower bound of Ψ. For $\forall \psi \in \Psi$, we have $\varphi \Rightarrow \psi$, and thus $\varphi^m \Rightarrow \bigwedge_{\psi \in \Psi} \psi^m$, which means $(\varphi^m)^c \Rightarrow (\bigwedge_{\psi \in \Psi} \psi^m)^c$. Thus $(\bigwedge_{\psi \in \Psi} \psi^m)^c$ is the glb of Ψ.

Combining the above arguments, we have proved that $\langle REM, \Rightarrow \rangle$ is a complete lattice. $\square$

From the proof of Theorem 6, it immediately follows that $(\bigvee_{\psi \in REM} \psi^m)^c$ is the least upper bound (lub) of REM, or the greatest element of REM. In terms of determining reuse, $(\bigvee_{\psi \in REM} \psi^m)^c$ is also called the most general equivalence class of reuse-ensuring matches, and $\bigvee_{\psi \in REM} \psi^m$ is a most general reuse-ensuring match. Theoretically, for any given specification match, we can prove or refute whether it is reuse-ensuring or not by checking if the given specification match implies a most general reuse-ensuring match. However, it is difficult to use $\bigvee_{\psi \in REM} \psi^m$ for this purpose. In the following discussion, we show that the *relaxed plug-in* match is also a most general reuse-ensuring match.†

Theorem 7 (Most General Reuse-Ensuring Match) $M_{relaxed-plug-in}(A, Q) = (Q_{pre} \to A_{pre}) \wedge (Q_{pre} \wedge A_{post} \to Q_{post})$ is a most general reuse-ensuring match.
Proof. We show that $M^c_{relaxed-plug-in}$ is the least upper bound (lub) of REM. In Example 5 above, we have shown that $M_{relaxed-plug-in}$ is reuse-ensuring, therefore, $M^c_{relaxed-plug-in} \in REM$. We now show that $M^c_{relaxed-plug-in}$ is an upper bound of REM.

(i) For any $c \in REM$, we have $c^m(A, Q) \wedge \{A_{pre}\}A\{A_{post}\} \Rightarrow \{Q_{pre}\}A\{Q_{post}\}$. That is, (1): $c^m(A, Q) \wedge S_{A_{pre}} \subseteq Dom.I_A \wedge S_{A_{pre}} | I_A \subseteq R_{A_{post}} \Rightarrow S_{Q_{pre}} \subseteq Dom.I_A \wedge S_{Q_{pre}} | I_A \subseteq R_{Q_{post}}$ (by Definition 10). Notice that in (1), component A is an arbitrary implementation satisfying specification $\langle A_{pre}, A_{post} \rangle$. For discussion purposes, we instantiate A to be $Dom.I_A = S_{A_{pre}}$ and $I_A = R_{A_{post}}$,

(ii) (1) is simplified as (2): $c^m(A, Q) \Rightarrow S_{Q_{pre}} \subseteq S_{A_{pre}} \wedge S_{Q_{pre}} | R_{A_{post}} \subseteq R_{Q_{post}}$.

(iii) According to Theorem 2, we have (3): $S_{Q_{pre}} \subseteq S_{A_{pre}} \Leftrightarrow Q_{pre} \to A_{pre}$.

† It should be noted that all the most general reuse-ensuring matches are logically equivalent, thus there is only one equivalence class of them in REM.

(iv) According to Definition 11, Theorems 4 and 2, we have (4): $S_{Q_{pre}} \rceil R_{A_{post}} \subseteq R_{Q_{post}} \Leftrightarrow Q_{pre} \wedge A_{post} \rightarrow Q_{post}$.

(v) Combining (2), (3), and (4), we have $c^m(A, Q) \Rightarrow (Q_{pre} \rightarrow A_{pre}) \wedge (Q_{pre} \wedge A_{post} \rightarrow Q_{post})$. That is, $c^m(A, Q) \Rightarrow M_{relaxed-plug-in}(A, Q)$, which means $c(A, Q) \Rightarrow M^c_{relaxed-plug-in}(A, Q)$.

Therefore, $M^c_{relaxed-plug-in}$ is an upper bound of REM. Since $M^c_{relaxed-plug-in} \in REM$, we have that $M^c_{relaxed-plug-in}$ is the least upper bound (lub) of REM. Thus $M_{relaxed-plug-in}$ is a most general reuse-ensuring match. $\square$

Theorem 7 answers our questions presented in Section 5.1. That is, there does not exist a *better* specification match than the *relaxed plug-in* match in determining reuse, nor can we refine the *guarded generalized predicate* match used in defining object-oriented behavioral subtyping (since in Example 8, we showed that $M_{relaxed-plug-in}$ and $M_{guarded-gen-pred}$ are logically equivalent).

Furthermore, using these results, we can revise Hoare's consequence rule to make it reuse-ensuring, thus enabling us to make proofs of reusability complete:

$$\frac{p \rightarrow p', \{p'\}C\{q'\}, (p \wedge q' \rightarrow q)}{\{p\}C\{q\}}$$

where p and q are the pre- and postconditions of a query program, respectively, and p' and q' are the pre- and postconditions of an existing component C.

5.6 Related Work

As mentioned previously, many projects have explored the use of specification matching to determine software reuse and object-oriented subtyping [RW91, JC92, JC93, JC95, ZW95, JC94, PA97, SF97, Ame91, LW94, DL96]. A number of matching criteria have been proposed to capture the reusability of a component for implementing a query specification. This paper describes a semantic foundation, based on relational semantics, for reasoning about specification matches and reusability, thereby providing a framework to evaluate various specification matches.

Mili *et al.* [MMM97] propose a refinement-based approach to component retrieval. They use relational specifications to represent components. A relational specification directly specifies the input/output relations of a component (function). Then they define refinement relation between two relational specifications as their basis for component storing and retrieval. Despite being expressed in different terms, their refinement relation has the same objective as those of various specification matches that we discussed in this paper, that is, to capture the notion of reusability through comparing two specifications. In essence, their refinement relation is equivalent to relaxed plug-in match. Like other specification matching work, they address the connection between their refinement relation and reusability in a rather intuitive way. Although we used relational interpretation as the basis for reasoning about specification matches, the *relation* in our work is defined over the program state space, rather than the pairs of input/output values. Moreover, the objective of our work is to find a sound foundation and framework to evaluate specification matching for reuse, rather than define yet another matching criteria. This distinguishes this current work from Mili *et al.*'s work and others'.

Relational semantics of programs was first introduced by Hoare and Lauer [HL74] and later was used to define semantics of Hoare logic [Cou90]. Our discussion of specification match and their semantic interpretation falls in the framework of Hoare logic, but we made some changes in our approach. First, we are not involved in the specific constructs of a program, instead, we are only concerned with the overall behavior. Therefore we did not discuss the interpretation of formulas in Hoare logic regarding specific program constructs. Second, and more importantly, the postcondition in Hoare logic is the function of only the final values of variables. This often makes specifications cumbersome since auxiliary variables have to be introduced. We adopt the approach that most current specification languages take, that is, we allow both initial and final values of variables to appear in a postcondition. Thus the interpretation of our postcondition is a binary relation over the state space, rather than a subset of the state space, as in the case of Hoare logic. Finally, in Hoare logic, the correctness formula is intended to capture the notion of partial correctness, rather than total correctness as we did in this paper. Therefore, the interpretation of the correctness formula in Hoare logic does not contain the conjunct $S_p \subseteq Dom.I_A$ of Definition 10 that ensures the termination of program execution.

5.7 Conclusions and Future Investigations

In this paper, a semantic foundation is established to reason about the connections between a specification match and its usefulness for determining reusability. Based on this semantic foundation, we proved that the set of all equivalence classes of reuse-ensuring matches together with the logical implication ($\Rightarrow$) operator constitute a complete lattice, and showed that the *relaxed plug-in* match is a most general (or a *best*) reuse-ensuring match. We also discussed and clarified some concepts in the context of the proposed semantic foundation.

We are incorporating the results of this paper into an ongoing project whose objective is to develop an automated approach to component-based software development [CC97a]. Specifically, the work described in this paper provides a formal foundation for applying specification matching-based methods to component evaluation, and simplifies the development of a *best* component evaluation method [CC97b].

Acknowledgments

The authors gratefully acknowledge the detailed comments from the reviewers that have helped us to improve the final version of this paper.

This work was supported in part by DARPA grant F30602-96-1-0298 (administered by Air Force's Rome Laboratory), and the National Science Foundation grants CCR-9633391, CCR-9407318, CDA-9617310, and CDA-9700732.

Bibliography

[Ame91]   America, P. Designing an object-oriented programming language with behavioral subtyping. In de Bakker, J. W., de Roever, W. P., and Rozenberg, G., editors, *LNCS*, volume 489, pages 60–90. Springer-Verlag, 1991.

[Bac88]   Back, R. A calculus of refinements for program derivations. *Acta Information*, 25:593–624, 1988.

[BvW98]   Back, R. and von Wright, J. *Refinement Calculus: A Systematic Introduction*. Springer Verlag, 1998.

[CC97a]   Chen, Y. and Cheng, B. H. C. Facilitating an automated approach to architecture-based software reuse. In *Proceedings of the IEEE 12th International Conference on Automated Software Engineering*, November 1997.

[CC97b]   Chen, Y. and Cheng, B. H. C. Formalizing and automating component reuse. In *Proc. of 9th IEEE Intl. Conference on Tools with Artificial Intelligence*, November 1997.

[Coh90]   Cohen, E. *Programming in the 1990s*. Springer-Verlag, 1990.

[Cou90]   Cousot, P. Methods and logics for proving programs. In van Leeuwen, J., editor, *Handbook of Theoretical Computer Science*, volume B: Formal Models and Semantics, chapter 15, pages 841–993. The MIT Press/Elsevier, 1990.

[Dij76]   Dijkstra, E. *A Discipline of Programming*. Prentice-Hall, 1976.

[DL96]   Dhara, K. K. and Leavens, G. T. Forcing behavioral subtyping through specification inheritance. In *Proceedings of the 18th International Conference on Software Engineering (ICSE'18)*, Berlin, Germany, March 1996.

[FS90]   Fejer, P. A. and Simovici, D. A. *Mathematical Foundations of Computer Science*, volume I: Sets, Relations and Induction. Springer-Verlag, New York, 1990.

[GCC98]   Gannod, G. C., Chen, Y., and Cheng, B. An automated approach for supporting software reuse via reverse engineering. In *Proceedings of 13th IEEE International Conference on Automated Software Engin eering (ASE'98)*, Honolulu, Hawaii, USA, October 1998.

[GH93]   Guttag, J. V. and Horning, J. *Larch: Languages and Tools for Formal Specification*. Springer-Verlag, 1993.

[Gra78]   Gratzer, G. *General Lattice Theory*. Birkhauser, Basel, 1978.

[Gri81]   Gries, D. *The Science of Programming*. Springer Verlag, 1981.

[Hes92]   Hesselink, W. H. *Programs, Recursion and Unbounded Choice*. Cambridge University Press, 1992.

[HL74]   Hoare, C. A. R. and Lauer, P. Consistent and complementary formal theories of the semantics of programming languages. *Acta Information*, 3:135–155, 1974.

[Hoa69]   Hoare, C. A. R. An axiomatic basis for computer programming. *Communications of the ACM*, 12(10), October 1969.

[JC92]   Jeng, J.-J. and Cheng, B. H. C. Using automated reasoning techniques to determine software reuse. *International Journal of Software Engineering and Knowledge Engineering*, 2(4), December 1992.

[JC93]   Jeng, J.-J. and Cheng, B. H. C. Using formal methods to construct a software component library. In *Lecture Notes in Computer Science*, volume 717, pages 397–417, September 1993.

[JC94]   Jeng, J.-J. and Cheng, B. H. C. A formal approach to reusing more general components. In *The Proceedings of IEEE 9th Knowledge-Based Software Engineering Conference*, September 1994.

[JC95]   Jeng, J.-J. and Cheng, B. H. C. Specification matching for software reuse: A foundation. In *SSR'95*. ACM SIGSOFT, ACM Press, April 1995.

[Jon80]   Jones, C. *Software Development: A Rigorous Approach*. Prentice-Hall International, 1980.

[Jon90]   Jones, C. B. *Systematic Software Development Using VDM*. Prentice-Hall International, 1990.

[LW90]   Leavens, G. T. and Weihl, W. E. Reasoning about object-oriented programs that use subtypes (extended abstract). In Meyrowitz, N., editor, *OOPSLA ECOOP '90 Proceedings*, volume 25(10), pages 212–223, October 1990.

[LW94]   Liskov, B. H. and Wing, J. M. A behavioral notion of subtyping. *ACM Transactions on Programming Languages*, 16(10), November 1994.

[MMM97]   Mili, R., Mili, A., and Mittermeir, R. T. Storing and retrieving software components: A refinement based system. *IEEE Transactions on Software Engineering*, 23(7), July 1997.

[Mor87]   Morris, J. A theoretical basis for stepwise refinement and the programming calculus. *Science of Computer Programming*, 9(3):287–306, 1987.

[Mor90]   Morgan, C. *Programming from Specifications*. Prentice Hall, 1990.

[PA97]   Penix, J. and Alexander, P. Toward automated component adaptation. In *Proc. of the 9th Intl. Conf. on Software Engineering and Knowledge Engineering*, June 1997.

[RW91]   Rollins, E. J. and Wing, J. M. Specifications as Search Keys for Software Libraries. In *Proceedings of the Eighth International Conference on Logic Programming*, June 1991.

[SF97]   Schumann, J. and Fischer, B. Nora/hammr: Making deduction-based software component retrieval practical. In *Proceedings of the 12th IEEE International Automated Software Engineering Conference (ASE97)*, Incline Village, Nevada, November 1997.

[Win90]   Wing, J. M. A specifier's introduction to formal methods. *IEEE Computer*, 23(9), September 1990.

[Wor92]   Wordsworth, J. B. *Software Development with Z*. Addison-Wesley Longman Ltd., 1992.

[ZW95]   Zaremski, A. M. and Wing, J. M. Specification matching of software components. In *3rd ACM SIGSOFT Symposium on the Foundations of Software Engineering*, October 1995.

Part Two
Object-Based Specification and Verification

6

Concepts of Behavioral Subtyping and a Sketch of Their Extension to Component-Based Systems

Gary T. Leavens

Department of Computer Science, 226 Atanasoff Hall
Iowa State University, Ames, IA 50011-1040 USA
leavens@cs.iastate.edu

Krishna Kishore Dhara

Bell Laboratories, Lucent Technologies
2f-247, 600-700 Mountain Ave
Murray Hill, NJ 07974-0636 USA
dhara@lucent.com

Abstract

Object-oriented systems are able to treat objects indirectly by message passing. This allows them to manipulate objects without knowing their exact runtime type. Behavioral subtyping helps one reason in a modular fashion about such programs. That is, one can reason based on the static types of expressions in a program, provided that static types are upper bounds of the runtime types in a subtyping preorder, and that subtypes satisfy the conditions of behavioral subtyping. We survey various notions of behavioral subtyping proposed in the literature for object-oriented programming. We also sketch a notion of behavioral subtyping for objects in component-based systems, where reasoning about the events that a component can raise is important.

6.1 Introduction

Component-based systems require a renewed emphasis on specification and verification, because if one is to build a computer system based on components built by others, then one must know what each component is supposed to do and trust it to carry out that task. Similarly, the builder of a component needs to know what behavior its users depend on, so that improvements in algorithms and data structures can be made.

A specification of a component can meet both these needs, since it acts as a contract between builders and their clients [LG86, Mey92]. The builders are obligated to make the component behave as specified, but gain the opportunity to use any data structures and algorithms that satisfy the contract. A client can only use the component through the specified interface given by the contract; in particular the client is prohibited from using hidden features. In return, the client gains the ability to treat the component abstractly, as a black box that behaves as specified.

6.1.1 Background

Traditionally, software has been specified using pre- and postconditions [Hoa69, Dij76, Hes92]. As is well-known, a procedure specification given in this style consists of two predicates. The *precondition* describes the states in which the procedure can be invoked; if procedures are modeled as relations between states (pre-state and post-states), then the precondition is the characteristic predicate of this relation's domain. The *postcondition* describes the transformation of pre-states into acceptable post-states; it is the characteristic predicate of the relation itself.

Abstract data types (ADTs) can also be specified using such specifications for their operations; these specifications are written using a mathematical abstraction of the values of objects of the type, called *abstract values* [FJ92, GHG+93, Jon90, LG86, OSWZ94]. To prove an implementation of such a specification is correct, one must be able to find an abstraction relation that relates the values of the objects used in the implementation to the abstract values, in such a way that the relationship is preserved by the operations, and is the identity on more fundamental types (like the integers) [Hoa72, LP97, Nip86, Sch90, SWO97].

For components in the sense of Microsoft COM or Java Beans, specification techniques are much less clear. Key features of components that are distinct from OO systems and that affect specification and verification are the following [Szy98, DW99].

- A component may provide more than one interface to its clients. For instance, it will typically provide an interface for other components (listeners) to register for the events that it may raise. However, each such interface can be specified separately.

- A component may not be self-contained, but may have some requirements on the context in which it must be used. However, one can treat these dependencies as extra parameters, as, for example, is done in OBJ [FGJM85, Gog84] and the RESOLVE family of specification languages [SWO97].

- A component will raise events (that is, invoke callbacks) during execution of its operations, for example when its instances experience state changes. Traditional specification languages ignore such higher-order behavior, although the refinement calculus [Bac88, Bv92, BvW98, Mor94, MV94, Mor87, Woo91] does provide a paradigm for specifying when such events are raised by using model (or abstract) programs. (But it is only recently that it has been applied in this area [BS97, Mik98a, MSL99].)

For example, an editor component might have a context dependency on a spell checker, and would raise events when the text is changed.

6.1.2 Specifications for Components

As we described above, the higher-order behavior of callbacks is a critical issue that distinguishes the specification of components from the specification of ADTs. By a *callback*, we mean a method that is invoked to handle some event; typically this method is in an object that is only registered as interested in the event at runtime.

Szyperski illustrates the pitfalls of callbacks with examples such as directories and a text models and views [Szy98, Section 5.5]. His directory example illustrates the complicating factor of callbacks sharply. Consider a `Directory` component with operations in its interface to add and remove files: `addEntry` and `removeEntry`. Unlike a simple, first-order OO ADT, these operations also raise events to notify listeners of changes in the directory. The listeners satisfy an interface named `DirObserver`. The class `Directory` also provides operations to register and unregister listeners for such events, which it inherits from its ancestor `DirObserverKeeper`. The immediate superclass of `Directory` is a class `RODirectory`, which is a subclass of `DirObserverKeeper`. `RODirectory` supplies methods `equals` and `thisFile` to observe directories.

However, if the specification for `Directory` does not take the callbacks into account, then there is no way to guarantee the postconditions of `addEntry` and `removeEntry`, since a callback can undo the work of either of them. In Szypreski's example, invoking `addEntry` with a file named "`Untitled`" breaks the contract because of the behavior of a callback that removes files named "`Untitled`." However, the caller (client) thinks that `addEntry` is broken when in fact the behavior of the callback is the one that caused the anomaly.

Szyperski gives a specification that prevents this problem by having a test function `inNotifier` that returns true when "a notifier call is in progress" [Szy98, page 56]. He adds preconditions to `addEntry` and `removeEntry` that require that `inNotifier` returns false; so that changes to directories can only occur when no notification is in progress. This is fine, but leaves one to wonder how the details can be formalized.

One way to formalize the specification of this example is to use both specification-only variables (also called ghost or model variables, see, for example Leino's work [Lei95]) and model programs (as in the refinement calculus). We present such a specification for the four types written in JML [LBR99] below.

Figure 6.1 specifies the type `DirObserverKeeper`. It is itself a fairly simple ADT.

Some notes on JML may be helpful. JML is a behavioral interface specification language. It specifies the interface of a Java module using Java syntax, and adds annotations to specify behavior. In JML, Java comments that start with an at-sign (@) mark annotations; JML treats the body of such comments as part of the specification, ignoring at-signs on the beginning of annotation lines.

As in Larch [GHG+93], specifications of behavior are written in terms of abstract values, which are given as the values of model variables in JML. In JML specification-only declarations use the keyword `model:`. The keyword `instance:`

```
import edu.iastate.cs.jml.models.*;

public interface DirObserverKeeper extends JMLType {
    /*@ public model instance boolean in_notifier
      @                              initially: in_notifier == false;
      @ public model instance JMLObjectSet listeners
      @                              initially: listeners != null
      @                              && listeners.equals(new JMLObjectSet());
      @ public invariant: listeners != null;
      @*/
    public boolean inNotifier();
    /*@ normal_behavior
      @    ensures: \result == in_notifier;
      @*/
    public void register(DirObserver o);
    /*@ normal_behavior
      @    requires: o != null;
      @    modifiable: listeners;
      @    ensures: listeners.equals(\old(listeners.insert(o)));
      @*/
    public void unregister(DirObserver o);
    /*@ normal_behavior
      @    requires: o != null;
      @    modifiable: listeners;
      @    ensures: listeners.equals(\old(listeners.remove(o)));
      @*/
}
```

Fig. 6.1. A JML Specification of a `DirObserverKeeper` Interface.

says that a field declaration, which in an interface would normally be **static**, is instead to be considered as an instance variable in each class that implements the interface. For example, in Figure 6.1, **in_notifier** and **listeners** are both *model variables*. The **initially** clauses give possible starting values for these model variables. The abstract values of these model variables are described, to the user, as either built-in Java primitive types (like **boolean**) or as a Java class with immutable objects. JML calls such classes *pure*; they are used to encapsulate the mathematical description of abstract values. An example of such a class is **JMLObjectSet**, which is found in the package **edu.iastate.cs.jml.models**. Such classes allow JML specifications to use Java expression syntax for invoking their operations, without compromising mathematical rigor. The operations (Java methods) are specified with **normal_behavior** clauses, which give the usual pre- and postcondition style specification over the model variables. Preconditions are introduced by **requires**, and postconditions by **ensures**. The **modifiable** clauses in the last two method specifications say that only the model variable **listeners**, and variables declared

```
public interface DirObserver {
  void addNotification(Directory o, String n);
  /*@ normal_behavior
    @    requires: o != null && o.in_notifier && n != null && n != "";
    @    modifiable: \everything;
    @    ensures: o.equals(\old(o));
    @*/
  void removeNotification(Directory o, String n);
  /*@ normal_behavior
    @    requires: o != null && o.in_notifier && n != null && n != "";
    @    modifiable: \everything;
    @    ensures: o.equals(\old(o));
    @*/
}
```

Fig. 6.2. A JML Specification of a `DirObserver` Interface.

to depend on it in an implementation [LBR99, Lei95], may have their value changed by invocation of one of these methods.

Figure 6.2 specifies the interface of directory observers, which are callback objects. The callbacks will be made when the model variable `in_notifier` of the directory that is being changed is true. The callbacks are permitted to do anything at all, except that they must terminate normally, and cannot modify the directory giving notice. The `\old(o)` in the postcondition represents the pre-state value of o.

Figure 6.3 specifies the interface `RODirectory`, for read-only directories. This interface extends `DirObserverKeeper`, and so inherits all of its specifications [DL96, LBR99]. It adds a model variable `entries`, which is a finite map from strings to file objects. The two `invariant` clauses specify these types. The `thisFile` operation is specified using case analysis; the first `requires` clause applies globally, but only one of the two specification cases that follow it will apply, depending on whether the name given is defined in the map `entries`. The `equals` operation is also respecified here; the use of "`also`" at the start of this specification is needed to remind the reader that this is a respecification.

Figure 6.4 gives the specification of the interface `Directory`, which adds `AddEntry` and `RemoveEntry` methods to its superclass `RODirectory`. Both specifications are similar, so let us consider the specification of `AddEntry`. It is given by a model program (hence it starts with `model_program`). The syntax of a model program like that of a Java *block* (statements surrounded by curly braces). As in the refinement calculus, the meaning is that a correct implementation must refine the model program. This model program in `AddEntry` contains two statements. The first is a `normal_behavior` statement, which is followed by a `for`-loop. The normal behavior statement ends at the semicolon (;) following `ensures`. It is a specification of what, in a refinement, some concrete code must accomplish. It says that `entries`

```
//@ model import edu.iastate.cs.jml.models.*;

public interface RODirectory extends DirObserverKeeper {
    /*@ public model JMLValueToObjectMap entries
      @         initially: entries != null
      @                     && entries.equals(new JMLValueToObjectMap());
      @ public invariant: entries != null && (\forall (JMLType o)
      @           entries.isDefinedAt(o) ==> o instanceof JMLString);
      @ public invariant: (\forall (JMLString s)
      @           entries.isDefinedAt(s)
      @             ==> entries.apply(s) instanceof Files.File);
      @*/
    public Files.File thisFile(String n);
    /*@ normal_behavior
      @    requires: n != null && n != "";
      @    {|
      @       requires: entries.isDefinedAt(new JMLString(n));
      @       ensures: \result.equals( (Files.File)
      @                                 entries.apply(new JMLString(n)));
      @     also
      @       requires: !entries.isDefinedAt(new JMLString(n));
      @       ensures: \result == null;
      @    |}
      @*/
    public /*@ pure @*/ boolean equals(Object oth);
    /*@ also
      @   normal_behavior
      @   {|
      @      requires: !(oth instanceof RODirectory);
      @      ensures: \result == false;
      @    also
      @      requires: oth instanceof RODirectory;
      @      ensures: \result ==
      @         (   entries.equals(((RODirectory)oth).entries)
      @          && listeners.equals(((RODirectory)oth).listeners));
      @   |}
      @*/
}
```

Fig. 6.3. A Specification of a RODirectory Interface.

is modified to add the given association. The **for**-loop is used to say, abstractly, how notifications are done. From this one can tell that when **addNotification** is called, the model variable **in_notifier** is true, and the association has already been added to the directory.

The technical "tricks" used in this specification were model (ghost) variables and model programs. By using these features, one can show both what callbacks can do and exactly the state in which they are called. The utility of model programs

```
//@ model import edu.iastate.cs.jml.models.*;

public interface Directory extends RODirectory {

  public void addEntry(String n, Files.File f);
  /*@ model_program {
    @   normal_behavior
    @     requires: !in_notifier && n != null && n != "" && f != null;
    @     modifiable: entries;
    @     ensures: entries != null
    @         && entries.equals(\old(entries.extend(new JMLString(n), f)));
    @     for (JMLObjectSetEnumerator e
    @                        = new JMLObjectSetEnumerator(listeners);
    @          e.hasMoreElements(); ) {
    @       in_notifier = true;
    @       ((DirObserver)e.nextElement()).addNotification(this, n);
    @       in_notifier = false;
    @     }
    @ }
    @*/
  public void removeEntry(String n);
  /*@ model_program {
    @   normal_behavior
    @     requires: !in_notifier && n != null && n != "";
    @     modifiable: entries;
    @     ensures: entries != null
    @         && entries.equals(\old(entries.remove(new JMLString(n))));
    @     for (JMLObjectSetEnumerator e
    @                        = new JMLObjectSetEnumerator(listeners);
    @          e.hasMoreElements(); ) {
    @       in_notifier = true;
    @       ((DirObserver)e.nextElement()).removeNotification(this, n);
    @       in_notifier = false;
    @     }
    @ }
    @*/
}
```

Fig. 6.4. A Specification of a `Directory` Interface.

in this setting was first made known to us by Büchi and Sekerinski [BS97]. For us, model programs seem more practical than other ways of specifying callbacks and higher-order procedures [EHL+94, EHMO91, Gog84]. Recently, other work on the refinement calculus has provided a more thorough treatment of this subject, including a modular reasoning technique that has been proved sound [MSL99].

6.1.3 Modular Reasoning

An important concern in both object-oriented and component-based programming is how to reason about extensions of programs. For example, suppose one has a method m that takes a `RODirectory` as an argument. If the implementation of m is correct with respect to its specification, then it should work correctly for `Directory` arguments. This is the notion of *modular reasoning*, which can be seen as a criteria for goodness of verification techniques [LW90, LW95, Lei95]. The basic idea for modular reasoning about OO programs is to:

- Assign to each expression in a program a static type that is an upper bound on the dynamic type of the expression's value. (That is, if the static type is T, then the value must have a dynamic type that is a subtype of T.)
- Reason about client code using the static types of expressions, as in standard reasoning about programs with ADTs.
- Prove that each subtype used in the program is a behavioral subtype of its supertypes [Ame87, AvdL90, Ame91, Dha97, LW93b, LW94, Utt92, UR92]. In simplest terms, this means that the subtype objects obey the specification of their supertype objects [DL96].

The advantage of modular reasoning is that unchanged methods do not have to be respecified or reverified when new behavioral subtypes are added.

6.1.4 Outline

The rest of this chapter is organized as follows. In Section 6.2 we consider the relationship between subtypes and behavioral subtypes. In Section 6.3 we survey the literature on behavioral subtyping in OO systems. We then discuss in Section 6.4 some ideas about subtyping for component-based systems. Finally, we offer some conclusions.

6.2 Subtyping and Behavioral Subtyping

In this section we define some important terms and make several distinctions among superficially-related concepts in OO languages that are important in understanding behavioral subtyping and how they differ from less OO concepts. In particular we distinguish metatypes and object types, and refinement and behavioral subtyping.

6.2.1 Classes, Types, and Specifications

A *class* is a program module that describes a set of potential *instances* or *objects*. In many languages, such as Java and Smalltalk, a class also describes a *class object*, which can be sent messages to create instances (in Smalltalk), and which also holds information common to all instances (such as the code for methods, the class name, and others). One can also make a distinction between instance methods and class methods; *instance methods* can be sent to an instance, while *class methods* are sent to class objects. We will use the term "class method" to refer also to the static methods and constructors of languages like C++ and Java.

A *type* is a static attribute of some phrase in a programming language. For example, numeric literals have a type such as `int`. In OO languages, both class objects and instances have types. The type of an instance is derived from the class declaration, and a structural rendering of such a type only involves the instance methods. Such a type corresponds to a Java interface, since it describes a protocol for manipulating objects; hence it is called an *object type*. The extension of an object type is thus a set of objects with a common protocol [GHJV95]. All the instances of a given object type can thus be sent the same set of messages (method calls with arguments) without generating a type error.

By contrast a class type or *metatype* describes the protocol of class objects. A structural rendering of such a type involves the types of class methods and the object types of the instances that the class can create.

Types can be viewed as degenerate specifications, since they give information about the syntax of methods (their names, and types of arguments, etc.), but do not (usually) involve behavior. By contrast, a *behavioral specification* describes both syntax and semantics, as seen in the preceding figures.

A behavioral specification of a metatype (that is, of a set of classes) involves both the specification of how objects are created (constructors in C++ and Java), class methods, and a specification of how instances behave in response to instance methods. By contrast, a behavioral specification of an object type (a Java interface) does not involve constructors or other class methods.

6.2.2 Refinement

Refinement is an important relationship on metatypes. It is a stronger relationship than behavioral subtyping, which relates object types.

Refinement is a relationship between behavioral specifications that is useful in developing programs from specifications [Mor94, Woo91]. The basic idea is that a *refinement*, C, of a specification, A, is a specification that is stronger than A in the sense that every correct implementation of C is also a correct implementation of A; thus, C will have no more correct implementations than A. Another way of thinking about a refinement is that the set of allowed behaviors of the refinement is a subset of the behaviors allowed by the original specification.

Refinement can also be extended to a relationship between implementations and specifications and between implementations. If one thinks of each implementation module as having a specification that describes its exact behavior, or if one uses a programming language as an (operational) specification language, then this idea, which is crucial to the refinement calculus, falls out. In this sense, one meaning of "a refinement" is "a correct implementation." Thus, we will say just "a refinement" for the longer phrase "an implementation of a refined specification" below.

For example, given a procedure specification, one can reason about the correctness of client code using its specification, without knowing anything about its implementation. Many different implementations may be linked into a program without changing the soundness of such reasoning, if each such implementation is a refinement of the specification used in reasoning. If one takes a total-correctness specification for a procedure g with precondition R_A and postcondition E_A, then a refinement must:

- have the same syntax (the same name, number of arguments, argument types, return type, and exception result types),
- a precondition R_C such that $R_A \Rightarrow R_C$, and
- a postcondition E_C such that the following holds.

$$(R_C \Rightarrow E_C) \Rightarrow (R_A \Rightarrow E_A) \tag{6.1}$$

See the paper by Cheng and Chen in this volume for further discussion of formula (6.1). This formula is weaker than the usual one for postconditions, which is that $E_C \Rightarrow E_A$ [Mor90]. The usual formula is both simpler and works in most practical cases. Note also that termination is implicitly required by both specifications, and so there is no explicit proof obligation to show termination.

For specifications given in terms of model programs, the techniques of the refinement calculus would be used instead of the pre- and postcondition rule described above.

For abstract data types, refinement means again that each implementation of refinement is an implementation of the original specification [Win83, GM94]. Such data type refinement can be mediated by a change in the way data is modeled [GM94, MG90, Mor94, Mor89]. One can use an abstraction function [Hoa72] or relation [LP97, Nip86, Sch90, SWO97] to translate between logical assertions in the theory of one abstract model and another. For example, suppose the specification C is a refinement of A, and C is stated using a theory T_C, which we assume includes the theory used to state the specification of A. Suppose that $r_{C \to A}$ is a relation between the models of C and A, so that $r_{C \to A}(c', a')$ holds when c' is related to a'. In the following we use the notations $x\,\hat{}\,$, x', and $x°$ to denote the pre-state, post-state, and arbitrary public state values of x (respectively). Then it must be that (again for total-correctness specifications):

- C and A have the same interface (the same name, class, and instance methods with the same number of arguments, argument types, and so on),

- using the theory of the specification of C, T_C, C's invariant implies A's

$$T_C \vdash \forall self : C . \exists x : A .$$
$$r_{C \to A}(self^\circ, x^\circ) \tag{6.2}$$
$$\land (invariant_C(self^\circ) \Rightarrow invariant_A(x^\circ))$$

- C's history constraint† must imply A's:

$$T_C \vdash \forall self : C . \exists x : A .$$
$$r_{C \to A}(self^\wedge, x^\wedge) \land r_{C \to A}(self', x') \tag{6.3}$$
$$\land (constraint_C(self^\wedge, self') \Rightarrow constraint_A(x^\wedge, x'))$$

- for each instance method, g, the specification of g in C must refine that of g in A via $r_{C \to A}$. For pre- and postcondition specifications, this means that:

  - g's precondition in A, pre_A^g, must imply the corresponding precondition in C:

$$T_C \vdash \forall self : C . \exists x : A .$$
$$r_{C \to A}(self^\wedge, x^\wedge) \tag{6.4}$$
$$\land (pre_A^g(x^\wedge) \Rightarrow pre_C^g(self^\wedge))$$

  - g's specification in C must be such that the following holds:

$$T_C \vdash \forall self : C . \exists x : A .$$
$$r_{C \to A}(self^\wedge, x^\wedge) \land r_{C \to A}(self', x') \tag{6.5}$$
$$\land (((pre_C^g(self^\wedge) \Rightarrow post_C^g(self^\wedge, self'))$$
$$\Rightarrow (pre_A^g(x^\wedge) \Rightarrow post_A^g(x^\wedge, x'))))$$

- each class method, f, in A is refined by the class method f in C via $r_{C \to A}$.

Besides dealing with model programs, the refinement calculus is a way of systematically deriving refinements [Bac88, Bv92, BvW98, Mor94, MV94, Mor87, Woo91]. Each such derivation is a small step, and is guaranteed to be correct. The calculus uses a wide-spectrum language in which programs are enriched by (nondeterministic) specification statements. In this way one may start the refinement process with a behavioral specification which consists of only a specification statement, and by making several refinement steps, arrive at completely executable code.

6.2.3 Subclasses, Subtypes, and Behavioral Subtypes

Refinement, as defined above, does not capture one key feature of OO programming: the use of message passing to achieve subtype polymorphism. One way to view this distinction is that refinement for abstract data types makes no distinction between metatypes and object types. Behavioral subtyping is essentially refinement of object types, whereas in common terminology, refinement of types refers to metatypes.

---

† A history constraint is a monotonic relation on pairs of states; it relates an earlier state to a later state [LW93b, LW94]. History constraints are useful in abbreviating specifications, and have implications for behavioral subtyping that are discussed below. In JML, history contraints are syntactically stated as if they related a pre-state and a post-state, although the semantics is more general.

	Relates	Inherits	Guarantees
Subclass	modules	fields, methods	data format matches
Subtype	object protocols	interface obligations	no type errors
Beh. Subtype	specifications	specifications	expected behavior

Fig. 6.5. Relationships.

However, let us step back for a moment, and discuss not the relation of refinement and behavioral subtyping, but the relationships of subclassing, subtyping, and behavioral subtyping.

Since classes, types, and behavioral specifications are, in our terminology, different kinds of things, it follows that subclassing, subtyping, and behavioral subtyping are different kinds of relationships. As summarized in Figure 6.5, a subclass relationship relates implementation modules, a subtype relationship relates object protocols, and a behavioral subtype relationship relates behavioral specifications. Subclasses inherit field and method declarations from superclasses, subtypes inherit interface obligations (to implement methods) from their supertypes, and behavioral subtypes inherit interface obligations and behavioral specifications from the specifications of their supertypes. Another way to look at this is in terms of the guarantees each kind of relationship makes. Roughly speaking, a subclass relationship guarantees some common data structures in objects (common field and method slots), a subtype relationship guarantees that no type errors occur when subtype objects are used in place of supertype objects, and a behavioral subtype relationship guarantees no surprising behavior occurs when subtype objects are used in place of supertype objects.

6.3 Notions of Behavioral Subtyping

Work on subtyping in type systems has important connections to behavioral subtyping. A behavioral subtype must be a subtype, since otherwise surprising behaviors (type errors) would arise. This makes sense if one thinks of structural typing as a weak behavioral specification. Two recent books describe type systems with subtyping for single-dispatch languages [AC96] and multiple-dispatch languages [Cas97].

The concept of behavioral subtyping seems to have been in the air in the late 1980s. The first edition of Meyer's book on OO software construction in Eiffel [Mey88] gives one of the first accounts of the idea. Unfortunately, Eiffel has an unsound definition of behavioral subtyping, because the language's type system has an unsound definition of subtyping [Coo89]. America gave the first sound definition of behavioral subtyping that appeared in print [Ame87] (reworked in [Ame91]); he emphasized the need for contravariance and gave a simple proof of the soundness of his rule based on Hoare's rule of consequence. The simple version of America's definition [Ame91, pp. 77–78], where the types of additional arguments and the result do not vary when a method is overridden in the subtype, uses a "transfer function" $\phi_{C \to A}$ from the abstract values of a subtype, C, to the abstract values of its supertype, A. Then it must be that:

- for each instance method g in A, g's precondition in A composed with the transfer function, $pre_A^g(\phi_{C \to A}(self\hat{\ }))$, must imply the corresponding precondition in C:

$$T_C \vdash \forall self : C . (pre_A^g(\phi_{C \to A}(self\hat{\ })) \Rightarrow pre_C^g(self\hat{\ })) \tag{6.6}$$

- for each instance method g in A, g's specification in C must be such that the following holds:

$$T_C \vdash \forall self : C . post_C^g(self\hat{\ }, self') \Rightarrow post_A^g(\phi_{C \to A}(self\hat{\ }), \phi_{C \to A}(self')) \tag{6.7}$$

The main difference between America's notion of behavioral subtyping and refinement is that it only applies to instance methods, and does not apply to class methods. America also showed how to extend the definition to deal with contravariant subtyping among the other parameters of a method and with subtyping of the result, by using the transfer functions for these arguments as well.

America's work (with van der Linden) in ECOOP/OOPSLA '90 [AvdL90] is interesting in its attempt to make behavioral subtyping statically checkable by using keywords to stand for behavioral properties.

6.3.1 Model Theory
6.3.2 For Types with Immutable Objects

Also in the late 1980s Leavens, in his Ph.D. thesis [Lea88, Lea90], showed how to use the notion of behavioral subtyping to do modular verification of OO programs [Lea91, LW90, LW95]. Leavens's definition of behavioral subtyping is model-theoretic. The basic notion is that of a coercion relation between models of abstract values [LP92], which has led to a precise model-theoretic characterization of behavioral subtyping for types with immutable objects [LP99].

Leavens's work is inspired by other model-theoretic treatments of behavioral subtyping and related ideas. A major influence is the work of Reynolds on category-sorted algebras [Rey83, Rey85]. This work forms the basis for a model-theory for multimethod languages, and a theory of subtyping based on homomorphic coercion functions (which can be generalized to homomorphic relations). The idea is that if C is a subtype of A, then there must be a coercion function from objects of type C to objects of type A, $\phi_{C \to A}$ that is preserved by the instance methods in the sense that, for example, for an instance method g that has types $A \to A$ and $C \to C$:

$$\phi_{C \to A}(g(s)) = g(\phi_{C \to A}(s)). \tag{6.8}$$

Category-sorted algebras make it possible to do modular reasoning about overloading and coercions. By generalizing static overloading to message passing (multimethod dispatch is just dynamic overloading), and coercions to subtyping, this theory also applies to OO languages with multimethods.

Another strain of model theory is based not on coercions, but on set inclusions. In such theories, the abstract values of a subtype are included in the abstract value set of each of its supertypes. Functions on such values exhibit subtype polymorphism, as a function works on any subset of its domain. Cardelli used such models in an early proof of the soundness of a type system with subtype polymorphism [Car88].

Goguen and Meseguer's Order-Sorted Algebra (OSA) [GM87], used inclusion models to help deal with subtyping in algebraic specifications. Bruce and Wegner adapted OSA to give a definition of behavioral subtyping for OO programming languages [BW90]. Such a definition says that, if one can construct a model where the set of subtype objects is a subset of the set of supertype objects, then the subtypes in question are behavioral subtypes.

The relationship between such models and models based on coercion is simple. Given a model based on coercions, one can construct an inclusion model by simply treating the set of abstract values of the supertype as the union of the sets of abstract values for their subtypes. If necessary, abstract values of each type can be "tagged" first, so that they can still be distinguished when part of a larger set. The functions that model the instance methods of the supertype can then be defined by cases, so that, for each type tag, the corresponding function from the coercion model can be run. In the other direction, one can simply take as coercion functions the inclusion function that maps each subset to its containing set.

The above construction shows that the key issue in constructing an inclusion model is not making the sets have the inclusion relationships, but in constructing the models of the instance methods.

6.3.3 Model Theory for Types with Mutable Objects

One common aspect of all the above model-theoretic approaches is that they deal with only types with immutable objects. An object is *mutable* if it has an abstract value that may vary over time.

Most OO programs contain types with mutable objects, and thus studying behavioral subtyping for such types is crucial. Though the basic idea of using a coercion relation remains valid when mutation is considered, the technical details are more complex, because mutable objects have a unique identity, and hence coercing an object from one type to another means not just creating a new value, but also associating the new value with the appropriate object identity. For this reason, Dhara's model-theoretic study [Dha97] uses coercion relations that relate not abstract values, but entire states.

Mutation also introduces the possibility of observing aliasing among objects and variables. In the presence of subtyping, one can create a state in which variables of the subtype and supertype share the same object. In such a case, if the subtype has more instance methods than the supertype, these extra methods might be able to change the shared object, when applied to the variable that has the subtype, in a way that is inconsistent with the supertype's specification [LW93b, LW94]. This problem can be dealt with in at least two ways.

Strong behavioral subtyping [LW93b, LW94] restricts the extra instance methods of a behavioral subtype to make only those state changes that are consistent with the state changes allowed by the supertype's specification. Liskov and Wing gave two different formulations of this idea. One formulation requires that each extra instance method of the subtype be supplied with a model program that shows how its effect on the abstract value can be achieved using only the instance methods of the supertype [LW93a, LW94]. Their second formulation [LW93b, LW94] requires the specification of the supertype to provide a "history constraint," which is a monotonic relation between states that says how the abstract values of that type may be changed by its instance methods; the extra instance methods of behavioral subtypes must respect the history constraint. For example, a Mutable Point type cannot be a strong behavioral subtype of an Immutable Point type, because the extra instance method that changes the state of a Mutable Point would not satisfy the history constraint of Immutable Point's specification.

However, strong behavioral subtyping allows the extra instance methods of a subtype to mutate an instance's state in ways that cannot be observed through a supertype's instance methods. For example, a Triple with two immutable components and an added mutable component can be a strong behavioral subtype of an Immutable Pair type.

Strong behavioral subtyping allows all forms of aliasing, and achieves soundness of modular reasoning, because even if a supertype and subtype variable share the same subtype object, manipulations of the object through the subtype's variable cannot be surprising. Using Liskov and Wing's first formulation, this is because any mutation done by the extra instance methods can be explained by the abstract programs for the extra instance methods. Using their second formulation, this is because in reasoning about what state changes may take place one is only allowed to use the history constraint, and that must be obeyed by subtypes.

Weak behavioral subtyping [Dha97, DL95], by contrast, achieves soundness by limiting aliasing. Direct aliasing between variables of a supertype and its subtypes is prohibited. A weak behavioral subtype may have additional instance methods that change the state of a subtype object in ways that could not be explained by the supertype's instance methods, or that would violate the supertype's history constraint. Of course, the supertype's instance methods must behave similarly in the subtype.

Because of the aliasing prohibitions of weak behavioral subtyping, a type of Mutable Pairs can be a weak behavioral subtype of an Immutable Pair type. This is sound for modular reasoning because a program can only manipulate the subtype objects through variables of one of these two types, not both. Hence, if an object is being manipulated through a variable of the supertype, then it must act like an instance of the supertype, since only the common methods can be used.

Weak behavioral subtyping thus allows more subtype relationships than strong behavioral subtyping. However, the price to be paid is that the programming language used must enforce the aliasing prohibitions described above [Dha97].

6.3.4 Proof Theory

Meyer [Mey88] and America [Ame87, Ame91] both gave proof-theoretic definitions of behavioral subtyping, which were described above. Both of these definitions, however, ignored the problem of aliasing.

Cusack [Cus91] uses Z schemas in her definition of specialization, which is similar to behavioral subtyping. She does not discuss the effects of extra instance methods of the subtype on the invariants of the supertype and does not deal with aliasing.

As described above, Liskov and Wing [LW93b, LW94] were the first to offer a notion of behavioral subtyping that takes aliasing into account. Although we described it in the model theory section above, their paper actually states the definition in proof-theoretic terms.

Dhara and Leavens made only small changes to the Liskov and Wing definition in their paper that related the notions of specification inheritance and behavioral subtyping [DL96]. This idea builds on the concept of specification inheritance found in Eiffel [Mey97] and also used by Wills [Wil92] to achieve behavioral subtyping. The idea is that subtypes inherit the specifications of instance methods of their supertypes; Dhara and Leavens gave an account of specification inheritance for model-based specification languages, and proved that it ensured behavioral subtyping. They also showed how different forms of specification inheritance were needed to produce strong and weak behavioral subtypes. However, they offered no proof that the definition of behavioral subtyping used was sound with respect to some model theory.

Abadi and Leino [AL97] extend a structural type system [Car88] by behavioral specification information to the types. They present a sound axiomatic semantic semantics and provide practical guidance on reasoning about OO programs. However, their approach is not modular.

Poetzsch-Heffter and Müller give a sound Hoare-logic for a sequential subset of Java, which handles recursion, class and interface types, subtyping, inheritance, and encapsulation [PHM99]. Their work is explained further in chapter 7 of this volume.

Lewerentz and his colleagues [LLRS95] use refinement calculus for OO modeling based on observations of types. They use coercion on attributes of their language, to relate the effect constructors and methods on the states of subtype and supertype objects. They do not consider aliasing or interference.

Utting [UR92, Utt92] defined behavioral subtyping using the refinement calculus. The refinement calculus offers a way to prove behavioral subtyping in this setting. His definition does not, however, allow for change of data representations.

The work of Mikhajlova and her coauthors [BMvW97, MS97, Mik98b] allows the sound verification of OO programs in a refinement calculus framework. The key concept is that of class refinement (called *correct subclassing*) which (as described above) is stronger than behavioral subtyping, since it involves class methods. Class refinement, in addition to providing the same guarantee against surprising behavior when objects of subclasses are manipulated, also allows one to verify programs that use class methods (and even expressions denoting class objects) to create new instances. However, treating subclasses as subtypes and behavioral subtypes collapses the distinctions shown in Figure 6.5. This restricts both subclass and subtype relationships. For example, treating subclasses as subtypes restricts the use of binary methods [BCC+95]. Conversely, treating subclasses as behavioral subtypes limits certain uses of inheritance; for example, Doubly-Ended Queue could otherwise be a subtype of Stack, even though it is more convenient for Stack to inherit from Doubly-Ended Queue [Sny86].

6.4 Behavioral Subtyping for Components

A common theme in work on behavioral subtyping is that objects of behavioral subtypes should be able to be manipulated without surprises, where surprises are defined relative to the specification of the supertype. Hence this method of modular reasoning is called *supertype abstraction* [LW95]. Therefore, if we wish to reason about the correctness of component-based systems using supertype abstraction, the key issue is the notion of behavioral subtyping for such systems. To sketch this, we propose looking at their specifications and making an analogy to OO programs.

In Section 6.1.2, we saw that, in general, model programs were needed to fully specify components. We can also consider the usual pre- and postcondition style specifications to be a special case of model programs, since such a specification can be considered to be a model program with a single specification statement.

Our approach for defining behavioral subtyping is based on refinement of these model programs. For both strong and weak behavioral subtyping the key idea is that the common instance methods of the subtype and each supertype must be such that each such method's model program in the specification of the subtype refines its specification in that supertype. This, and requirements that the invariant and history constraint (for the common methods) of the subtype imply those in each supertype, is enough for weak behavioral subtyping. For example, the type

`Directory` is a weak behavioral subtype of `RODirectory`. (We hope to formally relate this to an extension of the refinement calculus [Mor94, MV94, Woo91] as future work.)

For strong behavioral subtyping, one approach is to require that the history constraint (for all the methods) of the subtype must imply that of each supertype [DL96, LW93b, LW94]. This limits what the extra methods can do in terms of mutation of the objects of the subtype, but does not place any limits on what events they may signal. Thus Liskov and Wing's other approach, of requiring a program that explains the effect of each additional instance method of the subtype in terms of the supertype's methods [LW93a, LW94], has more promise. Indeed, the refinement calculus paradigm makes it clear what must be verified to prove strong behavioral subtyping; that is, that for each additional instance method, m, of the subtype, there must be some model program, p_m, such that p_m is expressed only using the methods of the supertype, and the specification of m refines p_m.

Using the second form of strong behavioral subtyping, the type `Directory` is not a strong behavioral subtype of the type `RODirectory`, because the type `RODirectory` has a mapping, from names to files that is visible to clients, but this mapping is modified by the instance methods of `Directory`. However, `RODirectory` is a strong behavioral subtype of `DirObserverKeeper`, as `RODirectory` just adds to the model fields of `DirObserverKeeper`.

6.5 Conclusions

In this chapter we have discussed the specification of component-based systems. We noted that a combination of model variables [Lei95] and model programs (as in the refinement calculus) seem adequate for specification of callbacks that occur in such systems [BS97]. Our notion of behavioral subtyping for components is based on these specifications, in that we require that behavioral subtypes obey the specifications of the instance methods of their supertypes. We sketched both weak and strong behavioral subtyping.

Clearly we have only given a sketch of what behavioral subtyping should be for component-based systems. Much work remains in fleshing out the details and proving that such notions permit sound modular reasoning.

Acknowledgments

Thanks to the anonymous referees and Joachim van den Berg for comments on an earlier draft of this paper. Thanks to Al Baker and Clyde Ruby for discussions about the JML examples used in this paper. Leavens's work was supported in part by the United States of America's National Science Foundation under Grant CCR-9803843.

Bibliography

[AC96]   Abadi, M. and Cardelli, L. *A Theory of Objects*. Monographs in Computer Science. Springer-Verlag, New York, NY, 1996.

[AL97]   Abadi, M. and Leino, R. A logic of object-oriented programs. In Bidoit, M. and Dauchet, M., editors, *TAPSOFT '97: Theory and Practice of Software Development, 7th International Joint Conference CAAP/FASE, Lille, France*, volume 1214 of *Lecture Notes in Computer Science*, pages 682–696. Springer-Verlag, New York, NY, 1997.

[Ame87]   America, P. Inheritance and subtyping in a parallel object-oriented language. In Bezivin, J. et al., editors, *ECOOP '87, European Conference on Object-Oriented Programming, Paris, France*, pages 234–242, New York, NY, June 1987. Springer-Verlag. Lecture Notes in Computer Science, Volume 276.

[Ame91]   America, P. Designing an object-oriented programming language with behavioural subtyping. In de Bakker, J. W., de Roever, W. P., and Rozenberg, G., editors, *Foundations of Object-Oriented Languages, REX School/Workshop, Noordwijkerhout, The Netherlands, May/June 1990*, volume 489 of *Lecture Notes in Computer Science*, pages 60–90. Springer-Verlag, New York, NY, 1991.

[AvdL90]   America, P. and van der Linden, F. A parallel object-oriented language with inheritance and subtyping. *ACM SIGPLAN Notices*, 25(10):161–168, October 1990. *OOPSLA ECOOP '90 Proceedings*, N. Meyrowitz (editor).

[Bac88]   Back, R. J. R. A calculus of refinements for program derivations. *Acta Informatica*, 25(6):593–624, August 1988.

[BCC⁺95]   Bruce, K., Cardelli, L., Castagna, G., Group, T. H. O., Leavens, G. T., and Pierce, B. On binary methods. *Theory and Practice of Object Systems*, 1(3):221–242, 1995.

[BJ95]   Broy, M. and Jähnichen, S., editors. *KORSO: Methods, Languages and Tools for the Construction of Correct Software*, volume 1009 of *Lecture Notes in Computer Science*, New York, NY, 1995. Springer-Verlag.

[BMvW97]   Back, R., Mikhajlova, A., and von Wright, J. Class refinement as semantics of correct subclassing. Technical Report 147, Turku Centre for Computer Science, December 1997. http://www.tucs.abo.fi/publications/techreports/TR147.html.

[BS97]   Büchi, M. and Sekerinski, E. Formal methods for component software: The refinement calculus perspective. In *Proceedings of the Second Workshop on Component-Oriented Programming (WCOP)*, June 1997. ftp://ftp.abo.fi/pub/cs/papers/mbuechi/FMforCS.ps.gz.

[Bv92]   Back, R. J. R. and von Wright, J. Combining angels, deamons and miracles in program specifications. *Theoretical Computer Science*, 100(2):365–383, June 1992.

[BvW98]   Back, R.-J. and von Wright, J. *Refinement Calculus: A Systematic Introduction*. Springer-Verlag, 1998.

[BW90]   Bruce, K. B. and Wegner, P. An algebraic model of subtype and inheritance. In Bançilhon, F. and Buneman, P., editors, *Advances in Database Programming Languages*, pages 75–96. Addison-Wesley, Reading, MA, August 1990.

[Car88]   Cardelli, L. A semantics of multiple inheritance. *Information and Computation*, 76(2/3):138–164, February/March 1988. A revised version of the paper that appeared in the 1984 Semantics of Data Types Symposium, LNCS 173, pages 51–66.

[Cas97]   Castagna, G. *Object-Oriented Programming: A Unified Foundation*. Progress in Theoretical Computer Science. Birkhauser, Boston, 1997.

[Coo89]   Cook, W. R. A proposal for making eiffel type-safe. *The Computer Journal*, 32(4):305–311, August 1989.

[Cus91]   Cusack, E. Refinement, conformance, and inheritance. *Formal Aspects of Computing*, 3:129–141, January 1991.

[Dha97]   Dhara, K. K. Behavioral subtyping in object-oriented languages. Technical Report TR97-09, Department of Computer Science, Iowa State University, 226 Atanasoff Hall, Ames IA 50011-1040, May 1997. The author's Ph.D. dissertation.

[Dij76]   Dijkstra, E. W. *A Discipline of Programming*. Prentice-Hall, Inc., Englewood Cliffs, NJ, 1976.

[DL95]   Dhara, K. K. and Leavens, G. T. Weak behavioral subtyping for types with mutable objects. In Brookes, S., Main, M., Melton, A., and Mislove, M., editors, *Mathematical Foundations of Programming Semantics, Eleventh Annual Conference*, volume 1 of *Electronic Notes in Theoretical Computer Science*. Elsevier, 1995. http://www.elsevier.nl/locate/entcs/volume1.html.

[DL96]   Dhara, K. K. and Leavens, G. T. Forcing behavioral subtyping through specification inheritance. In *Proceedings of the 18th International Conference on Software Engineering, Berlin, Germany*, pages 258–267. IEEE Computer Society Press, March 1996. A corrected version is Iowa State University, Dept. of Computer Science TR #95-20c.

[DW99]   D'Souza, D. F. and Wills, A. C. *Objects, Components, and Frameworks with UML: The Catalysis Approach*. Object Technology Series. Addison Wesley, Reading, MA, 1999.

[EHL+94]   Edwards, S. H., Heym, W. D., Long, T. J., Sitaraman, M., and Weide, B. W. Part ii: Specifying components in RESOLVE. *ACM SIGSOFT Software Engineering Notes*, 19(4):29–39, Oct 1994.

[EHMO91]   Ernst, G. W., Hookway, R. J., Menegay, J. A., and Ofgen, W. F. Modular verification of Ada generics. *Computer Languages*, 16(3/4):259–280, 1991.

[FGJM85]   Futatsugi, K., Goguen, J. A., Jouannaud, J.-P., and Meseguer, J. Principles of OBJ2. In *Conference Record of the Twelfth Annual ACM Symposium on Principles of Programming Languages*, pages 52–66. ACM, January 1985.

[FJ92]   Feijs, L. M. G. and Jonkers, H. B. M. *Formal Specification and Design*, volume 35 of *Cambridge Tracts in Theoretical Computer Science*. Cambridge University Press, Cambridge, UK, 1992.

[GHG+93]   Guttag, J. V., Horning, J. J., Garland, S., Jones, K., Modet, A., and Wing, J. *Larch: Languages and Tools for Formal Specification*. Springer-Verlag, New York, NY, 1993.

[GHJV95]   Gamma, E., Helm, R., Johnson, R., and Vlissides, J. *Design Patterns: Elements of Reusable Object-Oriented Software*. Addison-Wesley, Reading, MA, 1995.

[GM87]   Goguen, J. A. and Meseguer, J. Order-sorted algebra solves the constructor-selector, multiple representation and coercion problems. In *Symposium on Logic in Computer Science, Ithaca, NY*, pages 18–29. IEEE, June 1987.

[GM94]   Gardier, P. H. B. and Morgan, C. A single complete rule for data refinement. In Morgan and Vickers [MV94], pages 111–126.

[Gog84]   Goguen, J. A. Parameterized programming. *IEEE Transactions on Software Engineering*, SE-10(5):528–543, September 1984.

[Hes92]   Hesselink, W. H. *Programs, Recursion, and Unbounded Choice*, volume 27 of *Cambridge Tracts in Theoretical Computer Science*. Cambridge University Press, New York, NY, 1992.

[Hoa69]   Hoare, C. A. R. An axiomatic basis for computer programming. *Communications of the ACM*, 12(10):576–583, October 1969.

[Hoa72]   Hoare, C. A. R. Proof of correctness of data representations. *Acta Informatica*, 1(4):271–281, 1972.

[Jon90]   Jones, C. B. *Systematic Software Development Using VDM*. International Series in Computer Science. Prentice Hall, Englewood Cliffs, NJ, second edition, 1990.

[LBR99]   Leavens, G. T., Baker, A. L., and Ruby, C. Preliminary design of JML: A behavioral interface specification language for Java. Technical Report 98-06h, Iowa State University, Department of Computer Science, December 1999.

[Lea88]   Leavens, G. T. *Verifying Object-Oriented Programs that use Subtypes*. PhD thesis, Massachusetts Institute of Technology, December 1988. Published as MIT/LCS/TR-439 in February 1989.

[Lea90]   Leavens, G. T. Modular verification of object-oriented programs with subtypes. Technical Report 90-09, Department of Computer Science, Iowa State University, Ames, IA, 50011, July 1990. Available by anonymous ftp from ftp.cs.iastate.edu, and by e-mail from almanac@cs.iastate.edu.

[Lea91]   Leavens, G. T. Modular specification and verification of object-oriented programs. *IEEE Software*, 8(4):72–80, July 1991.

[Lei95]   Leino, K. R. M. *Toward Reliable Modular Programs*. PhD thesis, California Institute of Technology, 1995. Available as Technical Report Caltech-CS-TR-95-03.

[LG86]   Liskov, B. and Guttag, J. *Abstraction and Specification in Program Development*. The MIT Press, Cambridge, MA, 1986.

[LLRS95]   Lewerentz, C., Lindner, T., Rüping, A., and Sekerinski, E. On object-oriented design and verification. In Broy and Jähnichen [BJ95], pages 92–111.

[LP92]   Leavens, G. T. and Pigozzi, D. Typed homomorphic relations extended with subtypes. In Brookes, S., editor, *Mathematical Foundations of Programming Semantics '91*, volume 598 of *Lecture Notes in Computer Science*, pages 144–167. Springer-Verlag, New York, NY, 1992.

[LP97]   Leavens, G. T. and Pigozzi, D. The behavior-realization adjunction and generalized homomorphic relations. *Theoretical Computer Science*, 177:183–216, 1997.

[LP99]   Leavens, G. T. and Pigozzi, D. An exact algebraic characterization of behavioral subtyping. To appear in *Acta Informatica*. Technical Report 96-15a, Department of Computer Science, Iowa State University, Ames, IA, 50011, November 1996, Revised November 1999.

[LW90]   Leavens, G. T. and Weihl, W. E. Reasoning about object-oriented programs that use subtypes (extended abstract). In Meyrowitz, N., editor, *OOPSLA ECOOP '90 Proceedings*, volume 25(10) of *ACM SIGPLAN Notices*, pages 212–223. ACM, October 1990.

[LW93a]   Liskov, B. and Wing, J. M. A new definition of the subtype relation. In Nierstrasz, O. M., editor, *ECOOP '93—Object-Oriented Programming, 7th European Conference, Kaiserslautern, Germany*, volume 707 of *Lecture Notes in Computer Science*, pages 118–141. Springer-Verlag, New York, NY, July 1993.

[LW93b]   Liskov, B. and Wing, J. M. Specifications and their use in defining subtypes. *ACM SIGPLAN Notices*, 28(10):16–28, October 1993. *OOPSLA '93 Proceedings*, Andreas Paepcke (editor).

[LW94]   Liskov, B. and Wing, J. A behavioral notion of subtyping. *ACM Transactions on Programming Languages and Systems*, 16(6):1811–1841, November 1994.

[LW95]   Leavens, G. T. and Weihl, W. E. Specification and verification of object-oriented programs using supertype abstraction. *Acta Informatica*,

32(8):705–778, November 1995.

[Mey88]   Meyer, B. *Object-oriented Software Construction*. Prentice Hall, New York, NY, 1988.

[Mey92]   Meyer, B. Applying "design by contract". *Computer*, 25(10):40–51, October 1992.

[Mey97]   Meyer, B. *Object-oriented Software Construction*. Prentice Hall, New York, NY, second edition, 1997.

[MG90]   Morgan, C. and Gardiner, P. H. . B. Data refinement by calculation. *Acta Informatica*, 27(6):481–503, May 1990.

[Mik98a]   Mikhajlova, A. Consistent extension of components in presence of explicit invariants. In Weck, W., Bosch, J., and Szyperski, C., editors, *Third International Workshop on Component-Oriented Programming (WCOP'98) held in conjunction with ECOOP'98*. TUCS General Publication Series, No. 10, July 1998.

[Mik98b]   Mikhajlova, A. Refinement of generic classes as semantics of correct polymorphic reuse. In *Proceedings of the International Refinement Workshop, and Formal Methods Pacific (IRW/FMP'98)*, Springer Series in Discrete Mathematics and Theoretical Computer Science, pages 266–285, New York, NY, Jul 1998. Springer-Verlag.

[Mor87]   Morris, J. M. A theoretical basis for stepwise refinement and the programming calculus. *Science of Computer Programming*, 9(3):287–306, December 1987.

[Mor89]   Morris, J. M. Laws of data refinement. *Acta Informatica*, 26(4):287–308, February 1989.

[Mor90]   Morgan, C. *Programming from Specifications*. Prentice Hall International, Hempstead, UK, 1990.

[Mor94]   Morgan, C. *Programming from Specifications: Second Edition*. Prentice Hall International, Hempstead, UK, 1994.

[MS97]   Mikhajlova, A. and Sekerinski, E. Class refinement and interface refinement in object-oriented programs. In Fitzgerald, J., Jones, C. B., and Lucas, P., editors, *FME '97: Industrial Applications and Stengthened Foundations of Formal Metohds*, volume 1313 of *Lecture Notes in Computer Science*, pages 82–101, NY, 1997. Springer-Verlag.

[MSL99]   Mikhajlov, L., Sekerinski, E., and Laibinis, L. Developing components in the presence of re-entrance. Technical Report TUCS-TR-239, TUCS - Turku Centre for Computer Science, February 1999.

[MV94]   Morgan, C. and Vickers, T., editors. *On the refinement calculus*. Formal approaches of computing and information technology series. Springer-Verlag, New York, NY, 1994.

[Nip86]   Nipkow, T. Non-deterministic data types: Models and implementations. *Acta Informatica*, 22(16):629–661, March 1986.

[OSWZ94]   Ogden, W. F., Sitaraman, M., Weide, B. W., and Zweben, S. H. Part I: The RESOLVE framework and discipline — a research synopsis. *ACM SIGSOFT Software Engineering Notes*, 19(4):23–28, October 1994.

[PHM99]   Poetzsch-Heffter, A. and Müller, P. A programming logic for sequential Java. In Swierstra, S. D., editor, *European Symosium un Programming (ESOP '99)*, volume 1576 of *Lecture Notes in Computer Science*, pages 162–176. Springer-Verlag, 1999.

[Rey83]   Reynolds, J. C. Types, abstraction and parametric polymorphism. In *Proc. IFIP Congress '83, Paris*, September 1983.

[Rey85]   Reynolds, J. C. Three approaches to type structure. In Ehrig, H., Floyd, C., Nivat, M., and Thatcher, J., editors, *Mathematical Foundations of Software Development, Proceedings of the International Joint Conference on Theory and Practice of Software Development (TAPSOFT), Berlin. Volume 1: Colloquium on Trees in Algebra and Programming (CAAP '85)*, volume 185 of *Lecture Notes in Computer Science*, pages 97–138. Springer-Verlag, New York, NY, March 1985.

[SBC92]   Stepney, S., Barden, R., and Cooper, D., editors. *Object Orientation in Z.* Workshops in Computing. Springer-Verlag, Cambridge CB2 1LQ, UK, 1992.

[Sch90]   Schoett, O. Behavioural correctness of data representations. *Science of Computer Programming*, 14(1):43–57, June 1990.

[Sny86]   Snyder, A. Encapsulation and inheritance in object-oriented programming languages. *ACM SIGPLAN Notices*, 21(11):38–45, November 1986. OOPSLA '86 Conference Proceedings, Norman Meyrowitz (editor), September 1986, Portland, OR.

[SWO97]   Sitaraman, M., Weide, B. W., and Ogden, W. F. On the practical need for abstraction relations to verify abstract data type representations. *IEEE Transactions on Software Engineering*, 23(3):157–170, March 1997.

[Szy98]   Szyperski, C. *Component Software: Beyond Object-Oriented Programming.* ACM Press and Addison-Wesley, New York, NY, 1998.

[UR92]   Utting, M. and Robinson, K. Modular reasoning in an object-oriented refinement calculus. In Bird, R. S., Morgan, C. C., and Woodcock, J. C. P., editors, *Mathematics of Program Construction, Second International Conference, Oxford, U.K., June/July*, volume 669 of *Lecture Notes in Computer Science*, pages 344–367. Springer-Verlag, New York, NY, 1992.

[Utt92]   Utting, M. *An Object-Oriented Refinement Calculus with Modular Reasoning.* PhD thesis, University of New South Wales, Kensington, Australia, 1992. Draft of February 1992 obtained from the Author.

[Wil92]   Wills, A. Specification in Fresco. In Stepney et al. [SBC92], chapter 11, pages 127–135.

[Win83]   Wing, J. M. A two-tiered approach to specifying programs. Technical Report TR-299, Massachusetts Institute of Technology, Laboratory for Computer Science, 1983.

[Woo91]   Woodcock, J. C. P. A tutorial on the refinement calculus. In Prehn, S. and Toetenel, W. J., editors, *VDM '91 Formal Software Development Methods 4th International Symposium of VDM Europe Noordwijkerhout, The Netherlands, Volume 2: Tutorials*, volume 552 of *Lecture Notes in Computer Science*, pages 79–140. Springer-Verlag, New York, NY, October 1991.

7

Modular Specification and Verification Techniques for Object-Oriented Software Components

Peter Müller and Arnd Poetzsch-Heffter

Fernuniversität Hagen, D-58084 Hagen, Germany

[Peter.Mueller, Arnd.Poetzsch-Heffter]@Fernuni-Hagen.de

7.1 Introduction

Component-based software development means reusing prefabricated components, adapting them to particular needs, and combining them to larger components or applications. Reusing components developed by other companies leads to a demand for high-level component specifications and for certification of the component quality. Most quality levels beyond syntactic and type correctness need techniques for formal specification and verification.

Component-based software development requires that the specification and verification techniques can handle modularity and adaptability. *Modularity* means that specifications need to support abstraction from encapsulated implementation aspects, that they remain valid under composition, and that they are sufficiently expressive for verifying properties of composed programs from the specifications of their components. *Adaptability* means that the programming and specification framework support techniques to adapt existing components to the needs and interfaces of other components.

In this article, we develop a formal modular specification and verification framework for OO-components. OO-programming provides a good basis for component technology. It supports adaption by subtyping, inheritance, and dynamic method binding. Classes form an appropriate basic unit for encapsulation and modularity on the level of types. To demonstrate our techniques, we use a Java subset as programming language and assume that a component is described by a package. Syntactically, composition corresponds to the import relation between packages.

The framework builds on specification variables to express abstractions, dependencies between abstract and concrete variables, pre-/postconditions for methods, and so-called modifies-clauses. The article makes two contributions: (1) It presents a formally founded, modular sound solution to the frame problem. (2) It develops a language-supported programming technique to control sharing and structure the object store. The rest of this section introduces the underlying approach and gives an overview of the article.

Specification Technique. Specifications of OO-components have to describe the functional behavior of methods, the effects to the object states, and invariant properties. The functional behavior is specified by pre-post pairs. The state modifications are specified by a modifies-clause listing all variables that are possibly affected by a method execution. Invariant properties are usually expressed by predicates that have to be maintained by nonprivate methods. However, to focus on the central ideas, we omit type invariants in this article. We assume that all properties necessary for the verification of a method are explicitly specified in the precondition.

In general, specifications cannot refer to concrete fields/attributes of objects: (1) Modularity requires that fields may be private and thus hidden to the user of a component. (2) Adaptability by inheritance and specialization leads to additional fields in subclasses (*extended state*). Since these additional fields are not known in the superclass, they cannot occur in the modifies-clauses of the superclass methods. On the other hand, subclass methods have to satisfy superclass specifications, in particular the modifies-clauses. Thus, without further techniques, a subclass method would not be allowed to modify the fields added in the subclass.

To solve these problems, we use abstract fields (corresponding to specification variables in procedural settings). Abstract fields allow one to express abstractions on the object state and to hide implementation details. The value of an abstract field depends on concrete fields and possibly other abstract fields. These dependencies are explicitly declared in the specification. Having the right to modify an abstract field F includes the right to modify any of the fields F depends on. Since subclasses can introduce dependencies for their new fields, subclass methods can gain the right to modify the extended state without violating the modifies-clause of the superclass.

Composition and Formal Foundation. Composition of packages leads to two particular problems: (1) Due to dynamic dispatch, a package P might invoke methods that are not present during the verification of P. (2) An abstract field F declared outside P might depend on a field which is modified by a method of P. Since F is not visible in P, this side-effect cannot be handled within the verification of P. For problem 1, we follow the classical solution and enforce behavioral subtyping. That is, subtype methods have to satisfy the specification of the corresponding supertype methods. This article addresses problem 2. The central contribution is a technique to control dependencies. By structuring the object store, we can exclude unwanted dependencies while retaining a powerful program model.

Attacking the above problems requires a precise notion of the meaning of interface specifications. In our work, the meaning of specifications is founded in an axiomatic language semantics (cf. [PHM98, PHM99]). Based on this semantics, we have proved that our specification constructs allow for modular verification.

Overview. Sec. 7.2 provides the formal foundations for programs and specifications. The specification of functional behavior is sketched in Sec. 7.3. The focus of Sec. 7.4 is on techniques to specify modifications of the object store. Sec. 7.5 presents a new method to control dependencies and sharing. A discussion of related work and the conclusions are contained in Sec. 7.6 and 7.7.

7.2 Foundations for Programs and Specifications

This section summarizes the relevant aspects of the used programming language and the specification primitives, and explains the formal semantics underlying specifications and proofs.

Programs and Specifications. To demonstrate the developed techniques, we use a sequential Java subset that contains classes, interfaces, subtyping, inheritance, dynamic binding, recursive methods, and instance variables. For simplicity, we assume that fields are **private**, and omit static fields.

A software component is assumed to be described by a Java package. A package declares a set of types and can import other packages. A type is declared either as an interface or as a class. As a running example, we use types from a tiny window toolkit, in particular an interface **Component**, representing the abstract behavior shared by all window components, and a class **Box**, representing a rectangular area on the screen (subclasses could for example extend **Box** to contain images):

```
interface Component {
    public abstract Dimension prefSize;
    public abstract Dimension defaultSize;
    public void reset();
    ...
}

class Box implements Component {
    private int width, height;
    private rep X.prefSize by [ $(X.width), $(X.height) ];
    public  rep X.defaultSize by [ 40, 70 ];
    public  void reset()  { width = 40; height = 70; }
    ...
}
```

Components have a preferred and a default size which are specified by the abstract fields **prefSize** and **defaultSize**. Abstract fields are part of the specification and may have types defined in the specification framework. The type *Dimension* in the example represents a pair of integers (denoted by [x, y]). Components provide a public method **reset** to set the preferred size to the default size. **Box** is a simple implementation of **Component**, that is, it inherits the abstract fields and provides implementations for the methods. **Box** declares two concrete fields **width** and **height** to store the dimensions. The first line with the keyword **rep** specifies that the preferred size of a **Box** is the pair of its fields. (We use $ to refer to the current object store in specifications. That is, $(X.F)$ denotes the object which is referenced by field F of object X in the current state. Explicitly denoting the execution state clarifies the meaning of specifications when two execution states are involved.) The second representation-clause specifies the default size. To keep the example small, we omitted aspects not related to the size of a component and assume that each type is contained in one package.

A package corresponds to a software component. It composes the imported packages and possibly adds further types. To reflect this view of composition, we require that the import relation is a partial order; that is, mutually recursive types have to be contained in one package. If a package P_1 imports a package P_0, all public program and specification elements of P_0 are visible in P_1, in particular those imported by P_0 from other packages. The *context* of a program or specification element consists of the package it is declared in and all directly or indirectly imported packages. Private program and specification elements are accessible only within their types and must not be used in public elements. For example, the representation-clause of `prefSize` in class `Box` must be private, because it refers to private fields.

In summary, the specification of a type consists of its abstract fields, depends-clauses (shown below), representation-clauses, and the method specifications. A method specification consists of a pre-post pair and a modifies-clause. In this article, we focus on these specification primitives. More elaborated specification constructs are, for example, discussed in [Lea96, PH97].

Formal Foundations. A formal foundation for the specification framework is necessary since (1) the semantics of specifications, in particular of modifies-clauses and dependencies, relies on some subtle points that require formal precision, and (2) a mathematical framework is needed to verify general properties of specification constructs, in particular their modularity properties. As formal foundation, we use an axiomatic semantics of the programming language. The meaning of interface specifications is expressed by triples of the corresponding programming logic (cf. [PH97, PHM99]). For brevity, we focus on the aspects relevant for this article.

To reason about execution states, a formal model of states is required. A state describes (1) the current values for the local variables and for the method parameters, and (2) the current object store. The types and values of the Java subset are formalized by the following data types:

$$
\begin{array}{ll}
\textbf{data type} & \textbf{data type} \\
\begin{aligned}
Type \quad = \quad & boolean\,T() \\
\mid \quad & int\,T() \\
\mid \quad & null\,T() \\
\mid \quad & ct(\ CTypeId\ ) \\
\mid \quad & it(\ ITypeId\ )
\end{aligned}
&
\begin{aligned}
Value \quad = \quad & b(\ Bool\ ) \\
\mid \quad & i(\ Int\ ) \\
\mid \quad & null() \\
\mid \quad & ref(\ CTypeId,\ ObjId\ ) \\
\tau : \ & Value \to Type
\end{aligned}
\end{array}
$$

Besides the predefined types `boolean`, `int`, and the type for the `null` reference, there are class and interface types where *CTypeId* and *ITypeId* denote suitable sets of type identifiers. The subtype relation on sort *Type* is defined as in Java and denoted by $\preceq$. Data type *Value* represents the set of values for the types. Values constructed by *ref* represent references to objects. The sort *ObjId* denotes some suitable set of object identifiers to distinguish different objects of the same type. The function τ yields the type of a value.

The state of an object is given by the values of its fields. We assume a sort *Location* for the (concrete and abstract) fields of all objects and functions

$$loc : \quad Value \times FieldDeclId \rightarrow Location \cup \{undef\}$$

where $loc(X,F)$ is defined as follows: If X is an object reference of a class type with field F, the corresponding location is returned. Otherwise loc yields *undef*. In the following, we write $X.F$ for $loc(X,F)$. *FieldDeclId* is the sort of field identifiers where two fields with the same name declared in different classes are represented by distinguished symbols. The type in which a field F is declared is called the *domain type* of F, denoted by $dtype(F)$; the type of F is called its *range type*. Accessibility of field F in type T according to the context conditions of Java is denoted by $accessible(F,T)$. In particular, F is only accessible in T if the domain type of F is imported by T's package. For simplicity, we require abstract fields to be public. To keep formulations short, we will speak of "a location L declared/accessible in type T" meaning that $L = loc(X,F)$ for some object X and some field F where F is declared/accessible in T.

The state of all objects and the information whether an object is alive (that is, allocated) in a program state is formalized by an abstract data type ObjectStore with sort *Store* and the following functions:

$\_\langle\_ := \_\rangle$	: $Store \times Location \times Value$	$\rightarrow Store$
$\_(\_)$	: $Store \times Location$	$\rightarrow Value \cup SpecSort$
$\_\langle\_\rangle$	: $Store \times CTypeId$	$\rightarrow Store$
new	: $Store \times CTypeId$	$\rightarrow Value$
$alive$	: $Value \times Store$	$\rightarrow Bool$

$OS\langle L := V \rangle$ yields the store that is obtained from OS by updating concrete location L with value V. $OS(L)$ yields the value of location L in store OS. For concrete locations, the result of $OS(L)$ is of sort *Value*; for abstract locations, the function yields a value of sort *SpecSort* which denotes the supersort of all sorts defined in the specification framework. Object creation is formalized by two functions: $OS\langle TID \rangle$ yields the object store that is obtained from OS by allocating a new object of type $ct(TID)$. $new(OS, TID)$ yields the reference to this object. If V is an object reference, $alive(V, OS)$ tests whether the referenced object is alive in OS.

The value of an abstract location $X.F$ in store OS is determined by its represents-clause. For a represents-clause **rep** `X.F` **by** `r(X,$)` declared in type T, we generate an axiom

$$\forall X, OS : \tau(X) \preceq T \wedge alive(X, OS) \Rightarrow OS(X.F) = r(X, OS)$$

The value of an abstract location $X.F$ can be modified only by updating a concrete location that $X.F$ depends on. In particular, we assume abstract locations not to depend on the liveness of objects. The other axioms of abstract data type ObjectStore are given in [PHM98].

In program specifications, we have to refer to types, fields, and variables, which is enabled by introducing constant symbols for these entities. In particular, we provide constant symbols for the types (of sort *Type*), fields (of sort *FieldDeclId*), and parameters as well as program variables (of sort *Value*). Furthermore, the symbol $ (of sort *Store*) is used to denote the current object store. A method m of type T is denoted by $T{:}m$.

7.3 Specification of Functional Behavior

A method specification has to cover two aspects: the functional behavior and the frame properties of the method. The specification of the functional behavior expresses the genuine task of a method, in particular the result a method returns. Frame properties describe which parts of the environment are left unchanged by a method execution. In this section, we describe the specification of functional behavior. Specification of frame properties is treated in the next section.

The functional behavior of a method is specified by a pre-post pair. For example, the functional behavior of the method **reset** in interface **Component** could be specified as follows:

```
void reset()
  pre    true
  post   $(this.prefSize) = $(this.defaultSize)
```

This specification demonstrates three important issues: (1) The behavior of **reset** is described in an abstract way without referring to any implementation. (2) The specification of functional behavior relies on frame properties: To reflect the intention that **prefSize** is set to **defaultSize** (and not vice versa), one has to specify that **defaultSize** remain unchanged. (3) Functional behavior may consist of wanted side-effects: **reset** modifies only the abstract field **prefSize** of the **this** object and does not return a value.

Behavioral Subtyping. Since objects of subtypes of a type T may occur in all places where T-objects are allowed, we have to guarantee that subtypes of T behave according to the specification of T. Otherwise we couldn't prove properties of types using T based on the specification of T. For this article, it is sufficient to require that the precondition of the supertype method implies the precondition of the subtype method and that the postcondition of the subtype method implies the postcondition of the supertype method. A detailed discussion of behavioral subtyping can be found in the chapter by Leavens and Dhara and in [DL96].

7.4 Specification and Verification of Frame Properties

This section investigates techniques to specify and verify frame properties. Based on abstract fields with explicit dependencies, we develop a formal semantics of modifies-clauses which meets the requirements of modular specification and verification. Finally, we discuss the application of the technique and illustrate a remaining problem.

7.4.1 Specification of Frame Properties

After explaining the frame problem, we identify the requirements imposed by modular specification and verification. We describe how explicit dependencies of abstract locations can be used to enhance the modifies-clause technique such that it is suitable for modular software development.

The Frame Problem. Specifications of functional method behavior in general leave large parts of method behavior unspecified. For example, `reset`'s specification does not specify whether the method affects `this.defaultSize` or `this.prefSize`. Since all objects of a program execution share one object store, method executions can have side-effects on the locations of all reachable objects. For verification, it is crucial to have precise information about side-effects. Those aspects of method behavior that concern the absence of side-effects are called the *frame properties* of a method. The problem of specifying frame properties is called the *frame problem*.

Modularity Requirements. If the entire program is known, the specification of frame properties is relatively simple since the developer has complete knowledge about all types and fields. Thus, it is possible to directly specify all locations that are modified by a method execution. Within a modular setting, the frame problem is more complicated for the following reasons:

(i) *Information hiding:* Private fields must not be contained in interface specifications. Thus, abstraction techniques have to be used to specify frame properties.

(ii) *Extended state:* The specification of frame properties must be loose enough to allow overriding methods to modify the extended state. On the other hand, they have to be rigorous enough to guarantee behavioral subtyping (see Sec. 7.3).

(iii) *Open Programs:* A program is called *open* if it can be extended by adding new types. that is, in component-based software development, every component is an open program since it is built to be extended. Therefore, it is never possible to know all types and fields, and frame properties cannot be specified by listing all modified locations.

In the sequel of this subsection, we describe how the modifies-clause technique can be enhanced to cope with these requirements.

Modifies-Clauses. The modifies-clause of a method m describes a set of (concrete and abstract) locations that characterizes all locations that may be modified by m. To cope with the modularity requirements above, we use the following informal meaning of modifies-clauses:

A method m may modify locations mentioned in its modifies-clause and those locations, the locations in the modifies-clause *depend on.*

An abstract location L_a *depends* on a location K if the value of L_a is represented in terms of the value of K. The problems described above can be solved by making these dependencies explicit as suggested in [Lei95]:

   (i) *Information hiding:* Instead of mentioning a location $X.F$ with a nonpublic field F in modifies-clauses, it is now possible to use an abstract location depending on $X.F$. Therefore, the permission to modify $X.F$ is granted without violating encapsulation.
  (ii) *Extended state:* Subclasses are allowed to introduce new dependencies for an inherited abstract field. Thereby, subtype methods can get the permission to modify fields of the extended state.
 (iii) *Open Programs:* This problem will be solved by imposing suitable restrictions on dependencies (see Sec. 7.4.2 and 7.5).

Explicit Dependencies. We require dependencies to be explicitly declared as part of the (public or private) interface of a type. For verification, these declarations are used to generate axioms specifying the depends-relation on locations. Since each program extension may declare further dependencies, the depends-relation in an open program is heavily underspecified.

An underspecified depends-relation has an important advantage over context-dependent depends-relations (that is, depends-relations that are—besides so-called *residues*—fully specified by the dependencies visible in a given context, cf. [Lei95]): Context-dependent depends-relations lead to a context-dependent meaning of modifies-clauses (see Subsec. 7.4.3) which causes two problems: (1) It is difficult to cover context-dependent specifications by Hoare-style programming logics. (2) Proofs for a smaller context do not necessarily carry over to larger contexts; modular soundness has to be proven for such techniques.

For modular verification, the (under-)specification of the depends-relation must guarantee four properties:

1. Consistency with Representation: Explicit dependencies reveal information about the locations that represent the value of an abstract location without giving away its actual representation. To be useful to decide which modifications of the object store might change the value of an abstract location, the value of an abstract location may only depend on locations it is declared to depend on. This is achieved by a proof obligation for every represents-clause.

2. Expressiveness: To prove that a location cannot be modified by a method, it is crucial to know which locations do not depend on each other. Since the depends-relation is underspecified, this information cannot directly be concluded from the specification of the depends-relation. We have to generate axioms expressing that certain locations do not depend on each other.

3. Modular Soundness: A verification technique is modular sound if all proofs of an open program stay valid for every *admissible* program extension. An extension is admissible if it satisfies behavioral subtyping and the additional axioms for the specification of the depends-relation. In our framework, modular soundness results from using underspecification: The programming logic can only verify properties of a program that hold in all admissible program extensions. To be reasonable, our technique has to ensure that the new axioms are consistent with the existing specification.

4. Modularity: With open programs and arbitrary dependencies it is neither possible to verify a method m w.r.t. its modifies-clause nor can the negation of the depends-relation be specified. Therefore, dependencies have to be restricted to allow for modular verification.

We discuss the above properties along with the formalization of dependencies and modifies-clauses in the next subsection.

7.4.2 Formalization of Dependencies

In this subsection, we present a formalization of the depends-relation.

Declaration of Dependencies. Dependencies are declared by so-called *depends-clauses* of the form depends $X.A$ on L, where X is a variable of sort *Value* and A is an abstract field. L is a location of the form $X.F$ or $\$(X.c).F$ where F is a concrete or abstract field and c is a concrete field. Following [LN97], we call these forms of dependencies *static* and *dynamic* dependencies, resp. These two forms provide enough expressiveness to specify linked object structures. On the other hand, they are restrictive enough to allow for syntactically checkable modularity rules (see below). The dependencies of an abstract location $X.A$ may be declared in several depends-clauses. Since A describes an abstraction of objects of the domain type of A, depends-clauses for $X.A$ may only occur in subtypes of the domain type of A. The access mode of a depends-clause is the most restrictive access mode of a mentioned field.

Modularity Rules. If a method $T{:}m$ modifies a concrete location L_c, one has to prove that all abstract locations L_a that are affected by this modification are covered by $T{:}m$'s modifies-clause. To enable such proofs, we have to enforce that L_a is accessible in all types in which L_c is. Since abstract fields have to be public, it suffices to enforce the following *authenticity* rule for every location L: *A location L must be accessible in the domain type of each location it depends on.* The requirement is trivially true for concrete locations, which depend only on themselves.

If program extensions can declare arbitrary dependencies, it is impossible to specify the negation of the depends-relation for an open program. Therefore, we introduce the following *visibility* rule: *If a location X.F depends on Y.E, the declarations of the involved depends-clauses must be contained in each package that contains both the declarations of F and E.*

Due to the structure of the depends-clauses, both requirements can be checked syntactically.

Formalization of the Depends-Relation. The depends-relation is formalized by the function

$$\_ \xrightarrow{\ \ } \_ : \quad Location \times Store \times Location \to Bool$$

For the definition of $\longrightarrow$, each depends-clause of the form **depends X.A on X.F** or **depends X.A on \$(X.c).F** contributes an axiom of the form

$$\forall X, OS : \tau(X) \preceq T \Rightarrow X.A \xrightarrow{OS} X.F \qquad \text{or}$$
$$\forall X, OS : \tau(X) \preceq T \Rightarrow X.A \xrightarrow{OS} X.c \wedge X.A \xrightarrow{OS} OS(X.c).F$$

where T is the type in which the depends-clause is declared, L is a location, and OS an object store. We assume $\longrightarrow$ to satisfy these axioms, and to be reflexive and transitive for all object stores.

Consistency with Representation. Based on $\longrightarrow$, we can formalize the proof obligation to check whether the dependencies of a location K are completely declared (see Subsec. 7.4.1). If K is associated with a representation and the modification of a location L affects the value of K, K must be declared to depend on L (the obligation is trivially true for concrete locations):

$$\forall OS, L, Y : \quad OS(K) \neq OS\langle L := Y \rangle(K) \;\Rightarrow\; K \xrightarrow{OS} L$$

Negation of the Depends-Relation. The modularity rules allow us to specify the negation for all pairs of locations declared in an open program $\mathcal{P}$ as follows: A location $X_0.F_0$ depends on a location $X_n.F_n$ if there is a sequence of locations $X_0.F_0, \ldots, X_n.F_n$ such that $X_i.F_i$ directly depends on $X_{i+1}.F_{i+1}$. Due to the structure of depends-clauses, X_{i+1} is either identical to X_i or obtained from X_i by reading location $X_i.c_i$. Therefore, we can characterize each path from X_0 to X_n by a regular expression $a_0 \ldots a_{n-1}$ where a_i is either ε or a *FieldDeclId* c_j. The set of all paths from an object X to any object Y such that $X.F$ depends on $Y.E$ can also be described by a regular expression $R(F, E)$. Union and Kleene closure are used to describe alternative and cyclic paths. The visibility rule guarantees that $R(F, E)$ is completely determined by the depends-clauses declared in any context that contains the declarations of F and E. Therefore, $R(F, E)$ can be specified by enumeration for all pairs (F, E) of a given context. We assume we have a function

$$\rho : Value \times Value \times Store \times RegExpr \to Bool$$

that expresses reachability of objects via paths described by a regular expression (for example, $\rho(X, Y, OS, cd) \Leftrightarrow Y = OS(OS(X.c).d)$).

To specify the negation of the depends-relation of an open program $\mathcal{P}$, we generate an axiom for every pair (F, E) of fields declared in $\mathcal{P}$:

$$\forall X, Y, OS : \neg \rho(X, Y, OS, R(F, E)) \Rightarrow \neg(X.F \xrightarrow{OS} Y.E)$$

These axioms are available for verification of type T if all fields named in R are accessible in T.

By the axioms for $\longrightarrow$ and its negation, the depends relation is completely specified w.r.t. all pairs of fields declared in an open program. However, parts of the specification may not be available for verification due to encapsulation.

Consistency of Program Extensions. To avoid contradictory specifications, the axioms generated for a new package P have to be consistent with the axioms generated for the imported packages. The specification of $\longrightarrow$ stays valid since all depends-clauses of an imported package are contained in the extended program. The specification of the negation stays valid since the value of $R(F, E)$ remains unchanged for all pairs of attributes (F, E) declared in an imported package: (1) types of P must not introduce direct dependencies among locations declared in imported types (visibility rule), and (2) types of P must not declare dependencies from locations declared in P on locations declared in imported types (authenticity rule). Therefore, neither direct nor transitive dependencies among locations declared in imported types can be introduced by P. That is, admissible extensions of an open program refine the specification of the depends-relation and its negation.

7.4.3 Formalization of Modifies-Clauses

Syntax. The modifies-clause for a method $T{:}m$ with implicit parameter *this* and explicit parameters $p_1, \ldots, p_n$ has the form **modifies** $M(this, p_1, \ldots, p_n, \$)$ where M is an expression of the specification language of sort *set of Location*. To be able to denote locations reachable from the parameters, M may depend on the current object store. We denote the set of locations of $T{:}m$'s modifies-clause with parameter objects $P_0, \ldots, P_n$ in store OS by $\mu(T{:}m, P_0, \ldots, P_n, OS)$.

Downward-Closures. If a method is allowed to modify a location K then it may also modify all locations K depends on. Following [Lei95], we call the set of locations on which K depends the *downward-closure* of K. Formally, the downward-closure δ of a set S of locations consists of all locations on which an element of S depends in an object store OS:

$$\delta(S, OS) =_{def} \{L \mid \exists K \in S : K \xrightarrow{OS} L\}$$

Like the depends-relation it refers to, the downward-closure is underspecified for open programs and context-independent. We use the term "a location L is covered by the modifies-clause of a method m in a store OS" to express that L is an element of the downward-closure of m's modifies-clause in OS. We omit the object store if it's clear from the context.

Meaning of Modifies-Clauses. The informal meaning of a modifies-clause M of method $T{:}m$ is: *Every location that belongs to an object that is allocated in the prestate of $T{:}m$ is either an element of the downward-closure of M or is left unchanged by $T{:}m$.* We formalize this meaning by translating a modifies-clause of method $T{:}m$ into a pre-post pair which has to be conjoined to $T{:}m$'s functional specification. The free variables OS and $P_0, \ldots, P_n$ are used to address the prestate values of the parameters in the poststate. All free variables in specifications are universally quantified over the whole pre-post pair. That is, to verify $T{:}m$ w.r.t. its modifies-clause, one has to prove that $T{:}m$ meets the following pre-post pair for *any* OS, P_i, X, and F:

pre $\$ = OS \wedge this = P_0 \wedge \bigwedge_{i=1}^{n} p_i = P_i$
post $alive(X, OS) \Rightarrow X.F \in \delta(\mu(T{:}m, P_0, \ldots, P_n, OS), OS) \vee OS(X.F) = \$(X.F)$

In addition to this pre-post pair, we require the verifier to show an additional proof obligation for every method invocation: If a method $T{:}m$ invokes a method n, n's modifies-clause in n's prestate has to be a subset of the downward-closure of $T{:}m$'s modifies-clause in $T{:}m$'s prestate. (Technically, the requirement is enforced by incorporating an appropriate proof obligation into the invocation rule of the programming logic.) Basically, this requirement is a consequence of the above meaning of modifies-clauses.† However, making this property explicit allows us to prove the modularity lemma below.

Behavioral Subtyping. Like any other pre-post pair, the specification stemming from a modifies-clause has to observe the rules of behavioral subtyping. This can be proved by showing that the modifies-clause of an overriding method is a subset of the downward-closure of the modifies-clause of the overridden method.

7.4.4 Verification of Frame Properties

In the last subsection, we introduced a specification technique for frame properties that is inherently modular sound. However, the usage of an underspecified depends-relation gives rise to the question whether the pre-post pair stemming from a modifies-clause can be proven in a modular way. Therefore, this subsection presents a lemma that allows for modular verification of modifies-clauses.

---

† It is a slightly stronger requirement for methods that modify a location and reestablish its initial value.

Modularity Lemma. To verify a method $T{:}m$ w.r.t. its modifies-clause, it is sufficient to prove the following pre-post pair.

pre $\$ = OS \wedge this = P_0 \wedge \bigwedge_{i=1}^{n} p_i = P_i$

post $alive(X, OS) \wedge accessible(F, T) \Rightarrow$ (∗)

        $X.F \in \delta(\mu(T{:}m, P_0, \ldots, P_n, OS), OS) \vee OS(X.F) = \$(X.F)$

Proof Sketch. We show that authenticity guarantees that the corresponding property holds for all locations *not* accessible in T:

pre $\$ = OS \wedge this = P_0 \wedge \bigwedge_{i=1}^{n} p_i = P_i$

post $alive(X, OS) \wedge \neg accessible(F, T) \Rightarrow$

        $X.F \in \delta(\mu(T{:}m, P_0, \ldots, P_n, OS), OS) \vee OS(X.F) = \$(X.F)$

The outline of the proof is as follows: $T{:}m$ can modify a (concrete or abstract) location $X.F$ only by (1) location update or (2) method invocation.†

Assume that $T{:}m$ updates a location L. If $X.F$ depends on L, authenticity ensures that F is accessible in T. Therefore, the above property is trivially true for $X.F$. Otherwise, $X.F$ is not affected by updates of L.

If a method n invoked by $T{:}m$ modifies $X.F$, $X.F$ is covered by n's modifies-clause since n is assumed to meet its specification. As described above, n's modifies-clause in n's prestate has to be a subset of the downward-closure of $T{:}m$'s modifies-clause in $T{:}m$'s prestate. Therefore, $X.F$ is also covered by $T{:}m$'s modifies-clause.

By simple programming logic, the conjunction of the two specifications above yields the pre-post pair stemming from the modifies-clause.

By the modularity lemma, the proof obligation for $T{:}m$'s modifies-clause can be reduced to the pre-post pair (∗). The restriction to accessible locations allows one to rely on a (besides encapsulation) complete specification of the depends-relation and therefore to prove the specification based on the information available in T's package.

7.4.5 *Using Modifies-Clauses*

In this subsection, we apply the techniques described above to the example of GUI components introduced in Sec. 7.2. We specify frame properties for interfaces and subtypes extending the state of their supertypes, and demonstrate the limitations of the techniques described so far.

Specification Example. Recall that method **reset** of interface **Component** sets the preferred size of a component to a default value. Besides that, it is assumed not to affect the object store:

```
public void reset() modifies {this.prefSize};
```

---

† In this context, a constructor call behaves like a method invocation.

To illustrate the modification of extended state, we revisit class `Box`. `Box` stores its dimensions explicitly in the fields `width` and `height`. Thus, X.`prefSize` depends on the `width` and `height` locations of X:

```
depends X.prefSize on X.width, X.height;
```

These dependencies allow `Box:reset` to modify the new fields (that is, the extended state).

Using Imported Types. To discuss a more realistic example of OO-programming, we extend the above program by a class `TextComponent`. `TextComponent` makes use of an imported type `StringBuffer` which implements mutable strings. We assume that `StringBuffer` contains one abstract field `length` representing the length of the string. A text component is supposed to display a string in a fixed font size. Thus, the preferred size of a text component depends only on the length of the string. `reset` sets the string to the empty string:

```
class TextComponent implements Component {
   private StringBuffer text;
   public  rep X.defaultSize by [ 10, 10 ];
   depends X.prefSize on $(X.text).length;
   public  void reset() { text.replace(0, text.length(), ""); }
   public  TextComponent(StringBuffer s) { text = s; }
}
```

This example reveals an important problem: With the new dependencies, `prefSize` is no longer authentic: In `StringBuffer`, the `length` field of `StringBuffer` is accessible, but `prefSize` is not, because the `StringBuffer` package does not import `Component`. The example shows that the authenticity rule forbids abstract fields to depend on fields of imported types, and thus reasonable reuse, which is unbearable for OO-programming.

The authenticity requirement is needed to prevent undetected modifications of fields. For example, a type T might also import `StringBuffer`. If `TextComponent` and T objects share a `StringBuffer` object, a method of T could modify `prefSize` via the shared string undetectably. With techniques that prohibit certain patterns of object sharing, we can refine the authenticity requirement to allow for reuse patterns like the example above. Such techniques are described in the following section.

7.5 Universes: Effective Control of Sharing

In this section, we analyze the situations in which nonauthenticity leads to undetectable modification of fields. To prevent such situations, we enhance Java's type system by so-called *universes*, which can be used to restrict object sharing. Based on these restrictions, we refine the relation between modifies-clauses and program extensions such that reuse is enabled. Furthermore, we discuss the resulting programming model.

7.5.1 Harmful Patterns of Sharing

The `TextComponent` example in the last section has demonstrated that the authenticity rule is too strong for modular program development. In particular, it entails two restrictions: (1) Abstract locations cannot depend on fields of imported types. Our solution to this problem is described in the sequel of this section. (2) Subclasses must not introduce new abstract locations that depend on inherited locations. If they did, inherited methods could modify these new locations without explicit permission. In the context of this article, the second restriction is a minor problem. Since its solution entails some technical subtleties, it is not presented here.

To reuse prefabricated packages, we definitely have to allow abstract fields to depend on fields of imported types. Imported methods must have the permission to modify the abstract fields by modifying locations they depend on (cf. the use of `StringBuffer:replace` in `TextComponent`). Therefore we have to refine the definition of authenticity and the meaning of modifies-clauses.

If both a nonauthentic location L and the locations it depends on are accessible in the caller of a method m, one can easily detect by verification that L might be modified by m. However, if we permit nonauthentic dependencies on imported fields in a general manner, m might modify a field without giving the caller a chance to detect this modification: Assume a type U which is imported by T and S. As illustrated in Fig. 7.1, T and S objects (depicted by boxes) can both reach a common U-location L (denoted by solid arrows). Nonauthentic locations A and B both depend on L (dashed arrows), that is, they are *codependent*. Let the modifies-clause of method $T{:}m$ contain location A. Since A depends on L, $T{:}m$ may modify L. However, this affects B although B is not contained in $T{:}m$'s modifies-clause.

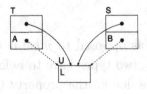

Fig. 7.1. Codependency.

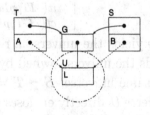

Fig. 7.2. Guards.

To prevent undetected modification of locations, objects can be placed into a so-called *guarded universe* or *universe* for short (denoted by the dashed circle in

Fig. 7.2). Each universe has a guard type G which guarantees that objects outside its universe can modify objects within only by methods of the guard. Thus, guards provide centralized access to guarded objects and can therefore be used to detect the kind of harmful codependencies described above. The next subsection describes universes and guards.

7.5.2 Universes

In the following, we present a type system and formal model for universes. Besides the sharing model enforced by universes, we describe related extensions to Java.

Type System and Formal Model. To restrict sharing, we divide the object store into several universes. We assume there is one instance of each reference type for each universe of a program. Two instances of type T in two different universes U and V are regarded as different types T_U and T_V. Thus, it is not possible to assign objects of type T_U to variables or fields of type T_V and vice versa. However, different instances of one type share a common implementation.

Besides the designated root universe which contains the whole object store, each universe U is associated with a type, the so-called *owner type* of U.† For simplicity, each class is the owner of at most one universe.

Universes form a hierarchic structure: There is one instance of every type for the root universe. Each instance can in turn be the owner of another universe and so on. Every owner of a universe enclosing universe U (including U itself) is called a guard of U. The guard of U that belongs to universe V is called *the guard of U w.r.t. V*. Universes are formalized by the following refinement of the data model described in Sec. 7.2:

data type

$$
\begin{array}{lll}
Universe & = & root() \\
         & | & mkuniv(CTypId)
\end{array}
$$

$$
\begin{array}{lll}
Type & = & booleanT() \\
     & | & intT() \\
     & | & nullT() \\
     & | & it(\ ITypId,\ Universe\ ) \\
     & | & ct(\ CTypId,\ Universe\ )
\end{array}
$$

$$
\begin{array}{lll}
univ : Type & \to & Universe \\
univ(\ it(\ ID,\ U)\ ) & = & U \\
univ(\ ct(\ ID,\ U)\ ) & = & U
\end{array}
$$

univ yields the universe a reference type belongs to (as opposed to *mkuniv* which yields the universe owned by a class). To be subtypes, two types have to belong to the same universe: $S \preceq T \Rightarrow univ(S) = univ(T)$. We denote the property that a universe U directly encloses universe V by $V \lhd U$. The reflexive, transitive closure of $\lhd$ is denoted by $\unlhd$.

Accessibility and Notation. Universes are private to their owner types: A type T_U of universe U is accessible only in other types of U and the owner type of U.

---

† Technically, it would be possible to associate universes with owner packages instead of types. That would grant more flexibility but leads to a more complex formal model for universes.

In particular, T_U must not be used in signatures of nonprivate methods or as range types of nonprivate fields in U's owner type.

Since each type T has access to at most two universes ($univ(T)$ and $mkuniv(T)$), we can use unprimed and primed type identifiers to refer to types of the enclosing and the owned universe, respectively. Note that an unprimed type of a universe U is identical to the primed type in the universe directly enclosing U. Since Java does not provide references to values, there is no need for primed versions of primitive types (for example, `int`). An occurrence of a primed type T' in a type S refers to the implementation of T in the universe owned by S. That is, all unprimed reference types in T's implementation are primed types w.r.t. S (there is no correspondence for primed types of T in S, since those types are not accessible in S).

In the following refined version of `TextComponent`, we store `StringBuffer` objects in a separate universe owned by `TextComponent`. Since primed type names must not occur in signatures of nonprivate methods/constructors, the constructor takes an unprimed `StringBuffer` object (see below for the constructor body):

```
class TextComponent implements Component {
    private StringBuffer' text;
    ...
    public TextComponent(StringBuffer s) {...}
}
```

Sharing Model. Universes guarantee the following invariant for every execution state: *If object X reaches object Y by a chain of references, then the universe of the type of X is equal to or encloses the universe of Y's type.* The invariant holds because (1) objects of type T_U (belonging to universe U) can be created only by types of U and U's owner type, and (2) a reference to an object of T_U cannot be passed to an object of a type not belonging to U except to U's owner type. Both properties are a direct consequence of the type and accessibility rules described above. For brevity, we omit a formal proof of this property.

The structure of the depends-clauses enforces that a location $X.F$ can only depend on $Y.E$ in state OS if X reaches Y in OS, and therefore, the universe of the type of X is equal to or encloses the universe of Y's type.

Language Extensions. To support universes, the Java type system has to be extended as described above.

Clone Operation. Since the universe type system does not allow one to pass references across universe boundaries (except to objects of owner types), we provide a special clone operation to still be able to exchange data across universe boundaries. This operation (1) clones a whole object structure (that is, performs a deep copy) and (2) moves the new structure from one universe to another. We provide an *upclone* and a *downclone* operation to clone objects and transfer the result from the primed to the unprimed universe respectively vice versa. These operations are denoted like method invocations (for example, `x.upclone()`). The static type of a clone operation is determined from the static type of its argument (by priming or unpriming).

In `TextComponent`, the constructor has to clone the `StringBuffer` parameter and move it to the primed universe: `text = s.downclone();`

Translation into Java. Although universes require some changes to the programming language, they are rather a specification technique than a language modification. Programs using universes can easily be translated into ordinary Java programs with identical behavior. To do that, we replace every primed type by its unprimed version and the clone operations by an invocation of the method `clone` with an appropriate cast. The `clone` method has to guarantee that its result is completely disjoint from its argument which can be enforced by a suitable specification for `Object:clone`. The result of the translation is an ordinary Java program which at runtime adheres to the partition of object stores enforced by universes.

7.5.3 A Weaker Definition of Authenticity

Universes have been introduced to enable reuse without permitting undetected modification of locations: Instead of simply importing a type T, a client imports T into a separate universe. Since the client is the guard of that universe, it controls access to T. To support this reuse pattern, the authenticity rule and the meaning of modifies-clauses have to be refined.

Authenticity. Locations outside a universe U must be allowed to depend on locations inside. With the above definition of authenticity this is not permitted since fields outside a universe are not accessible in types inside. An object of universe V can modify locations of a universe U enclosed by V only via invoking a method m of U's guard w.r.t. V. To meet its specification, m has to guarantee in particular that V-locations are not modified undetectedly. Therefore, every location of V depending on a U-location must be accessible in the guard of U w.r.t. V.† This is achieved by the following refined authenticity rule. *If $X.F$ depends on $Y.E$ and U and V are the universes containing the types of X and Y then: (1) if $V = U$, then $X.F$ must be accessible in the domain type of E, and (2) if $V \lhd U$, then $X.F$ must be accessible in the guard of V w.r.t. U.* Requirement 1 corresponds to the old authenticity requirement. Requirement 2 enforces the accessibility in guards described above. Both requirements can be checked syntactically.

---

† Recall that the sharing model of universes guarantees that $V \trianglelefteq U$ (cf. Subsec. 7.5.2).

Negation of the Depends-Relation. To avoid contradictions, the axioms generated for the negation of the depends-relation have to be adapted to the weaker form of authenticity:

$$\forall X, Y, OS : univ(\tau(X)) = univ(\tau(Y)) \wedge \neg\rho(X, Y, OS, R(F, E)) \Rightarrow \neg(X.F \xrightarrow{OS} Y.E)$$

The new visibility rule only has to hold for pairs of locations belonging to the same universe. With the new rules, it is again guaranteed that program extensions do not introduce axioms contradicting the specification of imported packages (by the argument described in Subsec. 7.4.2).

Modifies-Clauses. Methods of a type inside a universe U must be allowed to change abstract locations outside by modifying locations they depend on, even if the locations outside are not covered by the modifies-clause. Therefore, we have to exclude locations of outer universes from the proof obligation stemming from the modifies-clause of $T{:}m$ (cf. Subsec. 7.4.3):

> **pre** $\$ = OS \wedge this = P_0 \wedge \bigwedge_{i=1}^{n} p_i = P_i$
> **post** $alive(X, OS) \wedge univ(dtype(F)) \trianglelefteq univ(T) \Rightarrow$
> $\qquad X.F \in \delta(\mu(T{:}m, P_0, \ldots, P_n, OS), OS) \vee OS(X.F) = \$(X.F)$

The adaption of the modularity lemma (cf. Subsec. 7.4.4) to the refined semantics of modifies is straightforward. The adapted proof makes use of the sharing properties enforced by universes (see Subsec. 7.5.2). In particular, it is important that methods of a type in universe U can only be invoked by types of U or U's owner type. If a type invokes a method of the same universe, the proof is as in Subsec. 7.4.4. Otherwise, an owner type invokes a method of the universe it owns. In that case, the new definition of authenticity guarantees that all abstract locations that might be affected by the method invocation are either declared in the modifies-clause of or accessible to the caller. Thus, we have traded flexible reuse for a slightly weaker semantics of modifies-clauses.

Example. In the text component example, the dependency

```
depends X.prefSize on $(X.text).length;
```

is now authentic because (1) `prefSize` is accessible in `TextComponent`, which is the domain type of `text`, and (2) the `length` field belongs to the primed universe of `TextComponent` (since the range type of `text` is `StringBuffer'`). That is, `TextComponent` is the guard of `length` w.r.t. the universe of `prefSize`. Therefore, `TextComponent` has a legal specification.

To modularly verify `TextComponent`, one has to guarantee that objects of type `StringBuffer'` cannot be shared among several text components. Otherwise, `reset` would modify the `prefSize` field of all text components sharing a `StringBuffer`. Such fine-grained sharing control can be achieved by appropriate type invariants, which are not dealt with in this article.

7.5.4 Programming Model

Universes allow for modular verification by restricting sharing of object structures. In this subsection, we describe the influence of universes on the programming model and discuss the limitations of the approach.

Authenticity requires using universes when a location depends on a location declared in an imported type. This requirement reveals three aspects of universes: (1) Universes are only required when there actually are dependencies. For example, container data structures such as lists of objects usually don't depend on locations of contained objects and can therefore be implemented conventionally. (2) Universes are not required when both the source and target location of a dependency are declared in the same package. In particular, this allows one to implement (mutually) recursive types. Therefore, universes provide far more flexibility than a part-of relation. (3) In addition to the situations where universes must be used to achieve authenticity, they are helpful to ease verification of many implementation patterns.

Authenticity and the use of universes, as described above, impose two limitations on programs: (1) With the universe model presented in this article, it is not possible to share universes and their locations among objects of different types (since universes are private to types). However, the accessibility of universes can be extended to packages (we omitted this generalization to obtain an easier formal model). This allows for sharing of universes among objects of types declared in the same package, and provides enough flexibility for most implementation patterns. (2) The clone operation is required to exchange information across universe boundaries. Besides the runtime overhead to copy objects, information about object identities is lost by cloning.

In summary, the authenticity requirement and universes do not enforce a major shift in the programming model: Universes are only required in designated situations and do still allow for many sharing patterns.

7.6 Related Work

Combinations of formal techniques and OO-concepts have been investigated w.r.t. different development and abstraction levels ranging from requirement and design specification languages (cf. for example [DvK92, CDD+89]) to executable assertions extending OO-programming languages ([Mey92]). Our approach lies in the middle of this range. Like the former frameworks it uses declarative techniques† to formalize pre- and postconditions, and aims to support complete specifications of functional properties. However the foci are different. Design frameworks concentrate on development steps (for example, refinement techniques, [LH92]). We want to specify and verify interfaces of components implemented in existing programming languages. Consequently, we have to deal with the less abstract semantics of pro-

---

† We use first-order logic in contrast to the model-based approach of VDM and Z.

grams, in particular with sharing which is essential in practice, but often neglected in design languages.

Our specification technique builds on the two-tiered approach introduced by Larch (cf. [GH93]). To be suitable for verification, we provide explicit abstraction. The formal semantics of interface specifications used in this article is presented in [PH97]. A similar semantics is used in the Larch/C++ language (cf. [Lea96]). The programming logic on which our specification technique is based is presented in [PHM98, PHM99]. The rest of this section discusses research related to the specific contributions of this article.

Frame Properties. [Lei95] provides a basis for our work by introducing explicit dependencies and downward-closures for modifies-clauses. In his approach, the translation of a modifies-clause into a pre-post pair depends on the context in which the translation takes place. Therefore, it is difficult to handle this semantics by Hoare-style programming logics. Furthermore, Leino's soundness proof does not yet cover dynamic dependencies.

An alternative approach to the extended state problem is presented in [Lei98]. Instead of abstract fields, so-called data groups are used to represent a set of concrete fields. Like abstract fields, data groups can be mentioned in modifies-clauses and provide support for information hiding and modification of extended state. They are a natural way to reflect a programmer's intention. In contrast to abstract fields, data groups do not have a value. This allows one to drop the authenticity requirement. But on the other hand, data groups cannot be used to specify functional behavior in terms of abstract values which is crucial for verification of OO-programs.

Type Systems for Sharing Control. [CPN98] and [Alm97] present type systems (so-called ownership types and balloon types) that can be used to partition the object store (into contexts and balloons, respectively) and provide flexible alias control. In contrast to universes, contexts and balloons are owned by objects instead of types which allows for a more fine-grained sharing control. However, our intention was to clarify the requirements for modular verification. Therefore, we wanted to use as little syntactic support as possible to put the focus on the essential semantics. Although type invariants can be used to express sharing properties, elaborated type systems can be used to dramatically decrease the verification effort. Therefore, they are a good supplement to the techniques presented in this article.

7.7 Conclusions

We presented modular specification and verification techniques for OO-software components. To enable modularity, specifications have to support abstraction from encapsulated implementation aspects, remain valid under composition, and be sufficiently expressive to verify properties of composed programs from the specifications

of their components. Concerning functional behavior of methods, behavioral sub-typing is a suitable technique to enforce modularity of specifications and proofs.

Information hiding, the extended state problem, and program extensions make modular specification of frame properties delicate. Based on abstract fields with explicit dependencies, we enhanced the modifies-clause technique to meet these modularity requirements. Our semantics enables one to verify a method w.r.t. its modifies-clause locally in the context of the method. Authenticity guarantees that locations declared outside this context are not modified by the method.

Since authenticity is too strong to allow for effective reuse, we introduced a type system providing universes. By preventing certain patterns of sharing and codependencies of locations, universes allow us to weaken the authenticity require-ment and enable reuse. The price for these benefits is that object structures have to be cloned to move data from one universe to another. Furthermore, objects usually cannot be shared among data structures implemented in different packages.

In a nutshell, the described techniques allow for modular specification and verifi-cation of functional behavior and frame properties. They can be extended to cover type invariants. Therefore, they provide a basis for formal treatment of object-oriented software components.

Acknowledgments

We'd like to express our gratitude to the anonymous reviewers who provided exten-sive and very valuable comments. Thanks also to Gary T. Leavens for his comments on an earlier version of this article.

Bibliography

[Alm97]   Almeida, P. S. Balloon types: Controlling sharing of state in data types. In Akşit, M. and Matsuoka, S., editors, *ECOOP '97: Object-Oriented Programming*, volume 1241 of *Lecture Notes in Computer Science*, pages 32–59. Springer-Verlag, 1997.

[CDD+89] Carrington, D., Duke, D., Duck, R., King, P., and Rose, G. *Object-Z: an Object Oriented Extension to Z.* North-Holland, 1989.

[CPN98]   Clarke, D. G., Potter, J. M., and Noble, J. Ownership types for flexible alias protection. In *Proceedings of Object-Oriented Programming Systems, Languages, and Applications (OOPSLA)*, volume 33(10) of *ACM SIGPLAN Notices*, October 1998.

[DL96]   Dhara, K. K. and Leavens, G. T. Forcing behavioral subtyping through specification inheritance. In *Proceedings of the 18th International Conference on Software Engineering*, pages 258–267. IEEE Computer Society Press, 1996.

[DvK92]   Durr, E. H. and van Katwijk, J. VDM++: A formal specification language for object-oriented design. In *TOOLS Europe '92*, pages 63–77, 1992.

[GH93]   Guttag, J. V. and Horning, J. J. *Larch: Languages and Tools for Formal Specification.* Springer-Verlag, 1993.

[Lea96]   Leavens, G. T. An overview of Larch/C++: Behavioral specifications for C++ modules. In Kilov, H. and Harvey, W., editors, *Specification of*

	Behavioral Semantics in Object-Oriented Information Modeling, chapter 8, pages 121–142. Kluwer Academic Publishers, Boston, 1996.

[Lei95]   Leino, K. R. M. *Toward Reliable Modular Programs*. PhD thesis, California Institute of Technology, 1995.

[Lei98]   Leino, K. R. M. Data groups: Specifying the modification of extended state. In *Proceedings of the 1998 ACM SIGPLAN Conference on Object-Oriented Programming, Systems, Languages, and Applications (OOPSLA '98)*, volume 33(10) of *ACM SIGPLAN Notices*, pages 144–153, October 1998.

[LH92]   Lano, K. and Haughton, H. Reasoning and refinement in object-oriented specification languages. In Madsen, O. L., editor, *ECOOP '92 European Conference on Object-Oriented Programming*, volume 615 of *Lecture Notes in Computer Science*, pages 78–97. Springer-Verlag, 1992.

[LN97]   Leino, K. R. M. and Nelson, G. Abstraction and specification revisited. The manuscript KRML 71 can be obtained from the authors, 1997.

[Mey92]   Meyer, B. *Eiffel: The Language*. Prentice Hall, 1992.

[PH97]   Poetzsch-Heffter, A. Specification and verification of object-oriented programs. Habilitation thesis, Technical University of Munich, January 1997. URL: www.informatik.fernuni-hagen.de/pi5/publications.html.

[PHM98]   Poetzsch-Heffter, A. and Müller, P. Logical foundations for typed object-oriented languages. In Gries, D. and De Roever, W., editors, *Programming Concepts and Methods (PROCOMET)*, 1998.

[PHM99]   Poetzsch-Heffter, A. and Müller, P. A programming logic for sequential Java. In Swierstra, S. D., editor, *Programming Languages and Systems (ESOP '99)*, volume 1576 of *Lecture Notes in Computer Science*, pages 162–176. Springer-Verlag, 1999.

8

Respectful Type Converters for Mutable Types

Jeannette M. Wing and John Ockerbloom

Computer Science Department
Carnegie Mellon University
Pittsburgh, PA 15213-3890

Abstract

In converting an object of one type to another, we expect some of the original object's behavior to remain the same, and some to change. How can we state the relationship between the original object and converted object to characterize what information is preserved and what is lost after the conversion takes place? We answer this question by introducing the new relation, *respects*, and say that a type converter function $K : A \to B$ *respects* a type T. We formally define *respects* in terms of the Liskov and Wing behavioral notion of subtyping; types A and B are subtypes of T.

In previous work we defined *respects* for immutable types A, B, and T; in this chapter we extend our notion to handle conversions between mutable types. This extension is nontrivial since we need to consider an object's behavior as it varies over time. We present in detail two examples to illustrate our ideas: one for converting between PNG images and GIF images and another for converting between different kinds of bounded event queues. This work was inspired in building at Carnegie Mellon the Typed Object Model (TOM) conversion service, in daily use worldwide.

8.1 Motivation

The tremendous growth of the Internet and the World Wide Web gives millions of people access to vast quantities of data. While users may be able to retrieve data easily, they may not be able to interpret or display retrieved data intelligibly. For example, when retrieving a Microsoft Word document, without a Microsoft Word program, the user will be unable to display, edit, or print it. In general, the type of the retrieved data may be unknown to the retrieving site.

Users and programs cope with this problem by *converting* data from one type to another, for example, from the unknown type to one known by the local user or program. Thus, to view the Word document, we could convert it to ASCII text or HTML, and then view it through our favorite text editor or browser. A picture in an unfamiliar Windows bitmap type could be converted into a more familiar GIF image type. A mail message with incomprehensible MIME attachments could be converted from an unreadable MIME-encoded type to a text, image, or audio type that the recipient could examine directly. In general, we apply *type converters* on (data) objects, transforming an object of one type to an object of a different type.

8.1.1 *What Information Do Type Converters Preserve?*

In converting objects of one type to another we expect there to be some relationship between the original object and the converted one. In what way are they similar? The reason to apply a converter in the first place is that we expect some things about the original object to change in a way that we are willing to forgo, but we also expect some things to stay the same. For example, suppose we convert a LaTeX file to an HTML file. We may care to ensure that the raw textual contents of the original LaTeX document are preserved, but not the formatting commands since they do not contribute to the meaning of the document itself; here the preserved information is the underlying semantics of the text contained in the document. Alternatively, if we convert a LaTeX file to a table-of-contents document, we may care to ensure that the number, order, and titles of chapters and sections in the original document are preserved, but not the bulk of the text; here the preserved information is primarily the document's structure.

The question we address in this chapter is "How can we characterize what information is preserved by a type converter?" Our answer is given in terms of the behavior of some type T. Informally, we say a *converter $K : A \to B$ respects type T* if the original object of type A and the converted object of type B have the same behavior when both objects are viewed (through appropriate abstractions) as a type T object. That is, from T's viewpoint, the A and B objects look the same. If the converter respects a type, then it preserves that type's observable behavior, as defined by the type's interface specification. This chapter formalizes the notion of *respectful type converters*.

Our particular formalization of *respects* exploits the *subtype* relationship that holds among types of objects. The Liskov and Wing notion of behavioral subtyping [LW94] conveniently characterizes semantic differences between types. If S is a subtype of T, users of T objects cannot perceive when objects of type S are substituted for T objects. Intuitively, if K respects type T, a supertype of both A and B, then T captures the behavioral information preserved by K.

In our previous work, "Respectful Type Converters" [WO99a] we defined the *respects* relation for conversions between immutable types only. (It was correspondingly based on a simplified version of Liskov and Wing's definition of subtype.) In this chapter, we present an enhanced version of our respects relation that captures

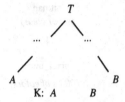

Fig. 8.1. Does Converter K Respect Type T?

important properties of conversions between mutable types. Specifically, for mutable types we say that a conversion *respects* a certain type T if an object with the converted value cannot be distinguished (using T's interface specification) from an object with the original value either at the time of conversion, or by analyzing any future computation on the object. That is, the future subhistory of the new object will not be inconsistent with the expectations raised by the past subhistory of the original object, given the constraints of type T.

Here is an example of why for some common ancestors, T, of A and B there may not exist respectful type converters from A to B (Figure 8.1). Consider a type family for images, depicted in Figure 8.2. Suppose that the PNG image and GIF image types are both subtypes of a pixel_map type that specifies the colors of the pixels in a rectangular region. GIF images are limited to 256 distinct colors; PNG images are not. Assuming the pixel_map type does not have a fixed color limit, then a general converter from PNG images to GIF images would not respect the pixel_map type: it is possible to use pixel_map's interface to distinguish a PNG image with thousands of colors from its conversion to a GIF image with at most 256 colors. On the other hand, suppose pixel_map is in turn a subtype of a more generic bitmap type that simply records whether a graphical element is set or clear. Suppose further that elements in a pixel_map are considered set if they are not black, and clear if they are black. As long as the PNG to GIF converter does not change any nonblack color to black (or black to nonblack), and otherwise preserves the pixel layout, there is no way for the bitmap interface to distinguish the PNG image from the GIF image that results from the conversion. Here then, the PNG to GIF converter respects the bitmap type.

8.1.2 *Typed Object Model Context*

At Carnegie Mellon we built a type broker, an instance of Ockerbloom's Typed Object Model (TOM) [Ock98], that provides a type conversion service. Our TOM type broker allows users in a distributed environment to store types and type conversion functions, to register new ones, and to find existing ones. It supports roughly 100

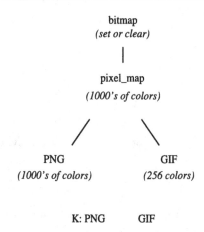

Fig. 8.2. A PNG to GIF converter that does not respect pixel_map might still respect bitmap. Conversely, it is easy to define a GIF to PNG converter that respects both pixel_map and bitmap.

abstract data types, a few hundred concrete data types, and over 300 type converters (including over 200 meaningful compositions of about 70 primitive converters). The kinds of types TOM supports today are different kinds of document types (for example, Word, LaTeX, PowerPoint, binhex, HTML) and "packages" of such document types (for example, a mail message that has an embedded postscript file, a tar file, or a zip file). The kinds of conversions TOM supports are off-the-shelf converters like *postscript2pdf* (that is, AdobeDistiller^{TM}), off-the-Web ones like *latex2html*, and some home-grown ones like *powerpoint2html*.

The website for Carnegie Mellon's TOM service is: http://tom.cs.cmu.edu/. As of May 1999, the number of accesses to the TOM conversion service stabilized to 5000 per month, which is an average of 167 per day. Accesses came from over 1000 sites in over 35 countries in six continents from all types of organizations including educational, government, and commercial institutions.

In designing the type hierarchy for this service, Ockerbloom made a deliberate decision to use only immutable types [Ock98], and hence our original paper [WO99a] on the *respects* relation ignored the complexities of mutability. However, Wing observed that though the objects are immutable, in their context of use—a distributed environment—the same problems of aliasing of mutable objects can arise [Win97]. For example, clients can access the same object through more than one naming scheme, for example, a URL, and a local file name; since objects are not necessarily uniquely named, this aliasing can lead to conflicting updates. Hence, in this chapter we investigate what *respects* means more generally, that is, in the presence of shared mutable objects.

Though our idea of respectful type converters was inspired by our use of TOM in the context of file and document converters, type converters show up in other contexts. Most programming languages have built-in type converters defined on primitive types, for example, *ascii2integer*, *char2string*, and *string2array[char]*. The real world is continually faced with painful, costly, yet seemingly simple conversions: the U.S. Postal System converted five-digit zip codes to five+four-digit zip codes; Bell Atlantic recently added a new area code necessitating the conversion of a large portion of phone numbers in Western Pennsylvania from the 412 area code to 724; payroll processing centers routinely need to convert large databases of employee records whenever extra fields are added to the relevant database schema; and of course, the infamous Year 2000 (Y2K) conversion problem is costing billions of dollars to fix [Jon98].

8.1.3 Roadmap to Rest of Paper

In this chapter we formally characterize the notion of when a converter *respects* a type. We first review in Section 8.2 background details leading up to the definition of Liskov and Wing's behavioral notion of subtyping [LW94]; this section is included to make this chapter self-contained. In Section 8.3 we exploit this notion of subtyping to define the *respects* relation between a converter and a type. In Section 8.4 we discuss in detail two examples to illustrate converters that do and do not respect types: one example of a type family for PNG and GIF images, and one for bounded event queues. We close with a discussion of related work and summary remarks.

8.2 Behavioral Subtyping

The programming language community has come up with many definitions of the subtype relation. The goal is to determine when this assignment

$$x: T := E$$

is legal in the presence of subtyping. Once the assignment has occurred, x will be used according to its "apparent" type T, with the expectation that if the program performs correctly when the actual type of x's object is T, it will also work correctly if the actual type of the object denoted by x is a subtype of T.

What we need is a subtype requirement that constrains the behavior of subtypes so that users will not encounter any surprises:

No Surprises Requirement: Properties of an object of a type T that users rely on should hold even if the object is actually a member of a subtype S of T.

which guarantees Liskov's *substitutability* principle of subtypes [Lis87]. In their 1994 TOPLAS paper "A Behavioral Notion of Subtyping" Liskov and Wing [LW94] formalized this requirement in their definition of subtyping. The novel aspect of their subtype definition is the ability to handle mutable types, and in particular, a type's *history* properties. Their specification logic limits the expressibility of history properties to be monotonic. For example, they can state that the bound of a queue stays the same but cannot state that it cyclically increases and decreases. Another example of a history property is that the value of an integer counter monotonically increases. They cannot state any liveness properties. We assume the same limitations herein.

Chapter 6 of this volume contains an extensive overview of many definitions of behavioral subtyping, including Liskov and Wing's. To provide background for our definition of *respects*, we first describe their model of objects and types, how they specify types, and then how they define the subtype relation. These definitions are all taken from the Liskov and Wing paper [LW94].

8.2.1 *Model of Objects, Types, and Computation*

We assume a set of all potentially existing objects, *Obj*, partitioned into disjoint typed sets. Each object has a unique identity. A *type* defines a set of *values* for an object and a set of *methods* that provide the only means to manipulate or observe that object.

Objects can be created and manipulated in the course of program execution. A *state* defines a value for each existing object. It is a pair of mappings, an *environment* and a *store*. An environment maps program variables to objects; a store maps objects to values.

$$
\begin{aligned}
State &= Env \times Store \\
Env &= Var \to Obj \\
Store &= Obj \to Val
\end{aligned}
$$

Given a variable, x, and a state, ρ, with an environment, $\rho.e$, and store, $\rho.s$, we use the notation x_ρ to denote the value of x in state ρ; that is, $x_\rho = \rho.s(\rho.e(x))$. When we refer to the domain of a state, $dom(\rho)$, we mean more precisely the domain of the store in that state.

We model a type as a triple, $\langle O, V, M \rangle$, where $O \subseteq Obj$ is a set of objects, $V \subseteq Val$ is a set of values, and M is a set of methods. Each method for an object is a *constructor*, an *observer*, or a *mutator*. Constructors of type τ return new objects of type τ; observers return results of other types; mutators modify the values of objects of type τ. A new object is one which does not exist in the domain of the state upon method invocation. An object is *immutable* if its value cannot change and otherwise it is *mutable*. A type is immutable if all of its objects are; otherwise it is mutable. We allow *mixed methods* where a constructor or an observer can also be a mutator. We also allow methods to signal exceptions; we assume termination exceptions, that is, each method call either terminates normally or in one of a number of named exception conditions. To be consistent with object-oriented language notation, we write $x.m(a)$ to denote the call of method m on object x with the sequence of arguments a.

Objects come into existence and get their initial values through *creators*. Unlike other kinds of methods, creators do not belong to particular objects, but rather are independent operations. They are the *class methods*; the other methods are the *instance methods*.

A *computation*, that is, a program execution, is a sequence of alternating states and transitions starting in some initial state, ρ_0:

$$\rho_0 \ Tr_1 \ \rho_1 \ \ldots \ \rho_{n-1} \ Tr_n \ \rho_n$$

Each transition, Tr_i, of a computation sequence is a partial function on states. A *history* is the subsequence of states of a computation.

Objects are never destroyed: $\forall \ 1 \leq i \leq n \ . \ dom(\rho_{i-1}) \subseteq dom(\rho_i)$.

8.2.2 Type Specifications

A type specification contains the following information:

- The type's name.
- A description of the set of values over which objects of the type ranges.
- For each of the type's methods:
  - Its name.
  - Its signature, that is, the types of its arguments (in order), result, and signaled exceptions.
  - Its behavior in terms of preconditions and postconditions.
- A description of the type's history properties.

Figure 8.3 gives an example of a type specification for GIF images. We give formal specifications, written in the style of Larch [HGJ+93], but we could just as easily have written informal specifications. Since these specifications are formal we can do formal proofs, possibly with machine assistance like with the Larch Prover [GG89], to show that a subtype relation holds [Zar96].

The GIFImage Larch Shared Language trait and the **invariant** clause in the Larch interface type specification for GIF images together describe the set of values over which GIF image objects can range. GIF images are sequences of frames where each frame is a bounded two-dimensional array of colors. The Appendix contains all traits used in all examples in this chapter, and here in particular, the GIFImage trait and those for frame sequences, frames, colors, and so forth.

A type invariant constrains the value space for a type's objects. In the GIF example, the type invariant says that a GIF image can have at most 256 different colors. (The *colorrange* function defined in GIFImage returns the range of colors mapped onto by the array.) The predicate $\phi(x_\rho)$ appearing in an **invariant** clause for type τ stands for the predicate: For all computations c, and for all states ρ in c:

GIF: **type**

uses GIFImage (gif **for** G)
for all g: GIF

invariant $\mid colorrange(g_\rho) \mid \leq 256$
constraint *true*

color *get_color* (i, j: int)
        ensures $result = overlay(g, i, j)$

bool *set_color* (i, j: int; c: color)
        modifies g
        ensures   **if** $\mid colorrange(changepixel(g_{pre}, i, j, c)) \mid \leq 256$
                then $c \in colorrange(g_{post}) \wedge g_{post} = changepixel(g_{pre}, i, j, c) \wedge$
                    $result = true$
                else $g_{pre} = g_{post} \wedge result = false$

frame *get_frame* (i: int)
        requires $1 \leq i \leq len(g)$
        ensures $result = g[i]$

end GIF

Fig. 8.3. A Larch Type Specification for GIF Images.

$$\forall x : \tau \ . \ x \in dom(\rho) \Rightarrow \phi(x_\rho).$$

Whereas an invariant property is a property true of all states of an object, a history property is a property that is true of all sequences of states that result from any computation on that object. A type constraint in a Larch interface specification defines the history properties of the type's objects. The two-state predicate $\phi(x_{\rho_i}, x_{\rho_k})$ appearing in a **constraint** clause for type τ stands for the predicate: For all computations c, and for all states ρ_i and ρ_k in c such that $i < k$:

$$\forall x : \tau \ . \ x \in dom(\rho_i) \Rightarrow \phi(x_{\rho_i}, x_{\rho_k})$$

Note that we do not require that ρ_k be the immediate successor of ρ_i in c. The GIF example has the trivial constraint *true*. In Section 8.4.2 we will give examples of types with nontrivial constraints.

The **requires** and **ensures** clauses in the Larch interface specification state the methods' pre- and postconditions respectively. To be consistent with the Liskov and Wing paper and the Larch approach, preconditions are single-state predicates and postconditions are two-state predicates. The **modifies** clause states that the values of any objects it does *not* list do not change; the values of those listed may possibly change. The absence of a **requires** clause stands for the precondition *true*.

The absence of a **modifies** clause means that the method cannot change the values of any objects.

The *get_color* method returns the color of the (i, j)th array element of g. The *overlay* function defined in GIFImage returns the color value of the (i, j)th array element of the last frame in the sequence that gives a value for (i, j); otherwise, it returns BLACK, a distinguished color value, introduced in the ColorLiterals trait. For example, if there are three frames in the frame sequence and for a given (i, j), the first frame maps the array element to BLACK, the second to RED, and the third does not map (i, j) to any color (because it is not within its bounds), then RED is returned. The *set_color* method modifies the GIF object g by changing the final color of pixel (i, j) to c, and returns true, if the change would not make the resulting GIF have more than 256 colors. Otherwise it leaves the GIF object unchanged and returns false. The *get_frame* method returns the ith frame of the GIF object's value.

To ensure that the specification is *consistent*, the specifier must show that each creator for the type τ establishes τ's invariant, and that each of τ's methods both preserves the invariant and satisfies the constraint. These are standard conditions and their proofs are typically straightforward [LW94].

8.2.3 The Subtype Relation

The subtype relation is defined in terms of a checklist of properties that must hold between the specifications of the two types, σ and τ. Since in general the value space for objects of type σ will be different from the value space for those of type τ we need to relate the different value spaces; we use an *abstraction function*, α, to define this relationship. Also since in general the names of the methods of type σ can be different from those of type τ we need to relate which method of σ corresponds to which method of τ; to define this correspondence we use a *renaming* map, ν, that maps names of methods of σ to names of methods of τ.

The formal definition of the subtype relation, $\preceq$, is given in Figure 8.4 †. It relates two types, σ and τ, each of whose specifications we assume are consistent. In the methods rules, since x is an object of type σ, its value (x_{pre} or x_{post}) is a member of S and therefore cannot be used directly in the predicates about τ objects (which are in terms of values in T). The abstraction function α is used to translate these values so that the predicates about τ objects make sense.

This definition of subtype guarantees that certain properties of the supertype—those stated explicitly or provable from a type's specification—are preserved by the subtype. The first condition directly relates the invariant properties. The second condition relates the behaviors of the individual methods, and thus preserves any observable behavioral property of any program that invokes those methods. The third condition relates the overall histories of objects, guaranteeing that the possible

† It is Liskov and Wing's "constraint"-based subtype definition, and is taken from Fig. 4 of [LW94].

DEFINITION OF THE SUBTYPE RELATION, $\preceq$: $\sigma = \langle O_\sigma, S, M \rangle$ is a *subtype* of $\tau = \langle O_\tau, T, N \rangle$ if there exists an abstraction function, $\alpha : S \to T$, and a renaming map, $\nu : M \to N$, such that:

(i) Subtype invariants ensure supertype invariants.

- *Invariant Rule.* For all computations, c, and all states ρ in c for all $x : \sigma$:
  $$I_\sigma \Rightarrow I_\tau[A(x_\rho)/x_\rho]$$

(ii) Subtype methods preserve the supertype methods' behavior. If m_τ of τ is the corresponding renamed method m_σ of σ, the following rules must hold:

- *Signature rule.*
  - *Contravariance of arguments.* m_τ and m_σ have the same number of arguments. If the list of i argument types of m_τ is a and that of m_σ is b, then $\forall i \,.\, a_i \preceq b_i$.
  - *Covariance of result.* Either both m_τ and m_σ have a result or neither has. If there is a result, let m_τ's result type be a and m_σ's be b. Then $b \preceq a$.
  - *Exception rule.* The exceptions signaled by m_σ are contained in the set of exceptions signaled by m_τ.

- *Methods rule.* For all $x : \sigma$:
  - *precondition rule.* $m_\tau.pre[\alpha(x_{pre})/x_{pre}] \Rightarrow m_\sigma.pre$.
  - *postcondition rule.*
    $$m_\sigma.post \Rightarrow m_\tau.post[\alpha(x_{pre})/x_{pre}, \alpha(x_{post})/x_{post}]$$

(iii) Subtype constraints ensure supertype constraints.

- *Constraint rule.* For all computations c, and all states ρ_i and ρ_k in c where $i < k$, for all $x : \sigma$:
  $$C_\sigma \Rightarrow C_\tau[\alpha(x_{\rho_i})/x_{\rho_i}, \alpha(x_{\rho_k})/x_{\rho_k}]$$

Fig. 8.4. Definition of the Subtype Relation.

histories (viewed abstractly) in the subtype specification are also possible histories in the supertype specification.

Figure 8.5 gives a type specification for pixel_map, which is a supertype of both GIF and PNG. To show that GIF is a subtype of pixel_map (Figure 8.2), we define the following abstraction function:

$$\alpha_G^{PM} : G \to PM$$
$$\forall i, j : \text{Integer} \,.\, \alpha_G^{PM}(g)[i, j] = overlay(g, i, j)$$

Using this abstraction function, the proofs that the invariant, signature, methods, and constraint rules either are straightforward to show or trivially hold. The only noteworthy aspect of pixel_map's specification is the nondeterminism specified for its *set_color* method, which is more liberal than that for both GIF images and PNG images (as we will see in Section 8.4). A call to *set_color* can always either fail pixel_map: **type**

uses PixelMap (pixel_map **for** PM)
for all p: pixel_map

invariant *true*
constraint *true*

color *get_color* (i, j: int)
　　　　ensures　$result = p[i, j]$

bool *set_color* (i, j: int; c: color)
　　　　modifies　p
　　　　ensures　$(result = false \land p_{pre} = p_{post}) \lor$
　　　　　　　　　$(result = true \land c \in colorrange(p_{post}) \land c = p_{post}[i, j] \land$
　　　　　　　　　　　$\forall k, l : Integer.(k \neq i \lor l \neq j) \Rightarrow p_{pre}[k, l] = p_{post}[k, l])$

end pixel_map

Fig. 8.5. A Larch Type Specification for Pixel Maps.

(making no change) or succeed (possibly adding a new color to the pixel_maps's color range). We exploit this nondeterminism later in our proofs.

8.3 Respects

8.3.1 Definition of Respectful Type Converter

Suppose we have two types $A = \langle O_A, V_A, M_A \rangle$ and $B = \langle O_B, V_B, M_B \rangle$. A converter, K, is a partial function from V_A to V_B. Thus when we say that a converter maps from type A to type B we mean more precisely that it maps the value space of type A to the value space of type B; for notational convenience, we continue to write the signature of K as $A \to B$. To ensure the converter is consistent with B's specification, the specifier should show that the values of V_B to which K maps satisfy B's type invariant.

Figure 8.6 gives the definition of the *respects* relation for a converter $K : A \to B$ and type T. The first two conditions (under **Methods**) state that the original value and the converted value are indistinguishable when viewed through the methods (in particular, the observers) of type T. Let a stand for y_{pre} used in the definition (the value of the object of type A before the call to T's method m). Then the first condition requires that m's precondition holds for a's abstraction under α iff it holds for the converted value of a abstracted under β. Thus from T's viewpoint, if m is defined for A's values, it should be defined for B's values, and vice versa. The second condition requires that m's postcondition holds for a's abstracted value under α iff it holds for the converted value of a abstracted under β. Thus, given

DEFINITION OF RESPECTS RELATION: Let $K : A \to B$ be a partial function mapping values of type A to values of type B. Let $A \preceq T$ and $B \preceq T$ and let $\alpha : A \to T$ and $\beta : B \to T$ be the abstraction functions for showing the corresponding subtype relations hold. Then *converter* K *respects* T if the following conditions hold:

- **Methods:** For each method m of T, and for all objects $x : T$, $y : A$, and $z : B$, and for all subcomputations $y_{pre} \ m_A \ y_{post}$ and $z_{pre} \ m_B \ z_{post}$, such that m_A and m_B are invocations of A's and B's corresponding methods of m, $y_{pre} \in dom(K)$, and $K(y_{pre}) = z_{pre}$:
  - (i) $m.pre[\alpha(y_{pre})/x_{pre}] \Leftrightarrow m.pre[\beta(z_{pre})/x_{pre}]$ and
  - (ii) $m.post[\alpha(y_{pre})/x_{pre}, \alpha(y_{post})/x_{post}]$
    $\Leftrightarrow m.post[\beta(z_{pre})/x_{pre}, \beta(z_{post})/x_{post}]$

- **Constraint:** For all integers i, j, and k, where $0 \leq i \leq j \leq k$, all histories $\rho_0...\rho_k$ and $\psi_0...\psi_k$, and for all objects $x : T$, $y : A$, and $z : B$ such that $y_{\rho_j} \in dom(K)$ and $K(y_{\rho_j}) = z_{\psi_j}$:
  $C_T[\alpha(y_{\rho_i})/x_{\rho_i}, \beta(z_{\psi_k})/x_{\rho_k}]$

Fig. 8.6. Definition of the Respects Relation.

that m is defined, then its observed state must be the same for A's values and B's values from T's viewpoint.

The last condition (labeled **Constraint**) requires that T's constraints between any two points of any history must be the same for an unconverted object of type A as for a converted object of type B. This is trivially true for two points before the conversion and for two points after the conversion; the condition more generally handles the case where one point, ρ_i, is before the conversion, and one point, ρ_k, is after the conversion, where the point of conversion is ρ_j. Thus, from T's viewpoint, the converted object's later abstracted states are consistent with the earlier abstracted states of the original object, given the history properties of T. To put it another way, now let a stand for y_{ρ_j} used in the definition. If T's history constraint holds, then an observer cannot tell that the object with the new value after conversion, $K(a)$, is any different from the object with the original value, a, before conversion.

These conditions together guarantee that T's behavior is preserved by the conversion of objects of type A to those of type B. Informally, T cannot distinguish between an object with the original value and an object with the converted value, even when taking the subsequent histories of the objects into account. Thus K *respects* T.

Claim 1 *If a and $K(a)$ abstractly map to the same value in T, i.e., $\alpha(a) = \beta(K(a))$ for all a in the domain of K, then the respects relation trivially follows.*

This special case is often useful in proofs that a converter respects a type, as we will see Section 8.4.

8.3.2 Discussion of Definition

The definition of the respects relation has a similar structure to the definition of the subtype relation. Like the subtype relation, the respects relation includes methods and constraint rules. The **Methods** rules show that the observable state of the original object and the object with the converted value are indistinguishable (from the respected type's point of view) at the time of conversion. The **Constraint** rule shows that the abstract history of the object with the converted value is consistent with the past abstracted history of the original object. Unlike the subtype relation, the respects relation does not need an invariant rule. Since both types A and B are subtypes of the respected type T, *all* objects of those types must conform to the invariants of T, by the definition of subtype, so restating the invariant rule here for particular A and B objects would be superfluous.

We considered various alternate definitions of the respects relation. One of them explicitly modeled a computation involving object $z : B$, and required it to correspond exactly to a computation involving object $y : A$, in rules like the ones above. Another did not explicitly consider histories or computations at all, but simply compared values of an object $y : A$ to values of a corresponding object $z : B$, and made sure the converted values of z matched the original values of y at every state. The first alternative was more complex than necessary; the second, too simplistic. Moreover, both failed to accommodate cases where the history of an object with a converted value diverges from that of an object with an original value, a situation we want (and need) to allow. (In the next section, we will see examples of this phenomenon. One common case occurs where one of the types in question is less constrained than the other.) The history of the original object and that of the converted object are allowed to diverge after the point of conversion, as long as both (abstracted) histories are consistent with the past (abstract) history of the original object, with respect to the respected type's constraints. As long as this consistency property holds, there should be "no surprises" from the respected type's point of view after a conversion.

8.4 Two Examples

The first example shows how our definition handles mutable methods, and hence mutable types. The second example goes one step further and shows how we handle history properties as specified in nontrivial constraint clauses.

8.4.1 PNG and GIF Example Revisited

Let us look at the PNG to GIF example more carefully. First, we give the type specification for PNG images and an abstraction function that enables us to argue that PNG is a subtype of pixel_map. Then we consider converters between PNG and GIF, to argue that no total converter from PNG to GIF respects pixel_map, but that some converters from GIF to PNG do.

The type specification for PNG images is given in Figure 8.7. Note we have a nontrivial application of the renaming map, ν, where $\nu(get\_corrected\_color) = get\_color$, and $\nu(set\_corrected\_color) = set\_color$. (Only some of the methods for PNG have corresponding supertype methods; the rest are left unmapped by ν.)

We are always allowed to set a PNG image's pixels to new colors, with no limit on the total number of colors in the image; this freedom follows from the trivial type invariant and $set\_corrected\_color$'s specification. In contrast, we are allowed to set a GIF image's pixels to new colors only when the total number of colors does not exceed 256. The nondeterminism in the pixel_map supertype (Figure 8.5) accommodates both subtype specifications. In particular, for PNG images, the color range grows as more colors are added, so that $set\_corrected\_color$ always successfully sets a color, if a coordinate is set within the PNG image's bounds. Moreover, although the pixel_map supertype does not have any concept of coordinate boundaries, its set_color method can fail for any reason, thus accommodating the behavior of PNG's $set\_corrected\_color$ in the case that the coordinates are out of bounds.

PNG images differ from pixel_map objects in two ways: (1) they are framed and (2) associated with each PNG object, p, is a "gamma" value, denoted $gamma(p)$, used in a *gamma correction* function, gc. The gamma correction function corrects for differences among monitors; some are dimmer than others and thus have different color balances. We abstract from the intricacies of gamma correction functions; for our purposes here, they take as arguments a color, an input gamma factor, an output gamma factor, and return a color. The constant, STDG, is the standard gamma value for normal monitors.

We define the following abstraction function to show that PNG is a subtype of pixel_map:

$$\alpha_P^{PM} : P \rightarrow PM$$

$$\forall i, j : \text{Integer} . \ \alpha_P^{PM}(p)[i,j] = \begin{cases} gc(p[i,j], gamma(p), STDG) \\ \quad if\, xmin(p) \le i \le xmax(p) \ \wedge \\ \quad\quad ymin(p) \le j \le ymax(p) \\ BLACK, \text{otherwise} \end{cases}$$

Consider a converter, $K : P \rightarrow G$, that maps values of PNG images to GIF values.

Claim 2 *There is no such converter that respects pixel_map, if the converter is defined for PNG images of more than 256 colors.*

Proof: A simple counting argument suffices. First we show that for a given PNG

PNG: **type**

uses PNGImage (PNG **for** P)
for all p: PNG

invariant *true*
constraint *true*

color *get_uncorrected_color* (i, j: int)
    requires $inframe(p, i, j)$
    ensures $result = p[i, j]$

gamma *get_gamma* ()
    ensures $result = gamma(p)$

int *get_xmin* ()
    ensures $result = xmin(p)$

... and similarly for *get_xmax*, *get_ymin*, and *get_ymax* ...

color *get_corrected_color* (i, j: int)
    ensures **if** $inframe(p, i, j)$
        then $result = gc(p[i, j], gamma(p), \mathrm{STDG})$
        else $result = \mathrm{BLACK}$

bool *set_corrected_color* (i, j: int; c: color)
    modifies p
    ensures $same\_bounds\_and\_gamma(p_{pre}, p_{post}) \wedge$
        if $inframe(p, i, j)$
        then $c = gc(p_{post}[i, j], gamma(p_{post}), \mathrm{STDG}) \wedge$
          $c \in colorrange(p_{post}) \wedge$
          $\forall k, l : Integer.(k \neq i \vee l \neq j) \Rightarrow p_{pre}[k, l] = p_{post}[k, l])) \wedge$
          $result = true$
        else $p_{pre} = p_{post} \wedge result = false$

end PNG

Fig. 8.7. A Larch Type Specification for PNG Images.

value, p, where $\mid colorrange(p) \mid = n$ and $n > 256$, its abstracted pixel_map value, $\alpha_P^{PM}(P)$, also has at least 256 colors. From the abstraction function, $\alpha_P^{PM}(p)[i, j] = gc(p[i, j], gamma(p), STDG)$, we know that every array element of p maps to some array element of $\alpha_P^{PM}(p)$. Furthermore, if two array elements in p have different colors, so do the corresponding cells in $\alpha_P^{PM}(p)$. To prove this, we show that if two gamma corrected colors are the same, then the original colors, c_1 and c_2, also have to be the same, that is,

Suppose
  1. $gc(c_1, gamma(p), STDG) = gc(c_2, gamma(p), STDG)$
By the "transitivity" and "reflexivity" properties of gamma correction functions (see the
  Appendix),
we know that
  2. $gc(gc(c_1, gamma(p), STDG), STDG, gamma(p)) = c_1$
By substitution in line 1, we get
  3. $gc(gc(c_2, gamma(p), STDG), STDG, gamma(p)) = c_1$
Yielding
  4. $c_2 = c_1$

So if there are $n > 256$ colors in p then there are also at least n colors in $\alpha_P^{PM}(p)$.

Next we show that the conversion of p to a valid GIF image value $K(p)$ would cause the GIF value to be observably different from the PNG value, when viewed through pixel_map's interface. $K(p)$ can have a maximum of 256 colors by the type invariant of GIF image. Furthermore, the abstraction mapping of $K(p)$ to a pixel_map value, $\alpha_G^{PM}(K(p))$, cannot add any colors to colorrange($K(p)$) (except for BLACK), since we see from the definition of α_G^{PM}, and hence by the definition of overlay, that every $c \in colorrange(\alpha_G^{PM}(K(p)))$ is either BLACK or one of the colors used in one of the frames of $K(p)$. Therefore, there exists some color c such that $c \in colorrange(\alpha_P^{PM}(p))$ and $c \notin colorrange(\alpha_G^{PM}(K(p)))$. It follows that there exists some i and j such that the result of calling pixel_map's observer, get_color with arguments i and j will differ between a call on the original PNG image from a call on the converted GIF image, that is, $\alpha_P^{PM}(p)[i,j] \neq \alpha_G^{PM}(K(p))[i,j]$ Therefore, the converter cannot respect pixel_map. □

It is possible, however, to have a converter from GIF images to PNG that respects the pixel_map type.

Claim 3 *There exist converters from GIF to PNG that respect pixel_map.*

Proof: By existence. Here is a converter from GIF to PNG:

$K : G \to P$
$K(g) = p$ *where*
  $xmin(p) = min(\{xmin(g[i]) \mid 0 \leq i < len(g)\}) \land$
  $xmax(p) = max(\{xmax(g[i]) \mid 0 \leq i < len(g)\}) \land$
  $ymin(p) = min(\{ymin(g[i]) \mid 0 \leq i < len(g)\}) \land$
  $ymax(p) = max(\{ymax(g[i]) \mid 0 \leq i < len(g)\}) \land$
  $gamma(p) = STDG \land$
  $\forall i, j : \text{Integer} .\ p[i,j] = overlay(g, i, j)$

Composing our converter with our abstraction function from PNG to pixel_map, for an original gif value, g, we get an abstracted converted pixel_map value, pm, such that

$$\forall i, j : \text{Integer} \ . \ pm[i,j] = \begin{cases} gc(overlay(g,i,j), STDG, STDG) \\ \quad if\, min(\{xmin(g[k]) \mid 0 \le k < len(g)\}) \le i \ \wedge \\ \quad i \le max(\{xmax(g[k]) \mid 0 \le k < len(g)\}) \ \wedge \\ \quad min(\{ymin(g[k]) \mid 0 \le k < len(g)\}) \le j \ \wedge \\ \quad j \le max(\{ymax(g[k]) \mid 0 \le k < len(g)\}) \\ BLACK, \textit{otherwise} \end{cases}$$

By the "reflexivity" property of gamma correction functions, we know that

$$gc(c, g, g) = c.$$

Furthermore, we know that from the definition of overlay that when i and j are beyond the bounds of any frames in a frameset, $overlay(g, i, j)$ is BLACK. In the definition above, whenever i or j are outside the respective minima or maxima, then (i, j) is outside any frame in the GIF. Therefore the definition above simplifies to

$\forall i, j : \text{Integer} \ . \ pm[i, j] = overlay(g, i, j)$

which is exactly the same abstraction function as is used to map the original GIF to a pixel map. The abstracted values are identical, so by Claim 1 (made at the end of Section 8.3.1), the conversion respects pixel_map. $\square$

Our assertion above may seem to go against our intuition, when we consider the further histories of the original GIF and the converted PNG. After all, the same sequence of mutations called at the pixel_map level can cause the histories of the original object and the converted object to diverge. Indeed, our type specifications for GIF and PNG mandate that the histories sometimes *must* diverge. Consider, for instance, an object o which at some state ρ has exactly 256 colors. Attempting to call *set_color* (within appropriate x and y bounds) with a 257th color *must* fail for the original GIF object, since it has a maximum of 256 colors. However, it *must* succeed for the converted PNG object, since *set_color* as defined on PNG images cannot fail if it is called within the x and y bounds of the image. From this point on, then, the histories of the original GIF image and the converted PNG image diverge.

For our conversion to respect pixel_map, however, it suffices that the GIF image and the converted PNG image, at the time of conversion, have identical *possible* futures from pixel_map's perspective. That is, we should not be able to tell, given only the mutations and requirements of pixel_map, that the object with the original value and the object with the converted value were different at the point of conversion. As long as this is true, programs expecting to operate on a pixel_map object will not encounter surprises if the object they operate on had been converted from a GIF to a PNG image.

Our pixel_map type has only one mutator, *set_color*. All we know about *set_color* is that any attempt to add a new color to a given pixel_map might succeed or might fail. Either outcome is possible from pixel_map's perspective, no matter how many

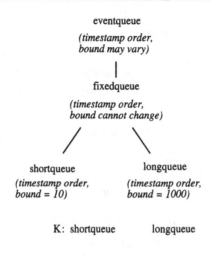

Fig. 8.8. A Queue Hierarchy.

colors are in a pixel map at a given time. So, from pixel_map's perspective, any sequence of pixel_map method calls on both an original GIF object and a converted PNG object will have the same possible future observed behaviors. Since the possible future histories of the PNG and GIF objects look the same from pixel_map's point of view, there will be no surprises when converting from GIF to PNG, if one assumes only the behavior specified in pixel_map.

8.4.2 Event Queues

The types in the previous example had invariants but no history constraints. In this section's example of an event queue type family (Figure 8.8), we look at a conversion between constrained types, and show which common supertypes the conversion respects, and which it does not.

At the root of the type hierarchy, we have an eventqueue type that models buffered event queues (Figure 8.9). We represent a value of an eventqueue object, q, as a pair, [*items, bound*], of a set of the buffered items and a bound. Events in the queue must be inserted in increasing timestamp order. The size of the queue buffer is bounded, but the bound is not directly readable or writable by the eventqueue type. New events (if they have appropriate timestamps) can be inserted into the queue unless the number of items already in the queue is equal to (or greater than) the bound. The eventqueue type also has the overall constraint that the event at the head of the queue at a state ρ_i has to have a timestamp less than or equal to the event at the head of the queue at any later state ρ_k. The constraint, however, does not require that its bound be fixed, so the bound can vary over time. (The specification subtly allows this possible mutation since the *insert* and *remove* methods each has

---

eventqueue = **type**

uses EventQueue (eventqueue **for** Q)
for all q: eventqueue

invariant $len(q_\rho.items) \leq q_\rho.bound$
constraint $timestamp(head(q_{\rho_i}.items)) \leq timestamp(head(q_{\rho_k}.items))$

bool *insert* (*e:* event)
      requires $timestamp(last(q_{pre}.items)) < timestamp(e)$
      modifies q
      ensures $len(q_{post}.items) \leq q_{post}.bound \wedge$
      if $len(q_{pre}.items) < q_{post}.bound$
            then $q_{post}.items = add(e, q_{pre}.items) \wedge result = true$
            else $q_{post}.items = q_{pre}.items \wedge result = false$

event *remove* ( )
      requires $q_{pre}.items \neq empty$
      modifies q
      ensures $q_{post}.items = tail(q_{pre}.items) \wedge result = head(q_{pre}.items) \wedge$
            $len(q_{post}.items) \leq q_{post}.bound$

int *size* ( )
      ensures $result = len(q_{pre}.items)$

end eventqueue

Fig. 8.9. A Type Specification for Event Queues.

---

a **modifies** clause; though no mention of changing the queue's bound is made in either of their postconditions, the presence of the **modifies** clause gives permission to implementors to change that part of the queue's value and simultaneously warns callers that they cannot rely on that part of the queue's value to remain the same. Even more subtly, the condition in the **if** ... **then** ... **else** clause for *insert* compares the length of the buffer of the queue's pre-state with the bound of the queue's *post*-state to account for the possibility of the bound changing as a side effect of calling *insert*.)

Let fixedqueue (Figure 8.10) be a subtype of eventqueue which adds the further constraint that the buffer bound cannot change. Again, there are no methods to read the bound directly. Two subtypes of fixedqueue, shortqueue and longqueue, further specify that the bound is fixed to be 10 and 1000 items, respectively (Figures 8.11 and 8.12). The **subtype** clause in a type specification includes an abstraction function, α, that relates subtype values to supertype values. Implicitly the clause requires that the subtype provides all methods of its supertype; any method not fixedqueue = **type**

uses EventQueue (fixedqueue **for** Q)
for all q: fixedqueue

invariant $len(q_\rho.items) \leq q_\rho.bound$
constraint $timestamp(head(q_{\rho_i}.items)) \leq timestamp(head(q_{\rho_k}.items)) \wedge$
$\qquad q_{\rho_i}.bound = q_{\rho_k}.bound$

bool *insert* (e: event)
$\qquad$ **requires** $timestamp(last(q_{pre}.items)) < timestamp(e)$
$\qquad$ **modifies** q
$\qquad$ **ensures** $q_{pre}.bound = q_{post}.bound \wedge$
$\qquad\qquad$ **if** $len(q_{pre}.items) < q_{post}.bound$
$\qquad\qquad$ **then** $q_{post}.items = add(e, q_{pre}.items) \wedge result = true$
$\qquad\qquad$ **else** $q_{post}.items = q_{pre}.items \wedge result = false$

event *remove* ( )
$\qquad$ **requires** $q_{pre}.items \neq empty$
$\qquad$ **modifies** q
$\qquad$ **ensures** $q_{post}.items = tail(q_{pre}.items) \wedge result = head(q_{pre}.items) \wedge$
$\qquad\qquad q_{post}.bound = q_{pre}.bound$

subtype of eventqueue
$\qquad \forall q : Q \ . \ \alpha(q) = q$

end fixedqueue

Fig. 8.10. A Type Specification for Fixed Queues.

---

renamed or redefined is "inherited" from its supertype as is. For example, short-queue's *insert* does not redefine fixedqueue's *insert*, but fixedqueue's does redefine eventqueue's.

Claim 4 *There is no conversion from shortqueue to longqueue, either partial or total, that respects fixedqueue.*

Proof: Consider a shortqueue object s in the domain of the conversion. By the definition of shortqueue, its bound must be 10. Suppose a conversion is made of s_{ρ_j}, yielding a longqueue value l_{ψ_j}. By the definition of the longqueue type, the bound of the converted object must be 1000. Now consider s_{ρ_i} prior to the conversion and the value l_{ψ_k} after the conversion. The constraint of fixedqueue is violated, since $s_{\rho_i}.bound \neq l_{\psi_k}.bound$, and fixedqueue's constraint prohibits the bound from changing between states. The **Constraint** *condition of the definition of respects does not hold. Hence, the conversion cannot respect fixedqueue.* $\square$

The histories of the converted object show the failure of the conversion to respect shortqueue = **type**

uses EventQueue (shortqueue **for** Q)
for all q: shortqueue

invariant $len(q_\rho.items) \leq q_\rho.bound \land q_\rho.bound = 10$
constraint $timestamp(head(q_{\rho_i}.items)) \leq timestamp(head(q_{\rho_k}.items))$

subtype of fixedqueue
$\qquad \forall q : Q . \alpha(q) = q$

end shortqueue

Fig. 8.11. A Type Specification for Short Queues.

longqueue = **type**

uses EventQueue (longqueue **for** Q)
for all q: longqueue

invariant $len(q_\rho.items) \leq q_\rho.bound \land q_\rho.bound = 1000$
constraint $timestamp(head(q_{\rho_i}.items)) \leq timestamp(head(q_{\rho_k}.items))$

subtype of fixedqueue
$\qquad \forall q : Q . \alpha(q) = q$

end longqueue

Fig. 8.12. A Type Specification for Long Queues.

fixedqueue. While it is possible to define a simple conversion from shortqueue to longqueue that contains exactly the same items, the conversion of its bound (from 10 to 1000) changes possible future behaviors of the longqueue object in ways not consistent with the fixedqueue constraints. Suppose, for instance, that we have a program that fills up a queue buffer to determine its size, and uses this information to allocate a fixed-size buffer of its own to store items pulled off the queue. At some later point, after more items have been added to the queue, the program empties the queue items into its own fixed-size buffer. If the queue bound has been increased by a conversion, the program may overflow its previously-allocated buffer, causing a crash or other errors.

To illustrate the incongruity above, we must track the behavior of the original object and the converted object over time, through the point of conversion. It is not enough simply to look at each state and to compare the original object's value and the converted object's value in that same state. In the queue example, the longqueue type is less constrained than the shortqueue type, and so some possible longqueue values are outside the range of any converter on shortqueue values. Once a conversion takes place, we need to reason about the object in terms of its longqueue values; moreover, it would be ill-defined in subsequent states to compare its longqueue value to any shortqueue value. However, we can allow such nonsurjective converters as long as the converted object's value does not violate constraints of the respected type.

For instance, it is possible to convert from shortqueue to longqueue in a way that respects the more general eventqueue type.

Claim 5 *There is a total conversion from shortqueue to longqueue that respects eventqueue.*

Proof: By existence. Here is such a converter:

$K : Q \to Q$
$K(q) = [q.items, 1000]$

To see whether this conversion respects eventqueue, we first check the method rules. The pre- and postconditions of the methods remove and size, and the precondition of the method insert, depend only on the items portion of the queue value, which is the same for both a shortqueue object s and a longqueue object l at the time of conversion. The insert method's postcondition depends in part on the post-state of bound, but since eventqueue allows bound to change on insert, eventqueue's specification permits either s or l's bound to change, and hence allows the operation to insert an item or not for either object. (While s and l will in fact behave differently based on the more constrained specifications of shortqueue and longqueue, the eventqueue specification itself cannot be used to tell that anything changed in the conversion.)

The only constraint of eventqueue is that the timestamp at the head of the queue not decrease over time. Let s_{ρ_i} be any value of s before the conversion, s_{ρ_j} be the value of s at the time of conversion, l_{ψ_j} be the value of l at the time of conversion, and l_{ψ_k} be any value of l after the conversion. Since shortqueue and longqueue are both subtypes of eventqueue, which includes the history constraint, we know that

   1. $timestamp(head(s_{\rho_i}.items)) \leq timestamp(head(s_{\rho_j}.items))$ *and*
   2. $timestamp(head(l_{\psi_j}.items)) \leq timestamp(head(l_{\psi_k}.items))$
Furthermore, by the definition of our conversion,
   3. $s_{\rho_j}.items = l_{\psi_j}.items$
so therefore
   4. $timestamp(head(s_{\rho_j}.items)) = timestamp(head(l_{\psi_j}.items))$
By transitivity, then,
   5. $timestamp(head(s_{\rho_i}.items)) \leq timestamp(head(l_{\psi_k}.items))$

Hence, the constraint rule is satisfied. Therefore, the conversion, K, as a whole respects eventqueue. □

Again, this result matches our expectations. The buffer-overflowing program mentioned earlier got into trouble only because the programmer assumed that the eventqueue's buffer bound would not change, and therefore allocated a fixed buffer for receiving events from the queue. Programmers that do not assume that the eventqueue's buffer bound is fixed should allow for arbitrarily many events to be emptied from the queue, and thus avoid the error of the previous program.

8.5 Related Work

There are notions of "respectful" conversions that are stronger or weaker than the one we present in this chapter; they may be more appropriate in certain situations.

In earlier work [WO99a], we gave a simpler model of respectful conversion for immutable types. Since the objects are immutable, there are no mutators or history properties to consider; hence, the predicates under the **Methods** condition are simpler and the **Constraint** condition is entirely unnecessary. We showed in that paper how the simpler model is useful for applications that retrieve and analyze data. When applied to mutable objects, however, the failure to consider history properties may produce behavior in the converted object that is inconsistent with the past behavior of the original object, as we saw in our queue example.

A longer version [WO99b] of this chapter contains informal descriptions of other real-world examples, including those used in the TOM context and those addressing the Y2K problem; it also contains a formal proof of the "no surprises" claim for pixel_map made at the very end of Section 8.4.1.

Applications that pass converted data back and forth between heterogeneous programs may require stronger guarantees on conversions. For example, the Mockingbird system [ACC97], defines a notion of *interconvertibility* where data conversions are fully invertible. With this policy, data converted to another format can always be converted back without loss of information. This concept corresponds in our model to a conversion between two representations of some type T, where the conversion respects type T. While interconvertibility makes it easy to exchange transformed data without risk of losing information, it is often too strong a constraint on conversions. Our model of respectful type conversions is more flexible. In respectful conversions, some information can be lost or changed in the conversion, provided that the information and behavior of the respected type is preserved.

8.6 Summary

In this chapter, we extended our earlier definition of a novel notion of *respectful type converters* to capture what behavior a conversion function preserves when transforming objects of one type to another; our extension deals with mutable types. We built on Liskov and Wing's notion of behavioral subtyping. Our notion of respectful type converters could probably be adapted for any other notion of subtyping (behavioral or not, dealing with mutable types or not).

Analyzing the types that a conversion respects allows developers to determine where programs will continue to behave normally after data is converted, and where they may behave unexpectedly or erroneously. Intuitively, if a conversion respects a type T, then after an object of type A is converted to an object of type B in a conversion that respects T, programs that operate on the objects using the interface and expectations of T will encounter no surprises. Programs that use more detailed interfaces or that rely on behavioral assumptions specified by A or B but not by T, however, may encounter problems. Reviewing the assumptions programs make about data and seeing what types conversions respect allow us to detect possible conflicts introduced by converted data, and to adjust programs appropriately.

Bibliography

[ACC97]   Auerbach, J. and Chu-Carroll, M. C. The Mockingbird System: A Compiler-based Approach to Maximally Interoperable Distributed Programming. Technical Report RC 20718, IBM, Yorktown Heights, NY, 1997.

[GG89]   Garland, S. and Guttag, J. An Overview of LP, the Larch Prover. In *Proceedings of the Third International Conference on Rewriting Techniques and Applications*, pages 137–151, Chapel Hill, NC, April 1989. Lecture Notes in Computer Science 355.

[HGJ+93]   Horning, J., Guttag, J. w. S. G., Jones, K., Modet, A., and Wing, J. *Larch: Languages and Tools for Formal Specification*. Springer-Verlag, New York, 1993.

[Jon98]   Jones, C. Bad Days for Software. *IEEE Spectrum*, 35(9):47–52, September 1998.

[Lis87]   Liskov, B. Data Abstraction and Hierarchy. In *OOPSLA '87: Addendum to the Proceedings*, 1987.

[LW94]   Liskov, B. and Wing, J. M. A Behavioral Notion of Subtyping. *ACM TOPLAS*, 16(6):1811–1841, November 1994.

[Ock98]   Ockerbloom, J. Mediating Among Diverse Data Formats. Technical Report CMU-CS-98-102, Carnegie Mellon Computer Science Department, Pittsburgh, PA, January 1998. Ph.D. Thesis.

[Win97]   Wing, J. Subtyping for Distributed Object Stores. In *Proceedings of the Second IFIP International Workshop on Formal Methods for Open Object-based Distributed Systems (FMOODS)*, pages 305–318, July 1997.

[WO99a]   Wing, J. M. and Ockerbloom, J. Respectful Type Converters. *IEEE Transactions on Software Engineering*, 1999. to appear.

[WO99b]   Wing, J. M. and Ockerbloom, J. Respectful Type Converters for Mutable Types. Technical Report CMU-CS-99-142, Carnegie Mellon Computer Science Department, June 1999.

[Zar96]   Zaremski, A. M. Signature and Specification Matching. Technical Report CS-CMU-96-103, CMU Computer Science Department, January 1996. Ph.D. Thesis.

Appendix: Larch Traits and Type Specifications

This appendix contains the following Larch specifications: Color trait for color literals, ColorSet trait for sets of colors, Frame trait, FrameSeq trait, GIFImage trait, Gammas trait, PNGImage trait, PixelMap trait, Event trait, event type, and EventQueue trait. Appendix A of the Larch Book [HGJ+93] contains traits for Boolean, Integer, FloatingPoint, Set, Deque, Array2, TotalOrder, and Queue, all of which we use below.

ColorLiterals: **trait**
    % A trait for N colors where BLACK = 0 and WHITE = 1 and N >> 256.
       Color **enumeration of** BLACK, WHITE, 2, ..., N-1
end ColorLiterals

ColorSet(Color, CS): **trait**
    includes ColorLiterals, Set (Color, CS)
end ColorSet

Frame(F): **trait**
    includes Array2 (Color, Integer, Integer, F), ColorSet (Color, CS)
    introduces
        $xmin, xmax, ymin, ymax : F \rightarrow$ Integer
        $colorrange : F \rightarrow CS$
        $inframe : F$, Integer, Integer $\rightarrow$ Boolean
    asserts for all $i, j :$ Integer, $f : F$
        $xmin(f) \leq xmax(f)$
        $ymin(f) \leq ymax(f)$
        $inframe(f, i, j) = (xmin(f) \leq i \leq xmax(f)) \wedge (ymin(f) \leq j \leq ymax(f))$
        $inframe(f, i, j) \Rightarrow f[i, j] \in colorrange(f)$
end Frame

FrameSeq(F, FS): **trait**
    includes Deque (Frame, FS)
    introduces
        overlay: FS, Integer, Integer $\rightarrow$ Color
        changepixel: FS, Integer, Integer, Color $\rightarrow$ FS
        colorrange: FS $\rightarrow$ CS
        __[__]: FS, Integer $\rightarrow$ F
    asserts for all $i, j, k, l:$ Integer, $c:$ Color, $f: F, fs:$ FS
        overlay(fs, i, j) = **if** $len(fs) = 0$ **then** BLACK **else**
            if   *inframe(last(fs), i, j)*
            then   *last(fs)[i, j]*
            else   *overlay(init(fs), i, j)*
        colorrange(empty) = {}
        $colorrange(fs \vdash f) = colorrange(fs) \cup colorrange(f)$
        $(fs \vdash f)[i] =$ **if** $i = len(fs \vdash f)$ **then** f **else** $fs[i]$
        $overlay(changepixel(fs, i, j, c), k, l) =$ **if** $i = k \wedge j = l$ **then** c **else** $overlay(fs, k, l)$
    exempting
        $\forall i :$ Integer $.$ $empty[i]$

$\forall i \leq 0 \; . \; fs[i]$

$\forall i \geq len(fs) \; . \; fs[i]$

end FrameSeq

GIFImage: **trait**
   includes FrameSeq (G **for** FS), ColorSet(Color, CS)
   asserts for all *g:* G
      BLACK $\in colorrange(g)$
end GIFImage

Gammas: **trait**
   includes FloatingPoint (Gamma **for** F)
   introduces
      $STDG: \rightarrow$ Gamma
      $gc :$ Color, Gamma, Gamma $\rightarrow$ Color
   asserts for all *c:* Color, *g, h, i:* Gamma
      $gc(c, g, g) = c$ "reflexivity"
      $gc(gc(c, g, h), h, i) = gc(c, g, i)$ "transitivity"
end Gammas

PNGImage: **trait**
   includes Frame (P **for** F), Gammas
   introduces
      $gamma:$ P $\rightarrow$ Gamma
      $same\_bounds\_and\_gamma:$ P, P $\rightarrow$ Boolean
   asserts for all *p, q:* P
      $same\_bounds\_and\_gamma(p, q) = (gamma(p) = gamma(q) \land$
         $xmin(p) = xmin(q) \land xmax(p) = xmax(q) \land ymin(p) = ymin(q) \land ymax(p) =$
  $ymax(q))$
 end PNGImage

PixelMap: **trait**
   includes Array2 (Color, Integer, Integer, PM), ColorSet (Color, CS)
   introduces
      $colorrange:$ PM $\rightarrow$ CS
   asserts for all *i, j:* Integer, *pm:* PM
      BLACK $\in colorrange(pm)$
      $pm[i, j] \in colorrange(pm)$
end PixelMap

Event: **trait**
   includes TotalOrder (Time **for** T)
   introduces
      $timestamp:$ Ev $\rightarrow$ Time

event: **type**
   uses Event (event **for** Ev)
end event

EventQueue: **trait**
   includes Queue (Ev **for** E), Event
      Q **tuple of** items: C, bound: Integer

Part Three
Formal Methods and Semantics

9

A Formal Model for Componentware

Klaus Bergner, Andreas Rausch, Marc Sihling, Alexander Vilbig, and Manfred Broy

Institut für Informatik, FORSOFT A1
Technische Universität München
80290 Munich, Germany
http://www4.informatik.tu-muenchen.de

Abstract

We present a formal model for component systems which provides precise mathematical definitions for concepts like component, interface, type and instance, as well as dynamic behavior and changes of system structure over time. Based on these concepts, we define the semantics of intuitive, commonly used graphical description techniques as an interpretation in terms of the presented system model. Several exemplary description techniques illustrate the feasibility of our approach.

9.1 Introduction

The essence of componentware is to build well-structured systems out of independently understandable and reusable building blocks. However, with the rise of pragmatic technologies like ActiveX [Mic98], JavaBeans [Jav99b], and Enterprise JavaBeans [Jav99a] as well as the growing interest in reuse and reengineering of legacy components it is evident that a solid, unified understanding and scientific models of componentware are still missing. Even central concepts like "component" or "interface" are defined and used in very different ways by different authors. Although existing Architecture Definition Languages, like Rapide [LKA+95], UniCon [SDK+95], or Wright [AG97] introduce these concepts on a more formal basis, they do not adequately consider all relevant behavior-related aspects of a component system and are sometimes difficult to apply in practice [NR99].

We believe that a clearly defined conceptual model designed for componentware development is essential, especially as a foundation for an overall componentware methodology comprising the integration of suitable graphical description techniques, tool support, and development process models [BRSV98]. Only then it is possible to answer typical questions like "What does this particular component do?", "Will these interfaces match?", and "Are these different system descriptions equivalent?" which are commonly posed during system development.

A fruitful discussion about such issues requires a precisely defined language as well as a comprehensive theory to reason about the behavior of a component system and its constituents. While a thorough treatment of the latter requirement is beyond the scope of this paper, we provide rigorous mathematical definitions for all essential concepts of componentware, and illustrate the translation of intuitive description techniques into this system model. Based on this common metamodel, many practical applications are conceivable, like the development of consistency checkers, transformation tools, and code generators. Moreover, it leads to a common understanding of the involved concepts and terminology.

9.2 Overview

Initially, the design and development of a concise formal system model for componentware has to consider the following main requirements:

Adequacy: On the one hand, the proposed system model should be able to represent the central concepts of existing, pragmatic componentware technologies like ActiveX or JavaBeans. It has to provide common abstractions for these concepts which are easily recognizable for the users of componentware technologies. On the other hand, it should be possible to map such a system model to existing formal theories of software systems. Thereby, a large part of proven, theoretical concepts may be applied or reused, providing a firm ground for the proposed system model.

Expressiveness: Like all systems, component-oriented systems may be characterized by structure and behavior, that is, the kind and organization of their constituents as well as the exchange of information and the resulting change of state and structure over time. The proposed system model should be able to express both aspects adequately, without imposing unnecessary or unrealistic restrictions on represented component systems.

Clarity: Given the previous requirements, the proposed system model should rely on a minimal number of basic concepts with clearly defined relations between them. This facilitates understanding, communication, and application of the model.

Obviously, these requirements are partly conflicting, thereby imposing a certain trade-off in the design of a proposed system model. For example, a faithful representation of a pragmatic componentware technology could require the introduction of a large number of detailed conceptual entities which in turn impedes the mapping to existing formal theories as well as the clarity of the model.

Regarding such trade-offs, we decided to restrict the model to a small number of basic concepts which are sufficiently abstract to incorporate most of the current technical componentware approaches. The presented model builds on related work on description techniques [Gro99, BHH+97] as well as existing models of distributed systems [Bro95, KRB96] based on the FOCUS methodology [BDD+92]. Its main concepts to model component-oriented systems are instances, types, and descriptions:

Instances represent the individual operational units of a component system that determine its overall behavior. A system consists of a family of component instances. Each of them has interface instances and is connected to other component instances by connections between these interface instances.

Types represent subsets of interface resp. component instances with similar properties. Each instance is associated to exactly one type.

Descriptions characterize types and thus all instances associated with them. They consider syntactical as well as behavior-related properties, like interface and component signature, expected input/output communication, and collaboration between different components.

Regarding the adequacy of such a model, it is important to note that all of these concepts are present in current technical and practical approaches to componentware. A typical JavaBeans component package [Jav99b], for example, may contain serialized component instances of different types (that is, Java classes) accompanied by Java byte code that defines their behavior. It also includes machine-readable signature descriptions of the contained component types, as well as arbitrary additional files with further information. Although the package format does not yet require standardized, machine-readable descriptions of the structural and behavioral properties of contained component types, such descriptions would be very valuable, both for human developers as well as for supporting development tools.

With respect to behavior, a component-oriented system may be further characterized by business-oriented and technical aspects. In order to fulfil a dedicated business functionality, the components of a system usually rely on a standardized technical infrastructure consisting, for example, of object request brokers [COR], Enterprise JavaBeans containers [Jav99a], databases, message queuing middleware, and so on. Most of the technical aspects as well as the details of the underlying technical protocols and services are not dealt with explicitly by application programmers. In the proposed model, the separation of business-oriented and technical characteristics is achieved by modeling the properties of the respective technical infrastructure within the behavior of interfaces, whereas abstract, business-oriented service protocols and the corresponding structural changes are associated with component behavior. This approach is similar to the concept of connectors in architecture description languages [AG97], which try to capture technical mechanisms and properties of connections.

The presentation of the proposed system model is structured as follows: Section 9.3 first introduces the basic concepts on the level of instances, and defines behavior with respect to communication and structure. Section 9.4 then considers types and descriptions. We provide a general formalization of these concepts and outline their interpretation for a number of exemplary descriptions. A brief section with a conclusion and an outlook about necessary future work is given at the end of the paper.

9.3 Instances

In this section, we introduce the instance part of the formal system model. An instance may be defined as an individual operational unit that exists in a running system. We distinguish between three different kinds of instances, namely component, interface, and connection instances. In the following subsections, we define and characterize these basic concepts and the relations between them.

9.3.1 Basic Concepts

Components are the basic building blocks of a component system at runtime. Each component instance possesses a set of interface instances which may be connected to other interface instances via connections. As described in Section 9.3.3, messages generated by a component flow via its interfaces and the corresponding connections to other interfaces and their components.

Figure 9.1 illustrates a possible snapshot of a component system with five components ($c1$ to $c5$) shown as rectangles, their interfaces ($i1$ to $i9$) shown as circles, and the connections between the interfaces shown as lines between them. This kind of diagram resembles the well-known object instance diagrams in UML [Gro99].

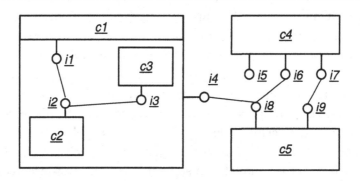

Fig. 9.1. Component Instance Diagram.

In order to uniquely address the elements of a component system, we introduce the disjoint, infinite sets *Interface*, *Component*, and *Connection*. Interfaces are associated with components via the total but not necessarily injective function *assigned*

$$assigned \quad : \quad Interface \to Component$$

This function is total as an interface cannot exist independently. It is associated with exactly one component. Note that *assigned* is generally not injective, as a component may have multiple interfaces.

A connection relates exactly two distinct interfaces. The total function *connIfs* determines which interfaces are related by a connection:

$$connIfs \ : \ Connection \rightarrow \{\{i, j\} \mid i, j \in Interface \land i \neq j\}$$

For a given interface, several different connections may exist. Thus, the presented model supports one-to-many connections between interfaces, as shown in Figure 9.1. Note that the elements of *Connection* represent symmetric connections between interfaces, as the set $\{i, j\}$ cannot be distinguished from the set $\{j, i\}$. Furthermore, the previous definition of *connIfs* excludes loop connections for a single interface. We also forbid multiple connections between the same two interfaces (cf. next section).

The remaining basic concept is component containment as illustrated by Figure 9.1: the components $c2$ and $c3$ are contained in component $c1$. This concept is modeled by the partial function *parent*

$$parent \ : \ Component \rightarrow Component$$

which returns for each component the parent component it is contained in. The function *parent* is partial since the top-level components of the system do not have a parent component. We require *parent* to be an acyclic function, as it is not possible for a component to contain itself or to be contained in one of its subcomponents. We also assume that there are no infinite chains of subcomponents in order to ensure that every subcomponent has a well-defined root component.

With regard to proper encapsulation of components, we exclude connections that cross a component boundary. Components may only be connected via their interfaces if one component is the parent of the other component or if they both have the same parent component (or no parent component at all). Connections from one interface of a component to another interface of the same component are not excluded. Formally, we obtain the following restriction on the set *Connection*:

$$\forall cn \in Connection, c, d \in Component, i, j \in Interface :$$
$$connIfs(cn) = \{i, j\} \land assigned(i) = c \land assigned(j) = d \Rightarrow$$
$$parent(c) = d \lor parent(d) = c \lor parent(c) = parent(d)$$

Note that top-level components without a parent component are also covered by this equation, as we use strong equality on components. In the example of Figure 9.1, a direct connection between the interfaces $i3$ and $i8$ would be invalid, as it violates the encapsulation boundary of component $c1$.

9.3.2 Time and System Configuration Histories

Like related formal models [KRB96], we work with discrete time and regard time as an infinite chain of time intervals of equal length. We use $\mathbb{N}^+$ as an abstract time axis, and denote it by T for clarity. Furthermore, we assume a time synchronous model because of the resulting simplicity and generality. This means that there is a global time scale that is valid for all parts of the modeled system.

We use *timed streams*, that is, finite or infinite sequences of elements from a given domain, to represent histories of conceptual entities that change over time. A *timed stream* (more precisely, a stream with discrete time) of elements from the set X is an element of the type $X^T =_{def} T \rightarrow X$. Thus, a timed stream maps each time interval to an element of X. The notation x_t is used to denote the element of the valuation $x \in X^T$ at time $t \in T$. By $x \downarrow t$ we denote the stream containing only the elements of the first t time intervals. Operators on streams induce operators on sets of streams by element-wise application.

Streams may be used to model the creation and deletion of instances in a system. Within a given time interval t, only finite subsets of the sets of all possible component, interface, and connection instances may exist in the system. Following our notational conventions, $interface \in \wp(Interface)^T$, $component \in \wp(Component)^T$, and $connection \in \wp(Connection)^T$ denote the changing subsets of instances that exist over time.

As already mentioned in the previous section, we exclude multiple connections between two interfaces in order to keep the resulting connection structure as simple as possible. Formally, this requires $connIfs|_{connection_t}$ to be injective for every subset $connection_t$. Furthermore, we require that a connection may only exist if both of its connected interfaces exist, as expressed by the following condition:

$$\forall t \in T : \forall cn \in connection_t : connIfs(cn) = \{i, j\} \Rightarrow i, j \in interface_t$$

Once a component, interface, or connection instance is removed from the system, it cannot be reactivated later. For a given interface i, this is stated by the condition:

$$i \in interface_t \wedge i \notin interface_{t+1} \Rightarrow (\forall n \in \mathbb{N}^+ : i \notin interface_{t+n})$$

Analogous conditions are required for components and connections. Obviously, the removal of a component, interface, or connection does not prohibit the creation of new components, interfaces, or connections with the same properties at a later time.

As expected for the containment relation, we require that once a parent component does not exist anymore, all its interfaces and subcomponents are removed from the system as well:

$$\forall c \in Component, t \in T : c \notin component_t \Rightarrow$$
$$(\forall x \in Component : parent(x) = c \Rightarrow x \notin component_t) \wedge$$
$$(\forall y \in Interface : assigned(y) = c \Rightarrow y \notin interface_t)$$

The basic concepts introduced above may now be used to describe the changing configuration space of a component system over time. Let $Conf^T$ denote the type of all system configuration histories. A given system configuration history $conf \in Conf^T$ consists of a timed stream of tuples

$$conf_t =_{def} (interface_t, component_t, connection_t)$$

which captures the changing sets of instances at different times during system execution.

Note that the functions *assigned* and *parent* do not depend on time and are therefore not part of the system configuration history. Thus, the model essentially only allows to consider the activation and deactivation of interfaces, components, and connections—it cannot handle mobile components which migrate to another parent component, for example. A more detailed formal model for mobile components may be found in [BGR+99].

9.3.3 Interface and Component Behavior

Components possess a behavior with respect to communication and structural changes: a component may send and receive messages via its interfaces, and it may change the connection structure of the system by creating or deleting interfaces, components, and connections. In the context of the presented model, interfaces are active entities with an associated behavior, too. In contrast to components, however, they may not change the connection structure of the system.

9.3.3.1 Interface Behavior

Based on the current FOCUS system model [BDD+92], sequences of messages represent the fundamental units of communication. Within each time interval components resp. interfaces receive message sequences arriving at their interfaces resp. connections, and send message sequences to their respective environment. In order to model message-based communication, we denote the set of all possible messages with M, and the set of arbitrary finite message streams with M^*. By $\langle\rangle$, $\langle a\rangle$ and $\langle a, b\rangle$ we denote the empty sequence, the one-element sequence containing only a, and the two-element sequence containing a and b, respectively. The notation $x\hat{\ }y$ is used to denote the concatenation of the two sequences x and y.

An interface merges multiple incoming-message sequences from its connections to a single message sequence for its assigned component. Likewise, it distributes the outgoing-message sequence from its assigned component to a number of outgoing-message sequences. A typical example is a *CORBAMethodServer* interface which serves a number of connected clients, buffering their method call requests so that the assigned component can handle them sequentially.

Figure 9.2 illustrates the behavior of the interface *i2*. It receives incoming-message sequences from the connections *cn2* and *cn3*, and creates a single message sequence for the component *c1* (and vice versa for the outgoing-messages).

Behavior Relation: Generally, the interface behavior of a system run may be represented by a pair relating its input history to its output history. We use the types *IfIn* resp. *IfOut* to denote an evaluation of the incoming- resp. outgoing-message sequences.

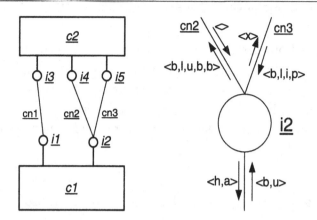

Fig. 9.2. Interface Behavior: Mapping Incoming to Outgoing Messages.

An interface receives messages from the component it is assigned to as well as from its attached connections, and sends messages in the opposite direction. Formally, the sequences of exchanged messages may be described by two relations

$$IfIn \quad =_{def} \quad M^* \times (Connection \to M^*)$$
$$IfOut \quad =_{def} \quad (Connection \to M^*) \times M^*$$

Given an input evaluation $(x, y) \in IfIn$ of interface i, x represents the stream of messages flowing from the component $assigned(i)$ to i, and y represents the multiple input streams for all the connections that connect to i. Note that the used connection evaluation functions are partial, as the behavior of a given interface generally depends only on inputs resp. outputs of a small subset from the set of all connections.

As an example, consider the input- and output-message sequences for interface $i2$ in Figure 9.2: During the given time interval, $i2$ receives the sequence $\langle h, a \rangle$ from its assigned component and sends the sequence $\langle b, u \rangle$ to it. At the same time, it receives the empty sequence $\langle \rangle$ and the sequence $\langle b, l, i, p \rangle$ from its connections $cn2$ resp. $cn3$, and sends the sequences $\langle b, l, u, b, b \rangle$ and $\langle x \rangle$ to them.

Complete input resp. output histories over time have the type $IfIn^T$ resp. $IfOut^T$. Accordingly, the behavior for all interfaces is provided by the function $ifBeh$

$$ifBeh \quad : \quad Interface \to \wp(IfIn^T \times IfOut^T)$$

which relates input histories to the corresponding output histories.

The behavior of an interface only depends on input streams from its attached connections which have to exist at the considered time. For instance, the behavior of interface $i2$ in Figure 9.2 does not depend on the streams sent via the connection $cn1$. Likewise, we have to ensure that an interface only sends messages on attached and existing connections. The following condition is used to express these restrictions on interface behavior:

$$ifBeh(i) \subseteq \{(ifIn, ifOut) \mid \forall t \in T :$$
$$ifIn_t \in (M^* \times (\{cn \in connection_t \mid i \in connIfs(cn)\} \to M^*)) \wedge$$
$$ifOut_t \in ((\{cn \in connection_t \mid i \in connIfs(cn)\} \to M^*) \times M^*)\}$$

Note that the previous definition of interface behavior relies on the evaluation of connections and does not directly relate input and output of connected interfaces. This would impose an unnecessary restriction on the expected behavior of connections. Within the presented model, it is possible for connections to drop or even invent arbitrary messages. Of course, the communication behavior has to be specified in more detail to model particular technical infrastructures.

Causality: In order to be realizable, we require interface behaviors to be *causal* (also called *time-guarded*). Intuitively, this property means that the output of an interface at a given point in time does not depend on input that arrives at the same time or later in the future. This is stated by the following condition for all time intervals t:

$$ifIn_a \downarrow t = ifIn_b \downarrow t \Rightarrow ifOutSet_a \downarrow t+1 = ifOutSet_b \downarrow t+1$$

where $ifIn_a$ and $ifIn_b$ denote two input histories in the behavior of an interface, and $ifOutSet_a$ and $ifOutSet_b$ denote the corresponding sets of related output histories (cf. [BDD+92] for a more detailed discussion of causality).

9.3.3.2 Component Behavior

A component receives a set of message streams from its assigned interfaces, and, depending also on the configuration history of the system, produces output message streams for its interfaces. Additionally, it may also change the connection structure of the system. This enables components to interact with other components in a flexible way to realize advanced functionality.

Figure 9.3 visualizes an example of an execution step of the component $c2$, including its incoming resp. outgoing message sequences and the resulting changes in the system configuration. The execution step is triggered by the current system configuration and the incoming-message sequences $\langle a \rangle$ via the interface $i4$ and $\langle \rangle$ via the interface $i5$. The execution results in changes to the system configuration—deletion of interface $i4$ with its attached connection to $i2$, and creation of component $c4$ together with its interface $i6$ and the corresponding connection to interface $i5$—and the outgoing message sequence $\langle o, x \rangle$ on interface $i5$.

Behavior Relation: Similar to interfaces, we describe the sets of incoming and outgoing message sequences of a component by two evaluation functions $CompIn$, $CompOut =_{def} Interface \to M^*$. Note that these evaluation functions are partial, in general, as the behavior of a component usually depends only on a small subset

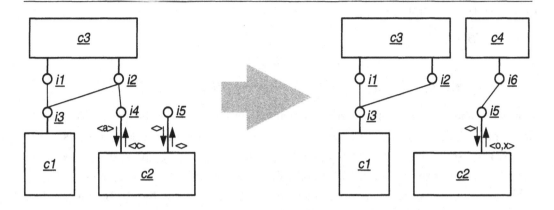

Fig. 9.3. Component Behavior.

of the set of all interfaces. Analogous to interface histories, complete component input resp. output histories over time have the type $CompIn^T$ resp. $CompOut^T$. In contrast to interface behavior, however, the behavior of a component also depends on the history of the system configuration $Conf^T$. Consequently, the behavior for all components is provided by the function

$$compBeh \quad : \quad Component \to \wp(CompIn^T \times CompOut^T \times Conf^T)$$

which assigns combinations of input, output, and configuration histories to each component of the system. Note that all components share the same configuration history.

A plausible restriction requires that only existing and assigned interfaces are relevant for component behavior at time t:

$$compBeh(c) \subseteq \{(compIn, compOut, conf) \mid \forall t \in T :$$
$$compIn_t, compOut_t \in (\{i \in interface_t \mid assigned(i) = c\} \to M^*)$$

Note that the required causality of component behavior may be stated by a condition analogous to the previously defined condition for interfaces (cf. Section 9.3.3.1). In the following paragraph, we state more restrictions on the behavior of components with respect to their composition.

Environments and Compositionality: So far, the presented model is highly noncompositional, as components may change the connection structure of arbitrary other components located anywhere in the system. Obviously, additional restrictions on component behavior with respect to structural changes are necessary to ensure the principle of encapsulation.

We first define the *immediate environment* of a component with respect to its components or more precisely connections by the functions

$$imCompEnv \; : \; Component \to \wp(Component)$$
$$imConnEnv \; : \; Component \to \wp(Connection)$$

The immediate environment consists of the component itself, its parent component, its subcomponents, as well as all brother and sister components and the connections between them:

$$\forall c, ec \in Component : ec \in imCompEnv(c) \Leftrightarrow$$
$$ec = c \vee parent(ec) = c \vee parent(c) = ec \vee parent(ec) = parent(c)$$
$$\forall c \in Component, en \in Connection : en \in imConnEnv(c) \Leftrightarrow$$
$$\forall i \in connIfs(en) : assigned(i) \in imCompEnv(en)$$

Figure 9.4 visualizes the immediate component environment of component $c1$: It consists of $c1$ itself, its child components $c2$ and $c4$, its brother component $c6$, and its sister component $c8$. If there existed a parent component of component $c1$, it would also be contained in the immediate environment.

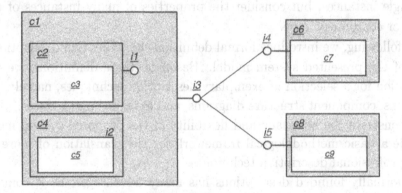

Fig. 9.4. Immediate Environment of Component $c1$.

This definition allows to restrict the structural behavior of a component to the creation resp. deletion of its assigned interfaces and the creation resp. deletion of components and connections in its immediate environment:

$$compBeh(c) \subseteq \{(compIn, compOut, conf) \mid \forall t \in T : conf_t \in$$
$$(\{i \mid i \in interface_t \wedge assigned(i) = c\} \times imCompEnv(c) \times$$
$$imConnEnv(c))\}$$

Note that creation and deletion of component instances, for example, does not mean that new elements are added to the set *Component*, but that $component_{t+1}$ contains a component not contained in $component_t$.

The previous restriction results in a compositional model of the structural changes inside a component, as they may only be affected by the component itself or by its immediate subcomponents. However, it is generally not possible to derive the overall behavior of a parent component from the individual behaviors of its subcomponents, because the parent component may react on them according to its own behavior. In current technical approaches, this additional overall component behavior is known as the "glue code" of the parent component.

9.4 Types and Descriptions

The basic concepts and their relations as covered in the previous sections provide mathematical definitions for the constituents of a component system at runtime. In order to be useful for practical development, however, such a formal model is not sufficient, as it requires experience in mathematical techniques, which most likely application developers and end users do not have. Therefore, additional concepts are needed to describe a component system in a more intuitive and illustrative way.

As already mentioned in Section 9.2, such descriptions usually not only characterize single instances, but consider the properties of many instances of the same interface or component type.

In the following, we introduce formal definitions for types and descriptions in the context of the presented system model. Based on these definitions, we outline a formalization for a selection of exemplary description techniques, namely signature descriptions, component structure diagrams, and extended event traces. Our intent is to demonstrate the adequacy and flexibility of the proposed system model, and to provide a basic methodological framework for the translation of more comprehensive, professional description techniques.

Using formally founded descriptions has many advantages, as it combines the rigour of formal methods with the intuitiveness of textual and graphical techniques that are widely used in practice. While end users can be protected from the intricacies of mathematical formulae, developers of description techniques and methodologists have the possibility to define consistency conditions and development steps in a precise and unambiguous way based on the formal foundation of the system model.

Ideally, the properties defined by descriptions are fulfilled for all described instances of the system. In practice, however, this goal is very difficult to reach, as it requires all descriptions to be consistent with each other as well as with the system's implementation. Currently, only very few descriptions may be checked or enforced statically—in general, this requires formally founded description techniques with adapted refinement and proof calculi that allow the verification or generation of code. In practice, extensive testing is usually performed instead. Such tests may be regarded as the dynamic validation of special test case descriptions.

9.4.1 Basic Concepts

In order to cover all kinds of descriptions in an abstract way, we introduce the infinite set *Description*. Each element of *Description* is represented by a syntactical notation which may be graphical, textual, or a combination thereof. Additionally, there exists an interpretation which translates the notation into terms of the formal system model, that is, a representation of the description's semantics. It precisely states the required properties of the described part of the system. Accordingly, we associate with each description a corresponding predicate which determines the fulfillment of these properties.

As mentioned previously, sets of similar interface and component instances are usually grouped together by *types*. Formally, we define the sets *ComponentType* and *InterfaceType* to be the infinite sets of component resp. interface types. We introduce two total functions *typeOf* which assign a unique type to each interface resp. component instance of the system.

$$typeOf \;\; : \;\; Component \to ComponentType$$

$$typeOf \;\; : \;\; Interface \to InterfaceType$$

Note that this simple formalization excludes instances with multiple types, as provided by certain technical componentware approaches that offer subtyping. Note furthermore, that *typeOf* does not depend on time; thus, it is not possible for an instance to change its determined type at runtime.

As explained in Section 9.2, descriptions may be explicitly assigned to certain types in order to state the desired restrictions on their instances. The assignment of a set of descriptions to a certain type is given by the following two functions:

$$descOf \;\; : \;\; ComponentType \to \wp(Description)$$

$$descOf \;\; : \;\; InterfaceType \to \wp(Description)$$

Figure 9.5 illustrates the resulting many-to-many relationship between instances, types, and descriptions.

Most descriptions are assigned to a single type. Signatures are a good example—as illustrated in Section 9.4.2, they define the set of admissible messages for the behavior of instances of a given, single type. Other descriptions, like extended event traces, consider the interaction of instances of multiple types. Consequently, they are assigned to all these types (cf. Section 9.4.5).

Note that a description may refer to a certain type without being explicitly assigned to it. An example are, again, signature descriptions—although they are assigned to exactly one type, they usually mention a variety of other types to characterize parameter and result values.

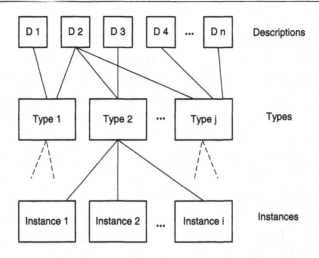

Fig. 9.5. Relation between Instances, Types and Descriptions.

9.4.2 Signature Descriptions

Signatures are a description technique widely used in software engineering. They are present in all current technical componentware approaches. Generally, signatures characterize the set of messages exchangeable at an interface. As such, they are fundamental for programmers as well as for composition tools. Most dynamic description techniques rely on the message sets defined within signatures, and many programming languages offer static type checking based on purely syntactical properties of the considered program. Good examples for signature descriptions are CORBA IDL files [COR, OH98] and Java interfaces [Fla96].

In the following, we demonstrate how interface signatures may be formalized based on the proposed formal system model. The presentation is structured in two parts: the first paragraph provides the translation of the example signature `Counter` into the corresponding predicate. The second paragraph generalizes the example, yielding a general predicate for arbitrary interface signatures.

Exemplary Translation: The following IDL fragment

```
interface Counter {
    long getSum();
    void setSum(long x);
    long increment();
};
```

introduces the IDL interface type `Counter` with its three methods `getSum`, `setSum`, and `increment`. We model this IDL fragment as a description *CounterIDL*, which is an element of the set *Description*. As the description characterizes all instances of the interface type *Counter*, it is explicitly assigned to it by stating

$$CounterIDL \in descOf(Counter)$$

For this example, we assume that method calls are translated to message sequences according to a simple scheme: A call of a method with a certain number of parameters is translated to a message sequence that starts with a method identifier and ends with the list of the actual parameters. The return value is translated to a message sequence of length one.

At a high level of abstraction, the given IDL method declarations in **Counter** restrict the possible input and output messages of the interface instances of type *Counter*, as given by the following two sets:

$$CounterInMsg = \{increment, getSum, setSum\} \cup \mathbb{N}$$
$$CounterOutMsg = \mathbb{N}$$

CounterIDL specifies that interface instances i of type *Counter* obey the given signature. Formally, this may be expressed as follows:

$$CounterIDL \in descOf(typeOf(i)) \Rightarrow \forall(ifIn, ifOut) \in ifBeh(i), t \in T :$$
$$ifIn_t \in (CounterOutMsg^* \times (Connection \rightarrow CounterInMsg^*)) \wedge$$
$$ifOut_t \in ((Connection \rightarrow CounterOutMsg^*) \times CounterInMsg^*)$$

Note that, in order to keep the example simple, this formalization neglects information about the grouping of method identifiers with their corresponding parameters and return values.

General Translation: In order to generalize the previous example for arbitrary IDL files, we first need to model the set of all IDL descriptions as $IDLText \subseteq Description$. An abstract mathematical representation of the information represented by an *IDLText* description is given by two functions $inMsg, outMsg : IDLText \rightarrow \wp(M)$. Interface instances which obey an *IDLText* description may thus be characterized by the predicate

$$fulfillsIDLText : IDLText \rightarrow (Interface \rightarrow \mathbb{B})$$

with the following definition

$$fulfillsIDLText(d)(i) \Leftrightarrow$$
$$d \in descOf(typeOf(i)) \Rightarrow \forall(ifIn, ifOut) \in ifBeh(i), t \in T :$$
$$ifIn_t \in (outMsg(d)^* \times (Connection \rightarrow inMsg(d)^*)) \wedge$$
$$ifOut_t \in ((Connection \rightarrow outMsg(d)^*) \times inMsg(d)^*)$$

Based on interface signatures, it is also possible to define component signatures. Following the relationship between interfaces and components as described in previous sections, a component signature is defined by the types of its assigned interfaces.

9.4.3 Component Structure Descriptions

As implied by the name, component structure descriptions are intended to describe the dynamic structural behavior of a component system. Due to the inherent problems associated with the presentation of large, dynamic graph structures, most of the current structural techniques are restricted to static configurations or system snapshots. The presented exemplary description technique is no exception: *Component Structure Diagrams* define the required static internal structure for components of a given type as shown in the example of Figure 9.6.

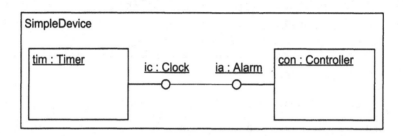

Fig. 9.6. Exemplary Component Structure Diagram.

This diagram visualizes the required internal white-box structure of component instances of type *SimpleDevice*. Internally, each component instance consists of two other components, *tim* of type *Timer* and *con* of type *Controller*, which are connected via a pair of interfaces. This diagram may be formalized as a description *SimpleDeviceCSD* ∈ *Description*. Although it mentions three component types (*SimpleDevice*, *Timer*, and *Controller*) and two interface types (*Clock* and *Alarm*), it is exclusively assigned to the component type *SimpleDevice* by stating

$$SimpleDeviceCSD \in descOf(SimpleDevice)$$

The translation of this description to a predicate on the system model results in the following formula:

$SimpleDeviceCSD \in descOf(typeOf(c)) \Rightarrow$

$\quad \exists tim, con \in Component, ic, ia \in Interface, cn \in Connection:$

$\quad typeOf(tim) = Timer \wedge parent(tim) = c \wedge$

$\quad typeOf(con) = Controller \wedge parent(con) = c \wedge$

$\quad typeOf(ic) = Clock \wedge assigned(ic) = tim \wedge$

$\quad typeOf(ia) = Alarm \wedge assigned(ia) = con \wedge$

$\quad connIfs(cn) = \{ia, ic\} \wedge$

$\quad (\forall t \in T : c \in component_t \Rightarrow$

$\quad\quad tim, con \in component_t \wedge ic, ia \in interface_t \wedge cn \in connection_t)$

Note that this predicate only states the required internal configuration, and does not exclude the presence of additional subcomponents. This results in underspecification and thus allows us to refine the diagram by adding further components, interfaces, and connections without violating the specification.

We refrain from generalizing this example to a general predicate for all component structure diagrams. Although this could be done following the presented approach, a complete formal treatment is beyond the scope of this paper.

9.4.4 Input/Output Behavior Descriptions

In this section, we consider a simple *state transition diagram* as an example for a component input/output behavior description technique. An exemplary component state transition diagram is shown in Figure 9.7.

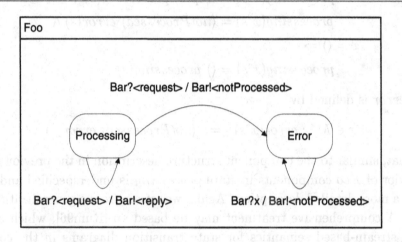

Fig. 9.7. Exemplary Component State Transition Diagram.

This diagram visualizes the input/output behavior of components of type *Foo* with respect to the communication of assigned interface instances of type *Bar*. The semantics of this diagram is as follows: whenever a *Foo* instance receives the message sequence ⟨*request*⟩ via a *Bar* interface, it either reacts by sending the message sequence ⟨*reply*⟩ on the same interface at the following time step, or it decides to stop message processing and continues sending ⟨*notProcessed*⟩ message sequences from there on.

This diagram may be formalized as a description $FooSTD \in Description$, which is explicitly assigned to the component type *Foo* by

$$FooSTD \in descOf(Foo)$$

The translation of this description to a system model predicate is expressed as

$$FooSTD \in descOf(typeOf(c)) \Leftrightarrow$$
$$\forall(compIn, compOut, conf) \in compBeh(c), \forall i \in Interface :$$
$$typeOf(i) = Bar \land typeOf(assigned(i)) = Foo \Rightarrow$$
$$compOut|_i = \langle\rangle\hat{~}processing(compIn|_i)$$

where $compIn|_i$ resp. $compOut|_i$ denotes the restriction of the component's complete input resp. output to the timed message stream corresponding to the interface i. The predicate employs two auxiliary functions:

$$processing, error \quad : \quad (M^*)^T \to (M^*)^T$$

The function *processing* is defined by

$$x = \langle request \rangle \Rightarrow$$
$$processing(x\hat{~}s) = \langle reply \rangle\hat{~}processing(s) \lor$$
$$processing(x\hat{~}s) = \langle notProcessed \rangle\hat{~}error(s) \land$$
$$x = \langle\rangle \Rightarrow$$
$$processing(x\hat{~}s) = \langle\rangle\hat{~}processing(s)$$

whereas *error* is defined by

$$\forall x \in M^* : error(x\hat{~}s) \quad = \quad \langle notProcessed \rangle\hat{~}error(s)$$

Note that, similar to the component structure description in the previous section, the behavior of *Foo* components in state *processing* is underspecified and may be refined in a more detailed description. Again, we refrain from a generalization of this example. A comprehensive treatment may be based on [Rum96], which considers a formal, stream-based semantics for state transition diagrams in the context of object-oriented systems.

9.4.5 Interaction Descriptions

Interaction descriptions specify the communication between two or more interfaces. They are useful for elaborating the decomposition of a system into individual interfaces and components, and for designing interaction patterns between a set of components as communication via their interfaces. Familiar interaction descriptions are Message Sequence Charts [IT93] as well as UML sequence and collaboration diagrams [Gro99]. The example of Figure 9.8 introduces a variation called *Extended Event Trace*.

This diagram visualizes the interaction between a set of components with an *Observer* interface and a component with an *Observable* interface. The communication follows the well-known design pattern from [GHJV95]: all registered observers

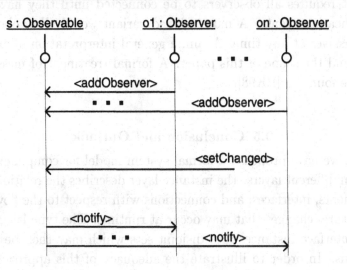

Fig. 9.8. Extended Event Trace: The Observer Pattern.

must be notified when one of them sends a **setChanged** message to the observed entity.

This diagram may be formalized as *ObserverEET* ∈ *Description*. In contrast to the previous descriptions, *ObserverEET* cannot be assigned to a single component or interface type. Instead, it is assigned to two interface types as *ObserverEET* ∈ *descOf*(*Observer*) and *ObserverEET* ∈ *descOf*(*Observable*), although we will only consider the communication obligations imposed on the *Observable* interface: For the interpretation of the diagram, we introduce two auxiliary functions

$$ifInConn, ifOutConn \quad : \quad Interface \times Connection \times T \rightarrow M^*$$

which return the input resp. output message sequences of a given interface's connection at a given time interval. Based on these functions, the diagram may be translated to the following logic formula:

$$ObserverEET \in descOf(Observable) \land typeOf(i) = Observable \Rightarrow$$
$$\forall t1, t2 \in T, cn1, cn2 \in Connection :$$
$$\quad t1 < t2 \land cn1 \in connection_{t1} \land cn2 \in connection_{t2} \land$$
$$\quad ifInConn(i, cn1, t1) = \langle addObserver \rangle \land$$
$$\quad ifInConn(i, cn2, t2) = \langle setChanged \rangle \Rightarrow$$
$$\exists t3 \in T :$$
$$\quad t2 < t3 \land cn1 \in connection_{t3} \land$$
$$\quad ifOutConn(i, cn1, t3) = \langle notify \rangle$$

Note that the previous formalization implies a rather strict observer-observable relation, as it requires all observers to be connected until they have received all pending notification events. A more relaxed variant would allow observers to disconnect themselves at any time. Again, a general interpretation of extended event traces is beyond the scope of this paper. A formal treatment of message sequence charts may be found in [BK98].

9.5 Conclusion and Outlook

In this paper, we have proposed a formal system model for component systems. It is organized in different layers: the instance layer describes the relations and behavior of components, interfaces, and connections with respect to the flow of messages and the structural changes that may occur at runtime. The type layer groups component and interface instances into disjoint sets which may then be characterized by descriptions. In order to illustrate the adequacy of this approach, we formalized a selection of simple exemplary textual and graphical description techniques for syntactic and behavioral properties. Our approach here is to translate these descriptions into predicates that impose restrictions on the described components.

In order to keep the presentation manageable and understandable, we deliberately chose to simplify certain concepts or even omitted unnecessary details. For example, it is desirable to employ structured messages instead of the flat set of messages M that was used throughout this paper. Moreover, the proposed model does not yet provide support for mobile components. In the context of our model, this could be done by allowing the containment relation *parent* to change over time. However, we believe this simple extension is not sufficient—a more general approach requires the introduction of a location concept, as proposed in [BGR+99].

Another restriction is more serious: the system model is not yet able to express the modification of a component's behavior, and its types and descriptions during runtime. Such modifications take place, for example, when a programmer introduces new types and descriptions, or when the implementation of a certain component is replaced during runtime. In the context of componentware, runtime and design time are not clearly distinguished, as configuration and adaptation tools and runtime environments allow the manipulation of running systems. An integrated formal model has to consider such modifications within the same time scale used to describe the 'normal' behavior of the system.

With respect to development methodology and description techniques, there remains much work to be done. First, it would be desirable to have a set of common interface specifications modeling the properties of existing technical middleware approaches. These specifications could then be used as exchangeable building blocks for communication while concentrating on business-oriented system functionality. Furthermore, a toolkit of coordinated, intuitive description techniques for componentware is required. The syntax and semantics should be precisely defined in terms of the system model as outlined for the exemplary description techniques in Section 9.4. Finally, methodical recommendations have to be provided, ranging from formal proof and refinement rules to consistency checks, test strategies, and overall process patterns.

It is our hope that the proposed system model is able to serve as a foundation for further work. Essentially, there are currently two kinds of conceivable extensions. On the one hand, additional concepts may be added to the system model itself, in order to represent the properties of existing technical approaches more adequately. On the other hand, the system model may be used as a foundation for a toolkit of carefully coordinated description techniques and a corresponding development methodology.

Acknowledgements

We thank Bernhard Rumpe and Bernhard Schätz for interesting discussions and comments on earlier versions of this paper.

Bibliography

[AG97]   R. Allen and D. Garlan. A Formal Basis for Architectural Connection. *ACM Transactions on Software Engineering and Methodology*, 6(3), 1997.

[BDD+92] Manfred Broy, Franz Dederichs, Claus Dendorfer, Max Fuchs, Thomas Gritzner, and Rainer Weber. The Design of Distributed Systems—an Introduction to FOCUS, http://www4.in.tum.de/proj/focus/Literature.html. Technical Report TUM-I9203, Technische Universität München, Institut für Informatik, January 1992.

[BGR+99] Klaus Bergner, Radu Grosu, Andreas Rausch, Alexander Schmidt, Peter Scholz, and Manfred Broy. Focusing on mobility. In Ralph H. Sprague, Jr., editor, *Proceedings of the Thirty-Second Annual Hawaii International Conference on System Sciences*. IEEE Computer Society, 1999.

[BHH+97] R. Breu, U. Hinkel, C. Hofmann, C. Klein, B. Paech, B. Rumpe, and V. Thurner. Towards a formalization of the unified modeling language. In *Proceedings of ECOOP'97*. Springer Verlag, LNCS, 1997.

[BK98]   Manfred Broy and Ingolf Krüger. Interaction Interfaces—Towards a scientific foundation of a methodological usage of Message Sequence Charts. In *Proceedings of the ICFEM 98*. IEEE Press, 1998.

[Bro95]   Manfred Broy. Mathematical system models as a basis of software engineering. *Computer Science Today*, 1995.

[BRSV98] Klaus Bergner, Andreas Rausch, Marc Sihling, and Alexander Vilbig. An integrated view on componentware—concepts, description techniques, and development process. In Roger Lee, editor, *Software Engineering: Proceedings of the IASTED Conference '98*. ACTA Press, Anaheim, 1998.

[COR]   Object Management Group CORBA. OMG website, http://www.omg.org.

[Fla96]   D. Flanagan. *Java in a Nutshell*. O'Reilly & Associates, Inc., 2nd edition, 1996.

[GHJV95] E. Gamma, R. Helm, R. Johnson, and J. Vlissides. *Design Patterns: Elements of Reusable Object-Oriented Software*. Addison-Wesley, 1995.

[Gro99]   UML Group. Unified Modeling Language. Version 1.3, Rational Software Corporation, 1999.

[IT93]   ITU-TS. *ITU-TS Recommendation Z.120: Message Sequence Chart (MSC)*.
             ITU-TS, Geneva, September 1993.

[Jav99a]   JavaSoft. Enterprise JavaBeans website,
             http.//java.sun.com/products/ejb/, 1999.

[Jav99b]   JavaSoft. JavaBeans website, http://java.sun.com/beans/, 1999.

[KRB96]   Cornel Klein, Bernhard Rumpe, and Manfred Broy. A stream-based
             mathematical model for distributed information processing systems: The
             SysLab system model. In J.-B. Stefani E. Naijm, editor, *FMOODS'96 Formal
             Methods for Open Object-based Distributed Systems*, pages 323–338. ENST
             France Telecom, 1996.

[LKA+95]   D. Luckham, J. Kenney, L. Augustin, J. Vera, D. Bryan, and W. Mann.
             Specification and Analysis of System Architecture Using Rapide. *IEEE
             Transactions on Software Engineering*, 21(4):336–355, 1995.

[Mic98]   MicroSoft Corporation. MicroSoft COM homepage,
             http://www.microsoft.com/com, 1998.

[NR99]   E. Di Nitto and D. Rosenblum. Exploiting ADLs to Specify Architectural
             Styles Induced by Middleware Infrastructures. In *Proceedings of the 1999
             International Conference on Software Engineering*. ACM Press, 1999.

[OH98]   Robert Orfali and Dan Harkey. *Client/Server Programming with Java and
             CORBA*. John Wiley & Sons, 2nd edition, 1998.

[Rum96]   Bernhard Rumpe. *Formale Methodik des Entwurfs verteilter objektorientierter
             Systeme*. PhD thesis, Technische Universität München, 1996.

[SDK+95]   M. Shaw, R. DeLine, D. Klein, T. Ross, D. Young, and G. Zelesnik.
             Abstractions for Software Architectures and Tools to Support Them. *IEEE
             Transactions on Software Engineering*, 21(4):356–372, 1995.

10

Toward a Normative Theory for Component-Based System Design and Analysis

David S. Gibson *(david.gibson@usafa.af.mil)*

Department of Computer Science, U.S. Air Force Academy
HQ USAFA/DFCS, 2354 Fairchild Drive, Suite 6K41
USAF Academy, CO 80840-6234 USA

Bruce W. Weide and Scott M. Pike *({weide|pike}@cis.ohio-state.edu)*

Department of Computer and Information Science, The Ohio State University
2015 Neil Avenue, Columbus, OH 43210-1277 USA

Stephen H. Edwards *(edwards@cs.vt.edu)*

Department of Computer Science, Virginia Tech
660 McBryde Hall, Blacksburg, VA 24061-0106 USA

Abstract

Component-based system design, like all modern engineering design, involves predicting and reasoning about the behavior of possible systems, that is, systems that have not been built yet. Similarly, component-level maintenance of these systems involves predicting and reasoning about the behavioral impacts of possible changes (for example, component substitutions). The need for tractable reasoning about system behavior and the central role of mathematical modeling in meeting this need together suggest a new framework for component-based system design: one that captures both the behaviors of components and systems and the meanings of associated symbolic design artifacts such as behavioral specifications. Such a framework is related intuitively to popular views of component-based systems from software architecture. It is related technically to more formal aspects of software engineering, such as formal specifications and formal semantics of programming languages.

Keywords: Component-based systems, engineering design, formal semantics, formal specifications, functional programming, mathematical modeling, parameterized programming, software architecture, software maintenance, templates, generics.

10.1 Introduction

Good engineers use a variety of general principles to guide system design. One such objective is design for predictability: try to design systems whose behaviors are

211

easy to analyze and understand. Here we use the term "predictability" in the sense that it is straightforward to predict the exact range of behavior that can arise from a system, and do not mean to imply that there must be a unique (deterministic) possible outcome.

The importance of this principle stems from the need to compare design alternatives. This requires the ability to analyze quickly the behaviors of many possible systems, most or all of which have not actually been built and thus may not be studied empirically. In other words, modern engineering involves both creative design *and* effective analysis.

One way to design systems with effectively analyzable behavior is to strive for the ***modular reasoning property***, that is, to design systems as assemblies of standard components whose behaviors are already understood in isolation. This must be done carefully enough that a system's behavior is predictable from the individual behaviors of its components and their *local* interconnections to other components.

What do we mean by "effectively analyzable"? In computer science there is a technical standard by which to judge such a property: a problem is considered ***intractable*** if the time required to solve it is not bounded by a polynomial in the size of the problem description. The implication of a problem being intractable is that even if it can always be solved in principle, it is infeasible or impractical to solve it except in limited special cases. If the problem of predicting the behavior of a system is intractable, then that system's behavior is not effectively analyzable.

We embrace the thesis that predicting software system behavior is intractable if the software lacks the modular reasoning property; this accounts for widely-reported difficulties faced by software engineers who are engaged in reverse engineering of legacy code [WHH95]. On the other hand, if the modular reasoning property holds then one can analyze and predict a software system's overall behavior without knowledge of how its components' behaviors are achieved. Only similar analyses of the components in isolation together with local composition rules are required, and such compositional analyses are relatively easy to carry out.

In this paper we explore some ramifications of the need for modular reasoning. We first consider component-based design of general engineered systems from the perspective of software engineers in Section 10.2. Concentrating on the modular reasoning property results in a preliminary proposal, elaborated in Sections 10.3 and 10.4, for a normative (that is, prescriptive) theory of design for component-based systems that applies not just to software but to other engineered systems. We suggest both a conceptual framework and a formal mathematical framework. The conceptual framework provides a way to think about component-based system design. The formal mathematical framework provides a way to express the required descriptions and analyses of component and system behavior. In Section 10.5 we discuss related work, and present some preliminary conclusions in Section 10.6.

10.2 Software Engineering and Traditional Engineering

Electrical, mechanical, and civil engineers routinely design and build physical systems from "components." It has, of course, occurred to software engineers that there is something to be learned from their experience (cf. [SW90]). Recently, the physical-system metaphor for software systems has been taken a step further: some software engineers should emulate architects, or even be called "software architects" [SS99]. Many now distinguish an entire subarea of software engineering as "software architecture" [SG96]. Even the "design patterns" literature [GHJV95] has an architectural lineage.

The physical-system engineering metaphor for software engineering clearly derives from component-based design in electrical engineering. This tradition apparently started with Doug McIlroy's proposal for a software component industry [McI76]. The electrical engineering metaphor is so appealing that it has been used repeatedly since then, even by one of us [WOZ91].

In this section we revisit the electrical engineering metaphor. We explain why it is superficially attractive and perhaps instructive, but ultimately misleading if elaborated too far. Then we briefly outline how an understanding of the role of mathematical modeling in modular reasoning about component-based systems leads to a new and different sense in which component-based physical and software systems are fundamentally similar.

10.2.1 The Electrical Engineering Metaphor: An Example

Here is a simple example to show how electrical engineers might think in terms of components. Certain resistors are available as standard components. The objective is to compose them into a two-terminal resistor network with a desired equivalent resistance. Figure 10.1 illustrates a particular design problem of this kind: Given only 500Ω and 300Ω resistors, construct the equivalent of a 1150Ω resistor.

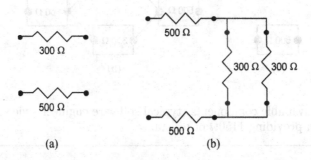

Fig. 10.1. (a) The available components (typical electrical engineer's view), and (b) a component composition providing 1150Ω of resistance.

Notice that Figure 10.1(a) leaves out an important available component that is used in Figure 10.1(b): wire. This is the physical "glue" for the resistor network. Couldn't one simply solder the resistor terminals (the dots) to each other directly to create the network? Logically this would work, but without a more flexible way to connect the resistors, it might not be physically possible to realize some compositions that are logically acceptable.

10.2.2 The Component-Connector Taxonomy

The presence of wires in the electrical engineering metaphor arises from an accidental property of the physical world we live in. Yet it seems to have led some software engineers who are searching for fundamental features of component-based software systems to distinguish *components* from *connectors*. Shaw and Garlan [SG96] have popularized this taxonomy† and the software architecture community has adopted it. Perhaps in part this acceptance comes because having the equivalent of wires is immensely helpful in block diagram layout: such drawings are subject to physical constraints similar to those of electrical-circuit layout.

It is clear that software engineers intend for devices such as resistors and wires of a *physical* electrical system to be metaphors for the components and connectors of a software system, which is a purely *logical* entity. However, the apparent unification of component-based physical and software systems, which this view seems to entail, is attractive. For one thing it means that software engineers can apply their intuitions about physical systems directly to software system design. Figure 10.2 shows how one might draw a software architecture-style block diagram similar to those in [SG96], using the component-connector taxonomy, to present the network of Figure 10.1.

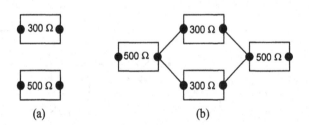

(a)   (b)

Fig. 10.2. (a) The available components (typical software engineer's view), and (b) a component composition providing 1150Ω of resistance.

The component-connector taxonomy for software systems seems to have other

---

† It is unclear how "connectors" could have arisen from the architecture metaphor, so we conclude that they are really left over from the earlier electrical engineering metaphor.

advantages as well. The most important is that it might give engineers who are designing and analyzing the *behavior* of hybrid physical/software systems a common conceptual framework in which to model and reason about those systems. Shaw and Garlan note the importance of understanding the behavior of component-based software systems, and thereby establish a goal for software architecture as a field [SG96, p. 4]:

At each level we find *components*, both primitive and composite; *rules of composition* that allow the construction of non-primitive components, or systems; and *rules of behavior* that provide semantics for the system. ... It is common for a description of a software system to include a few paragraphs of text and a box-and-line diagram, but there are neither uniform syntax nor uniform semantics for interpreting the prose and the diagrams.

Shaw and Garlan describe several kinds of box-and-line diagrams that have been used by software engineers, and give informal semantics for some of them. Notably, however, the component-connector taxonomy:

- sheds little light on what is common to all component-based systems—both physical and software systems—except that one can draw similar-looking block diagrams of them;
- provides at best an ad hoc and nonuniform framework for "syntax" (composition rules) and "semantics" (behavioral reasoning rules) for component-based systems; and
- gives a designer no guidance whatsoever about how to achieve the crucial modular reasoning property.

The Shaw/Garlan book introducing software architecture is descriptive, based largely on a survey of what software engineers actually do in practice. It is not surprising that the authors found the component-connector taxonomy hiding inside many designs. This view arises naturally from high-level block diagrams that all engineers tend to draw. It is hard to *avoid* adopting the component-connector taxonomy and trying to leverage it, as others—including one of us—had done before [SW88]. But because of the weaknesses mentioned above, we are not sure it is the right way to approach engineering design in general, or software design in particular.

10.2.3 ACTI: A Different Taxonomy

Despite the superficial advantages of the component-connector taxonomy in terms of drawing block diagrams, the software architecture community has not managed to achieve the dream of a uniform syntax and semantics for component-connector assemblies. So, in this paper we suggest an entirely different view of component-based systems. We call this taxonomy **ACTI**, for **abstract and concrete templates and instances** [Edw95]. ACTI also entails a point of view, a formal model, and an associated design approach, which we illustrate with an example.

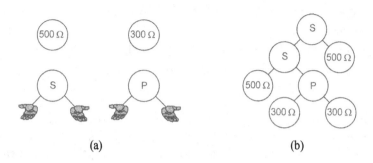

Fig. 10.3. (a) The available components (ACTI view), and (b) a component composition providing 1150Ω of resistance.

ACTI is a model of modular, parameterized subsystems that offers strong support for reasoning about collections of interacting components. It has been heavily influenced by the large body of work on formally characterizing module systems in programming languages [Mac86, Mog89, MT94, Jon96]. Intuitively, it separates the world of components across two dimensions. First, an *abstract* component is a description of behavior (for example, a specification), while a *concrete* component implements behavior (for example, an implementation). Second, a *template* is a parameterized component (for example, a generic module, or a functor in Standard ML terms), while an *instance* is not parameterized (for example, an ordinary module, or a structure in SML terms).

Figure 10.3 shows how ACTI might be used in the two-terminal resistor-network design problem. The components in Figure 10.3(a) are of two kinds: instances (shown as circles) and templates (shown as circles with "arms" and open hands). The instances are the resistors, and the templates are series S and parallel P components. The only composition rule for these components is that you may place at most one circle into each hand, as illustrated in Figure 10.3(b).

ACTI does not dictate a particular concrete syntax for design diagrams. Frankly, we normally do not recommend using clipart as in Figure 10.3, but the pictures here are meant to convey the (valid) impression that there is something quite different about this taxonomy compared to the component-connector taxonomy. The topological differences between Figures 10.2(b) and 10.3(b) help reveal this even without the hands.

In the following two sections, we outline our mathematical framework after first explaining intuitively how the ACTI taxonomy offers advantages over the component-connector taxonomy:

- ACTI explains the features that are *fundamentally* common to all component-based systems—both physical and software systems.

- ACTI offers a uniform framework for "syntax" (composition rules) and "semantics" (behavioral reasoning rules) for component-based systems.
- ACTI leads directly to designs having the modular reasoning property.

10.3 The Intuition Behind ACTI

There are three main problems to be solved in reasoning about the behavior of a component-based system:

(i) Describe the behavior of each component in isolation by developing a mathematical model of the behavioral features of interest.

(ii) Use the mathematical models of the components, along with information about how they are composed, to construct a mathematical model of the behavior of the composite system.

(iii) Define and enforce composition rules for the components so that legal composite structures result in local composition rules for the components' mathematical models.

Solutions to the first two problems are necessary for any kind of reasoning about system behavior from component behaviors. The requirement for addressing problem (iii) is more subtle because it has to do not with what is *possible* but what is *practical* for large systems [WHH95]. The remainder of this section compares the component-connector approach with the ACTI approach along these three dimensions.

10.3.1 Reasoning About Behavior Using Component-Connector Ideas

Initially, let us consider reasoning about behavior using component and connector ideas. From this perspective, the components in Figure 10.2 mirror the physical pieces in Figure 10.1. Point (i) above is addressed by modeling the behavior of each resistor (component) as a nonnegative real number: its resistance. Similarly the wire (connector) is modeled as a resistance value of zero. Point (ii) is addressed by using knowledge of all the point-to-point connections in the network to drive the construction of a set of simultaneous equations, based on Ohm's Law, which can then be solved for the equivalent resistance between the two terminals of interest. Point (iii), however, is not addressed. The component-connector framework gives us no leverage in terms of modular reasoning about the equivalent resistance of the network because the set of equations describing the overall system behavior models a global feature of the system interconnection structure.

Moreover, in terms of uniformity this approach is clearly lacking. The "syntax rules" are specific to the particular kinds of components and connectors at hand, that is, to resistors and wires. They reflect what can be done directly with the physical artifacts, not what can be done with the mathematical models for the behavioral properties of interest. The "behavioral rules" for component composition are equally specialized to these particular components. Moreover, they are not local but instead depend on the global pattern in which the components are assembled.

10.3.2 Reasoning About Behavior Using ACTI Ideas

In the ACTI approach, on the other hand, the available components are selected without direct regard to the physical situation. These components are "standard" because they reflect the underlying mathematical model of resistance-network behavior—which of course is *related* to the physical situation being modeled but is not identical to it. Each resistor component is an ***instance*** because its behavior does not depend on any parameters that might be introduced through component composition. This is the same as in the component-connector approach.

What is different is that there are no wires to connect resistors in this view. They are replaced by series and parallel (S and P) components, which are ***templates***, that is, ***parameterized components***. These components are implemented by physical connection patterns with behaviors that can be understood in isolation and be modeled by functions from pairs of nonnegative reals to nonnegative reals: the resistance of R_1 and R_2 connected in series is $R_1 + R_2$; and the resistance of R_1 and R_2 connected in parallel is $R_1 R_2 / (R_1 + R_2)$.

So problems (i) and (ii) are addressed, and problem (iii) also is solved because the mathematical model of the system behavior involves modular composition of the mathematical models of the components. Note that a local change in the design (for example, replacing the topmost S component with P) entails only a local change in the resulting system mathematical model, and the re-analysis resulting from such a change does not start from scratch.

Moreover, the "syntax rule" that you may place at most one circle into each hand is not specific to this set of components. It *always* applies and always means that you may bind actual to formal parameters; here, that you may bind a nonnegative real number to each of the formal parameters of the S and P functions. The "behavior rule" for the composite structure is likewise not specific to this set of components. The behavior of a composition of components is *always* produced by applying the behaviors of the templates to their actual parameters in that assemblage. No ad hoc "syntax rules" are needed to decide which compositions are legal and therefore meaningful; no ad hoc "behavioral rules" are needed to reason about the behavior of the composite system given the behaviors of the components.

This example suggests a high-level strategy for coming up with appropriate components for a particular domain:

(i) Develop a mathematical model that adequately captures the system properties of interest.

(ii) Examine the key constants and operators in the mathematics involved in step (i), and develop components whose mathematical models closely match these constants and operators. Some components are instances, that is, constants; some are templates, that is, operators with formal parameters.

(iii) Use the standard "syntax rule" that components are composed only by binding actual to formal parameters of templates, subject to type-matching and behavioral restrictions on the template parameters.

(iv) Use the standard "behavioral rule" that the behavior of an instance in isolation is described by its mathematical model; the behavior of a template is described by a function; and the behavior of an instantiated template is obtained by applying the template's behavioral function to the mathematical models of its actual parameters.

10.3.3 Observations

Four observations are in order here. First, to one who is already familiar with research on module systems for programming languages, the notion of using parameterized implementations or specifications within the realm of software is nothing new. Indeed, the module-like subsystem features of ACTI have been heavily influenced by past work in this area. The primary difference in this context is generalizing the idea from software constructs to the wider arena of parameterized subsystems in general system design.

Second, to a software engineer, ACTI from this 10,000-foot level might look just like functional programming (FP) using different terminology. Indeed there are similarities both because FP and ACTI seek to achieve the modular reasoning property and because they share certain underlying mathematical features. In fact, the FP paradigm can be considered one example of an ACTI-based software engineering methodology. Nevertheless, there are important differences that may not be apparent from the simple resistor example:

- The components that can be combined using this model can be subsystem-level components, not just simple data types. This is composition on a much larger scale than the perspective many practitioners (naively) hold of FP, and is akin to treating modules as first class entities [Jon96].
- Although the module composition mechanisms in ACTI share the same roots as category-theoretic explanations of module systems based on FP research, the behavior captured within individual ACTI components is characterized via relations instead of functions.
- ACTI components can have state that changes over time, and the behavior provided by a component can affect that state. This naturally supports imperative descriptions of implementation details.
- ACTI supports constructing and describing a mathematical model of a component's behavior—an abstract description of the capabilities it provides. This is

distinct from and in addition to providing an actual implementation mechanism
for achieving that behavior.

- Unlike the situation in most conventional programming languages, in ACTI, a
  subsystem *never* has any implicit dependencies, and never depends directly on any
  external definitions—all external dependencies are described through an explicit
  "importation" interface.

While FP certainly fits within this framework, other paradigms can also be applied.
An imperative language framework that fits within the ACTI model, RESOLVE
[SW94], makes it both technically and practically possible to reason modularly
about the behavioral effects of software component composition and substitution
[EHMO91, EHO94, Hey95, Gib97]. Software engineers following this discipline can
create state-oriented explanations of behavior for mutable objects that support procedural operations with relational behavior—yet still have the modular reasoning
property.

Third, physical layout of design diagrams simply does not matter for mathematical modeling of software system behavior, except possibly when the diagram will
also be used as the "blueprint" for physically constructing a device. For example,
suppose an ACTI-aware electrical engineer needs to take into account magnetically-
induced coupling between the electrical properties of two nearby parallel wires. This
physical-level designer might have to include components whose implementations
are, say, nearby parallel wires, among the components to be used in solving design
problems. In other words, to the extent that physical proximity or other physical
relationships participate in the mathematical modeling of relevant behavior, the
features of the mathematical model might suggest different components than are
available off-the-shelf based on traditional design techniques.

Finally, we recognize that the ACTI approach might seem unfamiliar and un-
natural to those experienced in traditional engineering design. But suppose electrical engineers, for example, were *taught* to use the ACTI approach, not traditional wiring diagrams, in an introductory circuit design course; and suppose that
the standard electrical components reflected the ACTI paradigm. Then except
where physical layout considerations were as important as the electrical properties, only circuit board layout designers (people or programs)—the implementers of
conceptual designs—would worry about physical wires or draw anything like Figure 10.1(b). There is no *inherent* reason that designers in electrical engineering
should prefer Figure 10.1(b) to Figure 10.3(b) as a way to express a design. In fact,
the way electrical engineering design is taught is probably at least as much a result
of "implementation-biased teaching" as software design instruction [LWBS99].

10.4 The Mathematical Framework Underlying ACTI

We now temporarily restrict our attention to software engineering because, for software components, the notion of behavior is well-understood and there is ample technical precedent for considering a general formal framework for defining behavior. Specifically, "behavior" is simply the *meaning*, or *semantics*, of a component. Consider a software system implemented in C++. For a typical operational program component such as a C++ class—a **concrete instance**, in ACTI terms— "meaning" normally is taken to be the operational behavior arising from the component at run time.

However, there are at least two other kinds of artifacts involved in modern component-based software systems:

- *Specifications* of operational program components, such as Larch [GH93], RE-SOLVE, or Z [Spi88] formal specifications, are used to record the required or intended behavior of operational program components.

- *Templates*, or generic (parameterized) components, such as Ada generic packages, C++ class templates, or RESOLVE realization modules, are *instantiated* to generate ordinary operational program components.

Although neither specifications—**abstract instances** and **abstract templates**, in ACTI terms—nor programming language templates—**concrete templates**, in ACTI terms—have behaviors in the same sense as ordinary operational components because they are not runtime entities, they are crucially important in design. A firm mathematical foundation for component-based system design must account for their meanings, and must explain how they are related to the meanings of operational program components where runtime manifestations can be observed.

Software systems are symbolic entities, so the standard notion of programming-language semantics makes these questions sensible. Other physical systems are not symbolic. But like software systems they clearly exhibit "behaviors," and their design documents *are* symbolic. So, while our development in this section refers primarily to software components and systems, the framework for defining component and system behavior and the meanings of other artifacts applies as well to component-based physical systems. We therefore intend the formal framework to:

- Help designers develop unified formal models of embedded system behavior, where the physical system being controlled and the software inside it must be analyzed and/or designed together.

- Help illuminate deeper connections between well-engineered physical systems and well-engineered software systems.

- Serve as a vehicle for phrasing future discussions about the fundamentals of component-based systems.

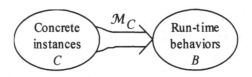

Fig. 10.4. $\mathcal{M}_C : C \to B$.

10.4.1 A Starting Point: Traditional Programming Language Semantics

We may begin developing such a framework by considering denotational semantics. In principle, it is relatively well understood how to define the semantics of operational program components in a programming language such as C or Pascal. Of course as a practical matter, defining the formal semantics for nearly any programming language is an enormous chore. What we seek is simply a mathematical framework in which such a semantics *might* be defined. This is illustrated in Figure 10.4. For each string that is an operational program component in the programming language (that is, an element of C), the semantic function $\mathcal{M}_C$ assigns to it a runtime behavior (that is, an element of B). In this paper we constrain neither the structure of B nor the semantic function $\mathcal{M}_C$, except to stipulate that $\mathcal{M}_C$ is total. With this starting point, we are now faced with the question of what specifications and templates mean, and how these meanings are connected to those of operational program components.

10.4.2 Relationships Between Components

The meanings of specifications and templates are necessary to precisely define key **behavioral relationships** involving operational program components, specifications, and templates that are central to understanding component-based systems [EGWZ97, Gib97]. Here is a quick *intuitive* overview of some of the most important mathematical relations that capture these properties, with C/C_i, S/S_i, and T/T_i taken to be operational program components, specifications, and templates, respectively:

- C_2 *uses* C_1: the behavior of C_2 depends on the behavior of C_1.
- C *implements* S: the behavior of C conforms to the behavior specified by S.
- S_2 *extends* S_1: any operational program component that *implements* S_2 also *implements* S_1.
- T *needs* S: T requires as an actual parameter some (any) operational program component that *implements* S.

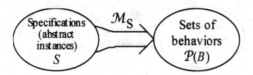

Fig. 10.5. $\mathcal{M}_S : S \to \mathcal{P}(B)$ (where $\mathcal{P}(B)$ is the power set of B).

The first relation, **uses**, is the usual connection between software components, where C_2 is a client of C_1. This connection allows $\mathcal{M}_C$ to be "constructed" bottom-up [Edw95]; if C_2 invokes some operation of C_1, then $\mathcal{M}_C(C_2)$ is defined in terms of $\mathcal{M}_C(C_1)$.

10.4.3 A Semantic Space for Specifications

In approaching the meaning of a specification, we expect intuitively that there may be many alternative operational components that conform to the behavioral description in a specification. We would like the meaning of a specification to capture the common features of these alternatives while also prescribing the behavioral limits it imposes. As a result, Figure 10.5 illustrates the meaning of a specification as the set of behaviors that we wish to allow for conforming implementations. Indeed this becomes the definition of the **implements** relation:

$$C \; \textbf{implements} \; S \equiv \mathcal{M}_C(C) \in \mathcal{M}_S(S)$$

The **extends** relation between specifications is defined similarly:

$$S_2 \; \textbf{extends} \; S_1 \equiv \mathcal{M}_S(S_2) \subseteq \mathcal{M}_S(S_1)$$

Consider a software-based example: suppose operational program component C is a procedure (with possibly relational, that is, nondeterministic behavior) and specification S is given by a precondition and a postcondition. We might consider a point in B to be a binary relation on a state space Σ (that is, a set of ordered pairs from $\Sigma \times \Sigma$), where (σ_1, σ_2) is in $\mathcal{M}_C(C)$ if and only if C is permitted to start with its environment in state σ_1 and, when doing so, might change its environment to state σ_2. The precondition and postcondition from S also define a binary relation $\rho(S)$ on Σ, where the precondition says where $\rho(S)$ is defined and the postcondition defines it there. We would define $\mathcal{M}_S(S)$ as the *set* of binary relations on Σ that are at least as defined as $\rho(S)$ and that are consistent with it where both are defined.

Notice that this framework lets us consider the meanings of specifications for systems other than programs. For example, Figure 10.5 and the definitions of **implements** and **extends** make sense even if C is the set of possible two-terminal

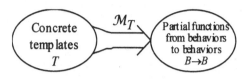

Fig. 10.6. $\mathcal{M}_T : T \to (B \to B))$.

resistor networks or cars or TV sets (or even mere descriptions thereof), B is the set of possible behaviors of two-terminal resistor networks or cars or TV sets, and S is the set of "instruction manuals" for how to use two-terminal resistor networks or cars or TV sets, respectively.

Our suggested semantic space for specifications might seem so simple as to be obvious or trivial, but the apparent simplicity is deceiving. There have been few attempts to address this problem in general, and even in the more limited domain of software, we have seen little previous work on the question of tying specifications' formal semantics to those of operational program components. Stand-alone specification languages such as Larch and Z have formal semantics, but in them a specification such as S above apparently would denote the single relation $\rho(S)$—which is in B, not in $\mathcal{P}(B)$ as in our framework. Instead, here we propose a semantic space for specifications that is a higher-order space, obtained directly and mechanically from B, but unrelated to the internal structure of B.

10.4.4 A Semantic Space for Templates

Building on this view, Figure 10.6 illustrates how we may view the semantics of templates. The meaning of a template is a partial function from behaviors to behaviors. This leads us to define the dependency relationship that is most important for a template, as follows:

$$T \; \textit{needs} \; S \equiv \mathbf{dom}(\mathcal{M}_T(T)) = \mathcal{M}_S(S)$$

The traditional view of a template in imperative programming languages is that it is a "transformation" that "generates" an operational program component when it is *instantiated*, that is, when it is given another operational program component as an actual parameter (multiple parameters can be packaged together). The actual parameter C typically cannot be just anything; it must implement some specification S. The resulting component C' then implements some (usually different) specification S'. This "macro expansion" view of a template is used by most compilers: C' can be obtained by substituting C for the template formal parameter wherever the latter occurs in the string T.

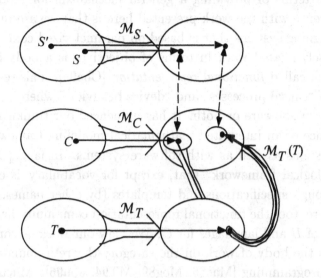

Fig. 10.7. The Meaning of Template Instantiation: Applying $\mathcal{M}_T(T)$.

The view suggested by Figure 10.6 differs subtly in that a template transformation is one of behaviors (on the diagram's right side), not of strings (on the left side) [Edw95]. Figure 10.7 illustrates how template instantiation works in this framework. Determining the meaning of T applied to an actual parameter C does not involve textual substitution of C for the formal parameter of T. The instantiation simply means $\mathcal{M}_T(T)(\mathcal{M}_C(C))$. This is exactly the approach taken by category-theoretic research on parameterized modules [Mac86, Mog89, Jon96]. The intended applicability of the framework to component-based physical as well as software systems emphasizes why it is significant that instantiating a template should not, in general, be viewed in terms of string substitution.

What about abstract templates—that is, parameterized specifications? The appropriate semantic space for these units is $\mathcal{P}(B) \rightarrow \mathcal{P}(B)$ [Edw95]. Similarly, the meanings of higher-order templates involve additional semantic spaces of higher-order functions, but remains within the same general mathematical framework.

10.5 Comparison with Related Work

We have seen little other work addressing the question of semantic spaces for general system artifacts or seeking an integrated formal treatment of the mathematical modeling of physical systems and software systems. One researcher working in this area is Manfred Broy [Bro98, Bro95], who is interested in providing a formal mathematical framework underlying commonly used development tools. His work uses "communication histories" to capture behavioral descriptions, similar to trace-based specifications, and he defines refinement relationships for his specifications. While this is related in terms of providing a general mechanism for modeling systems, the crucial difference with the work presented here is that we are proposing a new approach to designing systems that is based on parameterized components.

The most closely-related work in terms of objectives is a body of artificial intelligence research called *functional representation* [Cha94]. This research explores understanding of "causal processes" and "device behavior," where a "device" might involve hardware or software or both. It has influenced our thinking by emphasizing the significance of an integrated mathematical modeling framework that deals with physical systems as well as with software systems. In fact, [CJ96] describes a "smallest ontological framework" that, except for vocabulary, is consistent with Figure 10.4. Though specifications and templates (by other names, of course) are central issues there, too, the functional representation community has concentrated on the structure of B and languages for C. We view our work as complementary.

Also related is the body of work on the category-theoretic foundations of module systems for programming [Mac86, Mog89, MT94, Jon96]. Much of the formal research in this area is centered around the language of Standard ML [MTH90] and extensions to it. SML includes a concrete template construct (functors) and has a formal semantic definition. This semantic framework is similar to ours at the level of Figure 10.7, and (as noted earlier) it seems possible to view SML and other functional languages as fitting within the ACTI framework. There are two major differences in terms of generality and potential complexity, however. First, SML does not include behavioral descriptions and so SML functors are only subject to syntactic restrictions. Second, to our knowledge the SML semantic framework has not been suggested or used as a general model for reasoning about nonsoftware system behavior. Although SML does not support parameterized specifications or higher-order templates, several proposed extensions to the language's module system lie in this direction (for example, [Jon96]).

One extention of SML is particularly related here: Extended ML (EML) [KST97, San91]. EML extends a "purely functional" subset of SML (that is, SML without its imperative features) with algebraically-based behavioral specifications, all with a formal semantic definition. The algebraic approach used for behavioral specifications in EML differs from the model-based, relational foundations of ACTI, however, and EML still differs from ACTI in most of the ways characterized in Section 10.3.

Most other work on integrating formal specifications into the software life-cycle relies on using one language for writing specifications (for example, Larch or Z) and another language for writing implementations (for example, Ada or C++) [KH96]. We have concentrated on a single integrated framework because it is difficult to pursue formal verification of correctness unless the semantics of specifications and implementations are defined together. An integrated semantic treatment seems essential to avoid pitfalls in reasoning about software systems [Coo78, EHMO91, Lea91, EHO94, LW94, SWO97].

Although there have been proposals for giving semantics to specifications or parameterized specifications (for example, [Rei93]), these proposals generally assume certain algebraic properties of the semantic spaces. ACTI assumes nothing about the structure of the underlying behavior/meaning space, B.

RESOLVE is unusual in that it is both a specification and an implementation language with modern features such as templates, some forms of inheritance, and so forth. The semantic spaces developed to date for RESOLVE component varieties do not directly follow the approach suggested here. They are based on the original ACTI formal model of software subsystems [Edw95], which has of course heavily influenced this paper.

We hope our claims about the importance of templates in component-based system design help encourage the software engineering formal methods community to consider templates more seriously. We (like Goguen [Gog84]) have concluded that templates are inevitably at the heart of component-based systems [Gib97], and templates routinely appear in (or, if not, are quickly proposed as additions to) modern programming languages. Yet the larger formal methods community has hardly considered them. We note that the centrality of templates also seems clear to nearly all of the FP community and to some of the functional representation community in AI—probably because they recognize the importance of the modular reasoning property.

10.6 Conclusions

The foundations of component-based systems require a rich, general, unified, mathematically rigorous, yet conceptually simple framework. Early (mostly implicit) attempts at developing such a framework postulate that software engineers should design systems the way traditional engineers do. This path inevitably leads to the conclusion that the conceptual foundations of component-based systems lie in traditional engineering; that the informal foundations for traditional engineering design just have to be elaborated a bit and made rigorous enough to handle reasoning about software systems.

Seeing little progress in this direction, we have sought another starting point. Another potentially fruitful approach entails the transfer of advanced concepts from component-based software engineering (such as templates, formal specifications, formal semantics) back to traditional engineering. We have proposed a new line of work in the foundations of component-based systems by explaining the ACTI taxonomy of components, describing how the ACTI model might influence design of component-based systems, and outlining the mathematical framework underlying ACTI.

Already we have successfully used the ACTI approach to design a variety of software components and systems built from them [SW94], including commercially-successful software products. We have not, however, applied the ACTI approach to any significant nonsoftware design problems; thus, validating the generality of the approach is an open problem. We hope this paper raises for the reader a long list of interesting questions and thereby serves as a catalyst by which we can interest others in helping to explore the foundations of component-based systems.

Acknowledgments

We appreciate helpful discussions with Stephan Blatti, B. Chandrasekaran, Gary Leavens, J. Henk Obbink, Murali Sitaraman, Neelam Soundarajan, and Michael Stovsky, and with Bill Ogden and the other members of the Reusable Software Research Group at The Ohio State University. These, and the anonymous reviewers' comments, have helped focus and improve an earlier version of this paper that appeared in *Proc. 1997 ESEC/FSE Workshop on Foundations of Component-Based Systems.*

We also gratefully acknowledge financial support from the National Science Foundation under grants CCR-9311702, DUE-9555062, and CDA-9634425, the Fund for the Improvement of Post-Secondary Education under project number P116B60717, and Microsoft Research. Any opinions, findings, and conclusions or recommendations expressed in this paper are those of the authors and do not necessarily reflect the views of the National Science Foundation, the U.S. Department of Education, or Microsoft.

Bibliography

[Bro95]   Broy, M. Mathematical system models as a basis of software engineering. In van Leeuwen, J., ed., *Computer Science Today*, vol. 1000 of *LNCS*, pp. 292–306. Springer-Verlag, New York, NY, 1995.

[Bro98]   Broy, M. Compositional refinement of interactive systems modelled by relations. In de Roever, W.-P., Langmaack, H., and Pnueli, A., eds., *Compositionality: The Significant Difference*, vol. 1536 of *LNCS*, pp. 130–149. Springer-Verlag, New York, NY, 1998.

[Cha94]   Chandrasekaran, B. Functional representation and causal processes. In Yovits, M., ed., *Advances in Computers*, vol. 38, pp. 73–143. Academic Press, 1994.

[CJ96]   Chandrasekaran, B. and Josephson, J. Representing function as effect: Assigning functions to objects in context and out. In *Working Notes AAAI-96 Workshop on Modeling and Reasoning with Function*, Portland, OR, Aug. 1996. AAAI.

[Coo78]   Cook, S. Soundness and completeness of an axiom system for program verification. *SIAM J. Comput.*, 7(1):70–90, Feb. 1978.

[Edw95]   Edwards, S. H. *A Formal Model of Software Subsystems*. PhD thesis, Dept. Computer and Info. Science, The Ohio State Univ., Columbus, OH, Mar. 1995.

[EGWZ97]   Edwards, S., Gibson, D., Weide, B., and Zhupanov, S. Software component relationships. In *Proc. 8th Annual Workshop on Software Reuse*, Mar. 1997.

[EHMO91]   Ernst, G.W., Hookway, R.J., Menegay, J.A., and Ogden, W.F. Modular verification of Ada generics. *Computer Language*, 16(3/4):259–280, 1991.

[EHO94]   Ernst, G.W., Hookway, R.J., and Ogden, W.F. Modular verification of data abstractions with shared realizations. *IEEE Trans. Softw. Eng.*, 20(4):288–307, Apr. 1994.

[GH93]   Guttag, J. and Horning, J. *Larch: Languages and Tools for Formal Specification*. Springer-Verlag, New York, NY, 1993.

[GHJV95] Gamma, E., Helm, R., Johnson, R., and Vlissides, J. *Design Patterns: Elements of Reusable Object-Oriented Software*. Addison-Wesley, Reading, MA, 1995.

[Gib97]   Gibson, D. *Behavioral Relationships Between Software Components*. PhD thesis, Dept. Computer and Info. Science, The Ohio State Univ., Columbus, OH, Oct. 1997.

[Gog84]   Goguen, J. A. Parameterized programming. *IEEE Trans. Softw. Eng.*, SE-10(5):528–543, Sep. 1984.

[Hey95]   Heym, W. *Computer Program Verification: Improvements for Human Reasoning*. PhD thesis, Dept. Computer and Info. Science, The Ohio State Univ., Columbus, OH, Dec. 1995.

[Jon96]   Jones, M. Using parameterized signatures to express modular structure. In *Conf. Record 23rd Annual ACM Symp. Principles of Programming Languages*, pp. 68–78. ACM Press, New York, NY, 1996.

[KH96]   Kilov, H. and Harvey, W., eds. *Specification of Behavioral Semantics in Object-Oriented Information Modeling*. Kluwer Academic Pub., 1996.

[KST97]   Kahrs, S., Sannella, D., and Tarlecki, A. The definition of Extended ML: A gentle introduction. *Theoretical Comput. Sci.*, 173:445–484, 1997.

[Lea91]   Leavens, G. Modular specification and verification of object-oriented programs. *IEEE Software*, 8(4):72–80, July 1991.

[LW94]   Liskov, B. and Wing, J. A behavioral notion of subtyping. *ACM Trans. Prog. Lang. Syst.*, 16:1811–1841, Nov. 1994.

[LWBS99] Long, T., Weide, B., Bucci, P., and Sitaraman, M. Client view first: An exodus from implementation-biased teaching. In *Proc. 30th SIGCSE Technical Symp. Computer Science Education*, pp. 136–140. ACM, Mar. 1999.

[Mac86]   MacQueen, D. Using dependent types to express modular structure. In *Conf. Record 13th Annual ACM Symp. Principles of Programming Languages*. ACM Press, New York, NY, 1986.

[McI76]   McIlroy, M. D. Mass-produced software components. In Buxton, J. M., Naur, P., and Randell, B., eds., *Software Engineering Concepts and Techniques*, pp. 88–98. Petrocelli/Charter, Brussels, Belgium, 1976.

[Mog89]   Moggi, E. A category-theoretic account of program modules. In Pitt, D. H., Rydeheard, D. E., Dybjer, P., Pitts, A. M., and Poigné, A., eds., *Category Theory and Computer Science*, vol. 389 of *LNCS*, pp. 101–117. Springer-Verlag, New York, NY, 1989.

[MT94]   MacQueen, D. B. and Tofte, M. A semantics for higher-order functors. In *5th European Symp. Programming*, vol. 788 of *LNCS*, pp. 409–423. Springer-Verlag, New York, NY, Apr. 1994.

[MTH90]   Milner, R., Tofte, M., and Harper, R. *The Definition of Standard ML*. MIT Press, Cambridge, MA, 1990.

[Rei93]   Reif, W. An approach to parameterized first-order specifications: Semantics, correctness, parameter passing. In Bjorner, D., Broy, M., and Pottosin, I., eds., *Formal Methods in Programming and Their Applications*, vol. 735 of *LNCS*, pp. 66–80. Springer-Verlag, New York, NY, 1993.

[San91]   Sannella, D. Formal program development in Extended ML for the working programmer. In *Proc. 3rd BCS/FACS Workshop on Refinement*, pp. 99–130. Springer-Verlag, New York, NY, 1991.

[SG96]   Shaw, M. and Garlan, D. *Software Architecture: Perspectives on an Emerging Discipline*. Prentice-Hall, Upper Saddle River, NJ, 1996.

[Spi88]   Spivey, J. *Understanding Z: A Specification Language and Its Formal Semantics.* Cambridge Univ. Press, Cambridge, UK, 1988.

[SS99]   Sewell, L. and Sewell, M. The profession of software architecture. *Software Tech News*, 2(3):16–19, Jan. 1999.

[SW88]   Stovsky, M. and Weide, B. Building interprocess communication models using STILE. In *Proc. 21st Hawaii Int'l Conf. Systems Sciences*, vol. 2, pp. 639–647, Jan. 1988.

[SW90]   Stovsky, M. and Weide, B. The role of traditional engineering design techniques in software engineering. In *Proc. 2nd Int'l Conf. Software Eng. and Knowledge Eng.*, pp. 84–89, Chicago, IL, June 1990. KSI.

[SW94]   Sitaraman, M. and Weide, B. Component-based software using RESOLVE. *ACM SIGSOFT Softw. Eng. Notes*, 19(4):21–63, Oct. 1994.

[SWO97]   Sitaraman, M., Weide, B., and Ogden, W. On the practical need for abstraction relations to verify abstract data type representations. *IEEE Trans. Softw. Eng.*, 23(3):157–170, Mar. 1997.

[WHH95]   Weide, B., Heym, W., and Hollingsworth, J. Reverse engineering of legacy code exposed. In *Proc. 17th Int'l Conf. Software Eng.*, pp. 327–331, Seattle, WA, Apr. 1995. ACM.

[WOZ91]   Weide, B. W., Ogden, W. F., and Zweben, S. H. Reusable software components. In Yovits, M. C., ed., *Advances in Computers*, vol. 33, pp. 1–65. Academic Press, 1991.

11

An Implementation-Oriented Semantics
for Module Composition

Joseph A. Goguen

Department of Computer Science & Engineering
University of California at San Diego, La Jolla, CA 92093-0114, USA
goguen@cs.ucsd.edu

Will Tracz

Lockheed Martin Federal Systems
Owego, NY 13827-3994 USA
will.tracz@lmco.com

Abstract

This paper describes an approach to module composition by executing "module expressions" to build systems out of component modules; the paper also gives a novel semantics intended to aid implementers. The semantics is based on set theoretic notions of tuple set, partial signature, and institution, thus avoiding more difficult mathematics theory. Language features include information hiding, both vertical and horizontal composition, and views for binding modules to interfaces. Vertical composition refers to the hierarchical structuring of a system into layers, while horizontal composition refers to the structure of a given layer. Modules may involve information hiding, and views may involve behavioral satisfaction of a theory by a module. Several "Laws of Software Composition" are given, which show how the various module composition operations relate. Taken together, this gives foundations for an algebraic approach to software engineering.

11.1 Introduction

The approach to module composition described in this paper can be used in many different ways. For example, it can be added to a programming language, by providing a simple module connection language (MCL) with "module expressions" that say how to manipulate and connect modules in the programming language. The general approach, called "parameterized programming" [Gog89], involves a module specification capability; however, programmers can specify as little of a module as they like, as long as they declare the syntax. The approach has been validated with experiments using LILEANNA (for Library Interconnect Language Extended with Anna, where Anna itself is an acronym for Annotated Ada) [Tra93a] on real examples. LILEANNA, which has Ada [Ada83] as its programming language and Anna [Luc90] as its specification language, is also used for illustrations in this paper.

Our semantics for module expressions uses simple set theoretic manipulations to define module composition operations. This semantics is intended to aid implementors of module composition facilities; hence it is not a denotational or axiomatic semantics in the usual sense. In particular, it does not directly address the semantics of statements or what happens at compile time or at runtime; instead, it is concerned with the semantics of modules and their interconnection, that is, with what happens at *module composition time*. For this reason, it abstracts away details of the languages used for specification and programming.

Module composition languages can be used at least two different ways:

(i) *descriptively*, to specify and analyze a given design or architecture (that is, the interfaces and interconnections of modules); and

(ii) *constructively*, to create a new design from existing modules, using operations that combine and transform modules.

Using an MCL descriptively is like using a blueprint: it tells you about the structure of a house; languages that provide only these capabilities are often called MILs, Module Interconnection Languages [PDN86]. Using an MCL constructively is like having robots build a (modular) house by following a blueprint. This facilitates reuse, helps to control evolution†, and can simplify the development lifecycle by eliminating detailed design and coding, provided a suitable library of modules with their specifications and interrelationships is available.

An Analogy with Functional Programming It may be helpful to think of module composition as functional programming with modules ([Bur85] gives a nice exposition of this idea). The analogy is appropriate because we are evaluating expressions, called *module expressions*, that say how to put together software components. The result of evaluating a module expression is a *value*, namely the composed system; it is built by applying module composition operations to subsystems, which are also values.

Under this analogy, modules have *types*, which we call *theories*. A theory is another kind of module that is used to describe both the syntax and semantics of modules that supply code. We write "C :: T" to indicate that a module C has the "large grain type" T; this involves more than the usual notion of type indicated by the notation "C : T," because (what we call) a *view* must be given from T to C, binding the formal symbols in T to actual symbols in C. Furthermore, the axioms in T should be satisfied by the corresponding implementations of the symbols in C. Views are also used in instantiating parameterized modules, to say how to bind

---

† The traditional waterfall model is a great oversimplification, because it omits the processes of feedback and reconstruction that occur in real projects. Research on the sociology of software development shows that the division of tasks into phases is to a large extent illusory; see papers in [JG94], especially [BS94, Gog94].

symbols of a parameterized module's interface theory to symbols (for example, types and operators) in the module used as an actual parameter.

The axioms in the theory of a module give rise to "proof obligations;" these are mathematical assertions that should be true in order for the program to work as expected. We do not recommend that proofs be required for normal programming, but rather that a "hook" be left, in case rigorous formal methods are required. Thus in normal programming, the axioms only document properties of interfaces that the designers and programmers considered especially important, and believed to be true, perhaps as the result of informal reasoning.

There are two kinds of type in LILEANNA: (1) purely syntactic types that correspond to programming language types, and (2) types in the sense of theories, that is, programming language types and operations encapsulated with axioms. Hereafter we will use the word "type" only for programming language types (although theoretical discussions may use the word "sort" for added clarity), and we will use the word "theory" for large grain "types" at the module level.

Some History The paradigm for module composition described in this paper is based on *parameterized programming* and *hyperprogramming* [Gog89, Gog90b] (the term *megaprogramming* has been used in the DARPA community [BS92, WWC92]). Because this approach involves modules for both specification and code, both kinds of module must be composed. Specifications are used as "headers" for code, and are combined with simple set theoretic operations. At the code level, composition may be done with intermediate compiled code, which is sent to the compiler backend after composition. LILEANNA uses DIANA (for "Descriptive Intermediate Attributed Notation for Ada") for this purpose [DIA83, Tra93b].

Although we avoid abstract algebra and category theory, both the module composition facility and its semantics as described in this paper are largely inspired by work done using such formalisms, including the Clear specification language [BG77], and the OBJ [GM96, GWMFJ] system. The approach in this paper differs from that of those languages in providing a constructive module composition facility for an imperative programming language, as contemplated for the CAT and LIL [Gog85] systems, which are ancestors of LILEANNA.

The set theoretic implementation oriented semantics in this paper is novel. Sannella [San82] gave a set theoretic semantics for Clear. The elegant work of Wirsing [Wir86] on the ASL kernel specification language also involved a set theoretic approach. Many papers have used institutions and category theory to achieve generality. However, it had seemed that the generality of institutions was incompatible with the specificity of set theory. This paper combines the best of both approaches. It also differs from most previous work in the algebraic specification tradition in that it is concerned with generating systems, rather than just specifying them, that is, it is constructive as well as descriptive. Another unusual feature is the use of information hiding in specifications and the resulting behavioral (that is, "black box") notion of satisfaction for views. Similar basic laws for composing specifications were first proved in [GM82] and later in [ST88]. Material from the present paper appeared in [Tra97], and its full version may be found at www.cs.ucsd.edu/users/goguen/ps/will.ps.gz, which includes all the proofs omitted here.

The next section describes some foundational concepts that are used throughout the paper. This is followed by two sections on horizontal composition (on specification modules, and on implementation modules and views) and then a section on vertical composition. The paper concludes with some results and lessons.

11.2 Foundational Concepts

The concepts in this section are necessarily rather abstract, because of our goal to treat any (suitable) combination of programming and specification language. Readers more interested in using modules than in how they are defined may skip ahead. We may abbreviate "if and only if" by "iff." If S is a set, then S^* denotes the set of all finite lists from S, including the empty list, denoted []. We use the notation $[a_1, ..., a_n]$ for a list with n elements

11.2.1 The Module Graph

The parts from which systems are constructed are called *modules*. Parameterized programming has two kinds of module: (1) *specification* modules, and (2) *implementation* modules, which are discussed in Sections 11.3 and 11.4, respectively. The following gives a first definition for the basic *module graph* data structure used throughout the paper, and gradually extended with further assumptions for new features.

Definition 1 A **module graph G** consists of a finite set N of nodes, called **module names**, a finite set E of edges, two functions, $d_0, d_1 : E \to N$, which respectively give the source and target node for each edge, plus an acyclic subgraph **H**, called the **inheritance graph**, having the same node set N as **G**; thus, the edges of **H**, called **inheritance edges**, are a subset I of E, and the source and target functions of **H** agree with d_0 and d_1 on I. We write $N < M$ if there is a path from N to M in **H**. We may use the notation $e : M \to M'$ to indicate that e is an edge with $d_0(e) = M$ and $d_1(e) = M'$. □

Intuitively, the edges of a module graph indicate relationships between modules, of which the most basic are those of inheritance, indicated by the edges in the inheritance subgraph. $N < M$ means that M inherits from N. This relation is transitive because the composition of two paths is another path. (The idea of module graphs originates in [Gog91].)

Assumption 2 There are a fixed module graph **G** and inheritance subgraph **H**. □

Another kind of relationship between modules is a *view*, which asserts that the target module satisfies the axioms given in the source module. The module graph **G** describes the resources available at a given moment for building systems, including both modules and knowledge about their properties and interrelations; the role of **G** is analogous to that of an environment for evaluating expressions in a programming language.

11.2.2 Signatures and Tuple Sets

We will later define signatures for declaring the syntax of modules, using the notion of tuple sets given below. In this recursive definition, (0) is the base and (1) is the recursive step. It may help to visualize tuple sets as ordered trees having sets on their leaf nodes.

Definition 3 A **tuple set** is either

(0) a set, or else
(1) a tuple of tuple sets.

Two tuple sets have the **same form** if and only if they are both sets, or else are tuples of the same length such that their corresponding components have the same form. More formally, $t \sim t'$ iff

(0) t and t' are both sets, or else
(1) t and t' are tuples of the same length, say n, and $t_i \sim t_i'$ for $i = 1, \ldots, n$.

We will use the notation $(t_1, \ldots, t_n)$ for a tuple having n components, called an n-tuple. The sets that occur as the bottom level components of a tuple set are called its **base sets**, and their elements are called its **symbols**. □

When we need pairs, triples, lists, etc. that are not tuples, we will use the notation $[t_1, \ldots, t_n]$. The ordered tree view of tuple sets allows us to use paths as selectors to the base sets of tuple sets. If Σ is a tuple set and p is a path to a leaf node, then we let Σ_p denote the base set that is attached to that leaf node.

Example 4 Any set is a tuple set, e.g., $\{1, 0, \{1\}, -\}$; so is any tuple of sets, e.g., $(\{a, b\}, \{1, 2\})$; so is any tuple of tuple sets, e.g., $(\{a, b, c\}, (\{a, b\}, \{1, 2\}))$; and so on recursively. The tuple set $(\{a, b, c\}, (\{a, b\}, \{1, 2\}))$ has symbols $a, b, c, 1, 2$. On the other hand, the tuple set $\{[0, 0], [-, 1]\}$ has as its symbols the lists $[0, 0]$ and $[-, 1]$, rather than $0, 1$, and $-$. □

Example 5 The various signatures used for equational logic are tuple sets. For unsorted equational logic, there is a set O of operator symbols, plus an assignment of an **arity** $a(o)$ to each $o \in O$. Since a is a function, it can be viewed as a set of pairs. Thus $\Sigma = (O, a)$ where a is a set of pairs $[o, n]$ where n is a nonnegative integer and $o \in O$, such that there is exactly one such pair for each $o \in O$.

To allow *overloading*, where the same operator symbol o occurs with more than one arity, we could let Σ be a set of pairs $[o, n]$, where n is a natural number giving the arity; we can then define O from Σ, as the set of all o's that occur in the pairs in Σ. (Note that here the pairs $[o, n]$ are not tuple sets, they are symbols.)

For many sorted (also called "heterogeneous") equational logic, signatures consist of a set S of *sorts* (that is, "types") plus a set $\Sigma_{w,s}$ of operator symbols of sort s and arity w, for each $s \in S$ and $w \in S^*$. Thus, a signature is a pair (S, r) where S is a set and r is a set of triples $[w, s, o]$ with $s \in S$, $w \in S^*$, and o an operator symbol. This formulation again allows overloading, in that a given operator symbol o can occur with more than one "rank" $[w, s]$. Ada operator declarations can be treated in a very similar way. $\square$

Definition 6 Two tuple sets, t, t' are **equal**, written $t = t'$, iff they have the same form and all their corresponding components are equal, that is, if and only if t and t' have the same number of components, say n, and $t_i = t'_i$ for $i = 1, \dots, n$. We define **inclusion** similarly: $t \subseteq t'$ iff t and t' have the same form, with say n components, and $t_i \subseteq t'_i$ for $i = 1, \dots, n$. Similarly, the **difference** (or the **union**) of two or more tuple sets, all of the same form, is formed by taking the difference (or union) of the tuple sets occurring as their components. $\square$

Because signatures are tuple sets, Definition 6 gives us a natural notion of subsignature: Σ is a **subsignature** of Σ' iff $\Sigma \subseteq \Sigma'$ as tuple sets. For example,

$$(H, (T, O, V, E), (T_1, O_1, V_1, E_1), A) \subseteq (H', (T', O', V', E'), (T'_1, O'_1, V'_1, E'_1), A')$$

if and only if $H \subseteq H'$ and $T \subseteq T'$ and $O \subseteq O'$ and so on.

Definition 7 Given tuple sets Σ, Σ' of the same form, then a **tuple set relation** $\Sigma \to \Sigma'$ is a tuple set of pairs of symbols, that is, a subset of $\Sigma \times \Sigma'$ (technically, we should also add the source and target tuple sets to this tuple set of pairs). A tuple set relation is a **tuple set map** iff each of its base sets is a relation that is actually a function. A tuple set map is **injective** or **surjective** iff each of its base set functions is. Similarly, a tuple set map is an **isomorphism** iff each of its base set functions is; in this case we may write $\Sigma \approx \Sigma'$.

Given a tuple set Ω and a tuple set relation $h \colon \Omega \to \Sigma$, let $\Omega * h$ be the tuple set with each symbol a in each base set B of Ω replaced by the corresponding symbols a' in pairs $[a, a']$ in the corresponding base set of h, for each symbol a in Ω, that is,

$$(\Omega * h)_p = \{a' \mid a \in \Omega_p \text{ and } [a, a'] \in h_p\} \, ,$$

where Ω_p denotes the base set of Ω at the end of the path p. We call $\Omega * h$ the **renaming** of Ω by h. We may use the same notation when no target signature is given, because a smallest signature that will work can always be recovered from a tuple set of pairs with symbols from Σ. $\square$

Although tuple sets of the same form are closed under set theoretic operations performed component-wise, a given class of signatures need not be:

Example 8 Let $S = \{a, b\}, S' = \{a\}, r = \{[ab, a, f], [a, a, g], [b, b, h]\}$, and $r' = \{[a, a, g]\}$; then $(S, r) - (S', r') = (\{b\}, \{[ab, a, f], [b, b, h]\})$ is not a signature. $\square$

Definition 9 Given a collection *Sign* of tuple sets called "signatures," let *Sign*$^-$ denote the smallest class of tuple sets that contains *Sign* and is closed under tuple set difference. The new elements of *Sign*$^-$ will be called **partial signatures**. $\square$

Example 10 A LILEANNA signature has the form (T, O, V, E), where

- T is the set of visible (that is, exported) type declarations,
- O is the set of visible (that is, exported) operator declarations (with their input and output types),
- V is the set of variable declarations (including types), and
- E is the set of exception declarations.

The declarations in Figure 11.1 form a *partial signature*, because the types **Integer** and **Boolean** are used but not declared (they are assumed to be imported). Here T contains **Stack**, O contains **Is_Empty**, **Is_Full**, **Push**, **Pop**, and **Top**, while E contains **Stack_Empty** plus **Stack_Overflow**, and V is empty. $\square$

```
type Stack;
function Is_Full ( S : Stack ) return Boolean;
function Is_Empty ( S : Stack ) return Boolean;
exception Stack_Overflow;
exception Stack_Empty;
function Push ( I : Integer; S : Stack ) return Stack;
function Pop ( S : Stack ) return Stack;
function Top ( S : Stack ) return Integer;
```

Fig. 11.1. LILEANNA Signature for Bounded Stack of Integers.

11.2.3 Institutions, Sentences, and Models

This subsection presents an abstract framework that allows many notions of signature and axiom for specifications, as well as of models for implementations. We achieve this generality by using an axiomatization of the notion of "logical system" called an *institution*. It is outside the scope of this paper to develop the details of any particular logical system, and then show that it satisfies the conditions below; to provide the necessary details would take many pages of formal semantics, which would add little to this paper. But there are good reasons to believe that such examples satisfy the definition (for example, see [GB92]), and hereafter we will assume that Ada with Anna satisfies the conditions below:

Definition 11 An **institution** satisfies the following:

0. There is a class† *Sign* of signatures.
1. For each signature Σ, there is a set $Sen(\Sigma)$ of *sentences* built using Σ.
2. For each signature Σ, there is a class $Mod(\Sigma)$ of Σ-**models**, which provide *interpretations* for the symbols in Σ.
3. For each signature Σ, there is a **satisfaction** relation between Σ-sentences and Σ-models, written $c \models_\Sigma a$, where c is a Σ-model and a is a Σ-sentence; we may omit the subscript Σ on $\models_\Sigma$ if it is clear from context. We pronounce $c \models a$ as "c satisfies a."
4. For any signatures Σ and Σ', there is a set $Map(\Sigma, \Sigma')$ of **signature maps** from Σ to Σ', where $h \in Map(\Sigma, \Sigma')$ may be written $h: \Sigma \to \Sigma'$. There is a **composition** defined for signature maps, a function $Map(\Sigma, \Sigma') \times Map(\Sigma', \Sigma'') \to Map(\Sigma, \Sigma'')$ for each $\Sigma, \Sigma', \Sigma''$, which is associative and has an identity 1_Σ in $Map(\Sigma, \Sigma)$ for each Σ. We use the notation $h; h'$ for the composition of h in $Map(\Sigma, \Sigma')$ with h' in $Map(\Sigma', \Sigma'')$. Then we have $(h; h'); h'' = h; (h'; h'')$ and $h; 1_{\Sigma'} = h$ and $1_\Sigma; h = h$ for suitable h, h', h''.
5. Given a signature map $h: \Sigma \to \Sigma'$ and a Σ-sentence a, there is a **renaming of a by h**, also called a **translation of a by h**, denoted $a * h$, which is a Σ'-sentence, such that $a * 1_\Sigma = a$ and $a * (h; h') = (a * h) * h'$, for $h: \Sigma \to \Sigma'$ and $h': \Sigma' \to \Sigma''$.
6. For each signature map $h: \Sigma \to \Sigma'$ and each Σ'-model c', there is a **renaming of c' by h**, denoted $c' * h$, a Σ-model such that $c' * 1_\Sigma = c'$ and $c'' * (h; h') = (c'' * h') * h$.
7. Given a Σ-sentence a, a Σ'-model c' and a signature map $h: \Sigma \to \Sigma'$, we require that $c' \models_{\Sigma'} a * h$ iff $c' * h \models_\Sigma a$ (this is called the **satisfaction condition**).

We say that a Σ-model c **satisfies** a set A of Σ-sentences iff it satisfies each one of them, and in this case we write $c \models_\Sigma A$. $\square$

Condition 0 just says that we have signatures for declaring notation to be used in sentences and models. In our examples, signatures have types, operators, private types, private operators, and exceptions. Condition 1. says there are sentences. In our examples, Σ-sentences are built using the types, operators and exceptions in Σ.

---

† This paper seeks to avoid being distracted by foundational problems, but of course we wish to ensure that everything is sound. For this reason, when we encounter collections that may be too large to be sets, we will speak of *classes*, in the sense of Gödel-Bernays set theory. Some other similar issues are discussed in the full version of this paper.

Condition 2 says there are concrete entities, for example, Ada programs, to which sentences can refer. In our examples, models provide concrete data representations for the types in Σ, concrete operators for the operator symbols in Σ, and so on. Condition 3 introduces the mechanism through which sentences can refer to models: a model may or may not satisfy a given sentence; then a set of sentences determines the class of all models that satisfy all the given sentences, that is, that meet the given requirements. Condition 4 introduces "signature maps," which allow you to change notation. The composition of two signature maps describes the change in notation resulting from first applying one and then the other. It is intuitive that such a composition operation should be associative, and should have an "identity" map that indicates the substitution of each nonlogical symbol in the signature for itself, that is, with no change in notation. Condition 5 introduces the renaming operation for sentences, and states two properties that intuition says it should have. Condition 6 gives the corresponding operation and properties for renaming models; it is interesting to notice the *reversal* of direction in model renaming. Finally, condition 7 gives a property relating sentence and model renaming through satisfaction; this condition essentially says that truth is invariant under changes of notation. Much more information about institutions can be found in [GB92].

Definition 12 A Σ-sentence a is a **semantic consequence** of a set A of Σ-sentences, written $A \models_\Sigma a$, iff $c \models_\Sigma a$ whenever $c \models_\Sigma A$, that is, iff every model that satisfies A also satisfies a; we may also say that A (**semantically**) **entails** a. Given sets A and A' of Σ-sentences, we say that A (**semantically**) **entails** A' (or that A' is a **semantic consequence** of A) iff every model that satisfies A also satisfies A', that is, iff $c \models_\Sigma A$ implies $c \models_\Sigma A'$ for all Σ-models c. $\square$

For many logical systems, there is a natural notion of *deduction* on sentences, denoted $\vdash$, such that $A \vdash a$ iff $A \models a$; this makes it easier to implement checks of satisfaction, although it must be noted that in general the satisfaction problem is undecidable.

Every notion of signature of which we are aware is a tuple set in the sense of Definition 3; see Examples 5 and 10. Also, in each case signatures are closed under union, intersection, and renaming. Moreover, every notion of signature map of which we are aware is a tuple set map in the sense of Definition 7. This motivates the following:

Assumption 13 Each signature in our fixed institution is a tuple set in the sense of Definition 3, and the class of all signatures is closed under $\cup$, $\cap$, and $*$. Also, signature maps are exactly the corresponding tuple set maps. $\square$

It follows that inclusions $\Psi \subseteq \Sigma$ correspond to signature inclusion maps $i \colon \Psi \to \Sigma$. If h is a signature inclusion $\Psi \subseteq \Sigma$ and c is a Σ-model, then we may write $c|_\Psi$ for $c * h$, and call it the **restriction** or **reduct** of c to Ψ; this agrees with the standard terminology in first order logic, but we may use this terminology and notation even when h is not an inclusion. We now extend renaming from individual sentences and models to classes of sentences and classes of models, respectively:

Definition 14 Let A be a class of Σ-sentences, let $\mathcal{C}'$ be a class of Σ'-models, and let $h\colon \Sigma \to \Sigma'$ be a signature map. Then let $A * h = \{a * h \mid a \in A\}$ and $\mathcal{C}' * h = \{c' * h \mid c' \in \mathcal{C}'\}$. Note that $\mathcal{C}' * h$ is a class of Σ-models.

A signature map $h\colon \Sigma \to \Sigma'$ is an **isomorphism** iff there is another signature map $g\colon \Sigma' \to \Sigma$ such that $h; g = 1_\Sigma$ and $g; h = 1_{\Sigma'}$. $\square$

11.3 Specification Modules

There are two kinds of specification module: (1) theories and (2) packages. Both have signatures, which give the syntax for the module. Theories define properties of other modules, while packages specify what is to be implemented. A specification module is attached to each module name (in the module graph $\mathbf{G}$) as a "header," to (partially) describe the implementations (if any) attached to that name; it should at least include declarations for what is exported.

Assumption 15 For each module name M in the module graph, there is given a specification module $Q(M)$, with a tag saying whether it is a theory or a package†. Both the signature and sentences of each module $Q(M)$ are from a given fixed institution, in the sense of Definition 11. $\square$

Note that different module names could refer to the same specification module; that is, it is possible that $Q(M) = Q(M')$ with $M \neq M'$. Note also that specification modules are tuple sets, because they are 4-tuples having two sets and two tuple sets as components (see Definition 16 below). For convenience, we may write M when we really mean the specification module $Q(M)$ that is assigned to the name M.

Definition 16 A **specification module** is a tuple of the form (H, Σ, Ψ, A), where

1. H is a set of module names (for its imported modules),
2. Σ is a partial signature (to declare its types, operators, and so on),
3. Ψ is a sub-partial signature of Σ, called the **visible signature**‡ (for its exported types, operators, etc.), and
4. A is a set of $(\Sigma \cup |H|)$-sentences (also called **axioms**), where
$$|H| = \bigcup_{N \in H} |Q(N)|\,,$$
   and where $\Sigma \cup |H|$ is required to be a signature.

---

† Technically, this means giving two functions from the node set N of $\mathbf{G}$: one function (namely Q) to the class of specification modules, and the other, let us denote it t, to the set $\{\mathtt{th}, \mathtt{pkg}\}$.

‡ The symbols in Σ but not in Ψ are "local" or "private" types, operators, variables, and others used in axioms to describe the semantics of operators, exceptions, and so on; they are not exported. This gives us an information hiding capability, in the sense of [Par72, GM97].

We may call Σ the **local signature** of M to distinguish it from the visible signature Ψ of M, and we may call $|M|$ the **flat visible signature** of M.

Let us write $H(M)$ for the H component of M, $\Sigma(M)$ for its signature, $\Psi(M)$ for its visible signature, and $A(M)$ for its axioms. We call M **atomic** if $H(M) = \emptyset$; note that in this case, $|M| = \Psi(M)$. Finally, we let

$$\|(H, \Sigma, \Psi, A)\| = \Sigma \cup |H| ,$$

and call it the **working signature** of the module; it contains all the symbols that can be used in the axioms of the module. Note that 4. above requires that $\|M\|$ be a signature. $\square$

It is convenient to say "the axioms of module M" as shorthand for the A component of the tuple $Q(M)$ associated to the name M, that is, $A(Q(M))$. Note that $|M|$ includes all the visible symbols that M inherits from other modules. Also note that the two definitions of $|\_|$ are recursive over the inheritance hierarchy, and co-recursive with each other. Note that the working signature includes only visible symbols from inherited modules, but includes hidden symbols from the signature of the current module. Definition 16 implies that inheritance is *transitive*, in the sense that if M_3 imports M_2 and M_2 imports M_1, then everything visible in M_1 is also imported into M_3. We do not require M_1 to appear in the import set of M_3, only that M_1 appear in the import set of M_2 and M_2 in that of M_3.

Example 17 Given module names M_1, M_2, M_3 with associated specification modules $Q(M_i)$ for $i = 1, 2, 3$, suppose that $H(M_1) = \emptyset$, $H(M_2) = \{M_1\}$, and $H(M_3) = \{M_2\}$. Then

$$\begin{array}{lll} |H_1| = \emptyset & |M_1| = \Psi_1 & \|M_1\| = \Sigma_1 \\ |H_2| = \Psi_1 & |M_2| = \Psi_1 \cup \Psi_2 & \|M_2\| = \Sigma_1 \cup \Psi_2 \\ |H_3| = \Psi_1 \cup \Psi_2 & |M_3| = \Psi_1 \cup \Psi_2 \cup \Psi_3 & \|M_3\| = \Sigma_1 \cup \Psi_2 \cup \Psi_3 \end{array}$$

$\square$

According to Definition 16, $|M| = \Psi \cup |H|$ can be a partial signature. For LILEANNA, this means in particular that the interface to a module may have operations that involve types that are hidden (that is, private). For example, a STACK module is likely to have its Stack type hidden, but its operations pop and push visible. This means that users of the module can pop and push all they like, but they cannot look directly at the results of these operations, which might, for example, be an ugly mass of pointers.

Definition 18 Given a signature Σ, a set A of Σ-sentences, and a subsignature Ψ of Σ, we let the Ψ-**theory** of A be defined by

$$Th_{\Psi}(A) = \{a \in Sen(\Psi) \mid A \models_{\Sigma} a\} .$$

Given a module $M = (H, \Sigma, \Psi, A)$, define $Th(M)$, called the **theory** of M, by

$$Th(M) \;=\; Th_{\|M\|}(A(M) \,\cup\, \bigcup_{N \in H(M)} Th(N))\,.$$

Similarly, we define the **visible theory** of M, denoted $Vth(M)$, by

$$Vth(M) \;=\; Th_{|M|}(Th(M))\,.$$

$\square$

Note that $Th(M)$ is defined recursively over the inheritance hierarchy, so as to include all the consequences of all inherited axioms. Note also that $Th(M) = Th_\Sigma(A)$ when M is atomic, by the convention about unions over the empty index set and the fact that $\|M\| = \Sigma$. Similarly, $Vth(M) = Th_\Psi(A)$. Finally, note that $Vth(M) \subseteq Th(M)$.

If M is the `STACK` module with type `Stack` hidden, then its equation

$$pop(push(I, S)) = S$$

isn't visible, and so can't be part of $Vth(M)$ (see Figure 11.3). However, this equation does have many visible consequences, which are equations of visible type, that would be part of $Vth(M)$, such as

$$top(pop(push(I, S))) = top(S)$$
$$top(pop(pop(push(I, S)))) = top(pop(S)).$$

Such themes are much further developed in hidden algebra [GM97, Gog91].

Lemma 19 Given sets A and A' of Σ-sentences and a subsignature Ψ of Σ, then $A \subseteq A'$ implies $Th_\Psi(A) \subseteq Th_\Psi(A')$; moreover, $Th_\Psi(Th_\Psi(A)) = Th_\Psi(A)$. However, it is *not* true that $A \subseteq Th_\Psi(A)$, because $Th_\Psi(A)$ only contains Ψ-axioms. Also, it is not true that $c \models_\Sigma A$ iff $c \models_\Sigma Th_\Psi(A)$. $\square$

Proposition 20 If M is a specification module then $|M| \subseteq \|M\|$, and if $H(M) = \{N\}$, then $|N| \subseteq |M|$. More generally, if $H(M) = H$, then

(Law 1) $\displaystyle\bigcup_{N \in H} |N| \subseteq |M|$,

and if† $N < M$ then $|N| \subseteq |M|$. $\square$

Assumption 21 The function Q defined on (the set of module names in) the module graph $\mathbf{G}$ is such that there is an inheritance edge from M' to M iff the name M' appears in the import set $H(M)$ of the specification module $Q(M)$ for M. Also, it is forbidden to inherit a theory into a package. $\square$

Notation 22 If M is a module that inherits a set H of modules, then we may use the notation M^H to emphasize the role of H; however, this superscript is not really needed, because H is already given in the associated specification module $Q(M)$. We may also write M^N when the inheritance set for M is $\{N\}$, M^{N_1, N_2} when it is $\{N_1, N_2\}$, etc. $\square$

```
theory ANY_TYPE is
    type Element;
end ANY_TYPE;

theory MONOID is
    type Element;
    function "*" ( X, Y : Element) return Element;
    − − |axiom
    − − |        for all X, Y, Z : Element: =>
    − − |                (X * Y) * Z = X * (Y * Z) ; −− associative property
    − − |axiom
    − − |        for all X : Element: =>
    − − |        exist I : Element: =>
    − − |                ( X * I = X ) and ( I * X = X ) ; −− identity property
end MONOID;

theory EQV is
    type Element;
    function Equal ( X, Y : Element ) return Boolean;
    − − |axiom
    − − |        for all E1, E2, E3 : Element =>
    − − |                Equal ( E1, E1 ),
    − − |                (Equal ( E1, E2 ) and
    − − |                Equal ( E2, E3 ) -> Equal ( E1,E3 )),
    − − |                (Equal ( E1, E2 ) -> Equal ( E2, E1 ));
end EQV;
```

Fig. 11.2. Some LILEANNA Theory Specifications.

Example 23 Figure 11.2 shows three LILEANNA specification modules. The first is a theory called ANY_TYPE; it has a single type **Element**, and nothing more; it can be satisfied by any module that has a type. The second theory, MONOID, contains a single type and one operation that takes two parameters of that type and returns a **Boolean** value. This theory also contains two axioms. The Anna "annotation" language uses conventions, stylized Ada comments (following the symbol --|) to assert formal semantics of this LILEANNA specification module. An Anna annotation consists of variable declarations, quantifiers, and boolean expressions, whose values are asserted to be true using the symbol "=>." The first axiom asserts the associative law for the operation *, and the second asserts the identity law. The third theory, EQV, for equivalence relations, is similar to MONOID in having a single type and three assertions for its operation, which are reflexivity, symmetry, and transitivity, given by three Anna assertions, separated by commas; the last two assertions use Anna's implication symbol "->."

Figure 11.3 shows a package specification called INTSTACK for a bounded stack of integers; it has some relevant exceptions, and it inherits the module INTEGER, which defines the integers with appropriate operations (that is, $h(\texttt{intstack}) = \{\texttt{integer}\}$). The axioms describe how the operations change the state of objects of type **Stack**. The exception annotations on the operations **Push**, **Pop** and **Top** specify when these exceptions are raised.

† Recall that this means that there is a path from N to M in the inheritance graph.

```
package INTSTACK is
     inherit INTEGER;
     type Stack;
     Stack_Empty : exception ;
     Stack_Overflow: exception ;
     function Is_Empty ( S : Stack ) return Boolean;
     function Is_Full ( S : Stack ) return Boolean;
     function Push ( I : Integer; S : Stack ) return Stack;
     - - | where
     - - |        Is_Full ( S ) => raise Stack_Overflow;
     function Pop ( S : Stack ) return Stack;
     - - | where
     - - |        Is_Empty ( S ) => raise Stack_Empty;
     function Top ( S : Stack ) return Integer;
     - - | where
     - - |        Is_Empty ( S ) => raise Stack_Empty;

     - - |axiom
     - - |        for all I : Integer; S : Stack =>
     - - |            not Is_Full ( S ) ->
     - - |                (Pop ( Push ( I, S ) ) = S) and
     - - |                (Top ( Push ( I, S ) ) = I );

end INTSTACK;
```

Fig. 11.3. LILEANNA Bounded Integer Stack Package Specifications.

Theory modules are not intended to be implemented, but instead are used to define interfaces and declare properties. For example, the theory MONOID an the appropriate interface for iterators over certain data structures (see [Gog89]). On the other hand, package modules like INTSTACK are intended to be implemented, and this may be done in a variety of ways. The module INTSTACK also illustrates the use of partial specifications, because no axioms are given for Is_Full.

The package INTSTACK illustrates three of Anna's formal specification mechanisms: subprogram annotations, exception annotations, and axioms. Anna also has object annotations, type and subtype annotations, propagation annotations, context annotations, "virtual functions," and package states in axioms. □

Proposition 24 If M^N is a specification module with $H(M) = \{N\}$, then $Vth(N) \subseteq Vth(M^N)$. More generally, if $H(M) = H$, then

$$(\text{Law 2}) \quad \bigcup_{N \in H} Vth(N) \subseteq Vth(M^H) \,,$$

and if $N < M$ then $Vth(N) \subseteq Vth(M)$. The same results hold for $Th(M)$. □

Example 25 As in Example 17, assume module names M_1, M_2, M_3 with associated specification modules $Q(M_i)$ for $i = 1, 2, 3$, such that $H(M_1) = \emptyset$, $H(M_2) = \{M_1\}$, and $H(M_3) = \{M_2\}$. Also assume that

$$\Sigma(M_1) = \{[a, 0], [b, 0], [c, 0]\} \quad \Psi(M_1) = \{[a, 0], [c, 0]\} \quad A(M_1) = \{a = b, \; b = c\}$$
$$\Sigma(M_2) = \{[f, 1]\} \qquad\qquad \Psi(M_2) = \emptyset \qquad\qquad A(M_2) = \emptyset$$
$$\Sigma(M_3) = \{[g, 1], [h, 1]\} \quad\;\; \Psi(M_3) = \{[g, 1]\} \qquad A(M_3) = \{g(x) = h(x)\}.$$

Then

$$Vth(M_1) = \{a = b, \; b = c, \; a = c, \; a = a, \; b = b, \; c = c, \; b = a, \; c = b, \; c = a\}$$
$$Vth(M_2) = Vth(M_1)$$
$$Vth(M_3) = Vth(M_1) \cup \{k(l) = k'(r) \mid k, k' \in \{g, h\}, \; l = r \in A(M_1)\} \, .$$

□

11.3.1 *Overload Resolution*

We will assume below that each symbol has a "true name" that is tagged with the name of the module where it is declared. Because it is awkward to use such names in practice, we want a parser that can recover the true name from a "nickname" that omits the tag; the process of finding the closest true name corresponds to what is called "dynamic binding" in the object oriented community.

Notation 26 Because signatures are tuple sets, the required tagging can be accomplished by replacing each symbol σ by the pair $[\sigma, M]$, where M is the specification module involved; we will write this more simply as σ_M. □

Forming a tuple set of such pairs can be seen as a new operation on tuple sets. But first we need an auxiliary notion:

Definition 27 Given a signature map $h \colon \Psi \to \Omega$ with $\Psi \subseteq \Sigma$ such that Ω is disjoint from $\Sigma - \Psi$, we can extend h to a map $\overline{h} \colon \Sigma \to \overline{\Omega} = \Omega \cup (\Sigma - \Psi)$ by defining $\overline{h} = h \cup (1_{\Sigma - \Psi})$. □

We do not always use the notation $\overline{h}$ explicitly, but instead just write h. This convention allows us to write $a * h$ when a is a Σ-sentence with $h \colon \Psi \to \Omega$ and $\Psi \subseteq \Sigma$, and to write $A * h$ when A is a set of Σ-sentences.

Definition 28 If T is a tuple set and M is a symbol, let T_M denote the tuple set having the same form as T with each symbol σ in a leaf node being replaced by the pair $[\sigma, M]$. If $Q = (H, \Sigma, \Psi, A)$ is a module, then let $Q\_M = (H, \Sigma\_M, \Psi\_M, A * \overline{r}_{\Sigma, M})$, where $r_{\Sigma, M}$ is a signature map from Σ to Σ_M having the same shape as Σ, with each symbol σ in a leaf node set replaced by $[\sigma, [\sigma, M]]$, and the overbar indicates its extension to $\|M\|$. □

Assumption 29 The symbols in the local and visible signatures of each specification module are tagged with the module name. If we let $Q_0(M) = (H, \Sigma, \Psi, A)$ denote the untagged form of the module associated to the name M, then $Q(M) = Q_0(M)\_M$. □

In particular, if Σ and Σ' are the local signatures of modules with distinct names M and M', respectively, then Σ and Σ' are disjoint.

Example 30 As in Example 17, assume module names M_1, M_2, M_3 with associated specification modules $Q(M_i)$ for $i = 1, 2, 3$, such that $H(M_1) = \emptyset$, $H(M_2) = \{M_1\}$, and $H(M_3) = \{M_2\}$. Also assume that

$$\Sigma(M_1) = \{[a, 0], [b, 0], [c, 0]\} \quad \Psi(M_1) = \{[a, 0], [c, 0]\}$$
$$\Sigma(M_2) = \{[a, 0], [d, 0]\} \quad \Psi(M_2) = \{[d, 0]\}$$
$$\Sigma(M_3) = \{[c, 0], [d, 0]\} \quad \Psi(M_3) = \{[c, 0]\} \ .$$

Then the "tagged" forms of these signatures are as follows:

$$\Sigma\_M_1 = \{[a, 0]\_M_1, [b, 0]\_M_1, [c, 0]\_M_1\} \quad \Psi\_M_1 = \{[a, 0]\_M_1, [c, 0]\_M_1\}$$
$$\Sigma\_M_2 = \{[a, 0]\_M_2, [d, 0]\_M_2\} \quad \Psi\_M_2 = \{[d, 0]\_M_2\}$$
$$\Sigma\_M_3 = \{[c, 0]\_M_3, [d, 0]\_M_3\} \quad \Psi\_M_3 = \{[c, 0]\_M_3\} \ .$$

□

We want a parser that will allow us to use the symbols that appear in $Q_0(M)$ as shorthand for the full notation that appears in $Q(M)$, that is, to use the simpler notation σ for a symbol σ_M in $Q(M)$. This parser should disambiguate a symbol σ occurring in M according to the following rules:

(i) if the symbol σ is declared in M, then σ is parsed as σ_M;

(ii) if σ is not declared in M but is declared in some modules inherited by M, then it is parsed as σ_N where N is the unique *least* module (in the sense that the path from N to M is shortest in **H** having this property) inherited by M that declares σ, if there is one;

(iii) otherwise, a parse error is produced for σ in M. (In this case, the label σ cannot be disambiguated by the parser, and should have been explicitly written σ_N for some module name N.)

11.4 Implementation Modules and Views

We are now ready to say what is an implementation for a given package specification module M. Note that we do not need to implement what is hidden inside of M. In fact, we take an implementation of a module to be a model of what it exports as well as everything it inherits. This provides a precise correctness criterion for code while avoiding many complications.

Definition 31 An **implementation** for a specification module $M = (H, \Sigma, \Psi, A)$ is an $|M|$-model C satisfying $Vth(M)$; in this case we say that C **satisfies** M, we write $C \models M$, and we may call C an M-**module**. Let $[\![M]\!]$ denote the class of all implementations for M, called the **denotation** of M. □

It is possible for C to implement M using hidden operations that are completely different from those in $\Sigma - \Psi$. We do not include such hidden operations in the signature of C, but our institution may be such that this information is already in C, for example, if models consist of Ada code. The following says that if the visible theories of two specifications are the same, then they have the same denotation. The second assertion implies that we can require compatibility with a prior implementation C_N of an inherited module N by imposing the condition that $C|_N = C_N$.

Proposition 32 Given specification modules M and M', then $|M| = |M'|$ and $Vth(M) = Vth(M')$ imply $[\![M]\!] = [\![M']\!]$.

Let M be a package specification module and let C be an implementation module for M. Then $C \models M$ implies $C|_{|N|} \models N$ for each $N < M$ in the module inheritance graph **H**. □

At a given point in a software development project, there may be zero or more implementation modules associated to a given module name M. These fit into the module graph structure that we are developing as follows:

Assumption 33 There is a partial function I from module names to lists of implementation modules, defined on the names of package specification modules, and not on those of theory specification modules. (Note that $I(M)$ may be the empty list.) Each implementation module in $I(M)$ defines an implementation for $Q(M)$, for each module name M in the module graph **G**. □

A view in LILEANNA is a signature map used to assert that some theory is satisfied by some other specification module; more technically, a view binds the "formal" symbols in the signature of the source theory to "actual" symbols in the target module, which may be either a theory or a package, in such a way that the proof obligations arising from the signature map are satisfied.

Definition 34 A **view** from a specification module $M = (H, \Sigma, \Psi, A)$ to a specification module $M' = (H', \Sigma', \Psi', A')$ is a signature map $h: |M| \to |M'|$ such that $\Psi * h \subseteq |M'|$ and $Th(M') \models_{\|M'\|} a * h$ for each $a \in Vth(M)$, that is, such that $Th(M') \models_{\|M'\|} Vth(M) * h$. In this case, we may write $h: M \to M'$. We may also call a view a **specification module map**. □

In practice, we often have $H \subseteq H'$, so that a view $h: M \to M'$ can be given by just a signature map $h: \Psi \to \Psi'$, which then extends to a map $\overline{h}: \Psi \cup |H| \to \Psi' \cup |H'|$, provided Ψ is disjoint from $|H|$. In this case, the proof obligations are just that $Th(M') \models_{\|M'\|} a * \overline{h}$ for each $a \in Th(A)$, i.e., that the translations of the visible consequences of axioms in A hold for any model of $Th(M')$. This means that some axioms in M, namely those involving "hidden" types and/or operations, need only "appear" to be consequences of the axioms in M'; that is, we are dealing with what is called "behavioral satisfaction," as is appropriate to the "black box" notion of module used in this paper. Techniques for proving this kind of satisfaction have been developed in hidden algebra [GM97, Gog91].

For example, in the example of a STACK module with type Stack hidden, the equation $pop(push(I, S)) = S$ is *not* satisfied by the standard implementation using an array and a pointer, but all of its visible consequences are. So a view from M as this STACK specification module to another more concrete specification module M' for stacks implemented with an array and a pointer would satisfy the condition of Definition 34, since everything in $Vth(M)$ is satisfied by M'.

Example 35 The LILEANNA code in Figure 11.4 gives the theory of partially ordered sets; the axioms say that the operation "<=" on objects of type Element is reflexive, transitive, and antisymmetric. The three views shown in Figure 11.5 are of the NATURAL numbers as a partially ordered set. The first, NATD, uses the Divide function as a partial order relation. The second, NATV, gives the usual linear ordering relation. The view NAT_OBV can be abbreviated as in NAT_DEF by leaving out the operation mapping, using the default view mechanism discussed briefly at the end of Section 11.4. □

```
theory POSET is
      type Element;
      function "<=" ( X, Y : Element ) return Boolean;
       --| axiom
          --| for all E1, E2, E3 : Element =>
               --| E1 <= E1,
               --| (E1 <= E2 and E2 <= E3 -> E1 <= E3),
               --| (E1 <= E2 and E2 <= E1 -> E1 = E2);
   end POSET;
```

Fig. 11.4. Theory of Partially Ordered Sets.

```
view NATD :: POSET => STANDARD is
      types ( Element => Natural );
      ops ( "<=" => Divides );
end NATD;

view NAT_OBV :: POSET => STANDARD is
      types ( Element => Natural );
      ops ( "<=" => "<=" );
end NAT_OBV;

view NAT_DEF :: POSET => STANDARD is
      types ( Element => Natural ); -- no ops map - take the default
end NAT_DEF;
```

Fig. 11.5. Views of Natural Numbers as POSETs.

Lemma 36 Given specification modules $M = (H, \Sigma, \Psi, A)$ and $M' = (H', \Sigma', \Psi', A')$, then a signature map $h: |M| \to |M'|$ is a view $h: M \to M'$ iff $Vth(M) * h \subseteq Vth(M')$. $\square$

Proposition 37 Every specification module inclusion is a view, and the composition of two views is a view. $\square$

Languages that support the parameterized programming paradigm of this paper can declare views; thus, views are "first class citizens," on the same level as modules. Because views are relationships between modules, it makes sense that they should be recorded as edges in the module graph, between the modules that they relate. This is formalized as follows:

Assumption 38 Each non-inheritance edge $e: M \to M'$ in the module graph **G** is labeled with a view denoted $Q(e)$ from $Q(M)$ to $Q(M')$, where $Q(M)$ is a theory. We may denote this view by just e. When the edge $e: M \to M'$ is an inheritance edge (that is, in case $M \in H(M')$), we let $Q(e)$, or just e, denote the inclusion view $Q(M) \to Q(M')$, which is given by the inclusion signature map $|M| \to |M'|$. $\square$

When the user feels there is an obvious view to use, it is annoying to have to write out that view in full detail. **Default views** capture the intuitive notion of "the obvious view" and often allow omitting part, or even all, of the details of a view. See [Gog89]. These have been implemented in OBJ3 [GWMFJ] and in LILEANNA.

11.5 Horizontal Composition

This section discusses LILEANNA's operations for putting specifications together at a single level of a system architecture, while the next section discusses how the layering of systems is handled.

11.5.1 Renaming Specifications

Definition 39 Given a specification module $M = (H, \Sigma, \Psi, A)$ and a signature map $h: \Psi \to \Psi'$, define the **renaming** or **translation** of M by h, denoted $M * h$, to be the specification module $(H, \Sigma * \overline{h}, \Psi', A * \overline{h})$, where the first $\overline{h}$ is $1_{\Sigma - \Psi} \cup h$ and the second $\overline{h}$ is $1_{(\|M\|) - \Psi} \cup h$, recalling Definition 27 and that $\|M\| = \Sigma \cup |H|$. $\square$

We may also use the notation $M * h$ when $\Psi(M) = \Psi$ and $h: \Psi' \to \Psi''$ with $\Psi' \subseteq \Psi$, by extending h to $\overline{h}$, starting from Ψ' instead of from Ψ. Similarly, we may use this notation when $\Psi \subseteq \Psi'$ by first restricting h to Ψ, that is, by extending $h^\diamond = \square_\Psi; h$, where $\square_\Psi$ denotes the "square" relation, consisting of all pairs from Ψ, instead of extending h. A more general notion is:

Definition 40 Given a signature map $h\colon \Sigma \to \Omega$ and $\Psi \subseteq \Sigma$, we can **restrict** h to Ψ by defining $h^\Diamond = \Box_\Psi; h.$ $\Box$

As with the overbar notation of Definition 27, we often do not use the notation $h^\Diamond$ explicitly, but instead just write h. This convention allows us to write $a * h$ when $a * h$ for a a Ψ-sentence with $h\colon \Sigma \to \Omega$ and $\Psi \subseteq \Sigma$. Note that if h in Definition 39 is not injective, then some types and operations may be "munged" together. Then the resulting single operation will have to satisfy the union of (the translated versions of) all the axioms for the operations that were identified.

Proposition 41 Given specification module $M = (H, \Sigma, \Psi, A)$ and signature maps $h\colon \Psi \to \Psi'$ and $h'\colon \Psi' \to \Psi''$, then

　　(Law 3) $M * 1_\Psi = M$,

　　(Law 4) $(M * h) * h' = M * (h; h')$.

$\Box$

11.5.2 Hiding and Enriching

We now discuss two operations on modules (or systems, or subsystems) that were not implemented in Clear or OBJ, although similar ideas were proposed for LIL in [Gog85]. These operations allow deleting some of the visible interface of a module, and also adding to it. LILEANNA syntax for the first operation is $M * (\texttt{hide } \Phi)$, and for the second is $M * (\texttt{add } \Phi, A)$, where Φ is a partial signature and A is a set of axioms.

Definition 42 Given a specification module $M = (H, \Sigma, \Psi, A)$ and a partial sub-signature $\Phi \subseteq \Psi$, we define $M * (\texttt{hide } \Phi) = (H, \Sigma, \Psi - \Phi, A)$, where it is required that $((\Psi - \Phi) \cup |H|)$ is a signature. In the special case where $\Psi = \Phi$, we may write $(\texttt{hide-all})$ for $(\texttt{hide } \Phi)$.

　　Given a partial subsignature Φ disjoint from $\|M\|$ and a set A' of $(\Sigma \cup \Phi \cup |H|)$-axioms, let $M * (\texttt{add } \Phi, A') = (H, \Sigma \cup \Phi, \Psi \cup \Phi, A \cup A')$, where it is required that $(\Sigma \cup \Phi \cup |H|)$ and $(\Psi \cup \Phi \cup |H|)$ are signatures. $\Box$

Note that $H(M * h) = H(M)$. Sometimes we want to know what axioms could have been translated to produce some of a given set of axioms.

Definition 43 Given a map $h\colon \Phi \to \Psi$ and a spec $M = (H, \Sigma, \Psi, A)$, let $h^{-1}(M) = (H, \Phi, \Phi, \overline{h}^{-1}(Vth(M)))$, where $\overline{h}\colon \Phi \cup |H| \to \Psi \cup |H|$ and $\overline{h}^{-1}(Vth(M)) = \{a \in Sen(\Phi \cup |H|) \mid a * \overline{h} \in Vth(M)\}$. We call $h^{-1}(M)$ the **inverse image module** of M under h. $\Box$

Proposition 44 Given $h\colon \Phi \to \Psi$ where $M = (H, \Sigma, \Psi, A)$, then $\overline{h}\colon \overline{h}^{-1}(M) \to M$ is a view.

If $M = (H, \Sigma, \Psi, A)$ and C is a $|M|$-model, then $C \models M * (\textbf{hide } \Phi)$ iff $C \models i^{-1}(M)$, where i is the inclusion of $\Psi - \Phi$ into Ψ. □

Thus, the specification modules $M * (\textbf{hide } \Phi)$ and $i^{-1}(M)$ are in a sense equivalent.

11.5.3 Renaming and Transformation for Implementations

Users of systems like LILEANNA in general are more interested in implementations than specifications. Hence we should investigate transformations of implementations. We first discuss renaming. As with condition 6. in Definition 11, renaming implementations moves in the opposite direction from that of the signature map involved, whereas for specifications it moves in the same direction. Thus, there is a duality between specifications and implementations, parallel to the duality between sentences and models, as reflected in the following:

Proposition 45 If $h: M \to M'$ is a view and C' is an M'-module, then $C' * h$ is an M-module. Let $[\![h]\!]: [\![M']\!] \to [\![M]\!]$ denote the function sending C' to $C' * h$. □

Copying and renaming of implementations is surprisingly powerful: it allows deleting functionality from an implementation, as well as adding new functionality defined using what is already present; it also allows making one or more new copies of items exported by a module.

Definition 46 Given a specification module $M = (H, \Sigma, \Psi, A)$, an implementation C for M, and a partial subsignature $\Phi \subseteq \Psi$, let i denote the inclusion of $\Psi - \Phi$ into Ψ. Then $C * \bar{i}$ is denoted $C * (\textbf{hide } \Phi)$. □

Example 47 Figure 11.6 shows a module transformation using renaming, hiding, and enriching: the package RECTANGLE is inherited, extended with the operation Side, with its type Rectangle renamed to Square, and its operations Length and Width hidden (but not removed!); an axiom has also been added. (This is based on an example in [Mey88].) □

```
package SQUARE is
       inherit RECTANGLE * (rename Rectangle => Square)
                         * (add function Side ( S : Square ) return Real)
                         * (hide Width, Length);
       -- | axiom
       -- |      for all S : Square =>
       -- |           Length ( S ) = Width ( S );
   end;
```

Fig. 11.6. Specifying a SQUARE Package as a Transformation of RECTANGLE.

More generally, if $h: M \to M'$ is not surjective (that is, there may be symbols p such that there is no symbol p' such that $p = h(p')$), then implementations for symbols in the visible signature of M' that are not the image of any symbol in the visible signature of M are dropped (or "sliced") from C' when $C' * h$ is formed.

Proposition 48 Given a specification module $M = (H, \Sigma, \Psi, A)$ and a $|M|$-model C, then $C \models M$ implies $C * (\texttt{hide } \Phi) \models M * (\texttt{hide } \Phi)$. $\square$

Rather than give a construction for adding functionality to an implementation, we give a *correctness criterion* that should be satisfied by any such construction. The reason for this indirect approach is that many different constructions are possible, depending on the language involved, on the compiler technology used, and even on the amount of effort that the implementor wants to undertake.

Definition 49 Given a specification module $M = (H, \Sigma, \Psi, A)$, an implementation C of M, a partial subsignature Φ disjoint from $\|M\|$, and a set A' of $(\Sigma \cup \Phi \cup |H|)$-axioms, then we write $C' = C * (\texttt{add } \Phi, A')$ iff $C' \models M * (\texttt{add } \Phi, A')$. $\square$

Note that C' is *not* unique. More generally, whenever h is not injective (that is, we can have $h(p) = h(p')$ for some symbols $p \neq p'$), $C' * h$ will have one or more extra copies of some items implemented by C'.

Example 50 Figure 11.7 shows the package SINGLE_LINKED_LIST enriched to DOU-BLE_INKED_LIST by adding the operation **Previous**. Some users might prefer to include Ada code directly in the module expression, but the current implementation of LILEANNA requires placing it in a separate file, which is translated to intermediate representation (DIANA), and then manipulated as specified by the module composition operations. $\square$

The operations for renaming, hiding and adding to implementations are very useful as part of a module connection language, because existing modules often do not do exactly what is wanted. Another useful operation on implementations has an apparently more *ad hoc* character, simply adding to the signature and code. For example, to add a new enumeration literal to an enumerated type, the LILEANNA syntax is:

$$C * (\texttt{add literal to } \langle TypeName \rangle, \langle Literal \rangle).$$

We have proved the satisfaction condition for implementation modules with respect to specification modules, but this paper is not the place for such a technical result.

11.5.4 Aggregation of Specifications

Module aggregation is the flat combination of modules. An important issue is sharing common inherited modules; to understand how sharing works under aggregation, recall that all symbols introduced in a module are tagged with the name of that module. By convention, modules that are inherited are *always shared*: If A and

```
package DOUBLE_LINKED_LIST is
    inherit SINGLE_LINKED_LIST * (rename SLList => DLList)
              * (add function Previous ( N : Node; L : List ) return Node
                    – – | axiom Next ( Previous ( N, L ) ) = N ;
                    – – | raise Invalid_Node => NOT_IN ( N, L );
                    – – | raise Invalid_Node => HEAD ( L );
                    – – code found in separate package due to
                    – – limitations on current implementation.
              )
end;

package MAKELIL is
        – – By convention, the code to be added is found in this
        – – separately parsed Ada package/DIANA AST.
        function Previous ( N : Node; L : List ) return Node is
            begin
                if Current.Value = N.Value and
                    Current.Next = N.Next then
                        raise Invalid_Node; – – At Head
                end if;
                while Current.Next /= null loop
                    if Current.Value = N.Value and
                        Current.Next = N.Next then
                            return Last; – – found
                    else – – move down list
                            Last := Current.Next;
                            Current := Last.Next;
                    end if;
                end loop; – – drop through if not found
                raise Invalid_Node;
            end;
end MAKELIL;
```

Fig. 11.7. Transforming SINGLE_LINKED_LIST to DOUBLE_LINKED_LIST.

B both inherit M, then the resulting value of the module expression $A + B$ (the aggregation of modules A and B) only has one copy of M; this is consistent with the way that Ada handles imports. Here is the formalization:

Definition 51 If $M = (H, \Sigma, \Psi, A)$ and $M' = (H', \Sigma', \Psi', A')$ are specification modules, then the **aggregation** or **sum** of M and M' is

$$M + M' = (H \cup H', \Sigma \cup \Sigma', \Psi \cup \Psi', A \cup A') \,.$$

For convenience, we may also use the notation $M \cup M'$ in some formulae. More generally, given specification modules $M_i = (H_i, \Sigma_i, \Psi_i, A_i)$ for $i = 1, \ldots, n$, let

$$\sum_{i=1}^{n} M_i = (\bigcup_{i=1}^{n} H_i, \bigcup_{i=1}^{n} \Sigma_i, \bigcup_{i=1}^{n} \Psi_i, \bigcup_{i=1}^{n} A_i) \,.$$

We may also use the notation $\bigcup_{i=1}^{n} M_i$. Notice that there are natural views $M_j \to M = \bigcup_{i=1}^{n} M_i$, which are just inclusions; we denote these J_j for $j = 1, \ldots, n$. $\square$

Notice that operators with the same name (say o) introduced in different modules are automatically "named apart" in the aggregation (that is, they are o_M and o_M', because of Assumption 29 about the names of symbols in modules.)

Proposition 52 Aggregation is associative, commutative and idempotent, that is,

(**Law 5**) $M + M' = M' + M$,

(**Law 6**) $M + (M' + M'') = (M + M') + M''$,

(**Law 7**) $M + M = M$,

(**Law 8**) $M \subseteq M + N$,

(**Law 9**) $N \subseteq M$ implies $M + N = M$.

$\square$

The idempotent (Law 7) law depends on the fact that the two modules not only have the same content, but also the same name. If $Q(M) = Q(M')$ with $M \neq M'$, then $M + M' = M$ does not hold. The main equality about inheritance follows directly from the definition, and then implies the laws below it:

Proposition 53 Given specification modules M_i for $i = 1, \ldots, n$, then

$$H\left(\sum_{i=1}^{n} M_i\right) = \bigcup_{i=1}^{n} H(M_i) .$$

Given specification modules M_1 and M_2 and a set H of module names,

(**Law 10**) $M^H + M'^H = (M + M')^H$,

(**Law 11**) $M^{N_1, N_2} = M^{N_2, N_1} = M^{N_1 + N_2}$,

(**Law 12**) $M^{N_1^H,\ N_2^H} = M^{(N_1 + N_2)^H}$,

(**Law 13**) $M^N + N = M^N$.

$\square$

Lemma 54 Let M and M' be specification modules. Then

$Th(M + M') = Th(M) \cup Th(M')$,

$|M + M'| = |M| \cup |M'|$,

$\|M + M'\| = \|M\| \cup \|M'\|$.

$\square$

Proposition 55 Given specification modules M_1, M_2 and signature map $h \colon \Psi_1 + \Psi_2 \to \Psi$, then

(**Law 14**) $(M_1 + M_2) * h = (M_1 * h) + (M_2 * h)$.

$\square$

Sometimes we need to aggregate two copies of the same module. This can be done with renaming, but it is useful to have a special notation:

Definition 56 Let M_i be specification modules for $i = 1, \ldots, n$. Then we define

$$\bigoplus_{i=1}^{n} M_i = \bigcup_{i=1}^{n} M_i \_i .$$

and we call this operation **separated aggregation**. When $n = 2$ we use the notation $M_1 \oplus M_2$.

Given specification module maps (that is, views) $P_i \colon T_i \to M$ for $i = 1, 2$, define $P = P_1 ! P_2 \colon T_1 \oplus T_2 \to M$ by $P(\sigma\_i) = P_i(\sigma)$ for $i = 1, 2$. Similarly, given specification module maps $P_i \colon T_i \to M$ for $i = 1, \ldots, n$, define $P = !_{i=1}^{n} P_i \colon \bigoplus_{i=1}^{n} T_i \to M$ by $P(\sigma\_i) = P_i(\sigma)$ for $i = 1, \ldots, n$.

Similarly, given specification module maps $h_1 \colon T_1 \to N_1$ and $h_2 \colon T_2 \to N_2$, define $h = (h_1 \oplus h_2) \colon (T_1 \oplus T_2) \to (N_1 \oplus N_2)$ by $h(\sigma\_i) = h_i(\sigma)$ for $i = 1, 2$. More generally, given $h_i \colon T_i \to N_i$ for $i = 1, \ldots, n$, define $h = \bigoplus_{i=1}^{n} h_i \colon \bigoplus_{i=1}^{n} T_i \to \bigoplus_{i=1}^{n} N_i$ by $h(\sigma\_i) = h_i(\sigma)$ for $i = 1, \ldots, n$. $\square$

Lemma 57 In the above definition, P is a specification module map. Furthermore, if each P_i is injective and if the images of each T_i in M are disjoint, then P is injective. $\square$

In some module composition laws, the two module expressions do not have the same signature, but instead define specifications that are isomorphic under a renaming of symbols. We make this precise as follows:

Definition 58 Let $M = (H, \Sigma, \Psi, A)$ and $M' = (H', \Sigma', \Psi', A')$ be specifications. Then we write $M \approx M'$ iff $H = H'$ and there is a signature isomorphism $h \colon \|M\| \to \|M'\|$ such that $\Sigma * h = \Sigma'$, and $\Psi * h = \Psi'$, and $A * h = A'$. $\square$

Proposition 59 Separated aggregation is commutative and associative, that is,

(**Law 15**) $M \oplus M' \approx M' \oplus M$,

(**Law 16**) $M \oplus (M' \oplus M'') \approx (M \oplus M') \oplus M''$.

$\square$

11.5.5 *Aggregation of Implementations*

Rather than give a construction for the aggregation of implementations, we again take the indirect approach of giving a correctness criterion that any construction for this aggregation should satisfy. But first, an auxiliary concept:

Definition 60 Given an implementation C satisfying $M = (H, \Sigma, \Psi, A)$, let the **complete specification** or **theory** of C be $Th(M, C) = (H, \Psi, \Psi, Th_{\Psi \cup |H|}(C))$, where $Th_{\Psi \cup |H|}(C) = \{a \in Sen(\Psi \cup |H|) \mid C \models a\}$. $\square$

Definition 61 Given package specification modules $M_i = (H_i, \Sigma_i, \Psi_i, A_i)$ and implementation C_i with $C_i \models M_i$ for $i = 1, \ldots, n$, then an implementation C is an **aggregation** or **sum** of the C_i iff it satisfies $\sum_{i=1}^{n} Th(M_i, C_i)$, and in this case we may write $C = \sum_{i=1}^{n} C_i$ (noting that C is *not* in general unique). $\square$

(Actually, the model corresponding to the sum of specifications M_i is the product $\prod_{i=1}^{n} c_i$ of the component models, but we use the sum notation anyway.) In LILEANNA, where DIANA trees are manipulated to construct implementations, the aggregation $C = C_1 + C_2$ is built in several steps. First, a new (null) Ada package is created and called C. Then a copy of the DIANA tree for C_1 is created (fully qualified to avoid potential name conflicts) and inserted into C. Then a fully qualified copy of the DIANA tree for C_2 is created and inserted into C. The procedure of aggregating n implementation modules is similar.

11.5.6 *Module Expressions and Make*

We have described a number of operations for modifying and combining modules, and we can use them to form complex expressions, involving many modules and operations. We call such expressions *module expressions*, and we can use them to describe systems and subsystems. But we can also *evaluate* module expressions; when this happens, the (sub)system described by the expression is actually *created*. Note that evaluating a module expression involves evaluating all its subexpressions. This process agrees with the analogy with functional programming in the introduction: module expressions are analogous to functional expressions that are combinations of previously defined functions. But in this case, the result of evaluating an expression is a software system, plus its specification, not just a function.

The LILEANNA "`replace`" operation can replace existing module elements with new implementations, thus extending module composition in a way that can evolve components and systems in a consistent, traceable manner. Although it might seem to violate the principles of parameterized programming, it has considerable benefits over using an editor to remove existing code and then insert new code.

The "`make`" operation takes a new name and a module expression as arguments. The result of executing this command is to evaluate the module expression, for both the specification and the code, allocate storage for the resulting code (this is called "elaboration" in the jargon of Ada), and assign it the given name. Thus, executing a `make` yields executable code, attached to an appropriate specification. This code can then be used in building other systems by evaluating other module expressions that include the name of the newly made module.

Example 62 Figure 11.8 illustrates how a module can be enhanced and refined by replacing parts of an implementation to make it more efficient; a new axiom is also added. The second part of Figure 11.8 generates partial instantiations (generic

Ada packages) of REDUNDANT_SENSOR. In Example 62, HIGH_RATE_VIEW is used to generate the parameterized module HIGH_RATE_GENERIC_SENSOR, which can be configured to provide redundancy handling for any two sensors types. (This is based on an example in [Mey88].) □

```
make SQUARE is
        RECTANGLE * (rename Rectangle => Square)
                  * (add function Side(S : Square) return Real)
                  * (replace (Area => Area) )
                          -- where the new function is implemented as:
                          -- function Area(S : Square) return Real is
                          -- begin
                          -- return Length(S) ** 2;
                          -- end;
                  * (replace (Perimeter => Perimeter) )
                          -- function Perimeter(S : Square) return Real is
                          -- begin
                          -- return Length(S) * 4;
                          -- end;
            -- | axiom
            -- |      for all S : Square =>
            -- |          Length(S) = Width(S);
    end;

make HIGH_RATE_GENERIC_SENSOR is
    REDUNDANT_SENSOR [ High_Rate_View ]
  end;

make REDUNDANT_INS_GENERIC_SENSOR is
    REDUNDANT_SENSOR [ S1_View , S2_View ]
  end;
```

Fig. 11.8. Making Some Modules.

Assumption 63 Module expressions are evaluated bottom up, for both specification and implementation modules. Whenever a subexpression is evaluated, it is given a new name and added to the module graph.

Moreover, whenever a module instantiation is evaluated, inclusion views from the body module and the actual parameter module to the resulting instantiation are added; the view from the body will be labeled "instance" and the view from the actual "actual-of." Similarly, whenever an aggregation $M = M_1 + \cdots + M_n$ is evaluated, inclusion views $J_j : M_j \to M$ are added to the module graph (for $j = 1, \ldots, n$) and labelled "summand-of." Finally, whenever a transformation $M * r$ is evaluated, then the new module $M * r$ is *linked* to the old module M by a non-view edge labelled "transformed-to." A sequence $M * r_1 * \cdots r_k$ of transformations can be treated as a single transformation for this purpose. □

This assumption concerns dynamic updating of the module graph, which thus serves as a database for a development project. Although Assumption 63 is stated in an informal way, unlike all our previous assumptions, it would be straightforward, though somewhat tedious, to formalize it, using for example, an abstract machine for graphs. However, we have decided that given our goal of helping implementors, this would not be worth the trouble, and indeed, would make it harder for many readers to understand our intention. Note that a transformation edge (from some M to $M * r$) in the module graph is *not* a view, but just a link.

11.6 Vertical Composition

Vertical structure concerns the structuring of a software system into "layers," where each layer calls upon resources provided by layers below it; that is, vertical structure provides "virtual machines" as resources for higher levels. The motivation for layering comes from the construction of large, complex systems, such as communication protocols (for example, TCP/IP) and operating systems, where it is convenient to implement higher level services using lower level services, where the lowest level services are far from the user but close to the machine. This motivation implies that inheritance under vertical composition should be *intransitive*, as opposed to the *transitive* inheritance of horizontal composition. Intuitively, passing operations from the "lower" interface of a layer to its "upper" interface violates the idea of layering; however (perhaps unfortunately), nothing prevents a given layer from "wrapping" some functionality from a lower layer and then exporting it.

Another implication of the layering motivation for vertical composition is that the horizontal structuring operations for aggregation, renaming, and so on do not make sense: only *access* to the visible signature of lower layers is allowed. Thus, the only vertical composition operations are parameterization and instantiation; all the other structure of a layer must come from horizontal composition. Since the point of layering is to provide access to a service, more than one module may need that access. Since modules have unique names, there is no difficulty in vertically instantiating two different modules with the same module V representing a vertical layer; V is then shared by these two modules; for example, $A(V) + B(V)$ has just one copy of V. Perhaps surprisingly, the machinery we have developed to treat hiding for horizontal structure is just as well suited for the semantics of vertical parameterization and instantiation.

Definition 64 A **(vertically) parameterized** or **generic specification module** with **(vertical) interface theory** R and **body** M is an injective specification module map $Q\colon R \to M$ where R is a theory. We write $M(Q :: R)$ and say M is **vertically parameterized by** Q; we may write $M^H(Q :: R)$ when $H(M) = H$. $\square$

Definition 65 Given a vertically parameterized specification module $M(Q :: R)$ with body (H, Σ, Ψ, A) and given a view $h\colon R \to N$, we let the **(vertical) instantiation** of M by h be defined by the formula

$$M(h :: N) = (M * h^\diamond) + (N * (\texttt{hide-all})) \, .$$

The view h again may be called a **fitting view**. We may also use the notation $M(h)$, or even $M(N)$ if h is clear from context. □

Notice that $M(H(h)) = H(M)$, since nothing from N is imported. We treat multiple vertical parameters exactly the same way that we did multiple horizontal parameters, using the operation $\oplus$ to combine interfaces and the operation $!$ to combine the fitting maps of actual parameters.

Proposition 66 Given vertically parameterized specification modules $M_1(Q_1 :: T_1)$ and $M_2(Q_2 :: T_2)$, and fitting views $h_1 : T_1 \to N_1$ and $h_2 : T_2 \to N_2$ such that N_1 and N_2 are distinct†, then

(**Law 18**) $M_1(h_1 :: N_1) \oplus M_2(h_2 :: N_2) = (M_1 \oplus M_2)(h_1 :: N_1, h_2 :: N_2)$,

and if M_1 and M_2 are distinct, then $\oplus$ in the left side above can be replaced by $+$, provided $=$ is also replaced by $\approx$,

(**Law 18a**) $M_1(h_1 :: N_1) + M_2(h_2 :: N_2) \approx (M_1 \oplus M_2)(h_1 :: N_1, h_2 :: N_2)$.

When $T_1 = T_2$, $Q_1 = Q_2$ and $N_1 = N_2 = N$ is shared (recall that this means the names N_1 and N_2 are equal, not just that they denote equal modules), then

(**Law 18b**) $M_1(h :: N) + M_2(h :: N) = (M_1 + M_2)(h :: N)$.

□

Definition 67 A (**horizontally and vertically**) **parameterized** or **generic specification module** with **vertical interface theory** R, **horizontal interface theory** T, and **body** M consists of two injective specification module maps, $P : T \to M$ and $Q : R \to M$, where T and R are theories. We will write $M[P :: T](Q :: R)$ and say that M is **horizontally parameterized by** P and **vertically parameterized by** Q. We may write $M^H[P :: T](Q :: R)$ when $H(M) = H$. □

Definition 68 Given a vertically and horizontally parameterized specification module $M[P :: T](Q :: R)$ with body (H, Σ, Ψ, A) and given views $g : T \to N$ and $h : R \to N'$, we let the **instantiation** of M by g, h be defined by the formula

$$M[g :: N](h :: N') = ((M * g^\diamond) * h^\diamond) + N + (N' * (\text{hide-all})) .$$

The views g, h may be called **fitting views**. We may also use the notation $M[g](h)$, or even $M[N](N')$ if g, h are clear from context. □

For example, $M^H[P :: T](V :: R)$ is a module inheriting a set H of module names, horizontally parameterized by P with interface theory T, and vertically parameterized by V with interface theory R.

† Recall this means the *names* N_1 and N_2 are different, even though they might be equal, that is, $N_1 \neq N_2$ even if $O(N_1) = O(N_2)$.

Example 69 Figure 11.9 shows the package LIL_STACK, which is parameterized horizontally by the theory ANY_TYPE, and is parameterized vertically by the theory LIST_THEORY, which itself is parameterized by the theory ANY_TYPE, which here is instantiated with the same "Item" as in the horizontal parameterization. This means that if the horizontal parameter is instantiated with (say) N, then the vertical must be instantiated with LIST_THEORY[N]. □

```
generic package LIL_STACK[ Item :: ANY_TYPE ] -- LILEANNA Package
    needs ( ListP :: LIST_THEORY[ Item ] ) is
    type Stack;
    includes Element as Stack;
    function Is_Empty ( S: Stack ) return Boolean;
    function Push ( E: Element; S: Stack ) return Stack (comm);
    function Pop ( S: Stack ) return Stack;
    function Top ( S: Stack ) return Element;
    - - |axiom
        - - | for all E: Element, S: Stack =>
            - - | Pop( Push ( E, S ) ) = E;
            - - | (Pop ( X ) and Is_Empty ( X ) ) => raise Stack_Underflow;
                            -- strong propagation annotation
            - - | raise Stack_Overflow => S [ in Stack ] = S [ out Stack ];
                            -- weak propagation annotation
end LIL_STACK;
```

Fig. 11.9. LILEANNA Generic Stack Package Example with Vertical Parameterization.

Assumption 70 If Q: $R \to M$ is a vertically parameterized module, then the injection Q appears as an edge in the module graph from R to M, labeled to indicate it is a vertical generic module. Vertical instantiations in module expressions are evaluated bottom up, like all other module composition operations, with evaluated subexpressions being given new names and added to the module graph. □

Proposition 71 Given a specification module $M[P :: T](V :: R)$ that is both vertically and horizontally parameterized, then for any instantiation by some g, h,

(**Law 19**) $H(M[g :: N](h :: N')) = H(M) \cup H(N)$.

□

11.7 Results and Lessons

The DSSA-ADAGE (Domain-Specific Software Architecture – Avionics Domain Application Generation Environment) project used LILEANNA to generate integrated avionics software subsystems, and to specify their layered architectures. The two most common module composition constructs used were renaming and instantiation, often in combination with simple vertical parameterization. The need for implementation-level module expression operations to "glue" low-level components together became apparent in this project, and so LILEANNA was extended to allow adding enumerated types, vertical structure, and explicit invocation of operations.

Because of the size of the decision space and the degree of configurability of these avionics subsystems, LILEANNA module expressions were not written by users. Instead, a Graphical Layout User Environment (GLUE) coupled with a constraint-based reasoning system was created to allow the user to select components and specify instantiation parameters (and capture design rationale). This information was represented as a decision tree and passed to another tool, MEGEN (Module Expression GENerator), which constructed the appropriate LILEANNA **make** statements.

With this approach, a complete avionics subsystem could be generated in about an hour, whereas over 10 hours had been required previously. While the anticipated benefits of parameterized programming were realized in generating more efficient code (often 20-30% faster), the real savings resulted from the structure imposed on the configuration process by GLUE. This tool removed some of the syntactic tedium of creating LILEANNA views as well as worries about violating module semantics. GLUE was especially useful in helping users configure the vertical structure of an application by selecting from families of implementations.

Acknowledgments

This research was supported in part by the Defense Advanced Research Projects Agency (DARPA) in cooperation with the US Air Force Wright Laboratory Avionics Directorate under contract # F33615-91-C-1788, the European Community under ESPRIT-2 BRA Working Groups 6071, IS-CORE (Information Systems COrrectness and REusability) and 6112, COMPASS (COMPrehensive Algebraic Approach to System Specification and development), Fujitsu Laboratories Limited, and the Information Technology Promotion Agency, Japan, as part of the R & D of Basic Technology for Future Industries "New Models for Software Architecture" project sponsored by NEDO (New Energy and Industrial Technology Development Organization).

Bibliography

[Ada83]   US Department of Defense, US Government Printing Office. *The Ada Programming Language Reference Manual*, 1983. ANSI/MIL-STD-1815A-1983 Document.

[BG77]   Burstall, R. and Goguen, J. Putting Theories Together to Make Specifications. In *Proceedings of Fifth International Joint Conference on Artificial Intelligence*, pages 1045–1058. Department of Computer Science, Carnegie-Mellon University, 1977.

[BS92]   Boehm, B. and Scherlis, W. Megaprogramming. In *Proceedings of Software Technology Conference 1992*, pages 63–82, April 1992.

[BS94]   Button, G. and Sharrock, W. Occasioned Practises in the Work of

            Implementing Development Methodologies. In Jirotka, M. and Goguen, J.,
            editors, *Requirements Engineering: Social and Technical Issues*, pages
            217–240. Academic Press, 1994.

[Bur85]   Burstall, R. Programming with Modules as Typed Functional Programming.
            In *Proceedings, International Conference on Fifth Generation Computing
            Systems*, 1985.

[DIA83]   Tartan Laboratories Incorporated. *DIANA Reference Manual, Revision 3*,
            1983.

[GB92]   Goguen, J, and Burstall, R.. Institutions: Abstract model theory for
            specification and programming. *Journal of the Association for Computing
            Machinery*, 39(1):95–146, January 1992.

[GM82]   Goguen, J. and Meseguer, J. Universal Realization, Persistent
            Interconnection and Implementation of Abstract Modules. In Nielsen, M.
            and Schmidt, E., editors, *Proceedings, 9th International Conference on
            Automata, Languages and Programming*, pages 265–281. Springer, 1982.
            Lecture Notes in Computer Science, Volume 140.

[GM96]   Goguen, J. and Malcolm, G. *Algebraic Semantics of Imperative Programs*.
            MIT, 1996.

[GM97]   Goguen, J. and Malcolm, G. A hidden agenda. *Theoretical Computer
            Science*, to appear. Also UCSD Dept. Computer Science & Eng. Technical
            Report CS97–538, May 1997.

[GWMFJ]   Goguen, J., Winkler, T., Meseguer, J., Futatsugi, K., and Jouannaud, J.
            Introducing OBJ. In Goguen, J. and Malcolm, G., editors, *Software
            Engineering with OBJ: Algebraic Specification in Action*. Kluwer, 1999. Also
            Technical Report, SRI International, 1986.

[Gog85]   Goguen, J. Suggestions for Using and Organizing Libraries in Software
            Development. In *Proceedings, First International Conference on
            Supercomputing Systems*, pages 349–360. IEEE Computer Society, 1985. Also
            in *Supercomputing Systems*, Steven and Svetlana Kartashev, Eds., Elsevier,
            1986.

[Gog89]   Goguen, J. Principles of Parameterized Programming. In *Software
            Reusability Volume I, Concepts and Models*, pages 159–225. Addison-Wesley
            Publishing Company, 1989.

[Gog90b]   Goguen, J. Hyperprogramming: A Formal Approach to Software
            Environments. In *Proceedings of Symposium on Formal Methods in Software
            Development, Tokyo, Japan*, January 1990.

[Gog91]   Goguen, J. Types as theories. In Reed, J.M., Roscoe, A.W., and Wachter,
            R.F., editors, *Topology and Category Theory in Computer Science*, pages
            357–390. Oxford, 1991. Proceedings of a Conference held at Oxford, June
            1989.

[Gog94]   Goguen, J. Requirements Engineering as the Reconciliation of Social and
            Technical Issues. In Jirotka, M. and Goguen, J., editors, *Requirements
            Engineering: Social and Technical Issues*, pages 165–200. Academic Press,
            1994.

[JG94]   Jirotka, M. and Goguen, J. *Requirements Engineering: Social and Technical
            Issues*. Academic Press, 1994.

[Luc90]   Luckham, D. *Programming with Specifications: An Introduction to ANNA,
            A Language for Specifying Ada Programs*. Texts and Monographs in
            Computer Science. Springer-Verlag, October, 1990.

[LvH85]   Luckham, D. and von Henke, F. An Overview of Anna, a Specification
            Language for Ada. *IEEE Software*, 2(2):9–23, March 1985.

[Mey88]   Meyer, B. *Object-oriented Software Construction*. Prentice Hall Publishing
            Company, 1988.

[Par72]   Parnas, D. Information Distribution Aspects of Design Methodology. In *Proceedings of 1972 IFIP Congress*, pages 339–344, 1972.

[PDN86]   Prieto-Díaz, R. and Neighbors, J. Module Interconnection Language. *Journal of Systems and Software*, 6(4):307–344, November 1986.

[San82]   Sannella, D. *Semantics, Implementation and Pragmatics of Clear, a Program Specification Language.* PhD thesis, University of Edinburgh, Computer Science Department, 1982. Report CST-17-82.

[ST88]   Sannella, D. and Tarlecki, A. Specifications in an Arbitrary Institution. *Information and Control*, 76:165–210, 1988. Earlier version in *Proceedings, International Symposium on the Semantics of Data Types*, Lecture Notes in Computer Science, Volume 173, Springer, 1985.

[Tra93a]   Tracz, W. LILEANNA: A Parameterized Programming Language. In *Proceedings of Second International Workshop on Software Reuse*, pages 66–78, March 1993.

[Tra93b]   Tracz, W. Parameterized Programming in LILEANNA. In *Proceedings of ACM Symposium on Applied Computing SAC'93*, pages 77–86, February 1993.

[Tra97]   Tracz, W. *Formal Specification of Parameterized Programs in* LILLEANNA. PhD thesis, Stanford University, 1997.

[Wir86]   Wirsing, M. Structured Algebraic Specifications: A Kernel Language. *Theoretical Computer Science*, 42:123–249, 1986.

[WWC92]   Wiederhold, G., Wegner, P., and Ceri, S. Toward Megaprogramming. *Communications of the ACM*, 35(11):89–99, 1992.

Part Four

Reactive and Distributed Systems

12

Composition of Reactive System Components

Kevin Lano, Juan Bicarregui, Tom Maibaum

Dept. of Computing, King's College London,
Strand, London WC2R 2LS
kcl@dcs.kcl.ac.uk

Jose Fiadeiro

Dept. of Informatics, University of Lisbon,
Campo Grande, 1700 Lisbon, Portugal
Jose.Luiz.Fiadeiro@di.fc.ul.pt

Abstract

In this paper we show how the Object Calculus of Fiadeiro and Maibaum can be used to specify reactive systems. This provides a modular, highly declarative, and abstract specification language, suitable for refinement using model-based design notations such as B or VDM.

In the Object Calculus, pre/post style specifications of the effect of actions can be given, together with temporal logic specifications of expected histories of behavior of the system. We show how such specifications can be translated directly into B modules and an executable implementation.

12.1 Introduction

Temporal logic is an established technique for the specification of reactive systems: it has the advantage of being declarative and supporting reasoning, and it is sufficiently expressive for many practical cases. The Object Calculus adds a strong concept of encapsulation and theory composition to a basic temporal logic formalism [FM91], which allows reactive system components to be separately specified, instantiated, and combined using category-theoretic operations, in particular, the co-limit construction:

"given a category of widgets, the operation of putting a system of widgets together to form some super-widget corresponds to taking the co-limit of the diagram of widgets that shows how to interconnect them" [GG78]

Using this integration of category-theoretic structuring and temporal or modal logics, the development of the Object Calculus has been carried out by research groups at Imperial College and the University of Lisbon over the last ten years. It has been taken up by other research groups and applied to systems of significant complexity, such as the steam boiler system described here.

In this paper we use examples from a case study of an established benchmark for formal methods, the steam boiler system, to illustrate the techniques of abstract and compositional specification using the Object Calculus.

A description of the steam boiler system can be found in [ABL97], together with different approaches to formal specification of it.

The purpose of the system is to produce a flow of steam from the boiler water tank, without letting the tank boil dry or overflow. Failures in the measuring devices involved (flow monitors on the water feed lines, steam level sensor, and water level sensor), the water pumps, and the communication system must be handled by an appropriate change of mode of the controller—in emergency situations this may involve a shutdown of the control system. Figure 12.1 shows the main components of the system.

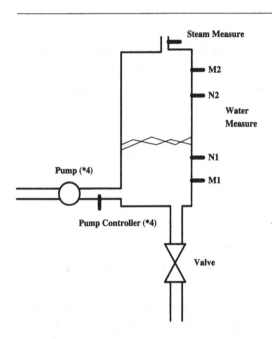

Fig. 12.1. Steam Boiler Components.

A specification in the object calculus [FM91] is constructed as a set of linked theories in a temporal logic. Formally, it is a diagram of objects in a category of theories and theorem-preserving morphisms. A theory consists of collections of *type* and *constant symbols*, *attribute symbols* (denoting time-varying data), *action symbols* (denoting atomic operations), and a set of axioms describing the types of the attributes and the effects, permission constraints, and other dynamic properties of the actions. The axioms are specified using linear temporal logic operators: ○

(in the next state), $\mathcal{U}$ (weak until), $\square$ (always in the future), and $\diamond$ (sometime in the future). There is assumed to be a first moment. The predicate *BEG* is true exactly at this time point.

$\bigcirc$ is also an expression constructor. If e is an expression, $\bigcirc e$ denotes the value of e at the beginning of the next time interval. e itself denotes its value at the beginning of the current interval. Several actions may execute in a given interval: the formula α where α is an action, denotes that α occurs in the current interval. We express the effects of actions via axioms of the form:

$$Pre \wedge \alpha \ \Rightarrow \ Post$$

where *Pre* is a precondition, a predicate over the current state, and *Post* describes the properties of the state that results from execution of α in a state satisfying *Pre*. It may use both $\bigcirc att$ and att for attributes att of the theory.

A wide variety of properties can be expressed using such a logic. In particular it seems appropriate for the specification of the steam boiler problem as the requirements of this system are expressed in terms of reaction cycles (intervals) where a collection of events (actions) occur, including inputs to the system, its internal reactions, and outputs from the system to the physical devices. Constraints between the events in a given cycle include that multiple *level* messages in a given interval should give rise to a transmission error:

$$\neg \ \exists_1 \ lev : \mathbb{Z} \cdot level(lev) \ \Rightarrow \ transmission\_failed$$

$\exists_1 \ x$ is the "exists a unique x" quantifier.

Constraints between events in successive cycles include that three successive *stop* messages give rise to a termination (in the same cycle as the third *stop*) [ABL97, p505]:

$$stop \wedge \bigcirc stop \wedge \bigcirc \bigcirc stop \ \Rightarrow \ \bigcirc \bigcirc terminate$$

and the protocol for failure detection and acknowledgment:

$$water\_measure\_failed \ \Rightarrow$$
$$(level\_failure\_detection \ \mathcal{U} \ level\_failure\_acknowledgment)$$

"If the water measure fails in the current cycle, the message *level_failure_detection* is repeated until a *level_failure_acknowledgment* message is received." The use of weak until means that there is no obligation for an acknowledgment message to ever be received†.

In order to support reasoning about the attributes which may change over a given interval, we associate to each action the set of attributes which it may change: its *write frame*. For each attribute att we then have a *locality axiom* Loc_{att} of the form

$$att = \bigcirc att \ \vee \ \alpha_1 \ \vee \ \ldots \ \vee \ \alpha_n$$

---

† Technically, this means that this property is a *safety* rather than a *liveness* property.

where the α_i are all those actions with *att* in their write frame.

Theories are connected by means of *theory morphisms* σ which map each attribute symbol *att* of the source theory S to an attribute symbol $\sigma(att)$ of the target theory T, each action α of S to an action $\sigma(\alpha)$ of T, and so forth. Each theorem of S must become a theorem of T under this translation:

$$\vdash_S \varphi \quad \text{implies} \quad \vdash_T \sigma(\varphi)$$

If φ is the locality axiom Loc_{att} for *att*, this means that no actions β (not in the image of σ) can be introduced in T which have $\sigma(att)$ in their write frames. Any action of T with $\sigma(att)$ in its write frame must be (or must always co-execute with) the interpretation of some action α of S where *att* is in the write frame of α in S.

This form of encapsulation is close to that of B [Abr96]: only operations declared in a given B module (machine) may directly write to variables declared in that module.

The central problem with the specification of reactive systems is obtaining a sufficiently abstract description to avoid the high numbers of states which make verification difficult. In particular, it should be possible to describe the allowed sequencing of phases and operations without coding up details of component implementations.

The Object Calculus formalism provides a suitable framework for the description of reactive system components, because such components are often of a generic nature, consisting of variations or enhancements of fundamental physical devices such as valves, tanks, pumps, and so on. Particular systems are built from a combination of these components. Thus the Object Calculus seems an appropriate formalism for their specification since it allows convenient extension, adaption, and composition of component specifications. Moreover, the key properties of such components concern their dynamic and reactive behavior, for which temporal logic is ideally suited.

In the following sections we illustrate the use of the object calculus in specifying the steam boiler control system.

12.2 Abstract Specification

At the most abstract level, all actions of a system can be assumed to occur in intervals without overlap. An interval at this level of abstraction represents a cycle of the concrete system.

A theory *SData* gives definitions of the types and constants used in the system, and will be included in each of the other theories:

Types
> $PState = \{running, off\}$
> $PCState = \{flow, noflow\}$
> $Condition = \{failed, operating\}$
> $@Pump = \{p1, p2, p3, p4\}$

Constants
> $M1 : \mathbb{N}$ /* *Minimum water level* */

$M2 : \mathbb{N}$ /* Maximum water level */
$N1 : \mathbb{N}$ /* Minimum normal water level */
$N2 : \mathbb{N}$ /* Maximum normal water level */
$W : \mathbb{N}_1$ /* Maximum steam production */
$C : \mathbb{N}_1$ /* Capacity of boiler */
$P : \mathbb{N}_1$ /* Capacity of pump */
$U1 : \mathbb{N}$ /* Max rate of steam increase */
$U2 : \mathbb{N}$ /* Min rate of steam increase */
$\tau : \mathbb{N}_1$ /* Sampling interval */

Axioms

$$M1 < N1 \wedge N1 < N2 \wedge N2 < M2$$

Each physical component has an associated *monitor* which provides an interface between it and the controller. This monitor is responsible for managing the protocol of communications between the controller and the components, and for detecting errors in data and communications.

The axioms of the monitor theory for the water measure formalise the requirements given in [ABL97, pages 500–509].

Attributes

    water_measure_condition : *Condition*
    water_quantity : $\mathbb{Z}$

Actions (With write frames presented as sets of attributes:)

    level(*lev* : $\mathbb{Z}$)   {*water_quantity*}
    water_measure_failed   {*water_measure_condition*}
    transmission_failed $\varnothing$
    transmission_failure $\varnothing$
    level_failure_detection $\varnothing$
    level_failure_acknowledgment $\varnothing$
    level_repaired   {*water_measure_condition*}
    level_repaired_acknowledgment $\varnothing$

Axioms

(i) Initially the water quantity is 0 and the measure is operating:

$$BEG \Rightarrow water\_quantity = 0 \ \wedge$$
$$water\_measure\_condition = operating$$

(ii) A water measure failure event occurs if we receive a *level*(*lev*) message with *lev* < 0 or *lev* > C:

$$\exists lev : \mathbb{Z} \cdot level(lev) \wedge (lev < 0 \vee lev > C) \Rightarrow$$
$$water\_measure\_failed$$

(iii) A transmission failure occurs if we do not receive a unique *level* message in the current cycle:

$$\neg \ \exists_1 lev : \mathbb{Z} \cdot level(lev) \Rightarrow transmission\_failed$$

Notice that this includes the case where no *level* message is received.

$$transmission\_failed \Rightarrow transmission\_failure$$

(iv) If a level measure failure occurs, the system must react by recording the failure:

$$water\_measure\_failed \;\Rightarrow\; \bigcirc water\_measure\_condition = failed$$

(v) The signal *level_failure_detection* must then be repeated until *level_failure_acknowledgment* is received:

$$water\_measure\_failed \;\Rightarrow\;$$
$$(level\_failure\_detection \;\mathcal{U}\; level\_failure\_acknowledgment)$$

(vi) A *level_repaired* signal resets the *water_measure_condition* attribute:

$$\neg\, water\_measure\_failed \wedge level\_repaired \;\Rightarrow\;$$
$$\bigcirc water\_measure\_condition = operating$$

(vii) and leads to the generation of a *level_repaired_acknowledgment*:

$$level\_repaired \;\Rightarrow\; level\_repaired\_acknowledgment$$

(viii) A valid water level event sets the value of *water_quantity*:

$$\neg\, water\_measure\_failed \;\wedge\; \neg\, transmission\_failed \;\Rightarrow\;$$
$$(level(lev) \;\Rightarrow\; \bigcirc water\_quantity = lev)$$

The theory of the steam measure monitor is identical in structure to the water measure monitor. Formally it is an isomorphic image under the morphism which maps C to W, *water_measure_condition* to *steam_measure_condition*, and so on.

A similar structure can be given for the theory of the pump, pump monitor, and the pump controller and its monitor. Indeed we can recognize a number of commonalities between the monitor theories (only the criteria for detecting sensor failures, and for recording the current state, are different). The theory *FailureManager* expresses these common elements:

Attributes
　　condition : *Condition*
Actions
　　component_failed　{*condition*}
　　component_repaired　　{*condition*}
　　failure_detection　∅
　　failure_acknowledgment　∅
　　repaired_acknowledgment　∅
Axioms
　　$BEG \;\Rightarrow\; condition = operating$
　　$component\_failed \;\Rightarrow\; \bigcirc condition = failed$
　　$component\_failed \;\Rightarrow\; (failure\_detection \;\mathcal{U}\; failure\_acknowledgment)$
　　$\neg\, component\_failed \wedge component\_repaired \;\Rightarrow\; \bigcirc condition = operating$
　　$component\_repaired \;\Rightarrow\; repaired\_acknowledgment$

This could be further subdivided into parts dealing with the communication protocol (axioms 3 and 5) and parts dealing with the recording of failure status (axioms 1, 2, and 4).

A theory *Transmission* has the form

Actions

$\quad$ *component_state*(*val* : $\mathbb{Z}$) $\quad \varnothing$
$\quad$ *transmission_failure* $\quad \varnothing$
$\quad$ *transmission_failed* $\quad \varnothing$

Axioms

$\quad \neg \; \exists_1 \; lev : \mathbb{Z} \cdot component\_state(lev) \; \Rightarrow \; transmission\_failed$
$\quad transmission\_failed \; \Rightarrow \; transmission\_failure$

where we regard the *PState* and *PCState* types as isomorphic to $\{0, 1\}$ as in [ABL97].

Therefore the *Water_Measure_Monitor* theory can be re-expressed in terms of *Transmission*, via the morphism *m7* of Figure 12.2:

$\quad component\_state(s) \; \mapsto \; level(s)$
$\quad transmission\_failed \; \mapsto \; transmission\_failed$
$\quad transmission\_failure \; \mapsto \; transmission\_failure$

and *FailureManager*, via the morphism *m1*

$\quad condition \; \mapsto \; water\_measure\_condition$
$\quad component\_failed \; \mapsto \; water\_measure\_failed$
$\quad component\_repaired \; \mapsto \; level\_repaired$
$\quad failure\_detection \; \mapsto \; level\_failure\_detection$
$\quad failure\_acknowledgment \; \mapsto \; level\_failure\_acknowledgment$
$\quad repaired\_acknowledgment \; \mapsto \; level\_repaired\_acknowledgment$

The attribute *water_quantity* and axioms to initialize and set this quantity are defined locally in *Water_Measure_Monitor*, and the axiom

$$\exists \, lev : \mathbb{Z} \cdot level(lev) \wedge (lev < 0 \vee lev > C) \Rightarrow$$
$$water\_measure\_failed$$

determining when a component failure occurs is also defined in this theory.

Similar constructions work for the pump and pump controller (flow monitor) components. Figure 12.2 shows the structure of this part of the system. Separate copies of the *FailureManager* and *Transmission* theories are included in each of the component theories, but we identify all the different *transmission_failure* actions so that a transmission failure in any component generates the same system error event. *SData* is also included into each of the theories shown in this diagram.

The theory of the controller then extends the co-limit† of the monitor theories with the following attributes and actions:

Types

$\quad CState = \{initialization, normal, degraded, rescue, emergency\_stop\}$

---

† A co-limit of a set of theories is the least theory which extends all of the set. It can be constructed as a union of their axioms, with identifications of symbols induced by any morphisms linking the theories.

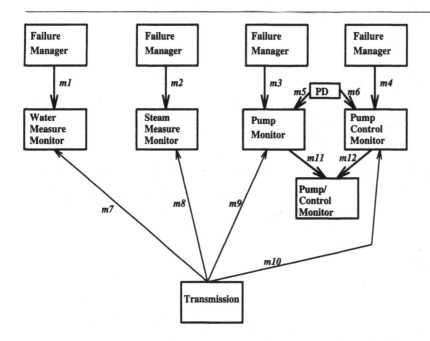

Fig. 12.2. Construction of Component Theories.

Constants

   $hazard\_level(\mathbb{Z}) : bool$
   $min\_level\_estimate(\mathbb{Z}, \mathbb{Z}) : \mathbb{Z}$
   $max\_level\_estimate(\mathbb{Z}, \mathbb{Z}) : \mathbb{Z}$

Attributes

   $cstate : CState$

Actions

   $react$ $\{cstate\}$
   $terminate$ $\{cstate\}$
   $stop$ $\varnothing$
   $steam\_boiler\_waiting$ $\varnothing$
   $physical\_units\_ready$ $\{cstate\}$
   $program\_ready$ $\varnothing$

Axioms

   Some example axioms of the controller are that a *terminate* event occurs if there have been three successive *stop* events, or if there has been a transmission error:

   $stop \wedge \bigcirc stop \wedge \bigcirc \bigcirc stop \;\Rightarrow\; \bigcirc \bigcirc terminate$
   $transmission\_failure \;\Rightarrow\; terminate$

   Given the new mode and water level, take appropriate action:

   $\bigcirc cstate = normal \;\vee\; \bigcirc cstate = degraded \;\vee$
   $\qquad \bigcirc cstate = initialization \;\Rightarrow$
   $\qquad\qquad\qquad (\bigcirc water\_quantity < N1 \;\Rightarrow\; increase\_flow) \;\wedge$
   $\qquad\qquad\qquad (\bigcirc water\_quantity > N2 \;\Rightarrow\; decrease\_flow)$

$\bigcirc cstate = rescue \Rightarrow$
$$(min\_level\_estimate(water\_quantity, steam\_quantity) < N1 \Rightarrow$$
$$increase\_flow) \wedge$$
$$(max\_level\_estimate(water\_quantity, steam\_quantity) > N2 \Rightarrow$$
$$decrease\_flow)$$

The specification can be validated via animation [Lan97]. The actions *increase_flow* and *decrease_flow* are general operations which will be interpreted as opening and closing certain pumps in the actual physical system.

12.3 Design and Implementation in B

The object calculus specification can be used as the basis of an implementation, using the B specification notation and development environment. B [Abr96] specifications of steam boiler components were defined from the above theories [Ali98]. The B specification was structured, where possible, in the same way as the RAL/Object Calculus specification.

Shared constants and types are placed in a *SData* machine corresponding to the *SData* theory. The implementation of *SData* defines the values of these constants to be those given by the simulation program that is found at the URL `ftp://ftp.fzi.de/pub/korso/steam_boiler/`:

```
MACHINE SData
SETS
  PState    = { running, off };
  PCState   = { flow, noflow };
  Condition = { failed, operating };
  CState    = { initialization, normal, degraded, rescue,
                emergency_stop };
  OPTOKEN   = { level_op, steam_op, stop_op, sbw_op,
                pur_op, pump_state_op, pump_control_state_op,
                pump_repaired_op, pump_control_repaired_op,
                level_repaired_op, steam_repaired_op,
                pfack_op, pcfack_op, lfack_op, sfack_op }
CONSTANTS
  M1, M2, N1, N2, W_max_steam, C_max_water,
  P_pump_capacity, U1, U2, tau
PROPERTIES
  M1: N & M2: N & N1: N & N2: N & W_max_steam : N &
  C_max_water : N & P_pump_capacity : N & U1: N & U2: N &
  tau : N &

  M1 < N1 & N1 < N2 & N2 < M2 &

  M2 ≤ C_max_water &
  C_max_water < 2147483646 &
  W_max_steam < 2147483646
END
```

IMPLEMENTATION *SDataI*
REFINES *SData*
PROPERTIES
  $M1 = 150$ & $M2 = 850$ &
  $N1 = 400$ & $N2 = 600$ &
  $W\_max\_steam = 13$ & $C\_max\_water = 1000$ &
  $P\_pump\_capacity = 10$ & $U1 = 1$ & $U2 = 1$ & $tau = 5$
END

12.3.1 Translation from Object Calculus to B

The most direct translation from object calculus theories to B machines involves the definition of flag variables $\alpha\_received : BOOL$ for each action α which may be sent to the system from the physical devices or operator. These flags identify if, within a given cycle, the action α has been sent to the control system. At the end of the cycle decisions are made on the basis of these flags to determine which messages the controller sends back to the physical devices, and what changes should be made to local attributes.

We also define flags i_issued for each internal action i which indicate if i has been generated in the current interval.

More generally, if actions α are parameterized by a type X, the flag variables are declared as $\alpha\_received : X \to BOOL$ or $\alpha\_issued : X \to BOOL$ in B.

Certain forms of axioms φ of a theory T can then be restated in terms of these flags, and become obligations $\tau(\varphi)$ on the behavior of an *end_of_cycle* operation of a corresponding machine M_T, or invariant constraints on the state of M_T. The *end_of_cycle* operation is the only operation of M_T which updates those variables of M_T which correspond to attributes of T.

The translation τ for terms is given in Table 12.1. τ commutes with the logical operators $\Rightarrow$, $\wedge$, etc. $[Act]Q$ is the B notation for "*Act* establishes Q"—the total

OC term e	B interpretation $\tau(e)$	Conditions
$\alpha(x)$	$\alpha\_received(x) = TRUE$	α external action, received
$\alpha(x)$	*end_of_cycle* invokes $\alpha(x)$	α external action, generated
$\alpha(x)$	$\alpha\_issued(x) = TRUE$	α internal action
att	*att*	*att* an attribute
$\bigcirc att$	$[end\_of\_cycle]att$	*att* an attribute

Table 12.1. *Interpretation τ of object calculus to B.*

correctness precondition of *Act* with respect to Q, which ensures that every execution of *Act* terminates in a state satisfying Q. This is also modal action logic notation [RFM91] for the identical concept.

The following forms of axiom of a theory T can all be translated into corresponding obligations on the B specification M_T using τ:

(i) $BEG \Rightarrow P(att)$ Interpreted as $[Init]P$ where $Init$ is the initialization of M_T and att denotes a vector of attributes of T

(ii) $P(att, x) \wedge \alpha_{ext}(x) \Rightarrow \beta_{int}(f(x, att))$ where ext and int subscripts denote external and internal actions, respectively, and $f : X \times V \to Y$ is some function from the product of the parameter type of α and the attributes of T to the parameter type Y of β. This is interpreted as an invariant

$$\forall x.(x \in X \wedge P(att, x) \wedge \alpha_{ext}\_received(x) = TRUE \Rightarrow$$
$$\beta_{int}\_issued(f(x, att)) = TRUE)$$

(iii) $P(att, x) \wedge \alpha_{ext}(x) \Rightarrow Q(att, x, \bigcirc att)$ This is interpreted as an obligation on end_of_cycle:

$$\forall x.(x \in X \wedge P(att, x) \wedge \alpha_{ext}\_received(x) = TRUE \Rightarrow$$
$$Q(att, x, [end\_of\_cycle]att))$$

(iv) $P(att, \beta_1, \ldots, \beta_n) \Rightarrow \gamma_{ext}$ where γ_{ext} is a generated external action. This is interpreted as an obligation

$$P(att, \beta_1\_issued = TRUE, \ldots, \beta_n\_issued = TRUE) \Rightarrow$$
$$end\_of\_cycle \supset \gamma_{ext}$$

$\alpha \supset \beta$ denotes that every execution instance of α contains an execution instance of β [Lan98].

(v) $P(att, x) \wedge \beta_{int}(x) \Rightarrow Q(att, x, \bigcirc att)$ This is interpreted as an obligation

$$\forall x.(x \in X \wedge P(att, x) \wedge \beta_{int}\_issued(x) = TRUE \Rightarrow$$
$$Q(att, x, [end\_of\_cycle]att))$$

(vi) $P(att, \beta_1, \ldots, \beta_n) \Rightarrow Q(att, \bigcirc att)$ This is interpreted as an obligation

$$P(att, \beta_1\_issued = TRUE, \ldots, \beta_n\_issued = TRUE) \Rightarrow$$
$$Q(att, [end\_of\_cycle]att)$$

Axioms of the form $\alpha \Rightarrow (\gamma \, \mathcal{U} \, \beta)$ can be dealt with separately, as we discuss below. Axioms involving past time operators on actions: $\bullet\alpha$, and so on, can be translated using flags $p\_\alpha\_received : BOOL$, initialised to $FALSE$ and with assignment $p\_\alpha\_received := \alpha\_received$ in the end_of_cycle operation.

As examples of the translation, in the water monitor, we can interpret axioms (iv), (vi), and (vii) as:

$$wmfailed\_issued = TRUE \Rightarrow$$
$$[end\_of\_cycle](water\_measure\_condition = failed)$$
$$wmfailed\_issued = FALSE \wedge level\_repaired\_received = TRUE \Rightarrow$$
$$[end\_of\_cycle](water\_measure\_condition = operating)$$
$$level\_repaired\_received = TRUE \Rightarrow$$
$$end\_of\_cycle \supset level\_repaired\_acknowledgment$$

respectively.

The initialization and operations of M_T are then defined in order to ensure these axioms hold. In the case of the water monitor, axiom (i) is ensured by the initialization

$$water\_measure\_condition := operating \parallel water\_quantity := 0$$

The B AMN statement $S = S_1 \parallel S_2$ where S_1 and S_2 are B AMN statements specifies that both the effects of S_1 and S_2 are to be achieved by S. Variable names appearing on the LHS of assignments and operation calls in S denote the value of the variable after execution of S, occurrences on the RHS denote the value of the variable at the beginning of execution of S.

M_T has an operation for each action e which may be input to the system described by the theory T. This operation sets the $e\_received$ flag to $TRUE$. Thus in the case of the water monitor, we have the code:

```
level(lev, sign)  =
     PRE lev :  ℕ & sign :  BOOL
     THEN
        level_received  :=  TRUE  ||
```

Axiom (iii)—nonuniqueness of level messages in a given cycle—requires the following code in *level*:

```
     IF level_received  =  TRUE
     THEN tfailed_issued  :=  TRUE
     END ||
```

$tfailed\_issued = TRUE$ indicates that there has been more than 1 *level* event received in the current cycle.

Axiom (ii)—invalid water data—is met by the following code in *level*:

```
     IF sign  =  FALSE or lev  >  C_max_water
     THEN wmfailed_issued  :=  TRUE
     ELSE water_quantity  :=  lev
     END
```

$wmfailed\_issued$ is a flag which identifies if the internal event $water\_measure\_failed$ has been generated in the current cycle.

The end_of_cycle operation inspects each of the flags describing which events have occurred, and sets attributes and issues output commands depending on their values.

For the water monitor, *end_of_cycle* includes the following tests and actions:

```
end_of_cycle =
  BEGIN
    IF level_received = FALSE or tfailed_issued = TRUE
    THEN transmission_failure
    END ||
    IF level_repaired_received = TRUE
    THEN level_repaired_acknowledgment
    END ||
    IF wmfailed_issued = TRUE
    THEN
        water_measure_condition := failed
    ELSE
      IF level_repaired_received = TRUE
      THEN
          water_measure_condition := operating
      END
    END ||
```

The three parts (separated by ||) of this operation are designed to satisfy the restated axioms (iii), (vii), and (vi), respectively.

All the *received* and *issued* flags are also reset to *FALSE* by this operation, ready for the next cycle:

```
    level_received := FALSE ||
    tfailed_issued := FALSE ||
    level_repaired_received := FALSE ||
    wmfailed_issued := FALSE || lfa_received := FALSE
```

The *until* condition in Axiom (v) of the water measure theory is coded using the following pattern. If an axiom has the form

$$\alpha \Rightarrow (\gamma \, \mathcal{U} \, \beta)$$

where α and β are actions received by the system, and γ an action generated, then define a new flag $\gamma\_until\_\beta : BOOL$ initialised to *FALSE* and add the following elements to the definitions of α and β:

```
α = α_received := TRUE ||
         ⋮
      γ_until_β := TRUE ;

β = β_received := TRUE ||
         ⋮
      γ_until_β := FALSE
```

The *end_of_cycle* operation then generates γ whenever the γ_until_β flag is true and β has not been received in the current cycle:

```
end_of_cycle  =  ...
    IF  γ_until_β  =  TRUE  &  β_received  =  FALSE
    THEN  γ
    END
```

In the case of the water monitor, α is the internal action *water_measure_failed*, β is *level_failure_acknowledgment* and γ is *level_failure_detection*, so we omit the operation definition for α, set *lfd_until_lfa* to *TRUE* in *level* when *wmfailed_issued* is set to *TRUE*, and the following code is put into *end_of_cycle*:

```
IF  lfd_until_lfa  =  TRUE  &  lfa_received  =  FALSE
THEN  level_failure_detection
END
```

The code which results from this direct translation combines several aspects—the communication protocol between the controller and the devices (axioms (v), (vii), for example), failure detection from invalid data (axiom (ii)), and transmission failure detection (axiom (iii)). It is a design choice whether to separate these aspects out into separate layers of machines, for example, placing transmission failure detection in one component, *Outer_Controller*, which handles other aspects depending directly on the patterns of messages received in a given cycle. The thesis [Ali98] develops this approach, showing how the object-oriented design pattern Chain of Responsibility can be used in the B context to implement such separation of fault detection and handling code from the main control code.

We can animate the B components, using the data settings in the simulator of `ftp://ftp.fzi.de/pub/korso/steam_boiler/`.

12.3.2 Composition of B Specifications

The structuring mechanisms of B provide a means of combining specifications of parts of a system into a specification of a complete system. However, they place restrictions on the allowed combinations of components, in order to simplify proof of correctness. A critical restriction is that at most one component C can invoke services from any other, S, say. That is, at most one B component may have a *INCLUDES S*, *EXTENDS S* or *IMPORTS S* clause in its text.

Therefore it is not possible to imitate the theory structure shown in Figure 12.2 because the *Transmission* theory would be *EXTEND*ed in each of *WaterMonitor*, *SteamMonitor*, and so on. Instead the separate machines *WaterMonitor*, *SteamMonitor*, *PumpMonitor* and *PumpControlMonitor* are textually aggregated, and their separate definitions of *end_of_cycle* combined using $\|$ to give a single definition for this operation in the resulting *Outer_Controller* machine. The *Outer_Controller* is then further extended with code to treat the additional controller axioms. For example, a flag *stop_count* : $\mathbb{N}$ could be used to record the number of *stop* messages sent to the controller:

```
stop =
     stop_received := TRUE
```

with the following code in *end_of_cycle*:

```
IF stop_received = TRUE
THEN
   IF stop_count ≥ 2
   THEN
        terminate
   ELSE
        stop_count := stop_count + 1
   END
ELSE
     stop_count := 0
END
```

Alternatively the axiom could be transformed into a past time version:

$$\bullet\!\bullet stop \wedge \bullet stop \wedge stop \Rightarrow terminate$$

and flags *p_p_stop_received* and *p_stop_received* used to determine the issuing of *terminate*:

```
IF stop_received = TRUE ∧ p_stop_received = TRUE ∧
      p_p_stop_received = TRUE
THEN
     terminate
END
```

12.3.3 Verification

Axioms of the form

$$P \wedge \alpha \Rightarrow \bigcirc Q$$

where P and Q are predicates not containing action symbols, are interpreted as obligations on the B specifications that

$$P \wedge \tau(\alpha) \Rightarrow [end\_of\_cycle]Q$$

As an example of verification, the axiom

$$water\_measure\_failed \Rightarrow \bigcirc water\_measure\_condition = failed$$

is valid in *WaterMonitor* because

$$water\_measure\_failed = TRUE \Rightarrow$$
$$[end\_of\_cycle](water\_measure\_condition = failed)$$

Similarly for other axioms of the form listed in Section 12.3.1.

12.4 Conclusion

We have shown that the Object Calculus can be used to provide a highly abstract and declarative specification of the behavior of the steam boiler. We have formalized most aspects of the system. An executable controller has been produced and tested against typical scenarios of use. B has been shown to be effective for industrial specification and to be comprehensible by 'average programmers.' We believe that the Object Calculus is also quite easy to relate to reactive system concepts and to notations such as statecharts, which it generalizes. The papers [BLM97a, BLM97b] describe how statecharts can be mapped to the Object Calculus.

Some specifications of [ABL97] address issues which we do not consider, such as the calculation of optimal control points or the probabilistic behavior of device failures. Our abstract specification adopts the approach of [CW] in working at the *macro* step level in order to simplify the description. The B design is at the *micro* step level. The Object Calculus description is also related to the rule-based approaches used in [BBD+] and [GDK], and suffers a similar problem of consistency obligations between rules. It is possible that a theory may be inconsistent (for example, the water monitor theory would be inconsistent if we had omitted the condition ¬ *water_measure_failed* from Axiom 6). This would be detected in the B specifications as a syntactic or semantic error. Our controller design model, like that of [BW], adopts a purely reactive system approach, whereby events are assumed to happen one at a time and are reacted to in the order of their arrival.

An alternative structuring approach would be to use a time-based partitioning of modules, whereby the actions relevant to the initialization phase of the steam boiler operation are placed in a theory separate from the actions and attributes of the running phase.

The mapping from Object Calculus to B is systematic (machines correspond to theories) but is not entirely automatic, since a design process is involved. Future work will classify different design choices for this translation, and relate B structuring formally to the Object Calculus. The Object Calculus has also been related to the UNITY approach for reactive system specification [LBFL97].

Other research directions include real-time extensions and durative actions, and deontic logic in order to handle failure states more naturally.

Bibliography

[ABL97]   Abrial, J. R., Borger, E., and Langmaack, H. *Formal Methods for Industrial Applications: Specifying and Programming the Steam Boiler Control*, volume 1165 of *Lecture Notes in Computer Science*. Springer-Verlag, 1997.

[Abr96]   Abrial, J. R. *The B Book: Assigning Programs to Meanings*. Cambridge University Press, 1996.

[Ali98]   Ali, M. B specification of steam boiler, 1998.

[BBD+]   Beierle, C., Börger, E., Durdanovic, I., Glässer, E., and Riccobene, E. Refining abstract machine specifications of the steam boiler control to well-documented executable code. Pages 52–78 of [ABL97].

[BLM97a] Bicarregui, J. C., Lano, K., and Maibaum, T. S. Objects, associations and subsystems: a hierarchical approach to encapsulation. In *ECOOP 97*, Lecture Notes in Computer Science. Springer-Verlag, 1997.

[BLM97b] Bicarregui, J. C., Lano, K., and Maibaum, T. S. Towards a compositional interpretation of object diagrams. In *IFIP TC 2 Working Conference on Algorithmic Languages and Calculi*. IFIP, 1997.

[BW] Büssow, R. and Weber, M. A steam-boiler control specification with statecharts and Z. Pages 109–128 of [ABL97].

[CW] Cuellar, J. and Wildgruber, I. The steam-boiler problem – a TLT solution. Pages 164–183 of [ABL97].

[FM91] Fiadeiro, J. and Maibaum, T. Describing, structuring and implementing objects. In *Foundations of Object-oriented Languages*, volume 489 of *Lecture Notes in Computer Science*. Springer-Verlag, 1991.

[GDK] Gaudel, M.-C., Dauchy, P., and Khoury, C. A formal specification of the steam-boiler control problem by algebraic specifications with implicit state. Pages 233–264 of [ABL97].

[GG78] Goguen, J. and Ginali, S. A categorical approach to general systems theory. In Klir, G., editor, *Applied General Systems Research*, pages 257–270. Plenum, 1978.

[Lan97] Lano, K. Specification of steam boiler controller in RAL/VDM^{++} and B. Technical Report ROOS Project Report GR/K68783-15, Dept. of Computing, Imperial College, London, 1997.

[Lan98] Lano, K. Logical specification of reactive and real-time systems. *Journal of Logic and Computation*, 8(5):679–711, 1998.

[LBFL97] Lano, K., Bicarregui, J., Fiadeiro, J., and Lopes, A. Specification of required non-determinism. In *FME 97*, Lecture Notes in Computer Science. Springer-Verlag, 1997.

[RFM91] Ryan, M., Fiadeiro, J., and Maibaum, T. S. E. Sharing actions and attributes in modal action logic. In *Proceedings of International Conference on Theoretical Aspects of Computer Science (TACS '91)*. Springer-Verlag, 1991.

13

Using I/O Automata for Developing Distributed Systems

Stephen J. Garland

MIT Laboratory for Computer Science,
545 Technology Square, Cambridge, MA 02139
garland@lcs.mit.edu

Nancy Lynch

MIT Laboratory for Computer Science,
545 Technology Square, Cambridge, MA 02139
lynch@theory.lcs.mit.edu

Abstract

This paper describes a new experimental programming language, IOA, for modeling and implementing distributed systems, plus designs for a set of tools to support IOA programming. The language and tools are based on the *I/O automaton model* for reactive systems, which has been used extensively for research on distributed algorithms. The language supports structured modeling of distributed systems using shared-action composition and levels of abstraction. The tools are intended to support system design, several kinds of analysis, and generation of efficient runnable code.

13.1 Introduction

Distributed systems are required to provide increasingly powerful services, with increasingly strong guarantees of performance, fault-tolerance, and security. At the same time, the networks in which these systems run are growing larger and becoming less predictable. It is no wonder that distributed systems have become very complex.

The best approach to managing the increased complexity involves organizing systems in structured ways, viewing them at different levels of abstraction and as parallel compositions of interacting components. Such structure makes systems easier to understand, build, maintain, and extend, and can serve as the basis for documentation and analysis. However, in order to be most useful, this structure must rest on a solid mathematical foundation. This is obviously necessary if the structure is to support formal methods of constructing or analyzing systems; however, even without formal methods, a mathematical basis is essential for precise understanding.

One reasonable mathematical basis is the *I/O automaton model* [LT87], which has

285

been used to describe and verify distributed algorithms and to express impossibility results (see, for example, [Lyn96]). Several aspects of this model make it good for such tasks. It is based on set-theoretic mathematics rather than on a particular logic or programming language. I/O automata are nondeterministic, which allows systems to be described in their most general forms. I/O automata have a simple notion of external behavior based on sets of traces of external actions. Moreover, I/O automata can be composed by identifying external actions, in a way that respects external behavior, and pairs of automata can be related using various forms of implementation relations that preserve external behavior. The model supports a rich set of proof methods, including invariant assertion techniques for proving that a property is true in all reachable states, forward and backward simulation methods for proving that one automaton implements another, and compositional methods for reasoning about collections of interacting components.

Also, the model has been extended to a *timed I/O automaton model* [LV96], which allows modeling of timing aspects of distributed systems, including timing assumptions and performance guarantees. Both I/O automata and timed I/O automata can be described using simple guarded-command-style pseudocode (see, for example, [LMWF94, Lyn96]).

Although I/O automata were originally developed for modeling theoretical distributed algorithms, in the past few years they have been used to model practical system components such as distributed shared memory services (for example, [FKL98, FGL+99]), group communication services [FLS97, DFLS98, HLvR99], and standard communication protocols like TCP [Smi97]. This work has resolved ambiguities and contributed proofs that systems meet their specifications. It has led to the discovery of problems, including logical errors in key algorithms in the Orca [BKT92], Horus [vRBM96], and Ensemble [HvR96] systems. Moreover, it has produced I/O automaton pseudocode that is close to actual system code: for example, some I/O automaton pseudocode for the Ensemble system [HLvR99] is similar to the actual ML code that appears in the system implementation.

Because the model and pseudocode have worked well in these case studies, we believe they can be made to play a significant role in developing real distributed systems. In this paper, we describe one way this might work.

Most of the work done so far using I/O automata has been carried out by hand. However, for these methods to play a serious role in system development, they will require computer tool support. So far, tool-based work with I/O automata has consisted mainly of using interactive theorem provers to verify invariant assertions and simulation relations (for example, [Nip89, SAGG+93, PPG+96, Arc97]) for I/O-automaton-based designs. The TAME system [AHS98] provides a high-level interface to the PVS theorem prover [ORR+96] for specifying and proving properties of a timed version of I/O automata. Other tool support for I/O automata includes the SPECTRUM programming language and simulator [Gol90].

13.2 General Design Guidelines

The tool support we are constructing begins with a simple formal language for modeling distributed systems using I/O automata, based on the guarded-command-style pseudocode already in use. Such a language should support the system designer in expressing his/her design at different levels of abstraction, starting with a high-level specification of the required global behavior and ending with a low-level version that can be translated easily into real code. The language should also allow the designer to decompose designs into separable components with clearly defined external behavior.

This language should be supported by a tools providing access to a full range of validation methods, including proof using an interactive theorem prover, simulation, and model-checking. These tools should allow designers to reason about properties of their designs at all levels of abstraction, and about relationships between different levels.

However, we would like more than just validation tools: we would also like tools for connecting verified designs to runnable distributed code. (Our experience with systems like Ensemble suggests that such connections are feasible.) Such tools would allow claims and proofs about designs to be carried over automatically to real distributed programs.

In particular, we believe that, with some well-chosen programmer input, real distributed code in a standard programming language like C++, Java, or ML, can be generated automatically from low-level I/O-automaton-based designs. The validation tools should be able to ensure that the final programs are correct, subject to assumptions about externally provided system components (for example, communication services). Runnable distributed code has already been generated by hand translation of some specific I/O-automaton-based distributed algorithm descriptions [Che97, Tau].

A programming environment based on such a language and tools could help mathematicians write distributed programs, and help programmers who are not mathematicians use mathematical methods in their work.

In this paper, we outline our design for such a programming environment and describe our progress on building a research prototype.

As a starting point, we have developed a candidate programming language, the IOA language, designed specifically to describe I/O automata and their relationships. IOA has evolved from the various forms of pseudocode used in previous work; it also uses ideas from SPECTRUM [Gol90]. It allows automata to be described using *transition definitions* (guarded commands) consisting of *preconditions* and *effects*. It allows explicit description of nondeterministic choice, composition, and levels of abstraction. It permits both declarative and imperative system descriptions. Although the IOA language may need to be enhanced later to increase its expressive power, we think it is a good starting point for developing a good programming environment.

We have also developed designs for a set of tools for validating and transforming IOA descriptions and for generating code from IOA descriptions. We are currently refining the designs and constructing prototypes. Key ideas of the high-level designs involve mechanisms for resolving nondeterminism, support for programming using levels of abstraction, and integration of externally provided system components, by modeling them as automata.

The rest of the paper is organized as follows. Section 13.3 contains a description of the IOA language. Section 13.4 contains an extended example—IOA programs for a toy distributed banking system. Section 13.5 contains a discussion of the language design. Section 13.6 contains an overview of our work on tools to manipulate IOA programs. Section 13.7 contains some conclusions. An earlier version of this paper (with more details) appeared as a technical report [GL98].

13.3 The IOA Language

13.3.1 The I/O Automaton Model

An *I/O automaton* is a labeled state transition system used to model a reactive system. It consists of a set of *actions* π (classified as *input, output,* or *internal*), a set of *states* s (including a nonempty subset of *start states*), a set of *transitions* of the form (s, π, s') that specify the effects of the automaton's actions, and a set of *tasks*, which are sets of locally controlled (that is, non-input) actions.† Input actions are *enabled* in all states. The operation of an I/O automaton is described by its *executions* $s_0, \pi_1, s_1, \ldots$, which are alternating sequences of states and actions, and its *traces*, which are the externally visible behavior (sequences of input and output actions) occurring in executions. One automaton is said to *implement* another if all its traces are also traces of the other. I/O automata admit a *parallel composition* operator, which allows an output action of one automaton to be identified with input actions in other automata; this operator respects the trace semantics.

Proof methods supported by the model include invariant assertion techniques for proving that a particular property is true in all reachable states, forward and backward simulation methods for proving that one automaton implements another (see, for example, [LV95]), and compositional methods for reasoning about collections of interacting components. For example, a *forward simulation* from automaton A to automaton B is a relation R between states of A and states of B that satisfies two conditions: (i) each start state of A is R-related to some start state of B, and (ii) for each step (s_A, π, s'_A) of A and each state s_B of B such that $(s_A, s_B) \in R$, there exists an execution fragment (that is, a sequence of steps) of B that "corresponds" to the step in a particular way. Namely, it has the same trace and leads to a state

---

† Tasks are used primarily to describe liveness; we will mostly ignore them here.

s'_B with $(s'_A, s'_B) \in R$. A summary of the model, its features for expressing system structure, and its proof methods, appears in Chapter 8 of [Lyn96].

The I/O automaton model is similar to the labeled transition system models used to define semantics for process algebraic languages like CSP [Hoa85] and CCS [Mil89]. In particular, those models also define parallel composition in terms of identifying external actions, and have trace-like notions of external behavior. Other languages for describing concurrent systems are based on different types of automata, with different notions of composition and external behavior; for instance, TLA [Lam94] and UNITY [CM88] are based on automata that combine via shared variables.

13.3.2 Language Design

The IOA language is designed to allow precise and direct description of I/O automata. Since the I/O automaton model is a reactive system model rather than a sequential program model, the language reflects this fundamental distinction. That is, it is not a standard sequential programming language with some constructs for concurrency and interaction added on; rather, concurrency and interaction are at its core.

The IOA language is designed to support both proving correctness and generating code. This leads to a tension in the design, because the features that make languages suitable for proofs (for example, declarative style, simplicity, and support for nondeterminism) differ from those that make them suitable for code generation (for example, imperative style, expressive power, determinism). Nondeterminism helps verification by allowing designers to validate designs in a general form. A simple language with a declarative style is easiest to translate into the input languages of standard theorem provers and easiest to manipulate in interactive proofs. On the other hand, programmers generally prefer a language with high expressive power. Moreover, a deterministic language with an imperative style is easiest to translate into runnable code.

The starting point for IOA was the pseudocode used in earlier work on I/O automata. This pseudocode contains explicit representations of the parts of an automaton definition (actions, states, transitions, and so on). Transitions are described using *transition definitions* (*TDs*) containing *preconditions* and *effects*. This pseudocode has evolved in two different forms: a *declarative style* (see, for example, [LMWF94]), in which effects are described by predicates relating pre- and post-states, and an *imperative style* (for example, [Lyn96]), in which effects are described by simple imperative programs.

In moving from pseudocode to a formally defined programming language, we made the following design decisions:

- Data types are defined axiomatically, in the style used by Isabelle [Pau93], the

Larch Prover (LP) [GG91, Gar94], PVS [ORR+96] and other theorem provers. This facilitates translation into theorem prover input languages. We provide definitions for built-in data types and allow the programmer to define new types, using the Larch Shared Language (LSL) [GH93].

- TDs can be parameterized and the values of the parameters constrained by predicates that we call "**where** predicates." A TD can have additional **choose** parameters, which are not formally part of the action name, but which allow values to be chosen to satisfy the precondition and then used in describing the effect.

- Since neither the declarative style nor the imperative style for describing TD effects is adequate for all purposes, we allow both, either separately or in combination. Thus, a TD effect may be described entirely by a program, entirely by a predicate, or by a combination: a program that includes explicit nondeterministic choices, followed by a predicate that constrains these choices.

- Imperative descriptions of effects are kept simple, consisting of (possibly nondeterministic) assignments, conditionals, and simple bounded loops. This simplicity makes sense, because transitions are supposed to be executed atomically.

- Variables can be initialized using ordinary assignments and nondeterministic choice statements. The entire initial state may be constrained by a predicate.

- Automaton definitions can be parameterized.

- There is an explicit notation for parallel composition. In order to describe values of variables in the state of a composed automaton, we use a naming convention that prefixes the name of each such state variable with a sequence of names designating the automata of which it is a part. Users can abbreviate some of these names by shorter or more mnemonic "handles." When there is no ambiguity, some of the automaton names or handles in the sequence may be suppressed.

- There are explicit notations for hiding output actions and asserting that a predicate is an invariant of an automaton or that a binary relation is a forward or backward simulation from one automaton to another.

Other languages, such as TLA, UNITY, and SPECTRUM, are similar to IOA in that their basic program units are transition definitions with preconditions and effects. However, effects in TLA are described declaratively, effects in UNITY and SPECTRUM are described imperatively, and we allow both. SPECTRUM also has other features in common with IOA; for example, it uses parameters similar to our **choose** parameters.

The IOA reference manual [GLV97] contains complete definitions of the syntax and semantics of IOA, as well as some sample programs.

13.3.3 A Simple Example: a Communication Channel

The following IOA program presents an abstract view of a reliable FIFO send-receive communication channel. A client can place a message in the channel via a

send action, after which the channel can deliver the message via a `receive` action. The specification says nothing about how the channel is implemented to ensure reliable delivery. It simply requires that messages are received in the order they are sent, with no duplicates or omissions.

```
automaton channel(i, j: Node, Node, Msg: type)
  signature
    input send(m: Msg, const i, const j)
    output receive(m: Msg, const i, const j)
  states queue: Seq[M] := {}
  transitions
    input send(m, i, j)
      eff queue := queue ⊢ m
    output receive(m, i, j)
      pre queue ≠ {} ∧ m = head(queue)
      eff queue := tail(queue)
```

The automaton is parameterized by two data types, **Node** and **Msg**, which can be instantiated to describe a set of indices for communicating nodes and a set of messages that can be sent; it is also parameterized by the indices i and j of the sending and receiving nodes. Its signature contains a single **send** and **receive** action for each m in M; the keyword **const** indicates that the values of i and j in these actions are fixed by the values of the automaton's parameters. Each channel automaton has a state consisting of a single variable, which holds an initially empty sequence of messages. Its actions are described in terms of their preconditions and effects, using the keywords **pre** and **eff**. An axiomatic definition of the sequence data type provides precise meanings for all other types and operations ({} denotes the empty sequence, and ⊢ appends an element to a sequence).

IOA can also be used to describe specific implementations for abstract channels, in which lower-level protocols ensure reliable message delivery. Furthermore, it allows a designer to assert that these protocols in fact implement the abstract channel, by defining a relation between the states of the high-level and lower-level automata.

13.4 Extended Example: a Distributed Banking System

In this section, we use IOA to describe a toy banking system in which a single bank account is accessed from several locations, using deposit and withdrawal operations and balance queries. We specify the system and its environment using two I/O automata, **A** and **Env**. **Env** describes what operations can be invoked, where, and when; it represents, for example, a collection of ATMs and customers interacting with those ATMs. Automaton **A** describes what the bank is allowed to do, without any details of the distributed implementation. We also give a formal description **C** of a distributed algorithm that implements **A**, in the context of **Env**. We give a specification **B** for an intermediate service describing stronger guarantees about what the bank does, and we use it to help prove that **C** implements **A** (in the context of **Env**). We also give IOA statements expressing some simple invariants and some

forward simulation relations between the levels. These programs illustrate most of
the language constructs.

The code in this section has been checked for validity using our front-end tools,
and its correctness has been proved using the Larch Prover.

13.4.1 Banking Environment

The automaton **Env** describes the environment for the banking system. It describes the interface by which the environment interacts with the bank (requests
and responses at locations indexed by elements of type I), and it expresses "well-
formedness conditions" saying that an operation at any location i must complete
before another operation can be submitted at i. **Env** simply keeps track, for each
i, of whether or not there is an outstanding operation at i, and allows submission
of a new operation if not.

The definition of **Env** is parameterized by the location type I. The output actions of **Env** are requests to perform deposit and withdrawal operations and balance
queries. Each request indicates a location i. Each deposit or withdrawal request
also indicates a (positive) amount n being deposited or withdrawn. The **where** predicates are constraints on the action parameters. The input actions of **Env**, which
will be synchronized with outputs actions of the bank, are responses **OK(i)** (to deposit and withdrawal requests at location i), and **reportBalance(n,i)** (to balance
queries).

The only state information is a flag **active[i]** for each location i, indicating
whether or not there is an active request at location i. The rest of the automaton
description consists of a collection of TDs that constrain when new requests can
be issued. An input at location i sets **active[i]** to **false**. An output is allowed
to occur at location i provided that **active[i]** is **false**, and its effect is to set
active[i] to **true**. In this description, **Int** and **Bool** are built-in types of IOA,
Array is a built-in type constructor, and the operator **constant** appearing in the
initialization is a built-in operator associated with the **Array** constructor.

```
automaton Env(I: type)
  signature
    input  OK(i: I),
           reportBalance(n: Int, i: I)
    output requestDeposit(n: Int, i: I) where n > 0,
           requestWithdrawal(n: Int, i: I) where n > 0,
           requestBalance(i: I)
  states active: Array[I, Bool] := constant(false)
  transitions
    input OK(i)
      eff  active[i] := false
    input reportBalance(n, i)
      eff  active[i] := false
    output requestDeposit(n, i)
      pre ¬active[i]
      eff  active[i] := true
    output requestWithdrawal(n, i)
      pre ¬active[i]
```

```
     eff active[i] := true
  output requestBalance(i)
    pre ¬active[i]
    eff active[i] := true
```

13.4.2 Weak Requirements Specification

Automaton **A** is an abstract, global description of the basic requirements on the behavior of the banking system. It simply records all deposits and withdrawals in a set of elements of data type **OpRec**. It allows a balance query to return the result of any set of prior deposits and withdrawals that includes all the operations submitted at the same location as the query. The response need not reflect deposit and withdrawal operations submitted at other locations.

A is parameterized by the location type **I**. The definition of **A** introduces several data types: Each **OpRec** is an "operation record" indicating the amount of a deposit or withdrawal—positive numbers for deposits and negative numbers for withdrawals—plus the location at which it was submitted, a sequence number, and a Boolean value indicating whether the system has reported the completion of the operation to the environment. Each **BalRec** is a "balance record" indicating the location at which a balance request was submitted and a value to be reported in response. An auxiliary specification **Total**, written in LSL, defines the function **totalAmount**, which sums the **amount** fields in a set of operation records. The type **Null[Int]** contains a special value **null**, which indicates the absence of a numerical value. It is used here to indicate that the return value has not yet been determined.

The external signature of **A** is the "mirror image" of that of **Env**—its inputs compose with **Env**'s outputs and vice versa. **A** also has an internal action **doBalance**, which calculates the balance for a balance query. The state of **A** consists of four variables: **ops** holds records of all submitted deposit and withdrawal operations (as **OpRecs**); **bals** keeps track of current balance requests (as **BalRecs**); **lastSeqno** contains an array of the last sequence numbers assigned to deposits or withdrawals at all locations; and **chosenOps** is a temporary variable used in one of the TDs.

The functions **insert** and **delete** are defined by the built-in data type **Set**. The program statements involving these functions look slightly complicated because the functions have no side effects. The function **nat2pos** (defined in the auxiliary specification **NumericConversions**) converts natural numbers (elements of built-in type **Nat**) to positive natural numbers (elements of built-in type **Pos**). The function **define** converts an element of any type **T** to an element of type **Null[T]**.

The action **requestDeposit** causes a new sequence number to be generated and associated with the newly requested deposit operation. The combination of the location at which the operation is submitted and the sequence number serves as an identifier for the operation. The requested deposit amount, the location and sequence number, and the value **false** indicating that no response for this operation has yet been made to the environment, are all recorded in **ops**. A

requestWithdrawal causes similar effects, only this time the amount recorded is
negative. A requestBalance causes a record to be made of the balance query, in
bals.

The action OK(i) is allowed to occur any time there is an active deposit or
withdrawal operation at location i; its effect is to set the **reported** flag for the
operation to **true**. The nondeterministic "**choose** parameter" x in its TD picks a
particular operation record x from the set ops. The action doBalance(i) is allowed
to occur any time there is an active balance query at location i; its effect is to choose
any set of operations that includes all those previously performed at location i, to
calculate the balance by summing the amounts in all the chosen operations, and to
store the result in the balance record in bals. Because we are currently using a
first-order language, without any special notations for set construction, the effect
expresses a set inclusion using an explicit quantifier. Finally, reportBalance reports
any calculated, unreported balance to the environment.

```
automaton A(I: type)
  type OpRec = tuple of amount: Int, loc: I, seqno: Pos, reported: Bool
  type BalRec = tuple of loc: I, value: Null[Int]
  uses NumericConversions, Total(OpRec, .amount, totalAmount), Null(Int)

  signature
    input requestDeposit(n: Int, i: I) where n > 0,
          requestWithdrawal(n: Int, i: I) where n > 0,
          requestBalance(i: I)
    output OK(i: I),
           reportBalance(n: Int, i: I)
    internal doBalance(i: I)

  states
    ops: Set[OpRec] := {},
    bals: Set[BalRec] := {},
    lastSeqno: Array[I, Nat] := constant(0),
    chosenOps: Set[OpRec]

  transitions
    input requestDeposit(n, i)
      eff lastSeqno[i] := lastSeqno[i] + 1;
          ops := insert([n, i, nat2pos(lastSeqno[i]), false], ops)
    input requestWithdrawal(n, i)
      eff lastSeqno[i] := lastSeqno[i] + 1;
          ops := insert([-n, i, nat2pos(lastSeqno[i]), false], ops)
    input requestBalance(i)
      eff bals := insert([i, null], bals)
    output OK(i)
      choose x: OpRec
      pre x ∈ ops ∧ x.loc = i ∧ ¬x.reported
      eff ops := insert(set_reported(x, true), delete(x, ops))
    output reportBalance(n, i)
      pre [i, define(n)] ∈ bals
      eff bals := delete([i, define(n)], bals)
    internal doBalance(i)
      pre [i, null] ∈ bals
      eff chosenOps := choose c
          where ∀ y:OpRec (y.loc = i ∧ y ∈ ops ⇒ y ∈ c) ∧ c ⊆ ops;
          bals := insert([i,define(totalAmount(chosenOps))],delete([i, null], bals))
```

Automaton **AEnv** is the parallel composition of automata **A** and **Env**, matching external actions:

```
automaton AEnv(I: type)
  compose A(I); Env(I)
```

The programmer can state invariants of **AEnv** within IOA. In the following invariant, the first clause implies that the value of the variable `lastSeqno[i]` is greater than or equal to all sequence numbers that have ever been assigned to operations originating at location i. The second clause implies that the sequence numbers assigned to operations submitted at location i form a prefix of the positive integers. The third and fourth clauses say that the environment's `active[i]` flag correctly indicates when an operation or balance query is active, and also say that only one operation is active at any location at any time. The final clause says that the location and sequence number together identify an operation in **ops** uniquely.

```
invariant of AEnv:
    ∀ x:OpRec (x ∈ ops ⇒ pos2nat(x.seqno) ≤ lastSeqno[x.loc])
  ∧ ∀ i:I ∀ k:Pos (pos2nat(k) ≤ lastSeqno[i]
                       ⇒ ∃ z:OpRec (z ∈ ops ∧ z.loc = i ∧ z.seqno = k))
  ∧ ∀ x:OpRec
      (   x ∈ ops ∧ ¬x.reported
       ⇒    active[x.loc]
          ∧ ∀ y:OpRec (y ∈ ops ∧ x.loc = y.loc ∧ ¬y.reported ⇒ x = y)
          ∧ ∀ b:BalRec (b ∈ bals ⇒ x.loc ≠ b.loc))
  ∧ ∀ b:BalRec
      (b ∈ bals ⇒    active[b.loc]
                   ∧ ∀ b1:BalRec (b1 ∈ bals ∧ b.loc = b1.loc ⇒ b = b1))
  ∧ ∀ x:OpRec ∀ y:OpRec
      (x ∈ ops ∧ y ∈ ops ∧ x.loc = y.loc ∧ x.seqno = y.seqno ⇒ x = y)
```

13.4.3 Strong Requirements Specification

Automaton B is very much like A, but imposes a stronger requirement, namely, that the response to a balance query include the results of all deposits and withdrawals anywhere in the system that complete before the query is issued. It does this by adding a state variable `mustInclude[i]` of type `Array[I, Set[OpRec]]` to A, by appending the statement

```
    mustInclude[i] := choose s where ∀ x:OpRec (x ∈ s ⇔ x ∈ ops ∧ x.reported)
```

to the effect of the `requestBalance(i)` TD, and by modifying the **choose** statement in the `doBalance(i)` TD to require the chosen set c of operations to include `mustInclude[i]`. The changed parts appear below.

```
automaton B(I: type)
  ...
  states
    ...
    mustInclude: Array[I, Set[OpRec]] := constant({})
  transitions
    input requestBalance(i)
      eff bals := insert([i, null], bals);
          mustInclude[i] := choose s where
              ∀ x:OpRec (x ∈ s ⇔ x ∈ ops ∧ x.reported)
    internal doBalance(i)
      pre [i, null] ∈ bals
      eff chosenOps := choose c where
```

$\forall$ y:OpRec (y.loc = i $\wedge$ y $\in$ ops $\Rightarrow$ y $\in$ c)
$\wedge$ mustInclude[i] $\subseteq$ c $\wedge$ c $\subseteq$ ops;
bals := insert([i, define(totalAmount(chosenOps))],delete([i,null], bals))

automaton BEnv(I: type)
  compose B(I); Env(I)

Informally, it is easy to see that **BEnv** implements **AEnv** in the sense that every trace of **BEnv** is also a trace of **AEnv**. Formally, this can be shown using a trivial forward simulation relation from **BEnv** to **AEnv**, namely, the identity relation for the state variables of **AEnv**. This relation can be expressed in IOA as follows, using our prefix naming convention for variables in a composition. Since there is no ambiguity, we can write, for example, **AEnv.active** and **A.ops** as abbreviations for the complete names **AEnv.A.active** and **AEnv.A.ops**, respectively.

forward simulation from BEnv to AEnv:
   AEnv.active = BEnv.active $\wedge$ A.ops = B.ops $\wedge$ A.bals = B.bals
 $\wedge$ A.lastSeqno = B.lastSeqno $\wedge$ A.chosenOps = B.chosenOps

13.4.4 Distributed Implementation

Now we describe a distributed implementation as an automaton C that is the composition of a node automaton CO(i) for each i in I, plus reliable FIFO send/receive communication channels channel(i,j) for each pair of distinct i and j in I, as described in Section 13.3.3. Each node automaton CO(i) keeps track of the set of deposit and withdrawal operations that it "knows about," including all the local ones. It works locally to process deposits and withdrawals, but a balance query causes it to send explicit messages to all other nodes. It collects responses to these messages and combines them with its own known operations to calculate the response to the balance query.

Since the automaton CO(i) corresponds to a location i, its action names are parameterized by i. Its **send** and **receive** actions are intended to match the same-named channel actions. In the state of CO(i), **ops** is maintained as a set of records with no **reported** field; each record is an element of a new type **OpRec1**. The information about which operations have been completed is kept locally in a separate variable **reports**, and is not sent in messages. Balance information is also recorded locally, as elements of a new type **BalRec1**, and never sent. Additional state variables keep track of request messages that have been sent, response messages that have been received, and response messages that must be sent. Specifically, the Boolean flag **reqSent[j]** is used to keep track of whether a **req** message has been sent to j, and the Boolean flag **respRcvd[j]** is used to keep track of whether a response has been received from j. The flag **reqRcvd[j]** is used to record that a request has just been received from j and is waiting to be answered. (Although these flag arrays are indexed by all of I, the flags for i itself are not really needed.) Since two kinds of messages are sent in this algorithm, we define a new message type **Msg** as the union of the two individual types.

```
automaton CO(i: I, I: type)
  type OpRec1 = tuple of amount: Int, loc: I, seqno: Pos
  type BalRec1 = tuple of value: Null[Int]
  type Msg = union of set: Set[OpRec1], req: String
  uses NumericConversions, Total(OpRec1, .amount, totalAmount), Null(Int)

  signature
    input requestDeposit(n: Int, const i) where n > 0,
          requestWithdrawal(n: Int, const i) where n > 0,
          requestBalance(const i),
          receive(m: Msg, j: I, const i) where j ≠ i
    output OK(const i),
           reportBalance(n: Int, const i),
           send(m: Msg, const i, j: I) where j ≠ i
    internal doBalance(const i)

  states
    ops: Set[OpRec1] := {},
    reports: Set[Pos] := {},
    bals: Set[BalRec1] := {},
    lastSeqno: Nat := 0,
    reqSent: Array[I, Bool] := constant(false),
    respRcvd: Array[I, Bool] := constant(false),
    reqRcvd: Array[I, Bool] := constant(false)

  transitions
    input requestDeposit(n, i)
      eff lastSeqno := lastSeqno + 1;
          ops := insert([n, i, nat2pos(lastSeqno)], ops)
    input requestWithdrawal(n, i)
      eff lastSeqno := lastSeqno + 1;
          ops := insert([-n, i, nat2pos(lastSeqno)], ops)
    input requestBalance(i)
      eff bals := insert([null], bals);
          reqSent := constant(false);
          respRcvd := constant(false)
    output OK(i)
      choose x: OpRec1
      pre x ∈ ops ∧ x.loc = i ∧ ¬((x.seqno) ∈ reports)
      eff reports := insert(x.seqno, reports)
    output reportBalance(n, i)
      pre [define(n)] ∈ bals
      eff bals := delete([define(n)], bals)
    internal doBalance(i)
      pre [null] ∈ bals ∧ ∀ j:I (j ≠ i ⇒ respRcvd[j])
      eff bals := insert([define(totalAmount(ops))], delete([null], bals))
    output send(req(x), i, j)
      pre ¬reqSent[j] ∧ [null] ∈ bals
      eff reqSent[j] := true
    output send(set(m), i, j)
      pre m = ops ∧ reqRcvd[j]
      eff reqRcvd[j] := false
    input receive(set(m), j, i)
      eff ops := ops ∪ m;
          respRcvd[j] := true
    input receive(req(x), j, i)
      eff reqRcvd[j] := true
```

We define C to be the composition of all the CO(i) and all the channels, with the communication actions hidden (to match the external signature of B), and CEnv to be the composition of C with the environment.

```
automaton C(I: type)
  compose CO(i) for i: I; channel(i, j, I, Msg) for i: I, j: I where i ≠ j
  hide send(m, i, j), receive(m, i, j) for m: Msg, i: I, j: I
```

```
automaton CEnv(I: type)
  compose C(I); Env(I)
```

CEnv has invariants analogous to those of **AEnv**, as well as trivial invariants saying that channels from nodes to themselves are never used. A new invariant says that any (deposit or withdrawal) operation that appears anywhere in the state (at a node or in a message) also appears in **ops** at its originating location. Other invariants express consistency conditions such as the following. (a) If there is a request in a channel, then there is an active query, the flags for sending and receiving are set correctly, there is only one request in that channel, and there is no response in the return channel. (These last two conclusions rule out messages left over from earlier balance queries.) (b) If there is a response in a channel, then there is an active query, the flags are set correctly, there is only one response in the channel, and there is no request in the corresponding channel. (c) The sending and receiving flags are set consistently. (d) If a response has been received, then a corresponding request was sent. We omit the IOA formulations of these invariants here; the technical report [GL98] contains them all.

To show that **CEnv** implements **BEnv**, we define a forward simulation relation from **CEnv** to **BEnv**. This uses a projection function `proj` from `OpRecs` to `OpRec1s`, defined in an auxiliary specification `Projections`, that just eliminates the `reported` component.

```
uses Projection

forward simulation from CEnv to BEnv:
    BEnv.active = CEnv.active
  ∧ ∀ x:OpRec
        (x ∈ B.ops ⟺    proj(x) ∈ CO(x.loc).ops
                     ∧ (x.reported ⟺ x.seqno ∈ CO(x.loc).reports))
  ∧ ∀ x:BalRec (x ∈ B.bals ⟺ [x.value] ∈ CO(x.loc).bals)
  ∧ ∀ i:I (B.lastSeqno[i] = CO(i).lastSeqno)
  ∧ ∀ i:I ∀ j:I ∀ x:OpRec
        (   [i,null] ∈ B.bals ∧ x ∈ B.mustInclude[i] ∧ x.loc = j ∧ j ≠ i
         ⇒    proj(x) ∈ CO(j).ops
            ∧ ∀ m:Set[OpRec1](set(m) ∈ channel(j,i).queue ⇒ proj(x) ∈ m)
            ∧ (CO(i).respRcvd[j] ⇒ proj(x) ∈ CO(i).ops))
```

The first four conjuncts define simple correspondences between the **ops**, **bals**, **lastSeqno**, and **active** components in **BEnv** and **CEnv**. The last conjunct says that, if there is an active balance query at location i, and if operation x, originating at another location j, is one of those that must be included in the query, then x must appear in certain places in the global state of **CEnv**. In particular, x must be in **ops** at location j, must be in any response message in transit from j to i, and, in case i has received a message from j, must be at location i. The existence of this forward simulation implies that **CEnv** implements **BEnv**, which in turn implies that **CEnv** implements **AEnv**.

13.5 Discussion of Language Design

Nondeterminism is an important feature of IOA, because it allows programmers to avoid restricting their designs unnecessarily. Reasoning about a design in a general form is desirable because it produces insights (and theorems) that may apply to many different implementations. Removing the "clutter" of unnecessary restrictions makes it easier to understand why designs work, because it is easier to see what correctness properties really depend on.

An important aspect of nondeterministic programming is allowing maximum freedom in the order of action execution. In specifications for interactive programs, considerable freedom in action order is often acceptable. Unlike traditional sequential programming styles, the guarded command style used in IOA makes it easy for programmers to constrain action order only when necessary.

Of course, control over action order is sometimes needed, particularly at lower levels of abstraction where performance requirements may force particular scheduling decisions. The current version of IOA lacks explicit control structures for describing such constraints. (In examples, these have generally been expressed using special *pc* or *status* variables to track progress in the sequential part of a computation.) It is likely that we will want later to enhance IOA with explicit support for specifying action order.

However, new research is needed to discover how best to do this. Standard sequential control constructs are neither sufficient nor entirely necessary. For example, reactive systems may contain threads that are intended to execute sequentially, but can be interrupted at any time; describing interactions between threads and interrupt-handling routines may require special control structures. On the other hand, guarded commands can be used to describe iteration, which suggests that some standard looping constructs can be avoided. In any case, to maintain simplicity and provability and to ensure consistency with the mathematical model, we think that new sequencing constructs should be added as pure *syntactic sugar*, that is, that there should be an unambiguous translation of the code with the additions into code without them.

Another possible improvement to IOA would add further local naming conventions. For instance, currently all of an automaton's state variables are global to all of its TDs; one could add variables whose scope is limited to a single TD. Also, currently all action names in a composition are global. One could also allow local action names, with a more flexible method of matching up names in a composition; SPECTRUM [Gol90] uses such a mechanism. A renaming operator for actions would also be useful.

It might also be desirable to add other "standard" programming language features to IOA. (The addition of some object-oriented features to I/O automata is described in [BH98].) However, we think that such features should be added judiciously, to avoid complicating the semantics of IOA. In particular, we think that such extensions should be made as syntactic sugar.

Similarly, it might be desirable to enrich the logical and mathematical features of IOA. We have chosen to base IOA on LSL, which uses the familiar syntax and semantics of first-order logic, so as to facilitate translation into the input languages of several different theorem provers. As a result, we must rewrite an informal statement such as $s := \{n : n < 10 \wedge a[n] > 0\}$ as an IOA statement

    `s := choose x where ∀ n: Int (n ∈ x ⇔ n < 10 ∧ a[n] > 0)`

that uses explicit quantifiers. Although theorem provers such as PVS and Isabelle provide richer notations than LP, we are not attracted to gaining expressive power by tying IOA too closely to less widely understood notations and type systems, which might limit the range of tools with which IOA could be employed. Instead, we envision two ways of gaining expressive power. One is to enrich IOA with syntactic sugar for particularly useful constructs. Another is to base IOA on the new Common Algebraic Specification Language (CASL) [CoF98] and leverage the work of others in translating CASL specifications into the input languages of different theorem provers. CASL is attractive because it is an emerging standard, has a richer type system than LSL, and provides better support for parameterized specifications.

A different, and more traditional, approach to constructing verified code has been to begin with a rich, expressive programming language, define formal semantics and proof rules, and try to use them for verification. We think that this approach has a serious problem: complicated languages have complicated semantics and complicated proof rules, which are difficult to think about and difficult to manipulate in proofs. The logical complexity of a design described in such a language becomes intertwined with the complexity of the language, making it hard to understand and verify the design. We think that a better approach is to begin with a very simple language that supports good proofs for high-level designs, and to add constructs carefully to obtain expressiveness.

13.6 Tools

In this section, we describe a set of tools to support IOA programming, and we describe our progress in building prototypes. For uniformity of presentation, we describe all tools in the present tense, although they are actually in various stages of development (as indicated at the end of each tool's description).

13.6.1 General Guidelines

We require that all tools be based formally on the mathematical model. The tools should be accompanied by theory to explain their operation, for example, theorems about the correctness of program transformations and theorems about the correctness and performance of generated code.

Not all tools need to be capable of processing the full IOA language. Some tools may only process restricted forms of programs, with the user responsible for transforming programs into the restricted forms.† This approach allows users to express their designs in the general IOA language, yet still utilize tools, like simulators and model checkers, that require restrictions. In particular, we believe that the user should help resolve scheduling decisions and other forms of nondeterministic choice when submitting a program to a simulator or code generator.

The most important use of the validation tools will be for checking safety properties. In fact, we propose de-emphasizing liveness properties in favor of considering *time bounds*, which yield sharper information, can be expressed formally as safety properties, and can be handled using standard assertional methods.†

The entire toolset, except for the theorem prover, should be usable by skilled programmers. Use of the theorem prover will require a fair amount of skill in logic and formal methods.

13.6.2 Basic Support Tools

The basic tools for IOA include a *front end*, consisting of a parser and static semantic checker, which produces an internal representation suitable for use by the other (*back-end*) tools. Other basic tools support structured system descriptions using composition and levels of abstraction.

To support composition, a *composer* tool converts the description of a composite automaton into *primitive form* by explicitly representing its actions, states, transitions, and tasks. The input to the composer must be a *compatible* collection of automata, which means, for example, that the component automata must have no common output actions. (This compatibility can be verified using other tools—in simple cases, the static semantic checker, and in more complicated cases, a theorem prover.) In the resulting automaton description, the name of a state variable is prefixed with the names (or handles) of the components from which it arises.

To support levels of abstraction, the tools provide facilities for defining and using *simulation relations*. When users argue that one automaton A implements another automaton B, they normally expect to supply a predicate relating the states of A and B. We think it is reasonable to expect the user to supply more, in particular, information relating *steps* of the two automata. Such information can be used by a theorem prover in establishing the correctness of a simulation relation (see Section 13.6.3), or by a simulator in testing its correctness (see Section 13.6.4).

For example, to show that a relation R is a forward simulation from A to B, the user can define, for each step (s_A, π, s'_A) of A (arising from a given TD), and for each state s_B of B such that $(s_A, s_B) \in R$, a "corresponding" execution fragment

---

† We use "user" to denote the user of the toolset, that is, the system designer, programmer, or program validator.

† Incorporating time bounds formally into IOA requires an extension to timed I/O automata, which is beyond the scope of this paper.

of B. One way he/she can specify this fragment is by providing, as a function of the given step and state, (a) a sequence of TDs of B, and (b) a way of resolving the explicit nondeterministic choices (those represented by **choose** statements and parameters) in those TDs. This function can be described using cases, based on a user-defined classification of the steps of A. To resolve nondeterministic choices, the user can supply subroutines. The programming environment provides an API for use in defining such step correspondences.

It is not always clear how to define the needed execution fragment solely as a function of the given step and state. For example, the definition of the fragment might depend on explicit nondeterministic choices or on the outcomes of conditional tests in the step of A. In such cases, the user can add *history variables* to A to record the relevant choices, and use the values of these variables in state s'_A in defining the fragment. The tools support the addition of such history variables.

We have implemented the front end already. Chefter's Master's Thesis [Che98] describes a design for the composer. Neither the composer nor support for levels of abstraction has been implemented yet.

13.6.3 Interfaces to Proof Tools

The toolset includes interfaces to existing theorem provers. The IOA language was designed for easy translation into axioms that can be used by interactive theorem provers. In this translation, all imperative statements in the effects of TDs, including assignment statements, **choose** statements, conditionals, and loops, are replaced by predicates relating poststates to prestates, and similarly for initial state descriptions. Other axioms are derived from formal definitions of the data types used in the automata.

Theorem provers can be used to prove validity properties for IOA programs and other user inputs (for example, that the set of choices for a nondeterministic assignment is nonempty, that automata being composed do not share output actions, or that actions specified by the user of the simulator are enabled) in cases where the properties are too hard to establish by static checking. Theorem provers can also be used to prove properties of data types used in automata, invariants of automata, and simulation relations between automata. Theorem provers must be able to process programs written in the full IOA language.

For example, showing that a relation R is a forward simulation from A to B involves showing a relationship between the start states of A and B and a relationship between the steps of A and B. The latter asserts, for each step of A and each state of B that is R-related to the pre-state in A, the existence of a "corresponding" fragment of B. Proving such an existence statement automatically is difficult for theorem provers, so the interface can ask the user to help by supplying explicit step correspondence information, as described in Section 13.6.2. The user can then use the theorem prover to verify that the specified sequence satisfies the requirements for a forward simulation: that the sequence is really an execution fragment, that it has the same external behavior as the given step, and that the final states are related by R. Our experience with proofs of distributed algorithms indicates that such step correspondence information greatly reduces the amount of interaction needed for the theorem prover to complete its work.

Initially, we are developing an interface to the Larch Prover. We have designed a translation scheme from IOA descriptions into LSL and used it manually to prove the invariants and simulation relations shown in Section 13.4 [GL98]. We have formalized the translation scheme (cf. [GLV97]) and are in the process of implementing it. Meanwhile, Devillers, working with Vaandrager, is writing a translation from IOA descriptions to the input language of PVS [Dev99].

The toolset also includes interfaces to existing model checkers. These interfaces only handle a restricted class of IOA programs. Although programs can be nondeterministic, they must be written in an imperative style and use only those data types provided by the model checker's input language.

So far, Vaziri has written a preliminary translation from a restricted class of IOA programs into PROMELA, the input language of the SPIN model checker [Hol91].

13.6.4 Simulator

The simulator runs sample executions of an IOA program on a single machine, allowing the user to help select the executions. The simulator is used mainly for checking proposed invariants and simulation relations.†

The simulator requires that IOA programs be transformed into a restricted form. The biggest problem in this transformation is resolving nondeterminism, which appears in IOA in two ways: *explicitly*, in the form of **choose** constructs in state variable initializations and TD effects, and *implicitly*, in the form of action scheduling uncertainty. The restricted form rules out both types of nondeterminism. We also assume that an IOA program submitted to the simulator is *closed* (that is, has no input actions) and is written in an imperative style. At most one (locally controlled) action may be enabled in any state; moreover, the user is expected to designate that action, as a function of the current state.

The tools provide support for getting programs into the required form. For example, the composer can be used to "close" an automaton by composing it with a user-defined "environment automaton" (like **Env** in Section 13.4.1). To resolve explicit nondeterminism, the system can generate probabilistic choices. Alternatively, the system can ask the user to provide explicit choices, for example, by adding a state variable containing a pseudo-random sequence and replacing nondeterministic choices by successive elements of this sequence. The theorem prover can be used to check that the provided choices satisfy any required constraints, expressed by **where** clauses, preconditions, and other predicates.

---

† There is an unfortunate clash of terminology here, between "simulator" and "simulation relation."

To remove implicit nondeterminism, the system can ask the user to constrain the automaton so only one action is enabled in each state; the user can do this, for example, by adding state variables containing scheduling information, adding extra preconditions for actions that involve the new variables, and adding new statements to the effects of actions to maintain the scheduling variables. The user should also provide a function that explicitly designates the next action to be simulated, as a function of the current state, in the form of a TD plus expressions giving values for the action's parameters. The programming environment provides an API for use in writing these functions, and the theorem prover can be used to verify that the designated action is enabled.

For example, if a set of actions is to be executed in round-robin order, then a scheduling variable can keep track of the (index of the) next action to be performed, the precondition of each action can be augmented with a clause saying that the indicated action is the one recorded by this variable, and the effect of each action can increment the index maintained by the variable. This strategy removes the scheduling nondeterminism, and an explicit function of the state describes the next action to be performed.

In order to simulate data type operations, which are defined axiomatically in IOA, the simulator needs actual code. For operations defined by IOA's built-in data types, the simulator uses code from class libraries written in a standard sequential programming language like C++ or Java. For operations (like `totalAmount` in Section 13.4) defined in auxiliary LSL specifications, the user can choose either to write these specifications in an executable algebraic style or to supply handwritten code. Although we do not plan to prove the correctness of this handwritten code, such proofs could be carried out using techniques of sequential program verification.

With all nondeterminism removed, the simulator's job is easy: starting from the unique initial state, it repeatedly performs the unique enabled action. That is, it uses the user-provided function to determine the next TD and parameter values, then executes that TD with those parameter values. Since there is no explicit nondeterminism, this uniquely determines the next state.

The simulator can be used to check that proposed invariants are true in all states that arise in the simulated executions. It can also check that a candidate relation R appears to be a simulation relation from A to B by performing a *paired simulation* of A and B, that is, by producing an execution of A as usual and using it to generate a corresponding execution of B. Specifically, for each simulated step of A, the simulator uses a user-specified step correspondence (see Section 13.6.2) to obtain a (proposed) execution fragment of B, then runs the steps of that execution fragment. As it runs those steps, the simulator checks that action preconditions are satisfied, that values used to resolve explicit nondeterministic choices satisfy the required constraints, that the fragment has the same external behavior as the given step, and that the relation R holds between the states of the two automata after the step and fragment.

Chefter's Master's Thesis [Che98] contains a detailed design for the basic simulator; she has also written a preliminary implementation in Java and produced a small library of hand-coded data type implementations. More recently, Ramirez has improved the simulator, this time starting from the intermediate language described in Section 13.6.2. It remains to enhance this newer version with more advanced capabilities, including the resolution of explicit and implicit nondeterministic choices and support for paired simulations.

13.6.5 Code Generator

Nearly all of the issues that arise in the simulator arise also for the code generator. New issues also arise because of distribution, the need to interact with externally provided communication services, and the need for good runtime performance.

The code generator generates real code for a target distributed system, which may be an arbitrary configuration of *computing nodes* and *communication channels*. The code generation scheme works directly from a low-level IOA language description of the system design, which can arise from a series of refinements starting with a high-level specification. This strategy allows the formal modeling and analysis facilities to be used to reason about the design until the last possible moment, when it is transformed automatically into a working implementation. The verification facilities can be used to ensure that the final implementation provably implements higher-level IOA descriptions, subject to assumed properties of externally provided services, of hand-coded data type implementations, and of the underlying hardware.

The code generation scheme produces runnable versions of *node automata* that can communicate via preexisting communication services such as TCP or MPI [MPI95], which are modeled by *channel automata*. Node automata typically model a combination of application-specific code and local pieces of communication protocols. A key to making this scheme work is obtaining clear IOA specifications of real communication services. Such definitions may be obtained by formalizing existing informal interface descriptions and recasting them, if necessary, in terms of shared actions.

The code generator, like the simulator, relies on the user to transform programs into a special form. As just described, programs provided as input to the code generator must match the given distributed system architecture. Node programs must also satisfy restrictions like those required by the simulator, although they need not be closed. That is, they should include neither explicit nor implicit nondeterminism. As before, the user should specify the next enabled action, as a function of the state.

We need another (technical) restriction to get a faithful system implementation. Atomicity requires that the effect of each transition occur without interruption, even if inputs arrive from clients or communication services during its execution. In our design, such inputs are buffered. In between running locally controlled actions,

the generated program examines buffers for newly arrived inputs, and handles some or all of them by running code for input actions. Since this delays processing inputs (with respect to when the corresponding outputs occur), it may upset precise implementation claims for the node automata. Therefore, we restrict node programs in order to avoid this risk. Stated in its strongest, simplest form, our restriction is that each node automaton A be *input-delay-insensitive*: its external behavior should not change if its input actions are delayed and reordered before processing.†
It is possible to weaken this requirement slightly, for example, requiring only that external behavior be preserved in "well-formed" environments, for example, only for blocking inputs. In this case, the actual environments of the node automata must satisfy these assumptions.

As for the simulator, the tools provide help in getting programs into the special form for the code generator. The general tools that support programming using levels of abstraction can be used to refine a design within the IOA framework until the required node-and-channel form is reached. IOA specifications for actual communication services like TCP and MPI are maintained in a library. Support for removing explicit (**choose**) and implicit (scheduling) nondeterminism is similar to that for the simulator. Like the simulator, the code generator uses a library of data type implementations.

For each node automaton, the code generator performs a source-to-source translation, translating the IOA code into a program in a standard programming language like C++ or Java. This program performs a simple loop, similar to the one performed by the simulator, except that it polls and handles input actions in between processing locally controlled actions. The code generator may translate the code at different nodes into different programming languages.

By insisting that IOA programs from which we generate code match the available computing hardware and communication services, and by requiring the node programs to tolerate input delays, we can achieve a faithful implementation without using any nonlocal synchronization, such as that required by earlier designs [Gol91, Che97].

Abstract Channels Before using the code generator, it is often helpful to describe a system design as a composition of application automata A_i and high-level *abstract channel automata* C_{ij}. Each C_{ij} is, in turn, implemented by lower-level automata D_{ij} and D_{ji}, representing real channels, composed with protocol automata P_{ij} and P_{ji}. For example, an abstract FIFO send/receive channel can be implemented in terms of an MPI service and an IOA protocol [Tau]. At this lower level of design, a node automaton N_i is, formally, the composition of the application automaton A_i and all the protocol automata P_{ij} (for node i) that appear in the channel imple-

---

† Formally, *traces*($A' \times$ *Buff*) must be a subset of *traces*(A), where A' is like A except that its inputs are renamed to internal versions, and *Buff* is a possibly-reordering delay buffer that takes the real inputs and delivers them later in their internal versions.

mentations. It is this composed automaton N_i that the code generator translates into a standard programming language. Figure 13.1 illustrates this design; in this figure, the composed automata N_i are encircled by dotted lines.

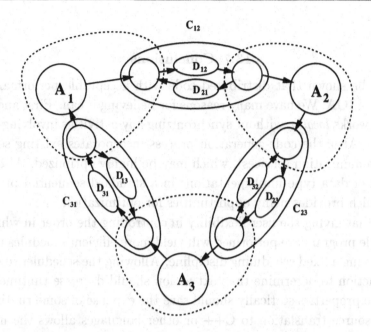

Fig. 13.1. An Implementation Using Abstract Channels Implemented by Real Channels.

Abstract channels provide flexibility: different abstract channels can be used with the same distributed system architecture, and the same abstract channels can be used with different architectures. The tools support programming with abstract channels by maintaining libraries of IOA descriptions of abstract and real channels, and libraries of IOA implementations of abstract channels in terms of real channels. The tools can also assist in proving the correctness of implementations of abstract channels.

Status of Code Generation Tauber has defined IOA models for external system services, including the console and a subset of MPI functions. In a first project on abstract channels, he has defined a protocol that implements reliable FIFO channels on top of MPI and proved the correctness of this protocol [Tau]. He has hand-translated sample distributed IOA programs using abstract channels into Java, and he has built an initial version of the code generator for a restricted subset of IOA, using MPI with a Java wrapper [BCF+99]. This initial version resolves action-scheduling nondeterminism using a simple round-robin scheduler.

Tauber and Tsai, with help from Ramirez and Reimers, are currently working on a reimplementation of the code generator. This version takes the IOA intermediate language as input instead of the source code, uses a flexible action scheduler, and does not restrict the use of action parameters, as does the initial version. The new version is constructed as a series of program transformations that use the composer and remove various kinds of nondeterminism.

13.7 Conclusions

It must still be shown that distributed code with acceptable performance can be obtained using IOA. We have many reasons for believing it can. First and foremost, our strategy works *locally*, without synchronizing any activities involving more than one machine. Also, the code-generation process incorporates existing services (for example, communication services), which may be highly optimized. Also, we allow hand coding of data type implementations in a standard sequential programming language, which provides many opportunities for optimization.

We think that giving the user flexibility in controlling the order in which actions of a local node program are performed will yield more efficient schedules than would arise from having a fixed scheduling discipline. Allowing the scheduler to call a user-provided function to determine the next action should decrease runtime overhead. Proving some properties statically should save the expense of some runtime checks.

Source-to-source translation to C++ or other languages allows the use of optimizing compilers for those languages. Also, IOA is sufficiently flexible to be used at different levels of abstraction, including a very low level that can permit detailed optimization within IOA itself.

Many research problems remain. For theorem prover support, an interesting problem is to devise specialized proof strategies for proving invariants, simulation relations, and IOA program validity properties, in order to reduce the amount of interaction needed in proofs. For model checker support, it would be useful to augment existing model checkers with additional data types so they can express a larger class of IOA programs. Also, one could develop support for exploring restricted subsets of an automaton's execution (for example, based on limiting the amount of asynchrony) in situations where the full automaton is too large to model check. Another interesting problem is to develop support for model checking proposed simulation relations, based on the notion of *paired simulation* described in Section 13.6.4. For the simulator, it would be useful to improve the support for resolving implicit nondeterminism by developing a library of built-in schedulers, and to develop an API to help users construct new schedulers.

For the code generator, research will be needed on improving performance and usability. For example, the target code for node programs could use multithreading to improve performance; however, this would make atomicity of actions harder to ensure and introduce concurrency control issues. Additional support for the user in resolving implicit and explicit nondeterminism could be developed. A more sophisticated, easier-to-use scheduling facility could be developed and integrated into the toolset.

Users can program in IOA at any level of abstraction. Low levels include more aspects of program behavior and so permit finer-tuned optimization. An interesting general problem is to determine how high a level of abstraction programmers can use and still obtain acceptable implementation performance.

Finally, research is needed in using these methods to generate prototype application systems, in evaluating these systems, in using the results of these experiments to improve the code generation methods, and in using the improved methods to develop useful distributed applications.

Acknowledgments

We thank Anna Chefter, Antonio Ramirez, Joshua Tauber, and Mandana Vaziri for their many contributions to this project, especially Josh for his help with Section 13.6.5. We also thank Michael Tsai and Holly Reimers for their programming assistance, and Jason Hickey, Martin Rinard, and Frits Vaandrager for their suggestions and encouragement. Garland's work was supported in part by NSF Grant CCR-9504248. Lynch's work was supported in part by DARPA contract F19628-95-C-0018 (monitored by Hanscom Air Force Base), AFOSR contract F49620-97-1-0337, NSF grants CCR-9225124 and CCR-9804665, and NTT Proposal MIT9904-12.

Bibliography

[AHS98]   Archer, M. M., Heitmeyer, C. L., and Sims, S. TAME: A PVS interface to simplify proofs for automata models. In *Workshop on User Interfaces for Theorem Provers*, Eindhoven University of Technology, July 1998.

[Arc97]   Archer, M., 1997. Personal communication.

[BCF+99]   Baker, M., Carpenter, B., Fox, G., Ko, S. H., and Lim, S. mpiJava: An object-oriented Java interface to MPI. In *Int. Workshop on Java for Parallel and Distributed Computing, IPPS/SPDP 1999*, San Juan, Puerto Rico, April 1999.

[BH98]   Bickford, M. and Hickey, J. Composition and inheritance for I/O automata using intersection types. Dept. of Computer Science, Cornell University, 1998.

[BKT92]   Bal, H. E., Kaashoek, M. F., and Tanenbaum, A. S. Orca: A language for parallel programming of distributed systems. *IEEE Trans. on Soft Eng.*, 18(3):190–205, March 1992.

[Che97]   Cheiner, O. Implementation and evaluation of an eventually-serializable data service. Master's thesis, Department of Electrical Engineering and Computer Science, Massachusetts Institute of Technology, Cambridge, MA, September 1997.

[Che98]   Chefter, A. E. A simulator for the IOA language. Master's thesis, Department of Electrical Engineering and Computer Science, Massachusetts Institute of Technology, Cambridge, MA, May 1998.

[CM88]   Chandy, K. M. and Misra, J. *Parallel Program Design: A Foundation*. Addison-Wesley Publishing Co., Reading, MA, 1988.

[CoF98]   The common algebraic specification language, April 1998.
           http://www.brics.dk/Projects/CoFI/Documents/CASL/Summary/.

[Dev99]   Devillers, M. Translating IOA automata to PVS. Preliminary Research
           Report CSI-R9903, Computing Science Institute, University of Nijmegen,
           the Netherlands, feb 1999.

[DFLS98]   DePrisco, R., Fekete, A., Lynch, N., and Shvartsman, A. A dynamic
           view-oriented group communication service. In *Proc. 17th Annual ACM
           SIGACT-SIGOPS Symposium on Principles of Distributed Computing*,
           pages 227–236, Puerto Vallarta, Mexico, June–July 1998.

[FGL⁺99]   Fekete, A., Gupta, D., Luchangco, V., Lynch, N., and Shvartsman, A.
           Eventually-serializable data service. *Theoretical Computer Science*,
           220(1):113–156, June 1999.

[FKL98]   Fekete, A., Kaashoek, M. F., and Lynch, N. Implementing sequentially
           consistent shared objects using broadcast and point-to-point
           communication. *Journal of the ACM*, 45(1):35–69, January 1998.

[FLS97]   Fekete, A., Lynch, N., and Shvartsman, A. Specifying and using a
           partitionable group communication service. In *Proc. 16th Annual ACM
           Symposium on Principles of Distributed Computing*, pages 53–62, Santa
           Barbara, CA, August 1997. Expanded version in Technical Memo
           MIT-LCS-TM-570, Laboratory for Computer Science, Massachusetts
           Institute of Technology, Cambridge, MA, 1997.

[Gar94]   Garland, S. J. LP, the Larch Prover, version 3.1, December 1994. MIT
           Laboratory for Computer Science.
           http://www.sds.lcs.mit.edu/~garland/LP/overview.html.

[GG91]   Garland, S. J. and Guttag, J. V. A guide to LP, the Larch Prover. Research
           Report 82, Digital Systems Research Center, 130 Lytton Avenue, Palo Alto,
           CA 94301, December 1991.

[GH93]   Guttag, J. V. and Horning, J. J., editors. *Larch: Languages and Tools for
           Formal Specification*. Springer-Verlag Texts and Monographs in Computer
           Science, 1993. With S. J. Garland, K. D. Jones, A. Modet, and J. M. Wing.

[GL98]   Garland, S. J. and Lynch, N. A. The IOA language and toolset: Support for
           designing, analyzing, and building distributed systems. Technical Report
           MIT/LCS/TR-762, Laboratory for Computer Science, Massachusetts
           Institute of Technology, Cambridge, MA, August 1998.
           http://theory.lcs.mit.edu/tds/papers/Lynch/IOA-TR-762.ps.

[GLV97]   Garland, S. J., Lynch, N. A., and Vaziri, M. *IOA: A Language for
           Specifying, Programming and Validating Distributed Systems*. Laboratory for
           Computer Science, Massachusetts Institute of Technology, Cambridge, MA,
           December 1997. http://sds.lcs.mit.edu/~garland/ioaLanguage.html.

[Gol90]   Goldman, K. J. *Distributed Algorithm Simulation using Input/Output
           Automata*. PhD thesis, Department of Electrical Engineering and Computer
           Science, Massachusetts Institute of Technology, Cambridge, MA, July 1990.

[Gol91]   Goldman, K. J. Highly concurrent logically synchronous multicast.
           Distributed Computing, 6(4):189–207, 1991.

[HLvR99]   Hickey, J., Lynch, N., and van Renesse, R. Specifications and proofs for
           ENSEMBLE layers. In Cleaveland, R., editor, *Tools and Algorithms for the
           Construction and Analysis of Systems* (Fifth International Conference,
           TACAS'99), volume 1579 of *Lecture Notes in Computer Science*, pages
           119–133, Amsterdam, the Netherlands, March 1999. Springer-Verlag.

[Hoa85]   Hoare, C. A. R. *Communicating Sequential Processes*. Prentice-Hall
           International, United Kingdom, 1985.

[Hol91]   Holzmann, G. J. *Design and Validation of Computer Protocols*. Prentice
           Hall Software Series, New Jersey, 1991.

[HvR96]   Hayden, M. and van Renesse, R. Optimizing layered communication
            protocols. Technical Report TR96-1613, Dept. of Computer Science, Cornell
            University, Ithaca, NY, November 1996.

[Lam94]   Lamport, L. The temporal logic of actions. *ACM Transactions on
            Programming Languages and Systems*, 16(3):872–923, May 1994.

[LMWF94]   Lynch, N., Merritt, M., Weihl, W., and Fekete, A. *Atomic Transactions*.
            Morgan Kaufmann Publishers, San Mateo, CA, 1994.

[LT87]   Lynch, N. A. and Tuttle, M. R. Hierarchical correctness proofs for
            distributed algorithms. In *Proc. 6th Annual ACM Symposium on Principles
            of Distributed Computing*, pages 137–151, Vancouver, British Columbia,
            Canada, August 1987.

[LV95]   Lynch, N. and Vaandrager, F. Forward and backward simulations—Part I:
            Untimed systems. *Information and Computation*, 121(2):214–233,
            September 1995.

[LV96]   Lynch, N. and Vaandrager, F. Forward and backward simulations—Part II:
            Timing-based systems. *Information and Computation*, 128(1):1–25, July
            1996.

[Lyn96]   Lynch, N. *Distributed Algorithms*. Morgan Kaufmann Publishers, Inc., San
            Mateo, CA, March 1996.

[Mil89]   Milner, R. *Communication and Concurrency*. Prentice-Hall International,
            United Kingdom, 1989.

[MPI95]   MPI: A message-passing interface standard,Version 1.1. Message Passing
            Interface Forum, University of Tennessee, Knoxville, June 1995.
            http://www.mcs.anl.gov/Projects/mpi/mpich/index.html.

[Nip89]   Nipkow, T. Formal verification of data type refinement: Theory and
            practice. In de Bakker, J. W., de Roever, W. P., and Rozenberg, G., editors,
            *Stepwise Refinement of Distributed Systems: Models, Formalisms,
            Correctness* (REX Workshop), volume 430 of *Lecture Notes in Computer
            Science*, pages 561–591, Mook, The Netherlands, May–June 1989.
            Springer-Verlag.

[ORR+96]   Owre, S., Rajan, S., Rushby, J. M., Shankar, N., and Srivas, M. PVS:
            Combining specification, proof checking, and model checking. In *CAV '96*,
            volume 1102 of *Lecture Notes in Computer Science*, pages 411–414. Springer
            Verlag, 1996.

[Pau93]   Paulson, L. C. The Isabelle reference manual. Technical Report 283,
            University of Cambridge, Computer Laboratory, 1993.

[PPG+96]   Petrov, T. P., Pogosyants, A., Garland, S. J., Luchangco, V., and Lynch,
            N. A. Computer-assisted verification of an algorithm for concurrent
            timestamps. In Gotzhein, R. and Bredereke, J., editors, *Formal Description
            Techniques IX: Theory, Applications, and Tools* (FORTE/PSTV'96: Joint
            Int. Conference on Formal Description Techniques for Distributed Systems
            and Communication Protocols, and Protocol Specification, Testing, and
            Verification), pages 29–44, Kaiserslautern, Germany, October 1996.
            Chapman & Hall.

[SAGG+93]   Søgaard-Andersen, J. F., Garland, S. J., Guttag, J. V., Lynch, N. A., and
            Pogosyants, A. Computer-assisted simulation proofs. In Courcoubetis, C.,
            editor, *Computer-Aided Verification* (5th Int. Conference, CAV'93), volume
            697 of *Lecture Notes in Computer Science*, pages 305–319, Elounda, Greece,
            June–July 1993. Springer-Verlag.

[Smi97]   Smith, M. *Formal Verification of TCP and T/TCP*. PhD thesis,
            Department of Electrical Engineering and Computer Science, Massachusetts
            Institute of Technology, Cambridge, MA, September 1997.

[Tau]   Tauber, J. A. IOA code generation—theory and practice. Manuscript.

[vRBM96]   van Renesse, R., Birman, K. P., and Maffeis, S. Horus: A flexible group communication system. *Communications of the ACM*, 39(4):76–83, 1996.

Printed in the United States
By Bookmasters